S0-ALG-490

COLOR LINES

11-12   The problem of mixed race

53-70   Graham on affirmative
actions for immigrants

176   Recognition of religious
groups in France

289   Lack of enforceability
of anti-discrimination laws

Single   49 . White workers begun
to maintain privileged status
produced by New Deal labor + economic
policies

55 Affirmative action
not extended until 1970s

COLOR LINES

AFFIRMATIVE ACTION,

IMMIGRATION, AND

CIVIL RIGHTS OPTIONS

FOR AMERICA

EDITED BY

JOHN DAVID SKRENTNY

THE UNIVERSITY OF CHICAGO PRESS

CHICAGO AND LONDON

JOHN DAVID SKRENTNY is associate professor of sociology at the University of California, San Diego. He is the author of *The Ironies of Affirmative Action: Politics, Culture, and Justice in America* (1996), also published by the University of Chicago Press.

The University of Chicago Press, Chicago 60637
The University of Chicago Press, Ltd., London
© 2001 by The University of Chicago
All rights reserved. Published 2001
Printed in the United States of America
10 09 08 07 06 05 04 03 02 01   1 2 3 4 5

ISBN: 0-226-76181-9 (cloth)
ISBN: 0-226-76182-7 (paper)

Chapters 1–5, 7, 8, and 10 originally appeared in *American Behavioral Scientist* 41, no. 7 (1998), © 1998 Sage Publications, Inc. Reprinted by permission.

Library of Congress Cataloging-in-Publication Data

Color lines : affirmative action, immigration, and civil rights options
for America / edited by John David Skrentny.
     p.   cm.
     ISBN 0-226-76181-9 (cloth : alk. paper)—ISBN 0-226-76182-7 (pbk. :
alk. paper)
     1. Affirmative action programs—United States. 2. Alien
labor—Government policy—United States. 3. United States—
Emigration and immigration—Government policy. 1. Skrentny,
John David.

HF5549.5.A34 C647   2001
331.13'3'0973—dc21
                                                                    00-010686

⊗ The paper used in this publication meets the minimum requirements of the American National Standard for Information Sciences—Permanence of Paper for Printed Library Materials, ANSI Z39.48-1992.

Contents

Preface and Acknowledgments

In the summer of 1997, I was invited by Neil Smelser and *American Behavioral Scientist* managing editor Laura Lawrie to edit a special issue of the journal on the topic of affirmative action. Because I was then—and still am—concerned about the dominance of polemical work on the issue and the policy and the relative dearth of empirical analysis, I seized the opportunity to bring together some of the leading scholars of the issue. I wanted to share with readers what the social scientists know. The theme of the volume was that facts and analysis of affirmative action policy development could add sources and foundations to the philosophical debates and help guide the long-running battle of the pundits in the news media and in Washington. My hope was to create a collection that would contain cutting-edge research on this important policy, bringing to light new perspectives and problems.

Through the work of the contributors, the special issue succeeded marvelously, I thought—I found that after it came out, I was constantly referring colleagues and students to articles in the volume. Two aspects of the volume also increasingly intrigued me. The first was that, in their own way, each of those articles discussed affirmative action, civil rights, and discrimination as these things affected ethno-racial groups other than just the abstract categories of "white" and "black." Almost all of the articles discussed other groups, often in historical context, from the white labor union members not included in the programs to the other nonblack ethnic groups included in the vast majority of affirmative action programs, particularly Latinos and Asian Americans. Second, one article included a cross-national comparison, and I realized that much could be learned if we moved beyond the usual America-centric, parochial approach to the study of civil rights.

In the fall of 1998, I sought to buttress the volume's treatment of diverse groups and to add cross-national comparisons through additional scholarly contributions. I also wanted to give the original authors a chance to reedit their chapters and give the whole collection wider publicity and accessibility as a book. In this process, new, more compelling themes emerged regarding the meaning, problems, and challenges of diversity in the twenty-first century. All of this is explained in the introduction.

This book owes everything, of course, to its superb interdisciplinary cast of contributors. My own contributions, the introduction and editorial work, owe much to the generosity of three fine university institutions. First, the project began while I was an assistant professor in the Department of Sociology at the University of Pennsylvania. There I received research support from a Research Foundation Grant, a Faculty Research Fellowship, and the Janice and Julian Bers Assistant Professorship, all of which gave me resources and time to get much of the project under way. The bulk of the work occurred while I enjoyed a year as a Laurance S. Rockefeller Fellow at the Center for Human Values at Princeton University. The finishing touches came after I arrived at the University of California, San Diego, where summer support helped see the book through to its end.

Although all contributors deserve my thanks, a few made special efforts beyond their individual chapters. Hugh Davis Graham was a guiding force in shaping the volume, and his energy, enthusiasm, and experience were invaluable at every stage of the project. I appreciated Jennifer Lee's professional advice and input on my thinking about how immigration and civil rights have intersected. My fellow aspirant to the someday-coveted title of Rust Belt Intellectual, Tom Sugrue (Tom is from Detroit while I am from the Gary, Indiana, area), was always willing to share his good judgment and offered helpful comments on my introduction. Steve Teles's various suggestions and his rare combination of keen intellect with razor-sharp wit helped sustain the project.

I thank Neil Smelser and Laura Lawrie for getting the ball rolling, and Sage Publications for giving permission to make this book. I am also grateful to work with the University of Chicago Press team: Doug Mitchell, Robert Devens, Leslie Keros, and Jane Zanichkowsky. The press's editorial expertise led to very helpful anonymous reviews—those reviewers deserve thanks as well—and smoothed the bumpy process required in bringing forth an edited volume.

Contributors

ERIK BLEICH is assistant professor of political science at Middlebury College. His research interests lie in the fields of race and ethnicity, ideas and policy making, and western European politics. His article "From International Ideas to Domestic Policies: Educational Multiculturalism in England and France" appeared in *Comparative Politics* in 1998. He is currently completing a book on British and French race policies.

LAWRENCE D. BOBO is professor of Afro-American studies and of sociology at Harvard University. He edited an issue of *Public Opinion Quarterly* on race (spring 1997), he is coauthor of *Racial Attitudes in America: Trends and Interpretations* (1997), and he is principal investigator on the Los Angeles Study of Urban Inequality, funded by the Ford Foundation and the Russell Sage Foundation.

FRANK DOBBIN is professor of sociology at Princeton University. He is studying the evolution of employer response to antidiscrimination law, changes in corporate structure since the 1960s, and the invention of business strategy among early railroads. His *Forging Industrial Policy* (1994) received the 1996 Max Weber Award from the American Sociological Association.

JOHN AUBREY DOUGLASS is a research fellow at the Center for Studies in Higher Education at the University of California, Berkeley. He is the author of a number of policy papers on higher education. Recent scholarly publications include *The California Idea and American Higher Education: 1850 to the 1960 Master Plan* (2000) and articles in *California Politics and Policy*, *History of Education Quarterly*, *American Behavioral Scientist*, the *European Journal of Education*, the *Journal of Policy History*, and the *History of Higher Education Annual*. He is currently working on the book *Affirming Opportunity*, a larger study of the development of affirmative action and the history of admissions at the University of California.

HUGH DAVIS GRAHAM is the Holland N. McTyeire Professor of History and a professor of political science at Vanderbilt University. His recent books include *The Civil Rights Era: Origins and Development of National Policy* (1990) and *Civil Rights and the Presidency* (1992). He is completing a new book, *Collision Course: The Strange Convergence of Affirmative Action and Immigration Policy in America*, to be published by Oxford University Press.

KYRA R. GREENE is a Ph.D. candidate in the sociology department at Stanford University. Her interests are political sociology and social stratification. She is working on a dissertation that explores the relation between protest cycles, the production of cultural and political resources, and the rise of the American disability rights movement.

ERIN KELLY is assistant professor of sociology at the University of Minnesota. She studies gender, organizations, and social policy. Her current work examines the adoption of corporate family policies from the early 1960s to the present.

GEORGE R. LA NOUE is director of the Project on Civil and Public Contracts, located at the University of Maryland, Baltimore County, and a professor of political science there. He received his Ph.D. in political science from Yale University and has held the Woodrow Wilson Danforth and Public Administration fellowships. He is the author or editor of four books, including *Local Officials' Guide to Minority Business Programs and Disparity Studies.* He has also written about minority business policies in the *Annals* of the American Academy of Political and Social Sciences, the *Columbia Human Rights Law Review, The Public Interest,* the *Journal of Policy History, Urban Lawyer,* and *Public Administration Review,* and he has contributed a chapter to *Racial Preferences in Public Contracting.*

JENNIFER LEE is assistant professor in the Department of Sociology at the University of California, Irvine. Her recent articles focus on immigrant entrepreneurship, black-immigrant competition, and hiring practices in inner-city neighborhoods. She is currently working on a book that examines race and ethnic relations in black neighborhoods among blacks, Jews, and Koreans.

MICHAEL LICHTER is currently a consultant for the County of Los Angeles, engaged in an evaluation of welfare reform in the county. He recently received a Ph.D. from the University of California, Los Angeles, Department of Sociology, and was a research fellow with the UCLA Center for the Study of Urban Poverty.

DEBORAH C. MALAMUD is professor of law at the University of Michigan, where she teaches and writes on labor and employment law and civil rights. Her articles on affirmative action and class and interethnic conflict have appeared in the *Journal of Legal Education, Ohio State Law Journal, Texas Law Review,* and *University of Colorado Law Review.* She is currently studying issues of class in New Deal social programs and has published an article on the subject in the *Michigan Law Review.*

SUNITA PARIKH is associate professor of political science at Washington University. She is the author of *The Politics of Preference: Democratic Institutions and Affirmative Action in the United States and India* (1997).

JOHN D. SKRENTNY is associate professor of sociology at the University of California, San Diego. He is the author of *The Ironies of Affirmative Action: Politics, Culture, and Justice in America* (1996). His current research includes a study of the linkages between national security policy, the black civil rights movement, and the "minority rights revolution" of the late 1960s and early 1970s.

THOMAS J. SUGRUE is Bicentennial Class of 1940 Professor of history and sociology at the University of Pennsylvania. He is the author of the award-winning book *The Origins of the Urban Crisis* (1996) and coeditor of *W. E. B. Du Bois, Race, and the City* (1998). He is currently writing a history of civil rights in the urban north and a general history of America in the twentieth century.

JOHN C. SULLIVAN is associate director of the Project on Civil Rights and Public Contracts. He received his J.D. from the University of Maryland Law School in 1983. He has been researching and writing about civil rights since 1990. With George R. La Noue, he has cowritten articles appearing in the *Columbia Human Rights Law Review*, the *Journal of Policy History*, and *Public Administration Review*. He has also written about racial preferences for newspapers such as the *Christian Science Monitor*. He has served as litigation consultant on more than fifteen court challenges to local preference programs around the country.

CAROL M. SWAIN is professor of law and of political science at Vanderbilt University. She is the author of *Black Faces, Black Interests: The Representation of African Americans in Congress* (1995), which was selected by *Library Choice Journal* as one of the seven outstanding academic books of 1994. *Black Faces* was also the winner of the 1994 Woodrow Wilson Prize, the winner of the 1995 D. B. Hardeman Prize for the best scholarly work on the U.S. Congress during the biennial period, and the co-winner of the V. O. Key Award for the best book published on southern politics. In addition, Swain is the editor of *Race Versus Class: The New Affirmative Action Debate* (1996). Her current book-in-progress is *Demographic Changes, Racial Preferences, and the Rise of White Nationalism*.

STEVEN M. TELES is assistant professor of politics at Brandeis University and has held posts at Harvard University, College of the Holy Cross, Boston University, Hamilton College, and the Institute of United States Studies, University of London. He is the author of *Whose Welfare? AFDC and Elite Politics* (1996) and the author of numerous scholarly articles and popular opinion pieces on subjects such as social security, U.S.-China relations, federalism, the British Labour party, and the public philosophy of liberalism. He is currently working on a book on pensions privatization in the United States and the United Kingdom, as well as being codirector (with Glenn

Loury and Tariq Modood) of a major international study, *Ethnicity and Social Mobility in the U.S. and U.K.*

ROGER WALDINGER is professor and chair, Department of Sociology, UCLA. He holds a B.A. from Brown University and a Ph.D. from Harvard University. Waldinger is the author of four books, most recently *Still the Promised City? African-Americans and New Immigrants in Postindustrial New York* (1986), which received the 1996 Best Book in Urban Politics award from the American Political Science Association and the 1998 Robert E. Park Award from the American Sociological Association, and *Ethnic Los Angeles* (1996), which received the 1997 Thomas and Znaniecki Prize from the American Sociological Association. He has completed two new books, *How the Other Half Works: Immigration and the Social Organization of Labor* (with Michael Lichter) and *Strangers at the Gates*, a collection of essays on new immigrants in urban America, both forthcoming from the University of California Press.

CHRISTINE MIN WOTIPKA is a doctoral candidate in the international comparative education program at the Stanford University School of Education. She expects to receive her Ph.D. in June 2001. While working on this chapter, she was a MacArthur Consortium fellow at the Center for International Security and Cooperation and a graduate dissertation fellow at the Institute for Research on Women and Gender at Stanford University. Her other research interests relate to cross-national analyses of women in science and engineering fields in higher education, women's studies programs, and human rights organizations.

Introduction

. . .

JOHN DAVID SKRENTNY

When the civil rights legislation and affirmative action regulations of the 1960s arrived, nearly all public attention to discrimination in the United States was on the plight of the descendants of black slaves, or Afro-Americans.[1] This was anything but surprising. For centuries, they suffered blatant, often vicious discrimination. They were gaining voting clout. They had organized effectively to gain public attention and sympathy. American political elites were concerned about the Soviet Union's anti-American propaganda, which highlighted the problems of Afro-Americans to an attentive world. And after the passage of the Civil Rights Act of 1964, Afro-Americans were involved in violent upheavals in the nation's cities that led to a series of "long, hot summers" throughout the middle and late 1960s, keeping issues of Afro-American opportunity on the national agenda.[2] Politicians often spoke of ending discrimination in American society, of creating opportunity for all, and of helping "minorities," but they really meant Afro-Americans.

Much has changed since the mid-1960s, and a fresh analysis is required. A new look at discrimination and the laws designed to prevent it is necessary because the American racial and ethnic scene has changed profoundly. On one hand, a large Afro-American middle class has formed (Thernstrom and Thernstrom 1997), while a large Afro-American lower class continues to suffer uniquely severe unemployment and social isolation (Massey and Denton 1993; Wilson 1987) as well as a deficit in acquired skills (Loury 1998). At the same time, Afro-Americans have lost their status as "the" minority in the United States. Although racial policy is still often debated in terms of blacks and whites, such debates now are anachronistic, even quaint. The explosive post-1965 growth of immigration, mainly from Latin America, Asia, and the Caribbean, has produced a very diverse and growing population of affirmative action–eligible groups that will increasingly strain the public justifications for that policy. These new immigrant groups, exhibiting greatly varying levels of education, income, and

1

achievement, play important and conflicting new roles in the lives of Afro-Americans. The new immigrants create economic opportunities through their enterprise, but they also become competitors and some-times discriminators. Further, not only the United States but the world has changed. Though Americans created their antidiscrimina-tion laws without insight into the experiences of other nations, they no longer have to do so. Indeed, they never had to—India has long had policies that resemble American affirmative action, and other coun-tries, such as France and Britain, are, like the United States, becom-ing increasingly multiethnic. These countries have now pursued their own policies to deal with issues of equal opportunity, leaving a track record to inform American policy makers on both the Left and the Right.

The purpose of this volume is to reexamine the issues of discrim-ination, civil rights, and affirmative action for American racial and ethnic groups in light of the new immigration and international de-velopments. Are we entering a new era of racial and ethnic harmony—or one of conflict? How did we get to our present situation, and what is the future of civil rights enforcement and affirmative action? What options exist to deal with problems of ethnic discrimination and representation? This volume brings together a variety of disci-plinary perspectives, including those of sociology, political science, history, and law, to shed the light of empirical research on the is-sues. The authors, including both critics and supporters of affirma-tive action, have concentrated their efforts on the presentation of facts for readers to consider for themselves. The focus is on affirma-tive action, a policy shrouded in both controversy and mystery, which lies at the center of debates about American equal opportunity policy.

The great Afro-American sociologist W. E. B. Du Bois stated in 1903 that the "problem of the twentieth-century is the problem of the color line" and showed a global view by describing the problem as "the relation of the darker to the lighter races of men in Asia and Africa, in America and the islands of the sea" (1997, 45). Yet even an observer as perspicacious as Du Bois did not foresee late-twentieth-century American demographic and policy changes. Continuing high immigration, discrimination, and officially designated affirmative-action minority groups will ensure that if the twentieth century had the problem of the color line, the twenty-first will have the problem of color lines.

Affirmative Action in Multiethnic America:
Policy History and Analysis

Making Discrimination Illegal

In 1964, Congress passed and President Lyndon Johnson proudly signed the Civil Rights Act. The law was intended to prevent discrimination in a variety of spheres of life, including public accommodations (Title II), institutions and programs receiving federal funds (Title VI), and most controversially, private employment (Title VII). Though each of these titles included broad prohibitions of discrimination on the bases of race, national origin, and religion (Title VII also included sex discrimination), the overwhelming focus of discussion was the problem of discrimination against Afro-Americans (Burstein 1998; Graham 1990).

The law does not explicitly define *discrimination*, but it appears that most members of Congress had in mind a commonsense understanding of the term. Throughout the southern states, Euro-Americans practiced obvious, open, intentional discrimination against Afro-Americans, interwoven through schools, work, and public life and based on belief in white supremacy. With the passage of the Civil Rights Act, this racial caste system became illegal. Title VII gave Afro-Americans the opportunity to complain to a new agency, the Equal Employment Opportunity Commission (EEOC), when they believed their race was used against them in job-seeking or promotion or when employers fired them. The EEOC was to investigate sworn complaints of discrimination and conciliate and persuade the guilty employers to hire without regard to the applicant's race. Failing here, individuals could sue on their own, or the Justice Department could initiate its own lawsuit where it found a "pattern or practice" of discrimination.[3]

The law contained a vaguely worded section that allowed some kinds of discrimination. If a hiring institution could claim that a job applicant's religion, sex, or national origin was a "bona fide occupational qualification," a necessary part of the job, then it was legal to prefer a particular background or sex. This loophole was not extended to race discrimination. Congress recognized no employment situations in which particular races or colors should be preferred.

These civil rights laws institutionalized a moral standard in the United States that discrimination was wrong. Polls show that Americans overwhelmingly supported the principle that race discrimination is wrong (Burstein 1998; Schuman, Steeh, and Bobo 1985), and they still do. Skeptics may doubt the sincerity of the support for nondiscrimination and argue that Americans are now only saying what they think is the "right" answer, but this claim dismisses a major development: supporting nondiscrimination is now the "right" answer (Brooks 2000).

Affirmative Action, Then and Now

Laws and regulations have developed that extend the Civil Rights Act of 1964 to ensure equal opportunity. These include the controversial affirmative action regulations and programs. Like the Civil Rights Act, they arose in the time when opportunity for blacks was the dominant issue, and the problem of opportunity for other groups, including Latinos, Asian Americans, and American Indians, was near the bottom of the national agenda.

It is difficult to provide one all-encompassing definition of affirmative action. It is important to keep in mind, for example, that there are affirmative action *regulations* that some firms contracting with the government are supposed to follow with their own affirmative action *programs.* Many other firms have their own voluntary affirmative action programs. There is added complexity, because the regulations have changed over time, and affirmative action programs have never been the same for different types of opportunity. Affirmative action in employment is not the same as the (mostly voluntary) programs in higher education or professional school admissions, and neither of these is identical to affirmative action in legally mandated contract set-asides or in Small Business Administration help for minorities.

Policy makers themselves have been confused. The earliest uses of the term *affirmative action* in the context of civil rights enforcement lacked clear intentions. The term appeared in John F. Kennedy's Executive Orders 10925 and 11114, prohibiting discrimination on the bases of race, national origin, and religion and requiring affirmative action to ensure nondiscrimination by government contractors. It appeared again in Title VII of the Civil Rights Act of 1964, as courts were empowered to order firms guilty of discriminating to take "affirmative action" to put discrimination victims in their rightful place. In 1965, the term was repeated in Lyndon Johnson's Executive Order 11246. In none of these instances was *affirmative action* clearly spelled out.

As Hugh Davis Graham points out in his essay in this volume, *affirmative action* seemed to mean what was later called "soft" affirmative action. But this was by no means clear. The executive orders and Title

VII list some activities that might be included, such as "hiring employees" and giving "back pay." The wording here suggested affirmative
action aimed at identifiable, individual victims of discrimination, but the
executive orders, which required promises of affirmative action *before* a
contractor was officially found to have discriminated, could not have
meant that. A Johnson administration memorandum dated January,
1964, highlights the confused nature of the policy.

The document, "Affirmative Action Commitment Under Executive
Orders 10925 and 11114," was meant to "acquaint government contractors with this requirement." It explained that affirmative action was "a
relatively new concept in contract management." There was nothing in
the provided definition that suggested color consciousness, later to be a
major drag on affirmative action's political support: "Affirmative action
means positive or firm or aggressive action as opposed to negative or
infirm or passive action. Affirmative action encompasses the steps necessary to insure that a contractor puts into practice his stated policies of
equal employment opportunity without regard to race, color, creed or
national origin." With a clear focus on Afro-Americans, the document
lists no fewer than twenty-five examples of affirmative action.

The simplistic quality of the suggestions reveals the nature of race
relations in the early 1960s, when discrimination was severe and open.
For instance, one suggestion for affirmative action was to "[e]liminate
segregated wash-rooms, cafeterias, smoking areas, locker-rooms, drink-
ing fountains, time clocks, pay-lines, contractor sponsored recreational
programs, etc." Another was a hallmark of soft affirmative action: employers should try "[p]ublication and dissemination of a written policy
of equal employment opportunity." Some of the stronger recommendations reveal both surprising differences with later beliefs about the
nature of discrimination and awareness of the taboo nature of color-
consciousness and preferences. For example, suggestion 9 gave no
preference to minorities: "Seek, employ and develop minority group
personnel, *as well as others*, in white collar classifications to insure that
the best talents and abilities of the nation's manpower resources are
utilized most advantageously" (emphasis added). Although in later years
most civil rights administrators saw the use of employment tests on
which Afro-Americans performed poorly as culturally biased and discriminatory, example 18 suggested, "Re-evaluate qualifications of lower
echelon minority employees to insure equal consideration for job progression based on standards and qualifications which should be no
higher or no lower than those established for white employees."[4] Still,
even in 1964 there was a harbinger of things to come: the document

closed by declaring that each contractor would have to devise its own plan to "achieve the maximum utilization of available manpower." In other words, affirmative action was not oriented toward some procedural justice, as was Title VII, but toward a substantive result.

It was not long before a combination of forces led to the development of the affirmative action we know today. Scholars and pundits frequently introduce affirmative action with the assumption that policy originators were trying to compensate Afro-Americans for centuries of discrimination. As I have argued elsewhere (Skrentny 1994, 1996), it is true that while enforcing Title VII federal courts have often ordered specific firms or public institutions to enforce racial hiring goals as compensation for past discrimination. Some civil rights groups also may have made compensation arguments. But the original justification for affirmative action in employment put forth by those implementing the policy was administrative pragmatism.[5] Civil rights enforcers said they needed an effective and efficient means of stopping *present* discrimination. This was very difficult to prevent when the government relied solely on promises by employers or charges made by aggrieved individuals. Others justified the policy as a means to quell the crisis of urban racial unrest in the late 1960s.

Soon after its creation, the EEOC began to monitor the racial and ethnic composition of the nation's workforces and encourage firms to undertake affirmative action to bring the proportions into balance. The EEOC was not alone in this task. Johnson's Executive Order 11246 had created the Office of Federal Contract Compliance (OFCC) to enforce the order. The OFCC would tackle a particularly stubborn problem, described in the chapter by Thomas Sugrue: the resistance to integration shown by construction unions. The OFCC eventually required construction firms with large government contracts to submit affirmative action plans along with their bids for projects. The plans had to include "goals and timetables," or good-faith promises to hire certain percentage ranges (goals) of minority workers by certain time periods (timetables). By 1970, the OFCC expanded these regulations to include all government contractors with contracts of at least $50,000 (Graham 1990).

Since 1970 there have come to be many different kinds of affirmative action regulations, programs, understandings, and purposes. As Erin Kelly and Frank Dobbin show in their contribution to this volume, firms (including those without government contracts) were faced with great uncertainty regarding requirements for compliance with civil rights laws and affirmative action regulations. The shifting political winds and changing occupants of the White House led to further complications. American firms have always had a lot of leeway in deciding how to fashion their affirmative action programs to satisfy the regulations. These efforts can range from color-blind to more specifically color-conscious methods. Just as Graham argues in chapter 2 that affirmative action developed its own political constituency among national, state, and local lawmakers, Kelly and Dobbin show that affirmative action developed a constituency among personnel and human resources officers in large firms. These officers maintained intra-firm pressure for affirmative action, helping to ensure that firms would support the policy even without government pressure. They often created specific affirmative action practices by copying each other, seeking some acceptable way of signaling compliance with the law. When the policy's uncertain political future threatened firms' affirmative action officers, they responded by crafting a rationale for the policy that was not even hinted at in 1964: the cultural diversity created by minority outreach and hiring would aid the bottom line.

Just as affirmative action in employment took different forms over time, affirmative action in other areas also has varied. Kelly and Dobbin present data showing that employment-related affirmative action has the most fluidity and is still often characterized by softness and inconsistency. In one of the very few studies of the origins of affirmative action in higher education, John Aubrey Douglass shows how affirmative action in the University of California's student admissions system became a highly rationalized, preferential process. It developed in the context of preferences based on less controversial criteria, such as geographical origin in the state. Admissions officers developed formulae based heavily on the race or ethnicity of applicants to remedy the problem of "underrepresentation." Douglass shows that the University of California turned to its policy as part of an effort to comply with state law and to fulfill its "social contract" of serving the entire state of California.

In the area of contract set-asides—another underanalyzed aspect of affirmative action policy—George La Noue and John Sullivan, like Graham, show a tendency for affirmative action to appear preferential and rooted in a model of proportional representation. Both chapters describe how affirmative action in government contract set-asides, the area where the Supreme Court has shown the most disapproval, has sometimes been motivated by political concerns and coalition-building. In short, there are and have been many affirmative actions and many different purposes of affirmative action.

Affirmative Action: The Growing Importance of New Color Lines

In all of these developments, virtually no scholarly or public attention has yet been paid to the issue of who should benefit from affirmative action. Although the policy always includes Afro-Americans and was developed to cope with their unique problems, it has formally included other groups from the beginning. In the mid-1960s, these were the "Spanish Americans," the "Orientals," and the "American Indians." The reasons these groups were included and others were not are obscure, but it is certain that few thought it was a matter of importance—the nonblack groups were small in the mid-1960s. These basic categorizations have allowed affirmative action to go beyond Afro-America to include Caribbean and African blacks, persons from Latin America, the Spanish Caribbean, and Spain, and Asians—but from eastern and southern Asia and the Pacific Isles only. Policy makers creating the "Oriental" or "Asian" category excluded Afghanistan, the former Soviet central and eastern republics, and the Middle East. Eskimos and Aleuts have joined American Indians as aboriginal beneficiaries of affirmative action. If the policy does not change and current demographic predictions come true, affirmative action programs will increasingly include nonblacks, mixed-race persons, and non-Afro-American blacks.

The chapters in part I, in addition to providing historical insights into the development of affirmative action policy, have some common elements. First, an overarching theme is that they show how the current dilemmas of affirmative action are rooted in the policy's very beginnings—a theme captured by Graham's phrase "unintended consequences." Second, they find dilemmas in affirmative action's targeted design and the differential achievement of American ethnic groups. The way affirmative action draws color lines has been, is now, and will be increasingly an object of contention in twenty-first-century America.

The historian Thomas Sugrue provides an original genealogy of the affirmative action controversy. Its origins, he argues, lie in the unintended consequences of the New Deal. President Roosevelt's New Deal policies worked to satisfy working class Euro-Americans' desire for security, but they left out Afro-Americans' desire for security with *equality*. The late 1940s through the middle 1960s saw Afro-American civil rights groups using a discourse of color-blindness to press for equality without regard to color. But early state-level Fair Employment Practice Commissions and the early federal civil rights protections did not immediately bring about equality—especially in trade unions. Roosevelt's pro-labor policies allowed the construction unions to become a solid step up on the socioeconomic ladder for thousands of Americans, including many Catholics of Irish or eastern and southern European descent. These Euro-Americans tended to maintain the trade unions as an ethnic niche for themselves. The federal government, though doing nothing to encourage these union men and their sons to go to college and seek white-collar and professional careers, responded with affirmative action designed to force the unions to bring in Afro-Americans. Sugrue concentrates on the efforts of the Kennedy administration. Though weak, confused, and mostly ineffectual, the threat that Kennedy's efforts symbolized produced a disproportionate emotional reaction from the unions. The result was local Afro-American leaders' adoption of a color-conscious discourse and support for the new affirmative action policy, while the unions used the old universalist civil rights language to resist. The chapter describes the roots and early history of affirmative action and shows how strongly a group can fight to maintain its niche, especially when Afro-Americans are the entering group.

Chapters by Hugh Davis Graham and by George La Noue and John Sullivan more directly explore the dilemmas of affirmative action's degree of ethnic inclusiveness by examining the meaning of continued immigration for affirmative action. Graham provides an overview of how affirmative action and immigration reform, previously unrelated and distinct policies, have become linked, producing sometimes troubling, unintended consequences. In some areas, for example, the linkage is especially pronounced: at the University of Michigan, a faculty affirmative action program had brought in many minority professors, but 18.8 percent of the black professors, 23.3 percent of the Latinos, and 56.1 percent of the Asians were foreign-born. One area of conflict developing in California involves Afro-Americans and Latinos and public employment. In many federal, state, and city jobs, Afro-Americans created an employment niche in which they are overrepresented. Some Latino leaders have pressed for full implementation of affirmative action in this context so that Latinos may get their fair share of these attractive jobs. Demographic forces are in place to make these kinds of conflicts increasingly frequent and divisive.

La Noue and Sullivan focus on affirmative action to help minority-owned businesses, which paradoxically aids groups with some of the highest business formation rates in America (Koreans being number one), as well as more disadvantaged Afro-Americans. Although the Korean businesses are often very small mom-and-pop outfits, staffed by family members, there is an important lesson in La Noue and Sullivan's study.[6] It seems clear that different minority groups have different tendencies to go into business and that discrimination cannot be the sole cause of the variation. Perhaps it is not even the primary cause of variation. America's minorities are certainly not equal, and many affirmative action–eligible groups have education levels considerably higher than both Afro- and Euro-Americans'. Supporters and critics of affirmative action have reason to pay attention to potential policy irrationalities. The routine inclusion of the standard array of affirmative action minorities in some city contract set-aside plans has been a factor in federal courts' recent suspicions of affirmative action. La Noue and Sullivan show, for example, that the Supreme Court struck down the minority business affirmative action plan of Richmond, Virginia, criticizing the "random inclusion" of various groups. Justice Sandra Day O'Connor explained, "there is absolutely no evidence of past discrimination against Spanish-speaking, Oriental, Indian, Eskimo, or Aleut persons in any aspect of the Richmond construction industry. . . . It may well be that Richmond has never had an Aleut or Eskimo citizen" (*City of Richmond v. Croson*, 488 U.S. 469 [1989], at 506).

Other provocative issues have emerged for affirmative action in the twenty-first century. As suggested above, a basic indicator of opportunity since the late 1960s has been the ratio of members of a given group in the population to those in some sphere of employment, business, or education. Underrepresentation of Afro-Americans implied discrimination. This inference, always controversial, is facing new difficulties as new groups are added to the mix. John Aubrey Douglass presents a close-up view of just how different at least some parts of America already are from that world of the late 1960s and 1970s when reliance on statistics to show underrepresentation or discrimination began. The University of California began to practice affirmative action in undergraduate admissions in part because it was already committed to representing all of the state of California. For years, it had sought representation of different geographical regions of the state. In a way, affirmative action was just a late-1960s spin on the century-old principle of the "social contract" of the state university. The difficulty was that admissions standards had to be considerably altered to achieve something like a proportional representation of Afro-Americans and Latinos. The regents of the university boldly decided to end affirmative action in 1995. Though rarely acknowledged, the University of California's affirmative action policy had produced by that time a surprising and curious situation: if the universities did succeed in getting a proportional representation of Afro-Americans and Latinos, Douglass shows, they would also guarantee an *underrepresentation* of Euro-Americans. This was because of the striking overrepresentation of Asian Americans in the state's universities. Did this make Euro-Americans a minority, and should a university committed to racial diversity seek to achieve a proportional representation of Euro-Americans? The very question is so at odds with the logic of affirmative action that it remains taboo. Maintaining affirmative action for Afro-Americans and Latinos while seeking a proportional representation of Euro-Americans would clearly require limiting Asian American opportunity.[7] Although the demise of racial and ethnic preferences at the University of California has led to a return to Afro-American and Latino underrepresentation on some of the giant university's most sought-after campuses, the issue will linger. Rather than reevaluating the logic and purposes of affirmative action for the "correct" representation, most political leaders and commentators simply ignore the facts of the new America.

The chapter by Kelly and Dobbin addresses these issues less directly, but the implications are equally provocative. The "diversity" rationale that has come to shape the understanding of affirmative action in the nation's largest firms was not created or intended by any government policy. Its independent emergence in higher education was similarly not the dictate of any government policy, though it received Supreme Court approval in *Regents of the University of California v. Bakke* (438 U.S. 265 [1978]). With the emergence of the diversity rationale, affirmative action has become separated from *discrimination*. This change invites minority politics from anyone in American society who can identify a context where their group's voice is not being heard. In an era of high levels of immigration of skilled, high-achieving nonwhite groups, Euro-Americans may soon be asking for special preferences to ensure diversity in some contexts. The oft-demonized WASPs, almost always assumed to be the dominant group, may engage in minority politics without having to prove "reverse discrimination." Of course, they may not, or they may use other identities, as have Christians and conservatives decrying their marginalization on the campuses of some leading universities (Tilove 1999, A21). But certainly the unintended opening is there, as are the conditions where it may be encouraged.

The lack of serious debate and analysis of the appropriate beneficiaries of affirmative action is surprising, and not only because of the problems described in the chapters that follow. There is, for example, the issue of categorizing mixed-raced persons. Despite the estimated 75 to 90 percent of Afro-Americans who have some European blood, Americans have, for more than a hundred years, pretended that anyone with almost any Afro-American ancestry is indeed "Negro," "black," or "African American" (Davis 1991, 21). Thus categorizing them for affirmative action has always been simple. But Americans have never used this "one drop rule" with Asians, nor with Latinos (a group that includes many whites), nor with American Indians. Immigration from Asia and Latin America is growing rapidly, and intermarriage rates between these groups and Euro-Americans are already very high. For example, for American-born persons under the age of forty, Jerry Jacobs and Teresa Labov found Filipinos marrying non-Hispanic whites at rates of 61 percent for males and 66 percent for females. For Japanese Americans, the figures were 44 and 54 percent, for Cubans 61 and 47 percent, and for Mexican Americans 31 and 28 percent, respectively (for blacks, the figures were much lower, 5 and 2 percent; Jacobs and Labov 1995). How Asian, and how Latino, does one have to be for inclusion in the programs? It is a question likely to make many Americans uncomfortable.

Afro-Americans and Immigrants in the Workplace

There may be new challenges for affirmative action from the new immigration, but what about the bedrock of American civil rights policy—the Civil Rights Act of 1964? Despite its celebrated status and public support, America's basic civil rights law may no longer be in tune with today's multiethnic and multiracial workplaces, vividly described in the chapter by Michael Lichter and Roger Waldinger and the chapter by Jennifer Lee. Of course, America has always been multiethnic. The workplaces of urban America in the 1910s and 1920s were both similar to and different from the Los Angeles and New York that the authors of part II describe at the end of the century. In the early twentieth century, Italians, Poles, Irish, Jews, Hungarians, Slovaks, Greeks, and many others rubbed elbows in cities such as New York, Chicago, Detroit, and Cleveland. All of these groups suffered some discrimination but also experienced some favored treatment over Afro-Americans on many occasions. There also was interethnic conflict in the workplace in 1920s America (Pacyga 1991; Philpott 1991; Waldinger 1996).

A similar situation exists in American cities today, with three major differences. First, the American manufacturing juggernaut that lured the southern and eastern European immigrants has been substantially replaced by smaller industrial concerns, services of various kinds, and retail stores (Sugrue 1996; Wilson 1996). Second, a developed regime of antidiscrimination and affirmative action policy is now in place.[8]

Third, the immigrants' origins have changed. Afro-Americans no longer compete only with ostensibly privileged Euro-Americans, but with disadvantaged members of other minority groups that are equally eligible for affirmative action programs. To be sure, many skilled and educated Afro-Americans are reinforcing their niche in the public sector. But the least skilled are increasingly competing with the new immigrants (Lim forthcoming; Waldinger 1996). Although the effects can be disputed, it is clear that the new immigration is changing the employment landscape in many areas where Afro-Americans are concentrated, and conflict and competition are inevitable.[9] The chapters in part II both find conflict among persons of color, a problem that suggests that future coalition-building based on nonwhite status will be no easy feat. The chapters also show that Euro-Americans have no monopoly on prejudice and ethnic preference.

First, Lichter and Waldinger show how different the America of the twenty-first century will be from the America that existed when civil rights laws were developed. They find that low-end employers in Los Angeles regularly rely on word-of-mouth hiring, a practice that leads them to hire the co-ethnics of their mostly Latino and Asian workforces. Further, where these jobs are desirable to Afro-Americans, they sometimes have difficulty fitting in with workers who are culturally different from themselves and even speak a different language. The Civil Rights Act made word-of-mouth hiring illegal when Euro-American employers and employees used it to shut Afro-Americans out of jobs.[10] But is it illegal, or as morally troubling, when one affirmative action–eligible minority group uses it in a way that excludes another?

Another aspect of early twenty-first-century America, however, is the new goal in hiring: make the workforce "diverse" enough to mirror the customer base. This goal is based in part on the new value on diversity that guides many larger firms, as described by Kelly and Dobbin, but also on simple customer preferences. Lichter and Waldinger describe how Los Angeles employers try to give customers of various cultural backgrounds co-ethnic service. Firms want their customers, who may be of Thai, Salvadoran, Chinese, or other descent, to be comfortable. This is different from the honoring of pre-1964 southern whites' preference for all-white service personnel—or is it? There is a paradox: many firms may pursue "diversity," but they do so to ensure that customers encounter only ethnic homogeneity.

The chapter by Jennifer Lee also details racially preferential hiring, but her research finds it occurring in New York, where there is a somewhat different dynamic. In New York City, stores owned by Korean Americans and Jewish Americans sometimes hire on the basis of color to deal with a customer base that is largely Afro-American. The reasons they do so are manifold. Koreans may hire blacks because they can more easily speak English to customers. Both Koreans and Jews want black employees to interpret the Afro-American client culture for them, and these employees also provide a symbol of "giving back" to the Afro-American local community, where there are sometimes sensitivities to the problem of outsiders taking locally derived profits to other communities. But the basic reason that these stores preferentially hire blacks is to serve as conflict-resolving "cultural brokers" that calm the sometimes tense situations that arise from misunderstandings between Korean or Jewish American shop owners and customers. Strikingly, the business owners prefer hiring *immigrant* blacks, rather than Afro-Americans. Blacks from the Caribbean or Africa have enough legitimacy in and understanding of the Afro-American community to be effective cultural brokers, and they also provide what the store owners perceive as a superior work ethic. In a way, race has become a bona fide occupational qualification, tied to obvious national-origin discrimination, perpetrated by groups often seen as victims of discrimination themselves in the past or present. None of this was, or could have been, foreseen by Congress when it passed its nondiscrimination law.

These chapters raise some important warning flags for Americans. First, any supporter of civil rights must be concerned by the finding that black immigrants and others frequently are preferred to Afro-Americans. Second, although it may not be surprising that recent immigrants from Korea might want to hire local people to deal with local customers, or that there is conflict between blacks in Los Angeles and recent immigrant arrivals, the similar use of "cultural brokers" by American-born store owners points to how different (and apparently incomprehensible) the inner-city Afro-American culture has become to third- or fourth-generation Euro-Americans.

We must also keep in mind, however, that although these studies find preferences for immigrants at entry-level jobs, this does not mean such preferences exist in other sectors. We still need more research on the treatment of American-born and immigrant blacks, Asians, and Latinos in skilled, professional, and white-collar positions, where discrimination likely still occurs. Research on a "glass ceiling" limiting promotions should also consider groups ineligible for affirmative action but who have faced discrimination or stereotypes in the past, such as Armenian, Italian, Jewish, Middle Eastern, and Polish Americans.

The Views of Multiethnic America

What about the views of the American people, especially the various minorities, on civil rights and affirmative action? For decades, students of public opinion have analyzed the views of Americans on issues of civil rights and affirmative action. But they developed theories based on, but rarely going beyond, analysis of the views of Euro-Americans and Afro-Americans on these issues. This volume contains two of the increasingly frequent but still-rare studies of the views and attitudes of Latinos and Asian Americans along with Euro- and Afro-Americans toward affirmative action.[11] The sociologist Lawrence Bobo brings the tools of public opinion analysis to examine the views of multiethnic America toward affirmative action, while the political scientist Carol M. Swain and her colleagues explore public attitudes through a focus group study. Although the methods and goals of the studies (and thus some of their findings) differ, the two chapters have themes in common. Although affirmative action programs do not formally differentiate between minority groups, those groups do differ in their views toward the policy, and they do so in ways that are not unpredictable. In addition, both studies express optimism regarding a future muting of the controversy over affirmative action, though for different reasons.

Assessing public opinion of affirmative action is a tricky business because, as with other policy issues, support varies considerably depending on question wording. This problem is compounded in the case of affirmative action, because the programs take many different forms. As Lawrence Bobo explains in his contribution to this volume, public opinion varies with the kind of affirmative action mentioned in surveys, with Euro-Americans showing support for some types. This is especially true when affirmative action is described as special job outreach and training for minorities or as scholarship programs targeted at minorities. Focusing on views of the policy when it aids blacks, he finds racial or ethnic differences in attitudes that are not reducible to socioeconomic and ideological factors. In other words, your ethnic or racial identity helps predict how you view the policy. Euro-Americans are most likely to see negative effects of affirmative action. Afro-Americans, the most disadvantaged group, are the least likely to see negative effects of affirmative action, while Latinos, though also benefiting from the policy, are less supportive, and Asian Americans, a group that benefits in many programs but is most like Euro-Americans on a variety of socioeconomic measures, fall between Latinos and Euro-Americans. Bobo moves beyond the old debates by criticizing the notion, developed in studies based solely on white and black attitudes, that resistance to affirmative action is either purely principled (affirmative action is a violation of individualism and merit) or evidence of racism. Bobo's more optimistic study suggests that views toward racial preferences are based on perceptions that opportunity is lost as a result of affirmative action. To the supporter of affirmative action, this is encouraging because such perceptions can change more easily than can moral principles. Showing that race or ethnic grouping matters in views of affirmative action, Bobo concludes with a claim new in the debate: "Affirmative action is about the place racial groups should occupy in American society."

Although public opinion studies offer important contributions, the survey format cannot fully illuminate the structures of American attitudes toward affirmative action and civil rights. Using a small sample but adding depth, the focus group research conducted by Carol M. Swain, Kyra Greene, and Christine Min Wotipka sheds new light. In their multiethnic study, Swain and her colleagues find widespread confusion about what is legal and what is required with affirmative action. Though quotas are illegal unless court-ordered, for example, there is a tendency among all groups to assume that affirmative action means quotas. The research, however, also seems to fit with Bobo's study as it finds Latinos and Asian Americans in between Afro- and Euro-Americans in the level of support for special preferences for minorities. Part of the reason for this varying level of support, the researchers surmise, stems from the different understandings of affirmative action and its purposes exhibited by different groups. One crucial factor appears to be the tendency among Afro-Americans to see affirmative action as the main policy to prevent everyday discrimination, and thus absolutely essential to their future, whereas Euro-Americans tend to see it as a boost to the unqualified. Asian American and Latino views of the policy and its purposes are ambiguous; it follows from this that their support level would be in between those of Euro-Americans and Afro-Americans. Swain's team also offers the only study to date to explore Americans' views of *which groups* should benefit from affirmative action. In their study, Latinos and Asian Americans did not display any emotional commitment to ensuring their inclusion in affirmative action. Asians did not even express awareness that they were included at all and did not offer stories of discrimination they suffered to justify inclusion. Latinos did claim to be victims of discrimination and stereotyping but did not connect, as did blacks, this present-day discrimination to the need for affirmative action.

An affirmative action based on class, targeted at the poor and not at particular races or ethnicities, has been criticized for a variety of reasons, often because it would not sufficiently address the problems of Afro-Americans (Appiah and Guttman 1996; Malamud 1997). Yet the Swain study suggests many Americans may agree with that policy's strongest proponent, Richard Kahlenberg (1997), that a class-based affirmative action is the better approach—at least, from a political standpoint. Swain, Greene, and Wotipka find that affirmative action would have the greatest support if it also benefited the poor and the disabled, regardless of race or national origin. Thus, if Bobo's research suggests that the way to reduce the controversy over affirmative action is to address Americans' concerns about the policy's distribution of opportunity, Swain's research suggests that making affirmative action available to the disabled and the poor is the way to reduce controversy.

Civil Rights and Affirmative Action beyond America

In the mid-1990s, many Americans began to reevaluate civil rights policy and especially affirmative action. The early political miscues by the Clinton administration energized conservative voters, leading to the rise of prominent conservative politicians. Republicans took control of Congress and aggressively sought new issues. Remarkably, however, during the Republican presidential primary of 1995–1996, when the strongest calls for ending affirmative action could be heard, there was virtually no discussion of the impact of immigration on affirmative action. The debate focused on arguably the neediest minority, the Afro-Americans.

Yet the affirmative action debate of 1995–1996 remained only a debate. The Republicans lost the presidential campaign, and Republican congresses chose not to attack the policy. Although some programs and regulations have been curtailed in executive actions, by referenda, or by the courts, especially at the state or local level, most federal programs have survived, partly as a result of President Clinton's defense of affirmative action. This defense was based on a comprehensive review of affirmative action regulations that ranged widely in its original discussions (Drew 1997, 289–96) but ended in a report prepared by George Stephanopoulos and Christopher Edley that focused obsessively on the question of whether affirmative action really led to quotas (Stephanopoulos and Edley 1995). As Graham shows in this volume, the report offers no analysis of the relation of immigration and affirmative action.

Another striking feature of that review was that there was no effort to look beyond America's borders for guidance on how to manage a multiethnic state. In a world filled with ethnic violence and separatist movements, Americans are justly proud of their relative success in creating a harmonious society of diverse groups. But the Clinton administration review missed out on some illuminating examples of different approaches to equal opportunity and nondiscrimination rights.

The Clinton review was typical. If American debates about civil rights, discrimination, and affirmative action have ignored the realities of American demographic changes, they have also been remarkably parochial. Neither the Left nor the Right in the United States has sought to learn from the experiences of other nations. In fact, India has had a kind of affirmative action for longer than the United States, and a much stricter form than that practiced here. And as European nations have become increasingly multiethnic they too have had to tackle the problem of discrimination, and they have chosen paths rather different than those chosen by the United States. Part IV of the book looks outside the United States for guidance on how the United States can improve its equal opportunity policy. The cases examined here range from a close approximation of an officially color-blind multiethnic society (France) to a society with a policy of strictly "soft" affirmative action (Britain) to a society with comprehensive, "hard" quota systems (India).[12] The case studies demonstrate the political consequences of different approaches to equal opportunity policy. They share a theme in that preferences for ethnic minorities always seem to be controversial, but the degree of resistance varies cross-nationally and over time.

It may be tempting to argue that in these cases demography is destiny, since the countries with the smallest percentages of minorities (Britain and France, each with about 5 percent of their populations of Asian, African, or Caribbean ancestry) have the fewest programs and the least preference, while the United States (with a 25 percent Latino and nonwhite minority population) and India (where lower castes can make up 50 percent of the population, depending on the state) have more programs and more preference. But this would be a mistake. First, if demography is destiny, then all countries would have the same affirmative action policies for women, and they do not. But a pure demographics argument is insufficient for ethnicity-based affirmative action as well. For example, although Britain and France have similar demographics, Britain has traveled partly down the road to affirmative action but then stopped, and France steadfastly adheres to a color-blind policy.

We begin with Britain, our cultural cousin in Europe. This former colonial power has experienced since the 1950s an influx of blacks from the Caribbean as well as Indians, Pakistanis, Bangladeshis, and other Asians. In dealing with problems of discrimination, British offi-cials looked to the United States as a model but so far have avoided American-style "hard" affirmative action. Steven M. Teles shows that the British have sought to avoid preferential types of affirmative action, but operating within these constraints, have found other possibilities as they work hard to ensure that nonwhite Britons can compete fairly with whites. The British, according to Teles, have not moved to preferential policies for a variety of reasons, including the lack of severe deprivation of its ethnic minorities, their status as immigrants whose very presence in the country remains controversial to many, and factors related to British political institutions. For example, the Labour Party has mobi-lized voters on the basis of class rather than ethnicity, and British femi-nists, who could take the lead in establishing preferential policies, have not sought them.

To American conservatives, the British are still committing the sin of color-consciousness by allowing targeted recruitment and training. To American liberals, they are making inadequate efforts. But with their more developed welfare state, the British may be doing more for their non-British-origin residents even without preferential affirmative ac-tion than the Americans are for their minorities. Even without the secu-rity guaranteed by a welfare state, Americans may look to Britain as a model for compromise. After all, the kinds of affirmative action that Americans in Bobo's study say they support closely mirror those already practiced in Britain.

Whereas Teles shows why Britain has not gone as far as the United States, Erik Bleich shows why France has stayed even further away from the American model. France has chosen a universalist, color-blind model to dominate public policy making. France has received numerous immigrants from North Africa and other nations but avoids ethnicity- or race-based affirmative action, such as preferences or goals. France does not even collect census statistics on the basis of ethnicity. The reasons include a strong cultural prohibition on ethnic categorization. Bleich argues that "in particular, there is a connection between race categorizations and the horrors of Nazism that is much stronger in France than in the United States." In addition, a credible threat from the far right in French politics has kept affirmative action off the agenda there, while the lack of ethnicity-based statistics obscures any severe problems that may exist for French minorities. While the British looked to the United States as a model, for the French the United States was an "anti-model" to be avoided (also see Bleich 1999).

France has pursued a road not traveled by the United States, though it could have been different. Color-blindness was close to orthodoxy among many civil rights leaders on the Left in the 1950s and early 1960s; the American Civil Liberties Union even lobbied to have all race questions removed from the 1960 census (Petersen 1987). Of course, in the United States, it is now the Right that believes color-blindness is the only acceptable model for society and civil rights law. Whether or not one believes that the French model is a good idea for France, Bleich cautions that it may not be applicable to the United States, given the very different histories and political institutions of the two countries. Still, the French case can give important insights on the nature and practicality of color-blind law in a multiethnic society.

The case of affirmative action in India may give support to both critics and supporters of American-style affirmative action. For the lower castes, India openly and unabashedly uses "reservations," which are, as Sunita Parikh shows, hard quotas. Parikh argues that the reservation policy is not simply the result of India having a large number of deserving beneficiaries. The policy actually had its origins in the British colonial regime and evolved into an important part of Indian coalition-building politics, where support for the policy serves as a litmus test for politicians seeking support from the "backwards" groups.

American critics of affirmative action might point out that India's reservation policies for the most disadvantaged castes have led to widespread conflict, often bloody and violent. Affirmative action supporters can point out that most of this conflict is in the past. Both sides might look with concern, however, at how affirmative action has become such a major part of political coalition-building in India. The Indian policies give preference to a very large percentage of the population, and all beneficiaries passionately care about maintaining the policies.[13] Although the lukewarm support that Bobo and Swain and her colleagues find among Latinos and Asian Americans suggests that the United States will not develop an ethnic coalition politics around affirmative action, this is not certain. There is some evidence that Republicans have avoided attacking the policy in part because they believe this would signal hostility to Latino groups that they want as voters, especially in populous states such as California (Skrentny forthcoming). In political coalition-building, politicians may pay more attention to the views of ethnic group leaders than to the views of ethnic group citizens, even if those views diverge, as they do for Mexican Americans (Skerry 1993). If the group leadership uses a politician's devotion to affirmative action as a litmus test for the leaders' support, the United States could follow the Indian pattern of ethnic coalition-building based on affirmative action.

The Legal Status of Affirmative Action and Title VII

The law professor Deborah C. Malamud closes the volume with an analysis of the legal standing of affirmative action and civil rights, focusing on the issues discussed in the previous chapters. She shows that if social scientists and political commentators have fallen behind the ethnic reality of America, legal development is not much further ahead. It is changing, however, rapidly and in surprising ways. Surveying the state of law regarding affirmative action, she shows, for example, that changing constitutional jurisprudence is producing an almost certainly unintended situation: legal defense of affirmative action for Afro-Americans is increasingly more difficult to achieve than defense of affirmative action for women. On the other hand, affirmative action for nonblack ethnic groups has run into some problems, as courts have found difficulties with the inclusion of groups who have not been shown to be victims of discrimination. Courts will increasingly be addressing these difficult issues; one uncomfortable judge already has considered which nations in South America are part of the definition of *Hispanic.*

Malamud observes that despite the embrace of "diversity" as a goal for many sectors of American society, especially employment, the courts have never said ethnic or racial diversity was a constitutionally accepted goal anywhere except in higher education. Public employers hiring on the basis of a diversity goal have not realized that there is different law for different domains. Further, she shows, hiring for diversity by private employers may also run afoul of the law, in this case, Congress's refusal in Title VII to allow employers to use race as a bona fide occupational qualification.

Surveying the current status of Title VII and research on immigrant hiring, she concludes that much of what is occurring in the urban workplaces of twenty-first century America, such as the reservation of jobs for particular minority races or ethnic groups or reliance on word-of-mouth hiring in immigrant communities, may be discriminatory and illegal. For a variety of reasons, this discrimination is rarely litigated. But does that mean it is not a problem? Malamud concludes that for those committed to integration, it is a problem. Whether Euro-Americans avoid hiring Afro-Americans, or immigrants avoid hiring them, or immigrant networks close off opportunities, the result is the same: Afro-Americans face uniquely limited opportunities. Further, she cautions that the notion of certain positions in society as appropriately the property of certain racial or ethnic groups "is a dangerous path if integration remains the desired goal."

Malamud's afterword, together with other chapters in the book, especially that of Graham, raises questions regarding the meaning of citizenship in twenty-first-century America. Recently, some scholars have described the rise of a rights model based on personhood and not on membership in a nation-state, noting that there are now "rights across borders" (Jacobson 1996) and a new "post-national membership" (Soysal 1994). Although citizenship is required in some affirmative action programs, it is not always required or noted, especially in programs that count anonymous numbers of minorities in a university or a firm.

Excepting Afro-Americans and American Indians, the vast majority of affirmative action–eligible persons, or their ancestors, came to the United States voluntarily. Should that matter? Should an immigrant or the descendant of affirmative action–eligible immigrants enjoy a preference because of the diversity that he or she may add to a top university or firm or because of past discrimination against persons in the same ethno-racial bloc, while a lower-income or poor citizen who is not eligible does not receive a preference? How could we make such distinctions while preserving our goal of equal opportunity? Should we exclude adult immigrants, who came here voluntarily, from affirmative action—even if they are naturalized citizens? The difficulties raised by questions of affirmative action and citizenship are made apparent in the law professor and former Clinton advisor Christopher Edley's mostly careful defense of affirmative action. Edley argues, first, that Latinos and Asian Americans should be included ("I have no doubt that the case remains strong for African Americans, Hispanics, and Asians"; Edley 1996, 174). Only a page later, he undercuts the point when he writes that we should consider the extent to which "these newcomers voluntarily assumed the burdens of 'otherness' in America." Edley suggests that "the voluntarily disadvantaged have a lesser claim on our solicitude if the remedy in question is the morally costly one of race-conscious decision making. All wrongs are not equally compelling" (175–76). This matter will command increasing attention in the years ahead.

Readers may, of course, disagree with some of the conclusions in this book. But it cannot be denied that American and world demographics and sociological dynamics will be different in the twenty-first century from what they were when the nation's civil rights laws and affirmative action regulations were created. We no longer have the problem of the color line, as Du Bois stated, but of color lines. Both sides in the affirmative action and civil rights debates, and Americans interested in equal opportunities in general, should see the work in this volume as an early notification. This book represents a first attempt to inform a coming—and inevitable—debate.

As it stands, the national conversation on civil rights and affirmative action, always oversimplified, is increasingly based on memory and not reality. Political commentators on both the Left and the Right, as well as the American public, continue to disregard the changing nature of the discrimination problem, civil rights law, and affirmative action in today's multiethnic, multiracial America. Though political leaders and commentators have never offered a consistent and clear justification for affirmative action, the focus of their justifications—Afro-Americans—was consistent. What does it mean for affirmative action when Afro-Americans are a "minority" minority? The courts have already cast a suspicious eye toward the perceived overinclusiveness of some affirmative action programs, as described in this volume. Who should be included in affirmative action? How should we decide? Is the policy as a whole an anachronism? To answer these questions, we must first study the issues. Because they have been obscured, it is not yet clear how the American public will view them. There is no doubt they are important and will become increasingly important.

Policy makers, take heed. Civil rights and ethnic inequality are issues that strike at the core of the nation's identity. Americans should have confidence that those making policy are informed of just how different the 2000s will be from the 1960s.

Notes

1. I follow Orlando Patterson in using *Afro-American* and *Euro-American* instead of *black/African-American* and *white*. Patterson points out that scientists have long known that there is no biological basis for "race" and that the term *African American* obscures the distinctive sociology of American-born persons of African descent, because it groups them together with the growing numbers of immigrants from the African continent and the Caribbean (Patterson 1997). *Euro-American* is gaining currency as a replacement for *white* to account for the fact that large percentages of Latinos are white (Skerry 1993, 2000) and to avoid the cumbersome term *non-Hispanic white*. Of course, the term is still imperfect since Latinos usually can also trace some ancestry to Europe.

There are many views on just how to label America's constituent ethnic and racial groupings. The contributors to this volume pursue their own ideas of appropriate labels.

2. On the mid-century increase in voting clout of Afro-Americans, see McAdam 1982 and Piven and Cloward 1977. On the civil rights movement's successful efforts to gain public attention, see Garrow 1978. On the relation of the civil rights movement to Soviet propaganda, see Dudziak 1988, Klinkner and Smith 1999, and Skrentny 1998. On the effects of 1960s urban unrest, see McAdam 1982 and Skrentny 1996.

3. In 1972, Congress passed the Equal Employment Opportunity Act, giving the EEOC the power to initiate lawsuits on its own.

4. See "Affirmative Action Commitment Under Executive Orders 10925 and 11114," in Lawson 1984, pt. II, reel 3, frame 809.

5. Another source for the widespread notion that affirmative action was created to compensate blacks is a much-cited speech by President Lyndon Johnson at the 1965 commencement of Howard University that was an eloquent justification of government-sponsored compensatory treatment. Johnson argued that "freedom is not enough" for American blacks and that fair competition required special help for this group long hobbled by discrimination. Johnson added that the next frontier was "equality as a fact and as a result" (Rainwater and Yancey 1967, 126), but there is no evidence that he had in mind the racial hiring goals, timetables, or quotas of affirmative action. The speech, written by Richard Goodwin and Daniel Patrick Moynihan, says not a word about affirmative action. It was much more in line with less controversial compensatory measures, such as the Head Start educational program and other monetary aid packages (Davies 1996). In other words, the most often-cited justification for affirmative action was not about affirmative action.

6. Though small, the Korean-owned firms, as well as Asian Indian- and Chinese-owned firms, made considerably more money than black-owned firms. For example, 1987 data for firms with no paid employees show that Korean firms had average gross receipts of $111,000, the Indian firms made $128,000, and the Chinese firms made $107,000. Black firms with no paid employees had gross receipts of $47,000. For only firms with paid employees, the statistics were as follows: Korean, $254,000; Indian, $317,000; Chinese, $281,000; and black, $200,000 (Portes and Rumbaut 1996, 74). For research on Korean-owned businesses, see Bates 1997; Kim 1981; and Yoon 1997.

7. Achievement by Asian Americans in higher education occurs at such high levels for a variety of reasons. One factor is simply that on average Asian American parents are more educated and wealthier than other groups. Research also indicates that Asian American children and their parents set higher educational achievement aspirations than other groups, and families devote more resources to preparation for higher education. Asian families are more likely than others to reserve a special part of the home for study, and the children spend more time on homework than those in other groups (Kao 1995). Some groups, such as the Vietnamese, may also have strong neighborhood networks and other resources—"social capital"—to keep children on the path to academic success. See Zhou and Bankston 1996, 1998.

8. Most federal civil rights laws and regulations only affect the larger employers (in the case of Title VII, those with at least fifteen employees), though state and municipal antidiscrimination laws have a wider reach.

9. The jury is still out on whether immigration helps, harms, or has no effect on op-

portunity for Afro-Americans. The immigration debate itself is ideologically confusing because conservatives and liberals can be found on both sides of the issue. For conservative arguments supportive of immigration, see Millman 1997 and Unz 1994. For the Left's argument that immigration is limiting the opportunities of Afro-Americans, see Steinberg 1995, 185–95. The Right, of course, also has arguments against immigration. See Beck 1996, chaps. 8 and 9. A moderate analysis can be found in Farley 1996, chap. 5; Hamermesh and Bean 1998.

10. See, for example, *NAACP v. Evergreen*, 693 F.2d 1367, 1369 (11th Cir. 1982); *Domingo v. New England Fish Co.*, 727 F.2d 1429, 1435–36 (9th Cir. 1984).

11. Owing to problems of sample size or a simple lack of interest, public opinion and focus group researchers have not disaggregated the four block groups, "Asian," "black," "Latino" and "white," into constituent ethnicities. In fact, it is easy to imagine large differences between ethnic groups within the ethno-racial blocks. I thank Karen Chai for this point.

12. Other nations have policies more or less resembling American-style affirmative action. Canada's affirmative action developed somewhat later than America's but is similar to it, according O'Connor, Orloff, and Shaver (1999). Lipset (1990) argues that affirmative action and multiculturalism in Canada in general are significantly harder, or stronger, than in the United States. Other nations with types of affirmative action include Australia (O'Connor, Orloff, and Shaver 1999), as well as Fiji, Malaysia, Nigeria, and Sri Lanka (Sowell 1990).

13. Of course, since it includes women of all colors plus the ethnic minorities, the American affirmative action is the most inclusive of all. The key difference is that affirmative action does not appear to be a salient concern for Euro-American women, and politicians seeking women's votes rarely advocate affirmative action to get them.

References

Appiah, K. Anthony, and Amy Gutmann. 1996. *Color conscious: The political morality of race.* Princeton: Princeton University Press.

Bates, Timothy. 1997. *Race, self-employment, and upward mobility.* Baltimore: Johns Hopkins University Press.

Beck, Roy. 1996. *The case against immigration.* New York: Norton.

Bleich, Erik. 1999. Problem-solving politics: Ideas and race policies in Britain and France. Ph.D. diss., Department of Government, Harvard University.

Brooks, Clem. 2000. Civil rights liberalism and the suppression of a Republican political realignment in the United States, 1972 to 1996. *American Sociological Review* 65:483–505.

Burstein, Paul. 1998. *Discrimination, jobs, and politics.* Chicago: University of Chicago Press.

Davies, G. 1996. *From opportunity to entitlement: The transformation and decline of great society liberalism.* Lawrence: University Press of Kansas.

Davis, F. James. 1991. *Who is black? One nation's definition.* University Park: Pennsylvania State University Press.

Drew, Elizabeth. 1997. *Showdown: The struggle between the Gingrich Congress and the Clinton White House*. New York: Touchstone.

Du Bois, W. E. B. [1903] 1997. *The souls of black folk*. Edited by David W. Blight and Robert Gooding-Williams. Boston: Bedford Books.

Dudziak, Mary L. 1988. Desegregation as a cold war imperative. *Stanford Law Review* 41: 61–120.

Edley, Christopher. 1996. *Not all black and white*. New York: Hill and Wang.

Farely, Reynolds. 1996. *The new American reality: Who we are, how we got here, where we are going*. New York: Russell Sage Foundation.

Frymer, P., and J. Skrentny. 1998. Coalition-building and the politics of electoral capture during the Nixon administration: African-Americans, labor, and Latinos. *Studies in American Political Development* 12:131–61.

Garrow, David. 1978. *Protest at Selma*. New Haven: Yale University Press.

Graham, Hugh Davis. 1990. *The civil rights era: Origins and development of national policy*. New York: Oxford University Press.

Hamermesh, Daniel S., and Frank D. Bean, eds. 1998. *Help or hindrance? The economic implications of immigration for African Americans*. New York: Russell Sage Foundation.

Jacobs, Jerry A., and Teresa Labov. 1995. Asian brides, Anglo grooms: Asian exceptionalism in intermarriage. Department of Sociology, University of Pennsylvania. Typescript.

Jacobson, David. 1996. *Rights across borders*. Baltimore: Johns Hopkins University Press.

Kahlenberg, Richard D. 1997. *The remedy: Class, race, and affirmative Action*. New York: Basic Books.

Kao, Grace. 1995. Asian Americans as model minorities? A look at their academic performance. *American Journal of Education* 103:121–59.

Kim, Illsoo. 1981. *New urban immigrants: The Korean community in New York*. Princeton: Princeton University Press.

Klinkner, Philip, with Rogers Smith. 1999. *The unsteady march*. Chicago: University of Chicago Press.

Lawson, Stephen F. 1984. *Civil rights during the Johnson administration, 1963–1969*. Frederick, Md.: University Publications of America.

Lim, Nelson. Forthcoming. On the backs of blacks? Immigrants and fortunes of African Americans. In *Strangers at the gate: The new immigrants in urban America*, edited by Roger Waldinger. Berkeley: University of California Press.

Lipset, Seymour Martin. 1990. *Continental divide*. New York: Routledge.

Loury, Glenn C. 1998. Discrimination in the post–civil rights era: Beyond market interactions. *Journal of Economic Perspectives* 12:117–26.

Malamud, Deborah, C. 1997. Assessing class-based affirmative action. *Journal of Legal Education* 47:452–71.

Massey, Douglas S., and Nancy A. Denton. 1993. *American apartheid*. Cambridge: Harvard University Press.

McAdam, Doug. 1982. *Political process and the development of black insurgency*. Chicago: University of Chicago Press.

Millman, Joel. 1997. *The other Americans: How immigrants renew our country, our economy, and our values.* New York: Viking.

O'Connor, Julia S., Ann Shola Orloff, and Sheila Shaver. 1999. *States, markets, families.* New York: Cambridge University Press.

Pacyga, Dominic A. 1991. *Polish immigrants and industrial Chicago: Workers on the South Side, 1880–1922.* Columbus: Ohio State University Press.

Patterson, Orlando. 1997. *The ordeal of integration.* New York: Civitas.

Petersen, William. 1987. Politics and the measurement of ethnicity. In *The politics of numbers,* edited by William Alonso and Paul Starr. New York: Russell Sage Foundation.

Philpott, Thomas Lee. 1991. *The slum and the ghetto: Immigrants, blacks, and reformers in Chicago, 1880–1930.* Belmont, Calif.: Wadsworth.

Piven, Frances Fox, and Richard Cloward. 1977. *Poor people's movements.* New York: Vintage Books.

Portes, Alejandro, and Rubén G. Rumbaut. 1996. *Immigrant America: A portrait.* 2d ed. Berkeley: University of California Press.

Rainwater, L., and W. L. Yancey. 1967. *The Moynihan report and the politics of controversy.* Cambridge: MIT Press.

Schuman, Howard, Charlotte Steeh, and Lawrence Bobo. 1985. *Racial attitudes in America.* Cambridge: Harvard University Press.

Skerry, Peter. 1993. *Mexican Americans: The ambivalent minority.* New York: Free Press.

———. 2000. *Counting on the census?* Washington, D.C.: Brookings Institution.

Skrentny, John David. 1994. Pragmatism, institutionalism, and the construction of employment discrimination. *Sociological Forum* 9:343–69.

———. 1996. *The ironies of affirmative action: Politics, culture, and justice in America.* Chicago: University of Chicago Press.

———. 1998. The effect on the cold war on African-American civil rights: America and the world audience, 1945–1968. *Theory and Society* 27:237–85.

———. Forthcoming. Republican efforts to end affirmative action: Walking a fine line. In *Durability and change: Politics and policymaking in the 1990s,* edited by Marc Landy, Martin Levin, and Martin Shapiro. Washington, D.C.: Georgetown University Press.

Sowell, Thomas. 1990. *Preferential policies: An international perspective.* New York: William Morrow.

Soysal, Yasemin. 1994. *The limits of citizenship.* Chicago: University of Chicago Press.

Steinberg, Stephen. 1995. *Turning back: The retreat from racial justice in American thought and policy.* Boston: Beacon Press.

Stephanopoulos, George, and Christopher Edley Jr. 1995. Affirmative action review: Report to the president. Washington, D.C.: Government Printing Office.

Sugrue, Thomas J. 1996. *The origins of the urban crisis.* Princeton: Princeton University Press.

Thernstrom, Stephan, and Abigail Thernstrom. 1997. *America in black and white: One nation, indivisible.* New York: Simon and Schuster.

Tilove, Jonathan. 1999. Christian at Harvard says paper nailed him to cross. *New Orleans Times Picayune,* 28 February.

Unz, Ron K. 1994. Immigration or the welfare state: Which is our real enemy? *Policy Review* 17:33–38.

Waldinger, Roger. 1996. *Still the promised city? African-Americans and new immigrants in postindustrial New York.* Cambridge: Harvard University Press.

Wilson, William Julius. 1987. *The truly disadvantaged.* Chicago: University of Chicago Press.

———. 1996. *When work disappears: The world of the urban poor.* New York: Vintage.

Yoon, In-Jin. 1997. *On my own: Korean businesses and race relations in America.* Chicago: University of Chicago Press.

Zhou, Min, and Carl L. Bankston III. 1996. Social capital and the adaptation of the second generation: The case of Vietnamese youth in New Orleans. In *The new second generation,* edited by Alejandro Portes. New York: Russell Sage Foundation.

———. 1998. *Growing up American: How Vietnamese children adapt to life in the United States.* New York: Russell Sage Foundation.

PART I

AFFIRMATIVE ACTION IN MULTIETHNIC AMERICA:

POLICY HISTORY AND ANALYSIS

1

Breaking Through:

The Troubled Origins of Affirmative Action

in the Workplace

. . .

Thomas J. Sugrue

Since the 1960s, the construction industry has been one of the most contested battlegrounds for racial equality, rights, and economic opportunity. Few sectors of the economy had fewer blacks than the unionized building trades. The Kennedy, Johnson, and Nixon administrations all identified the construction industry as the primary target for their evolving policy of affirmative action. Those efforts culminated in 1969 with the Nixon administration's Philadelphia Plan, an effort to break open Philadelphia's notoriously exclusive construction unions that became a model for nationwide affirmative action mandates. In the aftermath of the Philadelphia Plan, affirmative action became a wedge issue in national electoral politics. Republicans attempted to exploit the growing rift between white hard hats and African American beneficiaries of workplace racial preferences. The fate of affirmative action as a federal policy has hinged, in large part, on the outcome of efforts to open the construction industry to racial minorities. But to make sense out of the debate over affirmative action in construction requires beginning the story well before 1969. The central issues in the affirmative action debate—rights, the role of government, and the nature of workplace racial division—have deep and tangled roots.

Understanding the affirmative action debate requires reexamining racial politics in the heyday of liberalism, from the New Deal through the mid-1960s. It was the promise and failure of post–New Deal antidiscrimination policies that generated northern protests, particularly in the early 1960s, that laid the groundwork for the emergence of affirmative action as a social policy. Liberal civil rights policies were inadequate to deal with the institutionally embedded forms of racial privilege in what I call the "niche of whiteness" in the construction industry. Building trades activists, opposed to even the mildest affirmative action programs, ironically embraced the rhetoric of post–World War II gradualist liberalism and fashioned an effective critique of the policies that threatened to undermine their workplace control and their economic advantage. The result was an impasse that continues to shape and limit the debate about affirmative action today.

Race, Rights, and Liberalism in the Post–New Deal Era

Understanding the emergence of racial preferences as an issue in the 1960s requires an excavation of the neglected history of post–New Deal liberalism. Affirmative action was not merely a consequence of 1960s-era racial upheavals. To be sure, it emerged in response to the upsurge of civil rights activism and racial unrest in the mid-1960s. It took shape in the hands of federal bureaucrats who had their own administrative imperatives. And it came to fruition because of Richard Nixon's desire to drive a wedge into the vulnerable Democratic Party coalition of blacks and labor. But alone these factors do not explain the rise of affirmative action. Rather, racial preferences were the consequence of institutional forms and ideological debates that played out in the United States in the 1940s, 1950s, and early 1960s.

Affirmative action was the product of the convergence of five major currents in post–New Deal liberalism. First was a racially divided rights consciousness that took shape during the New Deal and World War II. Second was a highly influential moralistic current of racial liberalism that took hold during the 1940s. Third was increasingly militant civil rights activism targeting employment discrimination, particularly in declining major northern cities, where working-class and poor blacks were frustrated at the glacial pace of black economic progress. Fourth was the persistence of liberals' faith that government should be the agent of moral reform and, more specifically, that such reform was best carried out by the executive branch, by detached bureaucrats who, allied with impartial experts, were best equipped to solve social problems. Fifth was deep-rooted white resistance to antidiscrimination efforts that threatened their racial privileges. In the remainder of the chapter, I will examine each of these themes in greater detail and consider their implications for current scholarship on affirmative action.

Two Rights Revolutions

The debate over affirmative action cannot be understood outside the context of the complex rights revolution that transformed the political landscape of post–New Deal America. Advocates of affirmative action rested their claims on an argument that racial preferences were necessary to achieve the full attainment of civil rights. They argued that blacks had been denied equal access to employment opportunities. White critics of affirmative action also evoked rights rhetoric: affirmative action, they contended, privileged blacks at the expense of their rights.

That both pro– and anti–affirmative action activists evoked the language of rights is a consequence of a transformation of political discourse in the mid-twentieth century. Beginning in the New Deal, blacks and whites alike came to view an empowered federal government as the guarantor of positive as well as negative rights. At the heart of the later New Deal was a sweeping redefinition of the relationship of government, entitlement, and citizenship, perhaps best summarized in Franklin Delano Roosevelt's "Second Bill of Rights" (1944). Roosevelt offered a sweeping revision of the freedoms guaranteed in the first ten constitutional amendments. Under the Bill of Rights, government power was to be checked; the government could not interfere in a citizen's lawful exercise of enumerated rights such as freedom of speech, religion, and assembly. Under the Second Bill of Rights, an activist government guaranteed the positive rights to "a useful and remunerative job," to "enough [income] to provide adequate food and clothing and recreation," to "a decent home," and to "adequate protection from the economic fears of old age, sickness, accident, and unemployment." The twin pillars of these newly enumerated rights, as President Roosevelt defined them, were "equality" and "security" (Roosevelt 1944).

Roosevelt offered perhaps the most articulate expression of a rights consciousness that was already deeply rooted by the mid-1940s. Workers—black and white alike—couched their political demands in the language of rights. They insisted that the government protect and defend their newfound rights. The workplace became one of the most important venues where the new rights revolution played out. Blue-collar workers, particularly those in trade unions (whose power and legitimacy had been bolstered by New Deal labor legislation), demanded secure employment—through seniority, high wages, and, increasingly, pensions and other benefits to buffer them from the vagaries of the economy. They pushed for government programs that would cushion them from unemployment and guarantee their security in retirement. But their conception of workplace rights was, from the outset, racially inflected. New Deal programs benefited blacks and whites unequally (Lieberman 1998; Quadagno 1994). Although black and white workers alike gained from unionization, whole sectors of the American economy were still largely closed to African Americans. But black workers still claimed the promise of the Second Bill of Rights, even if it was largely honored in the breach. In the postwar years there emerged a powerful movement to demand racial equality in the workplace. Black activists, like their white counterparts, used rights talk to legitimate their agenda. The black and white versions of rights collided forcefully in postwar America. For many white workers who had battled to protect their livelihoods from insecurity, black demands for inclusion were profoundly threatening. The course of postwar liberalism was to accede to workers' demands for security but to give little more than lip service to the ideal of equality. The result was, as the legal scholar William Forbath (1994, 1805) has suggested, "a broken constitutional link between economic and racial justice." Blacks, drawing from the newfound rights language, demanded equality; whites demanded security.

Racial Liberalism and the Elusive Goal of Equality

The new rights rhetoric proved a powerful tool in the hands of advocates of racial equality. In the aftermath of World War II, civil rights organizations began to direct their energies toward the elimination of employment discrimination. A combination of rights consciousness rooted in the New Deal and antiracist rhetoric unleashed during World War II and the Cold War delegitimated racial prejudice to a degree unimaginable even a decade earlier. By the 1940s, civil rights activists had turned toward the Democratic Party and to local, state, and federal governments to solve the problem of racial inequality.

Despite the rhetorical shift in attitudes about race and rights, despite the universalistic rhetoric of the New Deal, racial inequality remained deeply entrenched in American labor markets after World War II, even in the urban North, the region that attracted millions of black migrants seeking economic opportunity after World War II. To be sure, the war witnessed a major transformation in the economic opportunities available to African Americans. Blacks were hired in unprecedented numbers in many key industries, in part because of the wartime shortage of labor, in part because of the pressure that civil rights groups put on the federal government to open federal positions to blacks during wartime (Klinkner and Smith 1999, 161–201). The war was, however, an extraordinary period. Between the mid-1940s and the early 1960s, black workers made fewer gains. They were disproportionately affected by the growing flight of capital away from the old industrial cities that had attracted black refugees from the South. And they were entrapped, by and large, in the poorest-paying and least secure jobs (Sugrue 1996a, chaps. 4–5). Because blacks were disproportionately found in unskilled positions and were low on the seniority queue or confined to predominately black, dead-end seniority lines, they were also, as a common adage had it, "last hired and first fired."

Wartime gains and postwar setbacks spurred black demands for stronger antidiscrimination measures. The quest for equal opportunity in the workplace became one of the leading arenas of postwar civil rights protest. Integrationist civil rights activists in the 1940s and 1950s offered a set of restrained, gradualist responses to racial discrimination and black unemployment and underemployment. The central strategy was to persuade employers to hire blacks in "breakthrough" jobs, primarily in white-collar and skilled jobs that had been formerly reserved for whites. Underlying this strategy was the belief that racism was at root an individual pathology that needed to be solved at the individual level through reasoned debate and education. "The Negro problem," wrote Gunnar Myrdal in his path-breaking book *The American Dilemma*, the single most influential guide for integrationists in the postwar decades, "is a problem in the heart of the American. It is there that the interracial tension has its focus. It is there that the decisive struggle goes on" (Myrdal 1944, lxxi). Drawing from Myrdal's thesis, rights activists assumed that racial segregation was an anomalous feature of American society that could be quickly eradicated through persuasion and education (Jackson 1990; Steinberg 1995). The presence of black "pioneers" in jobs that had been all-white preserves would break down the racial status quo by demonstrating to skeptical whites that blacks were capable of work in any sector of the economy. If a firm hired a single black, a mortal blow would be struck against discrimination.

The principles of the "breakthrough" strategy extended to the legislative arena. In the aftermath of World War II, civil rights activists throughout the country lobbied for the creation of permanent Fair Employment Practices Committees, modeled after President Franklin Delano Roosevelt's wartime antidiscrimination agency. The FEPC, its advocates argued, would provide a governmental wedge to open the labor market to African Americans. Proposed FEP laws were the outgrowth of liberal social science and labor law. The FEP approach dealt with discrimination on a case-by-case basis, under a model of arbitration derived from labor law. Under proposed FEP laws, a parajudicial system of arbitrators would hear individual grievances and, if necessary, require employers to take corrective measures. On the federal level, FEPC laws proved impossible to pass. Thwarted on the national level by southern members of Congress who blocked every effort to revitalize the Fair Employment Practices Commission, liberals turned toward state and local governments, which they hoped would be more hospitable.

Michigan was typical among northern states that passed Fair Employment Practices laws. Civil rights advocates battled for more than a decade to pass a statewide law prohibiting employment discrimination (Fine 1996). In Michigan, as in most northern states, a majority of Republicans opposed FEP legislation out of fear that civil rights laws would interfere with businesses' managerial prerogative to hire and upgrade employees as they chose. The need to conciliate conservative opposition and the liberals' fears of controversy led to compromise. Liberals, already inclined toward gradualistic responses, watered down FEP proposals to win the support of wavering moderate Republicans. The resulting state FEP law offered symbolic challenges to the racial status quo but ultimately had little effect. Like most state FEP laws, Michigan's relied on a grievance-based model and put a great deal of emphasis on education as the means to combat racial discrimination. In addition, the state FEP commission was underfunded and understaffed (Sugrue 1996a).

One major difficulty of antidiscrimination laws was that they left lily-white workplaces such as the building trades, chemical manufacturers, brewers, and family-owned businesses almost untouched. As do immigrant entrepreneurs today (see chapters 6, 7, and 13 in this volume), these firms relied primarily on personal references, kinship networks, and church and neighborhood groups. Employers often announced job openings by word of mouth. They depended on their current workers to recruit new workers. In many such firms, unions screened prospective employers through apprenticeship programs and hiring halls, tapping ethnic and familial networks. Since blacks and whites intermarried in very small numbers, seldom lived in the same neighborhoods, rarely worshipped at the same churches, and infrequently attended the same schools, blacks were almost entirely closed out of the referral networks that provided whites with knowledge about prospective jobs (Sugrue 1996a). Hiring officers and unions could plausibly claim that they did not engage in discrimination. Few, if any, blacks applied for their jobs.

Under the FEP model of discrimination, a grievance had not occurred unless an individual black had applied for a job and had been rebuffed.

However weak FEP laws were, they enlisted the power of government in the battle against workplace discrimination. Such laws provided civil rights groups with a new ally. Emboldened by the promise of equal employment opportunity but frustrated by the limitations of the FEP laws, activists began, gradually, to push for more rigorous antidiscrimination laws. By the late 1950s, they were joined by race relations experts, lawyers, and government bureaucrats who began to see the weaknesses in the FEP model of antidiscrimination and began to argue for an emphasis on disparate impact rather than continuing to seek elusive evidence for disparate treatment of minority job applicants (Moreno 1997). Perhaps most important, gradualist racial liberalism, whatever its failures, unleashed and legitimated growing African American militancy on civil rights issues.

Black Unrest

The limitations of state FEP laws and the gradualism of the postwar integrationists became quickly evident to African American workers and to civil rights activists. Whole sections of American industry remained overwhelmingly white, most notably the skilled trades, clerical, retail, and sales work, and construction work. As northern cities began to lose jobs through automation and deindustrialization beginning in the 1950s, blacks were hit especially hard (Sugrue 1993). Throughout the 1950s, black unemployment rates remained double those of whites; black youth unemployment began to rise in the late 1950s. State and local FEP laws seemed to have little discernible impact on the structure of urban labor markets.

The demand for more stringent antidiscrimination laws was greatest in the urban North, where blacks were doing better than in the South but where the gap between the promise of racial equality and the reality of workplace discrimination was obvious. By the late 1950s in many northern cities, black activists began to push at the limits of antidiscrimination law. Civil rights organizations such as the National Association for the Advancement of Colored People (NAACP) witnessed the overthrow of a generation of moderates by a younger, more populist cohort of activists. Many northern civil rights activists, emboldened by southern civil rights activism, began to carry their demands northward. In Philadelphia, a new generation of activists chafed impatiently against the persistent racial discrimination that plagued the city's labor market.

In 1960 and 1961, a group of black ministers began leading boycotts against local employers, such as Sun Oil Company and Tasty Kake, that continued to discriminate against black workers. In 1962 and 1963, the Congress of Racial Equality (CORE) spearheaded pickets at city and federally funded construction projects, demanding that building con-tractors hire skilled black workers (Meier and Rudwick 1973).

Similar changes took place in Detroit. The Motor City's NAACP chapter, the nation's largest during World War II, hemorrhaged mem-bers throughout the late 1940s and early 1950s as middle-class leaders purged left-leaning activists and embraced the gradualist agenda of ra-cial liberals. By the early 1960s, a new generation of more militant activ-ists had taken over the NAACP and begun picketing respected employ-ers such as First Federal Bank and General Motors. A parallel effort emerged among black United Auto Workers (UAW) activists who cre-ated the Trade Union Leadership Council (TULC) in 1957. The TULC activists resisted the underrepresentation of blacks in union of-fices and demanded that the UAW break open the skilled trades to black workers (Sugrue 1996a; Korstad and Lichtenstein 1988). In Detroit, as in Philadelphia, black ministers moved beyond 1950s-era demands for breakthrough jobs and demanded that firms hire African Americans in clerical and sales positions. Similar efforts took hold in Chicago, Cleve-land, Newark, New York, and Boston (Meier and Rudwick 1973). In-deed the early 1960s witnessed a wave of black protest throughout the North that focused on employment discrimination. Increasingly, pro-testers targeted federal contractors working on government office buildings, public schools, and urban renewal sites, where blacks did not share in the job boom created by 1960s-era federal largesse.

Federal Response

Already in the 1950s, the federal government had made halting efforts toward responding to discrimination in government contracts. Presi-dent Dwight D. Eisenhower had impaneled a commission to investigate discrimination in government contracts. Eisenhower's efforts were, however, small in scale and short on accomplishment. It took the events of the early 1960s to push reluctant government officials to strengthen and revise antidiscrimination law. The first steps toward a systematic antidiscrimination policy came in the Kennedy administration, with Ex-ecutive Orders 10925 and 11114. Kennedy was himself a gradualist on matters of civil rights. In the Senate during the 1950s, he had allied himself with conservative southern Democrats who were reluctant to upset the racial status quo. Kennedy had backed a tepid version of the Civil Rights Act of 1957, one that would have done little to undermine Jim Crow in the South (Stern 1992). As a president who was elected by a razor-thin margin, who relied on the support of key southern committee leaders in Congress, and who feared his party's loss of the "solid south," Kennedy was careful to avoid alienating southern Democrats. But two other countervailing forces were at work in his administration: the continued pressure of civil rights organizations for racial equality and Kennedy's desire for technocratic solutions to complex social problems.

Kennedy turned to executive orders for a solution to the problem of racial inequality. His efforts were more symbolic than effective. He hoped to diffuse increasingly militant civil rights protests without taking the politically risky step of advocating sweeping civil rights legislation. Executive Order 10925, in which he first used the term affirmative action, mandated that contractors make efforts to hire minorities on government contracts (Graham 1990). But tensions over employment discrimination only grew during the Kennedy years, as antidiscrimination protests spread from city to city. In 1963, after weeks of protest at government-funded construction sites in Philadelphia, New York, and Cleveland, in the aftermath of protests and violence in Birmingham and in the wake of months of accelerating civil rights protest, Kennedy began to move toward civil rights legislation (Stern 1992). In the spring he ordered Labor Secretary Willard Wirtz to enforce nondiscrimination in federally sponsored apprenticeship programs; on June 22, 1963, he issued Executive Order 11114, prohibiting discrimination against minorities in construction firms that held government contracts. That summer, Kennedy administration officials also began drafting the legislation that would culminate in the 1964 Civil Rights Act (Graham 1990).

Kennedy's solution to the crisis of 1963 fit well with the liberal proclivity to turn to administrative solutions to pressing social problems. His hope was that the federal government could succeed where the states and localities had failed: by resolving the problem of racial inequality in an uncontroversial arena, immune from the vagaries of the electoral system and not subject to the intense partisanship and the conflict within the Democratic Party that had hamstrung earlier civil rights efforts. Kennedy's efforts to resolve the problems of racial discrimination also left government agencies with significant discretion over the meaning of such vague phrases as "positive measures" (Executive Order 10925) and "affirmative action" (Executive Order 11114). Under Executive Order 11114, contractors had to provide access to books, records, and accounts to demonstrate compliance with antidiscrimination laws and "affirmative action" in employment (see Skrentny's introduction to this volume). At the heart of Kennedy's effort against employment discrimination was a tension between the growing demand of civil rights organizations for strong and effective civil rights measures and the increasing reluctance of federal officials to enact any laws that might be perceived as race-based quotas (Graham 1990). Fears about the political costs of enacting a quota system carried into the Johnson administration. The landmark Civil Rights Act of 1964 gave increased power and discretion to federal agencies to investigate and challenge workplace discrimination but left unresolved a major problem that would vex reformers: how to ensure that employers went beyond the tokenism that had plagued antidiscrimination efforts in the postwar decades without resorting to hard and fast numerical requirements for numbers of minority hires.

The Building Trades and the Battle over Affirmative Action

Kennedy's Executive Orders, the Civil Rights Act of 1964, Lyndon Johnson's Executive Order 11246 (strengthening Kennedy's efforts), and subsequent attempts to challenge discriminatory labor markets met with mixed success. Affirmative action efforts were most far-reaching within federal government agencies themselves, where minorities established beachheads of employment in the 1960s. By the 1970s, some private-sector employers began to embrace affirmative action, under the threat of federal lawsuits, by consent decree, or to forestall potential litigation. In addition, certain private-sector employers voluntarily expanded their minority workforces, particularly to expand their markets among minority and international customers and to handle personnel and regulatory matters that required interaction with racially diverse government agencies (Kelly and Dobbin, this volume). But resistance to affirmative action in the workplace persisted across the economy. Many white workers feared that affirmative action privileged minority workers at their expense (Rieder 1989, 254–55).

The fiercest opposition to affirmative action came from workers and employers in the building trades—and the most concentrated federal efforts to break down workplace discrimination came in the construction industry. Affirmative action in the construction industry became the Vietnam of civil rights. The battle started with great optimism. Liberal reformers believed that if racial exclusion were defeated in the construction industry, it could be vanquished anywhere. That optimism proved unfounded. What ensued was a drawn-out series of skirmishes that resulted in few clear victories. Affirmative action efforts were quickly bogged down in the quagmire of the informal labor market that prevailed in the construction industry. The earliest struggles over affirmative action revealed the limits of the postwar liberal rhetoric of civil rights. The fate of early affirmative action in the building trades also has implications for those considering questions of civil rights and workplace diversity in today's increasingly complex racial and ethnic labor markets.

Why did the building trades prove to be so resistant to antidiscrimination efforts after World War II? Why were they the target of civil rights activists in the early 1960s and of the early and persistent affirmative action efforts? The answer lies in the structure of the labor market in construction. The building trades are a textbook example of the employment niche, a sector of the economy dominated by a single group and characterized by a long history of exclusion of competing groups (Model 1993; Waldinger 1996). Mutually reinforcing processes of group identity formation and economic advantage made the building trades extremely resistant to change. While civil rights efforts and macroeconomic changes during and after World War II had accomplished a gradual transformation in the racial composition of many workplaces, the building trades remained a glaring exception. In response to Kennedy's relatively weak executive orders, labor leaders perfected an emotional anti–affirmative action rhetoric.

A Niche of Whiteness

Three characteristics shaped the labor market in the building trades. First, exclusivity kept wages relatively high and maintained a robust demand for construction workers. In many cities in the postwar era, skilled union construction workers were scarce, particularly during economic booms. In Detroit in 1947, the average age of union carpenters was fifty-seven (Sugrue 1996a). Builders and contractors regularly complained about a shortage of qualified construction workers and paid a premium in wages to their journeymen and apprentices. Second, employers' reliance on union hiring halls met internal labor market imperatives to create a reliable and loyal workforce while minimizing recruitment costs. Third, hiring practices drew from and reinforced communal, religious, and ethnic networks. In the early twentieth century, many building trades unions were dominated by a single ethnic group, such as Italian masons and plasterers and Irish plumbers. But by the mid-twentieth century, ethnic identities began to wane with rising rates of intergroup marriage, residential dispersion, and political incorporation, particularly during the New Deal and World War II (Kazal 1995; Cohen 1990). In this context, building trades unions grew more heterogeneous ethnically while remaining exclusive nonetheless. In northern cities, building trades became a *niche of whiteness*, drawing their membership from ethnically diverse European American communities. Kinship still mattered, but union references also came from neighborhood friendship networks, schoolmates, and connections forged in churches and parochial schools. All of these networks shared one element: they did not include African Americans.

The lack of African American representation in the unionized building trades was not for a lack of effort. In fact, many southern blacks migrated to the North with significant experience in construction labor. In every northern city, construction work was the second or third largest employer of African Americans. But black construction workers worked in two separate arenas: in nonunion black-owned (or self-owned) construction firms that worked on the margins of the booming postwar construction economy or in predominantly black union locals in inferior positions such as common laborers, hod-carriers, and bricklayers. These jobs were both poor-paying and insecure. Black construction workers made between one-half and two-thirds of what white construction workers earned and worked fewer days out of the year.

The long past of ethnic solidarity and racial exclusion in the building trades provided formidable obstacles to affirmative action's architects. Affirmative action, I argue, was a necessary tool to breach the exclusive boundaries of the building trades. But the fierce resistance that it faced, even in its earliest stages, foreshadowed struggles to come. It proved enormously difficult to challenge informal processes of hiring—through personal and ethnic networks and family connections—to include members of "out" groups such as racial minorities. Before affirmative action, it was nearly impossible for civil rights advocates to break into tight ethnic niches because of the absence of evidence that building trades unionists had intended to discriminate. Under most Fair Employment Practices laws of the 1940s and 1950s, a lack of minority workers was insufficient evidence of workplace discrimination. Civil rights activists had to prove that employers and unions had deliberately excluded minority workers. In the absence of formal, bureaucratically administered rules governing hiring and promotion that relied on statistical evidence of minority representation, and without a change in union members' perceptions of opportunities for further upward mobility, it would have been nearly impossible to open the exclusive building trades to minority workers. Many construction workers saw their craft as a form of property, as an inheritance to be passed from father to son. But even with such rules in place, the niche of whiteness in the building trades proved extraordinarily resistant to change.

There were many reasons for the difficulty of breaking down patterns of racial discrimination in the building trades. Above all was the confluence of the interests of both workers and employers in maintaining the racial status quo. White workers were deeply hostile to new black hires in construction. Black workers hired through affirmative action plans faced harassment, ostracism, and sometimes outright physical attacks on the job (Schneirov 1993, 105,108). The vehemence of white opposition to affirmative action was the consequence of its simultaneous challenge to the solidaristic culture of the workplace and to the economic self-interest of white workers on the job. But worker resistance to workplace integration was not alone sufficient to maintain racial homogeneity in the workplace. Employer interests mattered enormously in shaping the racial composition of a workplace (Sugrue 1996b). In the construction industry, employers could not trust that formal procedures and quotas would serve their internal labor market concerns as well as did informal hiring mechanisms. Affirmative action threatened the interests of employers and white workers simultaneously. What made affirmative action so difficult to implement was the confluence of grassroots, working-class resistance to it and employers' interest in maintaining the status quo.

The Rhetoric of Anti–Affirmative Action Politics

In one of the many ironies of affirmative action, white workers in the construction industry embraced the rhetoric of the post–World War II racial liberals to defend racially exclusionary hiring practices. White workers in the construction industry came to understand their job security and status as hard won "rights" that were under threat by affirmative action programs. Government-mandated antidiscriminatory hiring and training programs threatened white workers' security. Perhaps nothing was more important to post–New Deal working-class politics and union organizing efforts than attempts to protect the workers' economic security through seniority rules, generous benefits packages, unemployment benefits, pensions, and a federal safety net. The right to organize unions, enshrined in the 1935 National Labor Relations (Wagner) Act, was an essential component of workers' struggle for security.

Many white workers, particularly in the skilled trades, saw federal antidiscrimination efforts in the 1960s as a threat to their hard-won security. In unions such as the building trades, affirmative action (however vaguely or precisely defined) undermined traditional union hiring practices wherein workers reinforced solidaristic cultures of kinship and ethnicity by hiring friends, co-ethnics, and relatives. White workers also feared that antidiscrimination laws would undermine the seniority system, one of the most significant gains of twentieth-century unionism. Without seniority, workers would be subject to the vagaries of the job market at points in the life cycle where they were most vulnerable.

White resistance to affirmative action also grew from a strategic use of a rhetoric of racial innocence, one that was often in inverse relation to the racial segregation of a workplace. The building trades provide the best example of this. When contractors and unions did respond to accusations that they practiced racial discrimination, they denied culpability. Contractors passed the blame for hiring practices to the building trades unions (although in most trades, contractors played a role in the selection of apprentices and in the screening of journeymen through joint union-contractor councils). Unions disavowed discriminatory intent, falling back on the position that their nepotistic hiring practices were race-neutral. Along the way, they entirely effaced the long history of discriminatory attitudes and practices that were prevalent in the culture of the skilled trades. But when they responded to accusations that their hiring practices were discriminatory, building trades representatives were seldom foolish enough to resort to overt expressions of racism. They offered a simple defense that was difficult to undermine: blacks did not apply. Unions did not turn away potential black members; they simply recruited among their own personal contacts. Racial liberals had no effective answer to the building trades' protestations of racial innocence: they had looked for evidence of discriminatory intentions to explain discriminatory results. The postwar racial liberals' construction of discrimination as a moral problem led white workers in the building trades to plea their innocence, however disingenuous that plea might have been. But it also allowed construction trades workers to elide the issue that discrimination in the building trades was primarily institutional in its origins, the result of the ways that racial inequalities were embedded in urban space and urban institutions.

White opposition to civil rights in employment drew from the rights language of the New Deal, just as had black demands for equal opportunity. Government intervention in the hiring hall violated their understanding of the proper role of government. Attempts to "force" the hiring of blacks threatened the right to a secure job that they had expected the government to protect. And interference in internal union governance was a violation of the right to organize guaranteed by the Wagner Act. A Philadelphia plumbers' union official railed against efforts to open the building trades to blacks: "The established and well-earned rights of white people are being imperiled in the fight of Negro leadership against unions" (*Philadelphia Bulletin* 1963c).

Increasingly, building trades critics of early affirmative action efforts embraced the language of civil rights. The government mandate that contractors hire minority workers was, in the words of one critic, "discrimination against white persons" (*Philadelphia Bulletin* 1963b). Joseph Burke, head of the all-white Sheet Metal Workers local in Philadelphia (one of the major targets of the Philadelphia Plan), staunchly opposed Kennedy's requirements that blacks be hired on government contracts. "They are asking me to say to a working white man, 'Get off the job because I want to put a Negro on.' I can never say that. Nor can I say to people out of work 'I can't put you to work because I have to put a Negro to work'" (*Philadelphia Bulletin* 1963b). In the union hiring hall, however, Burke and his counterparts had regularly made choices—pitting one group against another. Had he substituted "Bill's cousin" or "a member of the Friendly Sons of Italy" or "Joe from Saint Cecelia's" for "Negro," the act of discrimination would have been so commonplace in the building trades as not to have elicited any protest. Building trades unions drew lines all the time—making distinctions between workers, sending away prospective workers in preference for the son or brother of a current member, favoring one worker on a job over another. To turn a prospective worker away empty-handed was part of an ordinary day at the hiring hall.

Moreover, federal antidiscrimination efforts raised workers' suspicion that their fate was in the hands of a distant, undemocratic bureaucracy that was willing to sacrifice their interests for the sake of African American gains. Kennedy's antidiscrimination measures were, in the words of one white unionist, "undemocratic, unreasonable, unwarranted, and unworkable," an insidious expansion of government power (*Philadelphia Bulletin* 1963a). Building trades union leaders evoked the specter of a tyrannical government trammeling the hard-won rights of the working man. A Philadelphia building trades union leader pledged that "we will accept no dictation from any government agency" (*Phila-*

delphia Bulletin 1963c.) Peter Schoemann, national president of the Plumbers Union, fiercely opposed federal demands for nondiscrimination. "We resent the use of the equal employment campaign as a reason for a federal takeover in an area where government does not belong" (*Philadelphia Bulletin* 1963c). The battle against equal employment opportunity eroded blue-collar support for government and was, perhaps, the most prominent manifestation of the antibureaucratic, antigovernment sentiment that was taking hold in many other arenas of American politics in the 1960s (Balogh 1996).

In addition, popular critics of racial preferences and disparate impact antidiscrimination laws claimed many of the premises of post–World War II racial liberalism as their own. Although building trades unions had practiced nepotism and hired co-ethnics, both forms of anti-meritocratic group preferences, they rushed to embrace a model of meritocratic individualism in the aftermath of mid-1960s civil rights reforms. To be sure, many building trades unions had long had minimal requirements for entry: many required a high school degree and basic numeracy. But in practice, the barriers to entry were low and local unions frequently bent rules. By the mid-1960s, however, building trades unions began to adopt various aptitude tests and interviews to determine eligibility for work.

The building trades protested too much. Their increasingly shrill denunciations of government "interference" conflicted with their simultaneous claim that they were nondiscriminatory. Whatever their resistance to equal employment opportunity, Kennedy's executive orders and the 1964 Civil Rights Act forced unionists to reconsider their hiring practices. In the aftermath of the Civil Rights Act, building trades unions made token efforts to open their ranks to blacks (Quadagno 1994). Union-sponsored "outreach programs" (efforts to recruit black apprentices through targeted advertising and informational events co-sponsored by civil rights groups) hearkened back to 1950s-style racial liberalism in their gradualism. Formerly lily-white unions could claim that they had opened their ranks to blacks, though the percentage of minority construction workers still remained very small (Hill 1974). Union outreach efforts may have generated good will in the 1950s, but by the late 1960s, they proved to be too little, too late for black activists. Civil rights groups grew increasingly impatient at the glacial pace of union desegregation and pressed for more far-reaching antidiscrimination efforts. Although there is little evidence that civil rights groups directly shaped the agenda of the government agencies that designed affirmative action directives, it is clear that in the context of what John

Skrentny (1996) calls "crisis management" in the late 1960s that black organizations would not simply rest content with small-scale, voluntary efforts to remedy workplace discrimination.

The growing pressure of civil rights groups was one part of the picture of the rise of affirmative action. Antidiscrimination protests took on new significance in the aftermath of the long hot summers of the mid-1960s. Between 1964 and 1968, American cities exploded in an unprecedented wave of black uprisings. In the atmosphere of crisis, government officials were desperate to contain the sources of racial unrest. They turned, quite naturally, to the still-unresolved problem of racial inequality in jobs and in housing. The Johnson administration's aborted Philadelphia Plan, resuscitated by Richard Nixon, offered riot insurance to uneasy white government officials. In the hands of Nixon, affirmative action became yet another wedge between white workers and blacks in the increasingly fractious Democratic Party (Skrentny 1996). Nixon's decision was more than a political calculation. It was the Republican's attempt to exploit deep-seated contradictions that were at the very heart of the post–New Deal liberal project.

By the time the Philadelphia Plan was implemented, building trades unionists had developed a powerful critique of affirmative action that would change little in the subsequent decades. The various "city plans" to open up the building trades met with limited success in the 1970s and 1980s (Hill 1974; Waldinger and Bailey 1991). African American workers expected to be treated harshly on the job, and even those who retained their jobs faced petty harassment and hostility from their co-workers. And a recent study of plumbers and pipe fitters found that affirmative action has "few defenders among white journeymen" (Schneirov 1993). Nearly a quarter-century after the Kennedy administration's first efforts to open up the construction industry to blacks, civil rights leaders continued to complain that the world of hard hats remained a predominantly white world.

Breaking open the building trades' niche of whiteness proved to be extraordinarily difficult because of the entangled combination of forces that preserved homogeneous networks that perpetuated white dominance in the industry. As long as personal references and nepotism remained untouched by civil rights legislation, even the most far-reaching federal efforts to open up the construction industry would meet with limited success. Despite optimistic evaluations of racial progress in the last half of the twentieth century (Thernstrom and Thernstrom 1998), many sectors of the labor market, notably the construction industry, remained disproportionately white. Persistent housing segregation

(Massey and Denton 1993), school segregation (Orfield and Eaton 1996), and low levels of interracial socialization and intermarriage (Patterson 1997) meant that few blacks would make their way into the hiring hall. Most important, the political rhetoric of affirmative action's critics naturalized the whiteness of the construction industry, leaving invisible the processes of racial exclusion that benefited construction workers and contractors. The postwar emphasis on morality and intention allowed critics of affirmative action to embrace universalistic ideals, couched in a powerful rights rhetoric, while continuing to profit from racial separation and isolation.

Rethinking Affirmative Action

Affirmative action remains one of the most fiercely contested legacies of the civil rights era. Yet its history, with the exception of studies of presidential policy, remains largely unwritten. In a short period of time (1963–1969) affirmative action moved from obscurity to prominence as the single most important federal policy for dealing with employment discrimination. The conventional narratives of affirmative action emphasize its role in the radicalization of the civil rights movement, its entanglement with growing black racial consciousness, and its alleged abandonment of a long-standing policy of "color-blindness" (Belz 1991; Detlefsen 1991; Glazer 1975). The rise of affirmative action, it is argued, led to the collapse of an integrationist liberalism and the rise of identity politics. It represented an unprecedented expansion of notions of "rights" from an emphasis on equality of opportunity to an emphasis on equality of outcome. It replaced an emphasis on merit with the preferential hiring of historically underrepresented minority groups, regardless of their qualifications. The result of affirmative action, argue Thomas and Mary Edsall, was that whites had "to absorb the penalties for past discrimination by other whites, ceding opportunities for employment and promotion to competing blacks." Affirmative action, they contend, created "zero sum solutions in which the gains of one group were losses for the other" (Edsall and Edsall 1991, 124). Most explanations of affirmative action begin with normative judgments about the policy's merits and fall back on moral arguments about the program's intentions and its implications for abstract theories of distributive justice. Clustering around the affirmative action issue are several major themes in twentieth-century American political history: liberal promises of racial equality, assumptions about the relation of workers to labor markets, assertions about race-consciousness versus color-blindness, and arguments about the proper scope of governmental activity. The most influential arguments (both Right and Left) about affirmative action rest on two assumptions. First, affirmative action represented a shift away from a "color-blind standard" toward a newly assertive racial identity politics. Second, the policy of racial preferences played a crucial role in weakening the liberal consensus that had dominated American politics since the New Deal by polarizing blacks and whites on matters of race (Rieder 1989).

Such views of affirmative action, I contend, are fundamentally ahistorical. They substitute a flattened image of the past—one of a "color-blind" Constitution and a golden age of racial cooperation—for the far more complicated and troubled history of racial liberalism in the post–New Deal era. Federally mandated affirmative action revealed deep fault lines that ran to the very core of New Deal liberalism; affirmative action brought into the open tensions that were barely visible beneath the patina of liberal "consensus" in post–New Deal America. Unionists railed against what they perceived to be the injustices of a policy that challenged white privilege in certain industries; civil rights organizations embraced it as an essential starting point in the conquest of racial inequality. Critics on the Right linked anti–affirmative action sentiments with growing discontent toward the structures of American government itself. At the heart of the battle over affirmative action was a debate about the very meaning of liberalism itself.

The issue of racial discrimination in the workplace revealed a deep-running fissure in mid-twentieth-century liberalism between white workers' demand for stable, secure employment and black workers' demand for racial equality. Affirmative action emerged not as the result of the "excesses" of black radicalism but as the consequence of liberals' long-standing failure to deliver on the promise of racial equality. The deep-rooted white opposition to affirmative action was at bottom a defense of a racial status quo that marginalized blacks in urban labor markets—a situation solidified by New Deal labor and economic policies that disproportionately benefited white workers. Affirmative action's critics masked their own unacknowledged identity politics in seemingly neutral, universalist rhetoric that they themselves had rejected only a few years earlier. Ironically, they embraced 1940s-style racial liberalism when it had lost its currency as a response to the crisis of the 1960s. The debate over affirmative action today continues to be mired in tensions that were presaged in mid-twentieth-century liberalism, whose legacies remain at the heart of the vexing problem of race, rights, and justice in modern America.

Acknowledgments

Thanks to Dana Barron, Thomas F. Jackson, Peter Siskind, and John Skrentny for comments on previous versions of this essay. I presented versions of this paper to interdisciplinary audiences at Boston University (Institute for Race and Social Division), Rutgers University (Political Science), the University of Michigan (History), the University of Pennsylvania (History and Wharton Department of Public Policy and Management), and Brandeis University (History), and I thank those audiences for helpful suggestions and comments. Parts of this essay appeared in "The Tangled Roots of Affirmative Action," *American Behavioral Scientist* 41 (April 1998): 886–97 and are reprinted by permission.

References

Balogh, Brian. 1996. Introduction to *Integrating the sixties: The origins, structures, and legitimacy of public policy in a turbulent decade*, edited by Brian Balogh. University Park: Pennsylvania State University Press.

Belz, Herman. 1991. *Equality transformed: A quarter-century of affirmative action*. New Brunswick, N.J.: Transaction Publishers.

Cohen, Lizabeth. 1990. *Making a new deal: Industrial workers in Chicago, 1919–1939*. New York: Cambridge University Press.

Dalfiume, Richard W. 1968. The "forgotten" years of the Negro revolution. *Journal of American History* 55:90–106.

Detlefsen, Robert R. 1991. *Civil rights under Reagan*. San Francisco: ICS Press.

Edsall, Thomas Byrne, and Mary D. Edsall. 1991. *Chain reaction: The impact of race, rights, and taxes on American politics*. New York: W. W. Norton.

Fine, Sidney. 1996. "A jewel in the crown of us all": Michigan enacts a fair employment practices act, 1941–1955. *Michigan Historical Review* 22 (spring): 19–66.

Forbath, William E. 1994. Why is this rights talk different from all other rights talk? Demoting the Court and reimagining the Constitution. *Stanford Law Review* 46:1771–1805.

Glazer, Nathan. 1975. *Affirmative discrimination: Ethnic inequality and public policy*. New York: Basic Books.

Graham, Hugh Davis. 1990. *The civil rights era: Origins and development of national policy, 1960–1972*. New York: Oxford University Press.

Hill, Herbert. 1974. Labor union control of job training: A critical analysis of apprenticeship outreach programs and the hometown plans. Institute for Urban Affairs and Research, Howard University, *Occasional Paper*, vol. 2, no. 1.

Jackson, Walter A. 1990. *Gunnar Myrdal and America's conscience: Social engineering and racial liberalism, 1938–1987*. Chapel Hill: University of North Carolina Press.

Kazal, Russell A. 1995. Revisiting assimilation: The rise, fall, and reappraisal of a concept in American ethnic history. *American Historical Review* 100:437–71.

Klinkner, Philip A., with Rogers M. Smith. 1999. *The unsteady march: The rise and decline of racial equality in America*. Chicago: University of Chicago Press.

Korstad, Robert, and Nelson Lichtenstein. 1988. Opportunities found and lost: Labor radicals and the early civil rights movement. *Journal of American History* 75:786–811.

Lieberman, Robert C. 1998. *Shifting the color line: Race and the American welfare state.* Cambridge: Harvard University Press.

Massey, Douglas S., and Nancy A. Denton. 1993. *American apartheid: Segregation and the making of the underclass.* Cambridge: Harvard University Press.

Meier, August, and Elliott Rudwick. 1973. *CORE: A study in the civil rights movement, 1942–1968.* New York: Oxford University Press.

Model, Suzanne. 1993. The ethnic niche and the structure of opportunity: Immigrants and minorities in New York City. In *The "underclass" debate: Views from history,* edited by Michael B. Katz. Princeton: Princeton University Press.

Moreno, Paul. 1997. *From direct action to affirmative action.* Baton Rouge: Louisiana State University Press.

Myrdal, Gunnar. 1944. *The American dilemma: The Negro problem and modern democracy.* New York: Harper Brothers.

Orfield, Gary, and Susan E. Eaton. 1996. Dismantling desegregation: The quiet reversal of *Brown v. Board of Education.* New York: New Press.

Patterson, Orlando. 1997. *The ordeal of integration.* New York: Civitas.

Philadelphia Bulletin. 1963a. The apprentice story, 10 June.

Philadelphia Bulletin. 1963b. OK accord with city, deny bias, 20 August.

Philadelphia Bulletin. 1963c. Plumbers reject compulsory rule against bias, 20 August.

Quadagno, Jill. 1994. *The color of welfare: How racism undermined the war on poverty.* New York: Oxford University Press.

Rieder, Jonathan. 1989. The rise of the silent majority. In *The rise and fall of the New Deal order,* edited by Steve Fraser and Gary Gerstle. Princeton: Princeton University Press.

Roosevelt, Franklin Delano. 1944. Message to Congress on the State of the Union (January 11). Reprinted in *The public papers and addresses of Franklin D. Roosevelt,* vol. 13. New York: Alfred Knopf, 1950.

Schneirov, Richard. 1993. *Pride and solidarity: A history of the plumbers and pipefitters of Columbus, Ohio, 1889–1989.* Ithaca: ILR Press.

Skrentny, John David. 1996. *The ironies of affirmative action: Politics, culture, and justice in America.* Chicago: University of Chicago Press.

Steinberg, Stephen. 1995. *Turning back: The retreat from racial justice in American thought and policy.* Boston: Beacon Press.

Stern, Mark. 1992. *Calculating visions: Kennedy, Johnson, and civil rights.* New Brunswick, N.J.: Rutgers University Press.

Sugrue, Thomas J. 1993. The structures of urban poverty: The reorganization of space and work in three periods of American history. In *The "underclass" debate: Views from history,* edited by Michael B. Katz. Princeton: Princeton University Press.

———. 1996a. *The origins of the urban crisis: Race and inequality in postwar Detroit.* Princeton: Princeton University Press.

———. 1996b. Segmented work, race-conscious workers: Structure, agency, and division in the CIO era. *International Review of Social History* 41 (December): 389–406.

Thernstrom, Stephan, and Abigail Thernstrom. 1998. *America in black and white: One nation, indivisible.* New York: Simon and Schuster.

Waldinger, Roger. 1996. *Still the promised city? African Americans and new immigrants in postindustrial New York.* Cambridge: Harvard University Press.

Waldinger, Roger, and Thomas Bailey. 1991. The continuing significance of race: Racial conflict and racial discrimination in construction. *Politics and Society* 19:291–324.

2

Affirmative Action for Immigrants?
The Unintended Consequences of Reform

. . .

HUGH DAVIS GRAHAM

In the early 1990s, against a backdrop of economic recession and rising job insecurity in the United States, public controversy over affirmative action and immigration policy intensified and, more significant, for the first time the two issues converged. Especially in California, where defense industry contraction and heavy immigration from Latin America and Asia increased economic anxiety, opponents of affirmative-action preferences and high levels of immigration linked their arguments. Nonminority Americans unfairly suffered rising unemployment, these critics held, because by hiring immigrants, employers bought cheap and docile labor and at the same time satisfied minority hiring requirements imposed by the government (Beck 1996; Brimelow 1995; Robb 1995).

In 1994, California voters passed Proposition 187, an initiative restricting access by illegal immigrants to welfare assistance and other public benefits. That same year, support for Proposition 187 helped California's Republican governor, Pete Wilson, win reelection. In 1995, the University of California Regents, encouraged by Wilson, an ex officio regent, prohibited affirmative-action preferences in admissions, employment, and contracts. In 1996, President Clinton signed a bill stripping significant welfare and health benefits from unnaturalized immigrants, and California voters passed an initiative, Proposition 209, banning affirmative-action preferences by state and local governments. In 1998, voters in Washington State passed a similar measure. News reports and press releases from groups opposing affirmative action featured stories of immigrants, legal as well as illegal, winning jobs through affirmative-action preferences (see Johnson 1994; Tilove 1994). It was absurd, critics contended, to grant preferences on the basis of ancestry to recently arrived immigrants, legal and illegal, as a compensatory remedy for historic discrimination in the United States.

News stories of immigrants winning affirmative-action benefits periodically revealed bizarre examples. The Fanjul brothers in Miami, for example—multimillionaire businessmen with large minority business set-aside contracts in Florida—fled Castro's revolution in 1960, yet retained their Cuban citizenship for tax-avoidance purposes (Cheshire 1995). The Rodriguez brothers, immigrants from Portugal and owners of three large construction and paving companies in the Washington, D.C., area, won 60 percent of the district's minority set-aside contracts from 1986 to 1990 (Schneider and Ragland 1992). A black businessman in Cincinnati, suing to prevent Governor George V. Voinovich from opening Ohio's minority contract set-aside program to Asian Indians, won a decertification order from the attorney general but lost in federal court, where Judge Tommy L. Thompson ruled that Asian Indians as "Orientals" were due the same privileges as blacks under affirmative action (Beck 1996). At the University of Michigan, the faculty senate discovered that large percentages of minority faculty recruited under the university's affirmative-action program were foreign-born—18.8 percent of black faculty, 23.3 percent of Hispanics, and 56.1 percent of Asian/Pacific Islanders (North 1995).

Supporters of affirmative action feared the conjoined opposition of antipreference groups and immigration restrictionists. Immigrant participation in affirmative action, according to Ricky Gaull Silverman, vice-chairman of the Equal Employment Opportunity Commission (EEOC), "is the ultimate nightmare of affirmative action. It is its Achilles heel" (Tilove 1994, A1). Lawrence Fuchs, former board member of the Mexican American Legal Defense and Education Fund (MALDEF), wrote in the *Washington Post* in 1995 that immigrant inclusion in affirmative-action programs "is an historical accident for which there is no possible justification" (Fuchs 1995, C2). Defenders of affirmative-action programs avoided the topic of immigrant participation. The Clinton administration's comprehensive review and defense of affirmative-action programs, produced by a presidential task force in 1995 on the heels of the Supreme Court's *Adarand* decision, nowhere mentioned immigration or immigrant participation (Stephanopoulos and Edley 1995).

Similarly, the major studies of immigration avoid discussing affirmative action. *The New Americans*, a study of the effects of immigration on American life released by the National Research Council in 1997, addressed controversial social issues such as job displacement, residential segregation, racial identification, crime, illegal immigration, and interethnic tensions, but nowhere mentioned affirmative action (National

Research Council 1997). The U.S. Commission on Immigration Reform, in its fall 1997 final report, was equally silent on affirmative action (U.S. Commission on Immigration Reform 1997).

The civil rights coalition, supporting both affirmative action and liberal immigration policies but anxious to avoid discussing their linkages, has been advantaged by the paucity of empirical data connecting the two fields of government social policy. To persons seeking systematic national data, statistical reports by government agencies offer abundant data on immigration patterns and, since the late 1960s, on racial and ethnic participation in affirmative-action programs. Evidence connecting immigration status to affirmative-action participation, however, is skimpy. Government agencies, employers, civil rights organizations, and the immigration rights bar have been anxious to avoid this connection. Since the early 1970s, for example, the EEOC's standard equal-employment reporting form for universities and colleges, EEO-6, required institutions to identify the citizenship status of all employees. In 1990, however, this requirement was dropped, without explanation.

Not surprisingly, scholarship has mirrored the dualism of the data. Social scientists have produced a massive body of literature on the two policy areas since the 1960s, yet studies exploring their relationship are rare. In the absence of systematic data and scholarly literature, this essay uses historical analysis of the parallel development of affirmative action and immigration policy since the mid-1960s to explain their unanticipated convergence and unintended consequences.

The Disjunction between Affirmative Action and Immigration Policy

From the perspective of the early twenty-first century, the political convergence of affirmative action and immigration policy is not surprising. The civil rights coalition has defended programs of aggressive affirmative-action enforcement and liberal immigration provisions, built since the 1960s under the effective lobbying umbrella of the Leadership Conference on Civil Rights. In the subsequent three decades more than 25 million immigrants arrived in the United States, three-fourths of them from Latin America and Asia. During the 1970s the development of affirmative-action policy extended remedies originally intended for African Americans to persons of Hispanic and Asian ancestry, irrespective of citizenship. The logic of coalition-building unites liberals and protected-class minorities behind expanding both affirmative-action benefits and, through immigration, minority populations eligible to receive them. The political implications of these converging trends were enormous. Yet neither trend was foreseen or even sought by policy makers during the 1960s (Graham 1990).

The controversial convergence of immigration and affirmative-action policies was an unintended consequence of two statutes, the Civil Rights Act of 1964 and the Immigration and Nationality Act of 1965, that were weakly linked at the time. Since the early 1920s, the nation's immigration law gave preferences to immigrants from mostly Protestant northern and western Europe and limited immigration from eastern and southern Europe and Asia. Liberal elites in the Kennedy-Johnson administration and Congress, pressed by Jewish and Catholic lobbies, supported immigration reform as a corollary of civil rights reform. But voters in the 1960s saw little connection between the campaign against racial segregation and foreign visa applications. To the American public, immigration issues dealt with which foreigners entered the gate to the promised land, whereas civil rights issues dealt with the claims and disputes of American citizens under the Constitution. Consequently, the civil rights and immigration reform issues in the 1960s differed markedly in political visibility. The civil rights struggle, featuring violent conflict, sectional cleavage, and fundamental constitutional confrontation, was high drama, a televised morality play watched closely around the globe, ending in triumph when reformers defeated the longest Senate filibuster in history. Immigration reform, on the other hand, was covered only routinely by the press and was scarcely noticed in the television newscasts. Unlike civil rights, it was not a significant factor in the polarized presidential election of 1964. The 1965 immigration law was a low-profile reform, featuring compromise and consensus in Washington. It was an inside-the-beltway adjustment engineered by liberal elites who pledged, and by all evidence sincerely expected, that its important symbolic reforms would bring little change in the number and origin of immigrants. Strikingly, there was virtually no organized opposition to the immigration bill (Reimers 1992).

Polls in the 1960s showed a steady erosion of racial, ethnic, and religious prejudice in America, and growing support (excluding white southerners) for federal policies enforcing individual rights, but little public demand for immigration reform. According to a 1965 Harris poll, only 24 percent of respondents favored increased immigration, while 56 percent were opposed; that same year, a Gallup poll showed 32 percent favoring decreased immigration, 42 percent for no change, and only 7 percent supporting an increase (Wagner 1986). Unlike black civil rights protest in the 1960s, or the feminist movement mobilizing in its wake, there was no grassroots social movement for immigration reform in America. Rather, it was the other way around: immigration reform, by unintentionally triggering an explosion of immigration, created conditions for future social movements.

This distinction between intended and unintended consequences set the immigration reformers of the 1960s apart from their civil rights counterparts. The civil rights and voting rights acts promised, and largely delivered, profound social and political changes. In a second reconstruction of the South, they "tore Old Dixie down." In selling immigration reform, however, the Johnson administration and congressional sponsors argued that although the immigration bill would abolish the government's national origin preference system, the practical result would be to maintain the status quo. Because most visa preferences under the new law would go to immediate family members, such as spouses, children, brothers and sisters, future potential immigrants would need to have close family ties in the United States, due to prior immigration, to gain entry. The new family reunification policy, reformers explained, would thus perpetuate traditional patterns of immigration—from eastern and southern Europe, source of the "Great Wave" immigration of 1880 to 1920—and continued low levels of immigration as well. Secretary of State Dean Rusk, testifying before Congress in 1964, estimated an annual average increase of only 63,000 immigrants above the 300,000 figure of recent years. Labor secretary Willard Wirtz, who supported the radical changes in labor law brought by the Civil Rights Act, anticipated no significant impact on labor markets from immigration reform. In the realm of public expectation and practical consequences, the civil rights and immigration reforms of the 1960s were distinguished by their differences.

Race, National Origin, and Citizenship

Despite these disjunctive historic factors, immigration and civil rights issues were intimately joined in liberal theory and constitutional doctrine. Classic natural rights liberalism held that all individuals were entitled to equal treatment under law, and historically, liberal reforms had attacked discrimination against individuals on account of group characteristics, especially race, religion, national origin, and sex. The benchmarks of American liberalism in the century following the Civil War were constitutional amendments, statutes, and Supreme Court rulings banning unequal treatment for victims of group prejudice—above all, African Americans, but also Catholics, Jews, Chinese, and persons of enemy national origin in wartime (Smith 1997).

Although the core targets of liberal reform were slavery and segregation, liberalism's simple, negative remedy—Thou Shalt Not Discriminate—offered protection to most victimized groups. The Civil War amendments spoke only of race. But the Fourteenth Amendment, by granting citizenship to "all persons born or naturalized in the United States," affirmed the tradition of *jus soli*, common among new world nations (Canada, the United States, and Australia), wherein citizenship derives from birth in the territory, as opposed to the old-world tradition of *jus sanguine*, wherein citizenship is derived from ancestral and blood ties (as in Germany, England, and Japan). The *jus soli* tradition in America, by accelerating the spread of citizenship to immigrant populations, reduced distinctions between citizens and noncitizens, including legal distinctions that would deny to immigrants the rights and benefits enjoyed by residents of many generations (Noiriel 1994; Schuck 1992; Schuck and Smith 1985; Soysal 1994). The U.S. Supreme Court in *Yick Wo v. Hopkins* (1886) ruled that the Civil War amendments applied "to all *persons* within the territorial jurisdiction, without regard to any differences of race, of color, or of nationality."[1]

By World War II, liberal lawmakers working to ban race discrimination routinely included *national origin* in their statutory language. Franklin Roosevelt's executive order of 1941 established the Fair Employment Practice Committee to protect workers against job discrimination on account of their "race, creed, color, or national origin." In 1945, New York's State Law Against Discrimination established a fair employment commission to protect workers against discrimination on the basis of "race, religion, or national origin"—a trend soon followed by most industrial states outside the South. President Kennedy's executive order of 1961, which first linked nondiscrimination to "affirmative action," directed government contractors to "take affirmative action to ensure that applicants are employed, and that employees are treated during employment, without regard to their race, creed, color, or national origin." The Civil Rights Act of 1964 repeated the race-and-national origin linkage in Title VI, on contract compliance, and also in Title VII on employment, where sex discrimination was also banned (Berger 1978, Graham 1992).

By 1965, when the principle of nondiscrimination was applied to immigration policy, Americans understood that civil rights reform mainly meant nondiscrimination against blacks, especially in the South. Race nondiscrimination presumably included Asians, but rather abstractly, because discrimination against Asians, severe prior to 1945, had eased following World War II and because there was no significant Asian civil rights movement. Nondiscrimination also presumably included, under national origins protection, Mexican Americans and Puerto Ricans, groups facing historic patterns of discrimination in the United States. But in 1965, the Hispanic civil rights movement, mobilizing in the 1960s at the local and regional level, had not yet reached the national agenda. Immigration had been so minimal since World War I that by the 1960s anti-immigrant sentiment was negligible.

Although the politics of African American protest held center stage in the mid-1960s and little attention was paid to national origin discrimination in domestic policy, constitutional developments had tied race and national origin discrimination tightly together. The Supreme Court in its rulings on segregation following World War II developed a doctrine requiring "strict scrutiny" for all laws classifying citizens by race or alienage. This meant that governments faced a virtually insurmountable task of demonstrating that the classification (racial segregation laws in the South, statutes barring Asian land ownership in the West) was essential to meet a compelling state interest. In 1971, a unanimous Court asserted in *Graham v. Richardson* that "classifications based on alienage, like those based on nationality or race, are inherently suspect and subject to close judicial scrutiny. Aliens as a class are a prime example of a 'discrete and insular' minority . . . for whom such heightened judicial solicitude is appropriate" (403 U.S. 365 (1971)). These developments in law and policy were consistent with the equal-treatment tradition of liberal nondiscrimination doctrine, which by the mid-1960s had won a strong national consensus. That consensus included the original Kennedy-Johnson meaning of affirmative action, which meant nondiscrimination enhanced by outreach programs (special recruiting, training, internships) targeted toward minorities and women. This was soft affirmative action, which expanded minority outreach into a gray area of targeted enticements but rejected reverse discrimination in favor of minorities.[2] The liberal consensus, however, did not extend to the minority preferences of hard affirmative action, which, by the inner logic of American interest-group liberalism, spread quietly outward during the 1970s to include new groups and ratcheted upward to benefit organized, advantaged clienteles.

From Soft to Hard Affirmative Action:
Spreading Outward and Ratcheting Upward

As John David Skrentny (1996) observes in *The Ironies of Affirmative Action*, the shift in federal civil rights policy from nondiscrimination to compensatory affirmative action following the urban riots of 1965–1968 occurred quickly and quietly, guided not by interest groups and elected officials but by judges and policy entrepreneurs in new enforcement subagencies. Alarmed by the racial violence, policy elites in Washington found leverage to speed job redistribution in the broad discretionary authority of the executive branch in procurement. They required government contractors to hire minority workers in rough proportion to their availability in the workforce, as in the Philadelphia Plan of 1969, or offered business benefits (subsidized loans, surety bonds) to minority entrepreneurs, as in the Small Business Administration's (SBA) section 8(a) program. These compensatory measures, which required preferential rather than equal treatment, were justified as remedies for past institutionalized discrimination. Challenged by nonminority business associations, the affirmative-action requirements were upheld between 1969 and 1971 by the federal courts, whose school integration rulings by then required race-conscious assignment of pupils and staff (Graham 1994; Skrentny 1996).

The shift during the Nixon administration to hard affirmative action focused on African American claims, but its success in the agencies and courts prompted other groups to seek similar advantages. The minority preferences of hard affirmative action were novel, but the interest-group bargaining that extended their benefits to other groups was traditional. By long practice in the American polity, temporary programs became permanent, programs established to benefit one group were spread to others, and programs designed to redistribute benefits downward were reshaped to aid highly organized and more affluent clienteles (Lowi 1969; J. Wilson 1989).

For these reasons, hard affirmative-action programs, a major component of the surge of social regulation brought by public law litigation and agency rule-making, spread rapidly after 1968 even under Republican presidents. The favored instrument of expansion in Congress was the Civil Rights Act's Title VI on contract compliance, where vague congressional language authorized agencies to write detailed enforcement regulations to redistribute benefits to racial and national origin minorities. This broad rule-making authority was extended to cover women in 1972, the physically and mentally handicapped in 1973, and

nonnative speakers of English in 1974–1975. During the Carter presidency, when Democrats controlled both elected branches in Washington, Congress for the first time since the Civil War era established a
racial classification and set explicit minority quotas. In 1977, without
hearings in either chamber, Congress by voice vote authorized the minority contract set-aside program.

The set-aside involved federal procurement contracts, specifically,
a $4 billion public works bill passed in 1977 to combat the recession.
That year, Congress set aside from normal competitive bidding requirements 10 percent of the appropriation, earmarking the funds for businesses owned by "Negroes, Spanish-speaking, Orientals, Indians, Eskimos, and Aleuts" (*Congressional Record* 1977). After the Supreme Court
upheld the 1977 minority set-aside in 1980 (in *Fullilove v. Klutznick*),
similar programs, totaling more than 230 by 1990, spread rapidly in
city and state governments. In these programs, especially in city governments controlled by minority coalitions and in universities, set-aside
targets tended to ratchet upward. The city government of Richmond,
Virginia, earmarked 30 percent of city contracts for minority business
enterprises (MBEs) without providing a rationale for the set-aside.[3] The
District of Columbia set aside 50 percent. Ohio State University set
aside 100 percent of its painting contracts for MBEs. During the Reagan
presidency, Congress extended minority set-aside requirements to the
large procurement budgets of the Departments of Transportation and
Defense. The Reagan administration, divided internally over the legitimacy of affirmative action, supported MBE programs for the same reason they appealed to Nixon—to build minority capitalism and appeal
to minority voters (Graham 1997; Shull 1993).

The Problem of Eligibility by Ancestry:
MBE Programs and Post-1965 Immigrants

In 1978, Congress for the first time provided a statutory basis for the
SBA section 8(a) program, begun administratively in 1968 in response
to the urban riots. In 1973, the SBA listed five groups—blacks, American Indians, Spanish Americans, Asian Americans, and Puerto Ricans—
"presumed" to be socially or economically disadvantaged and hence automatically eligible to participate (House 1973). The subsequent expansion of the section 8(a) program illustrates both the political pragmatism
and the theoretical incoherence that characterized the expansion of affirmative action beyond its core African American clientele.

Representative Parren Mitchell, an African American Democrat from Baltimore and the leading congressional policy maker for MBE programs, omitted Asian Americans from the list of presumptively eligible minority groups in the 1978 SBA law. The following year, the SBA, responding to lobbying by Asian American groups, included Asians in a broadened new category, Asian Pacific Americans. It included persons with ancestors in Cambodia, China, Guam, Japan, Korea, Laos, Northern Marianas, Philippines, Samoa, Taiwan, the U.S. Trust Territory of the Pacific, and Vietnam. This enumeration, like all previous such designations, was made without formal hearings or agency rationale.

During the 1980s, eleven groups petitioned the SBA for presumptive eligibility in the section 8(a) program. Petitions were successful for persons with ancestry from India (1982), Tonga (1986), Sri Lanka (1988), and, in 1989, Indonesia, Nepal, and Bhutan. The SBA rejected petitions for Hasidic Jews (1980), women (1982), disabled veterans (1987), Iranians (1989), and Afghans (1989). La Noue and Sullivan (1994), in their study of the section 8(a) program, found that the SBA used criteria arbitrarily, excluding some groups (Iranians, Afghans) as too narrowly based on an individual nation and lacking evidence of "long-term" prejudice and discrimination in American society, while admitting many other groups with the same characteristics.

For Asian groups especially, economic disadvantage was a particularly problematic criterion (see chapter 4). Using income data for the late 1960s, economist Thomas Sowell calculated the median family income of the major racial and ethnic groups (Sowell 1983). Sowell found that Americans of Japanese ancestry ranked second in the nation in family income (behind Jews) and that Chinese ranked fourth (behind Poles). Of the eight national-origin groups ranked above the national average in family income, English were seventh and Irish were eighth. Of the seven groups ranked below the national average, American Indians were last (60 percent of the national average), then blacks (62 percent), Puerto Ricans (63 percent), and Mexicans (76 percent).

Sowell's study captured the pre–World War I immigration and demonstrated the economic success of Japanese and Chinese Americans despite generations of severe discrimination. Post-1965 immigrants from Asia, far less subject to discrimination, showed mixed patterns, ranging from high levels of education and prosperity in the United States (Korea, Taiwan, Indonesia, India) to economic hardship (Cambodia, Laos, Vietnam). Thus in the same year (1969) that the Nixon administration, through the affirmative-action requirements of the Philadelphia Plan, committed the federal government to a norm of proportional representation for minority groups in the workforce, the census data showed that Japanese and Chinese Americans, although racial minorities suffering severe historic discrimination in America, were economically successful. Minority racial status per se, which brought presumptive eligibility for affirmative-action preferences to remedy historic discrimination, made no sense as a proxy for economic disadvantage even in 1969.

Historically, Asian Americans had not participated actively in political organizations and interest-group bargaining, including affirmative-action programs. Hispanic rights organizations mobilized aggressively in the 1970s but concentrated on bilingual education, a form of affirmative action that, unlike minority preference programs in employment, contracts, and admissions, dealt with a benefit (native-language instruction) that few Americans sought. For these reasons, African Americans dominated the early affirmative-action programs. In the section 8(a) program, for example, black-owned firms far outnumbered firms owned by competing minorities in the approved SBA pool. In fiscal 1981, black-owned firms won two-thirds of the $1.8 billion disbursed by federal agencies (see table 1). Women, the major beneficiaries of soft affirmative action (nondiscrimination plus aggressive recruiting and outreach), were marginal participants in preference-based programs. The SBA did not presume them to be disadvantaged, as it did the racial and ethnic minorities (La Noue and Sullivan 1994). Only 96 (4 percent) of the SBA's 2,264 MBE firms in 1981 were owned by women.

Given the political context of the section 8(a) program, the 1981 distribution of participants by race and national origin is not surprising. The General Accounting Office report, like all such government

TABLE 1

Minority-Owned Firms Certified as Presumptively Eligible by the Small Business Administration for the 8(a) MBE Program, Fiscal Year 1981

Minority	Number	Percentage
Black	1,418	62.6
Spanish American	451	19.9
Asian	164	7.2
American Indian	133	5.9
Puerto Rican	38	1.7
Eskimo and Aleut	4	.2
Other	56	2.5
Total	2,264	

Source: General Accounting Office, *The SBA 8(a) Procurement Program—A Promise Unfulfilled* (8 April 1981).

studies, makes no reference to citizenship or to the immigration status of participants (General Accounting Office 1981). Yet, accelerating immigration in the 1980s shifted the balance of eligible participants. During the decade 8.6 million immigrants came to the United States (an estimated 2 million of them illegal), 78 percent of them from Asia and Latin America. Whereas in 1965 the United States admitted about 115,000 persons from Third World countries, representing just under half of the total number of immigrants, by 1991 the number of such immigrants, including legalized undocumented aliens, had increased by more than a factor of 14 to 1.68 million, making up more than 90 percent of all immigrants (Krikorian 1994). By 1995 the foreign-born in America numbered 24.6 million (4 to 5 million of them illegal upon entry), 44 percent of them Latin American and 24 percent Asian. During fiscal year 1995, the SBA reported to Congress that the ethnic heritages of the 6,002 firms participating in the $5.8 billion section 8(a) program were as follows: black, 47 percent; Hispanic, 25 percent; Asian, 21 percent; Native American, 6 percent; and other, 1 percent (U.S. Small Business Administration 1995).[4] United States Census data on the foreign-born population for 1996 showed that 16 million of the 24.6 million foreign-born residents were noncitizens, yet they remained eligible for minority preferences under many affirmative-action programs (U.S. Bureau of the Census 1997). This trend was explosive with political possibilities, even though evidence of immigrant participation was episodic and anecdotal.

Rising Tensions between Blacks, Hispanics, and Asians

In the 1980s, news reports of black-Hispanic tension and violence concentrated on the Cuban influx in the Miami area, especially in Liberty City. In 1992, the most violent urban riot in the nation's history broke out in Los Angeles. Triggered by the jury acquittal of Los Angeles policemen accused of beating an African American suspect, Rodney King, and initially likened to the Watts riot of 1965, the Los Angeles eruption assumed the proportions of an immigration riot, since half of the arrested rioters were Hispanic, and most of the torched businesses were Korean-owned (Cannon 1997; Miles 1992). Hispanic organizations in Los Angeles increasingly had complained that blacks used affirmative action to entrench themselves in the civil service bureaucracy. With half of Angelenos foreign-born and more than 40 percent speaking Spanish at home, Hispanic rights organizations demanded that affirmative-action preferences reflect the city's new demographics (Skerry 1989,

1993). In the wake of the Los Angeles riot, Congressman Luis V. Gutierrez (Democrat-Illinois), a Puerto Rican elected in 1992 in a newly redistricted Hispanic-majority district in Chicago, requested a General Accounting Office study of government affirmative-action programs. The GAO in 1993 reported that blacks were heavily overrepresented and Hispanics underrepresented in the U.S. Postal Service (General Accounting Office 1993). In the GAO study, a representation index of 100 indicated demographic parity between groups (blacks, for example, holding 15 percent of jobs in the civilian workforce and also 15 percent in the postal service).

In Chicago, the GAO found, the representational index for blacks in Postal Service jobs was 439, meaning they were overrepresented in postal jobs by a factor greater than four. For Hispanics the index was 33 (an index lower than 50, according to the EEOC, showed extreme underrepresentation). The index for Asians in Chicago was 56. For whites, it was 20. In Los Angeles, the Postal Service index for blacks according to the GAO study was 646. For Hispanics it was 42, for Asians, 145, and for whites, 16. Nationwide, the representational index for Postal Service employment was 204 for blacks, 169 for Asians, 85 for whites, and 76 for Hispanics.

The GAO study offers only one small window, a rare glimpse into the demographic consequences of one of the oldest and largest affirmative-action programs (there were 678,000 postal employees in 1993). In this program, complaining Hispanic organizations had the strongest case for underrepresentation. But they had the weakest claims to a compensatory remedy originally intended for the descendants of African slaves. The GAO's Postal Service study illustrates both the advantages blacks enjoyed from political entrenchment in affirmative-action bureaucracies and the disadvantages blacks increasingly encountered from market forces in a global economy with heavy immigration. Economists debate the overall effect of immigration on the American economy, but many agree that large-scale immigration by low-skilled workers since the 1960s has reduced job opportunities and pay for inner city African Americans (Borjas 1994; McCarthy and Vernez 1997). William Julius Wilson (1996), in his book *When Work Disappears*, found that Chicago-area employers commonly preferred Hispanic and Asian workers and avoided hiring urban blacks. Jennifer Lee studying New York City and Michael Lichter and Roger Waldinger examining Los Angeles (see chapters 6 and 7 in this volume) show that the pattern is not confined to Chicago. Similar patterns of immigrants displacing native-born workers have been seen in construction, garment-making, hotel, restaurant, janitorial, and agricultural employment (Briggs 1993; Waldinger 1996).

The Unintended Consequences of Reform

All three of the major civil rights reforms of the mid-1960s—the Civil Rights Act of 1964, the Voting Rights Act of 1965, and the Immigration and Nationality Act of 1965—produced consequences that in many ways reversed the expressed intentions of their legislative sponsors. The Civil Rights Act, couched in liberalism's classic idiom of nondiscrimination and equal individual rights, led to affirmative-action preferences for protected-class minority groups. Similarly, the Voting Rights Act, guaranteeing equal access to the ballot box, led to the creation of "minority majority" electoral districts under Justice Department and federal court directives. And the Immigration and Nationality Act of 1965, despite supporters' sincere disclaimers, led not to a modest increase in European immigration but rather to a boom in immigration from Latin America and Asia. All three laws, to be sure, quickly accomplished their intended objectives—the Civil Rights Act and Voting Rights Act broke the back of Jim Crow segregation in the South, and the immigration reform ended the national origins quota preferences. But it was the unintended consequences that led to convergence between civil rights and immigration policy.

During the 1970s and 1980s this growing, and surprising, convergence strengthened both reform forces. New rights-based organizations, such as the MALDEF, worked in tandem with the American Civil Liberties Union and the NAACP's Legal Defense and Educational Fund (the model for MALDEF) to expand civil rights remedies and liberalize immigration and naturalization policies. When the "rights revolution" during the 1970s mobilized new constituencies to join the civil rights coalition—feminists, Hispanics, Native Americans, the handicapped—the Leadership Conference on Civil Rights, coordinating the lobbying of more than 165 rights-based organizations by 1980, became one of the most powerful forces in Congress. In the 1980s this coalition generally prevailed despite the efforts of the Reagan and Bush administrations. The civil rights coalition won surprising legislative victories against Republican presidents in 1982, 1988, and 1991. The immigration rights coalition turned restrictionist efforts into statutes in 1986 and 1990 that considerably expanded immigration. Also during the 1980s, federal courts in rulings on immigration policy abandoned their historic pattern of deference to the "plenary power" of Congress and its agent, the Immigration and Naturalization Service (INS). In *Plyler v. Doe* the Supreme Court in 1982 barred states from denying public education to the undocumented children of illegal aliens (457 U.S. 202 (1982)). Federal judges also invalidated key INS policies and enlarged the procedural rights of aliens resisting expulsion (Schuck 1992).

By the 1990s, however, the convergence of affirmative action and immigration policies drew increasing public resentment toward both. Opinion polls showed large majorities opposing preference policies based on race or ancestral origin. The federal courts, beginning in 1989, sharply narrowed the scope of affirmative-action remedies in government contracting, college admissions, and electoral districting. The unique moral force of affirmative action's original public rationale, as a temporary remedy to compensate for the lingering, institutionalized effects of past discrimination against the descendants of slaves, was eroded when preferences were extended to newly arrived immigrants from Latin America and Asia.

The result for Americans at the century's end has been an unhappy stalemate in a two-tiered system of policy making where the liberal co-alition has the advantage in the inside-the-beltway world of legislative committees and government agencies, and their opponents have the upper hand in the voting booth and in opinion polls. In the middle sit the federal courts, where conservative majorities in the 1990s began applying strict scrutiny standards to both racial and alien classifications in public policy. The result, ironically, has been to narrow affirmative-action remedies, of which blacks have been the chief beneficiaries, while broadening protection for immigrants, whether legal or illegal.

In this situation, African Americans have reason for the pessimism that contemporary polls suggest. The unintended consequences of the reforms of the 1960s strengthened the bargaining power of African American interest groups in the 1970s and 1980s but weakened it in the 1990s. For the greatly expanded black middle class, this alliance was fruitful in the 1970s and 1980s but soured in the 1990s. For the black urban poor, whose lives were largely untouched by affirmative-action programs, large-scale immigration had many negative economic effects. On balance, immigrant participation in affirmative-action programs has been destabilizing.

Historically, African American leaders such as Frederick Douglass, Booker T. Washington, and W. E. B. Du Bois had opposed importing cheap foreign-born labor to compete with native-born workers. But the 1960s encouraged a new "people of color" solidarity that paid political dividends for a generation. The immigrant success ethos, however, with its emphasis on hard work, merit, and social assimilation, clashed with hard affirmative action's emphasis on historic victimhood, reparations, and racial entitlement. These tensions were underlined in the 1990s by Asian American challenges to affirmative-action preferences in university admissions. As the twentieth century neared its end, historic tensions reasserted themselves, thus setting apart the quarter-century following the legislative breakthrough of 1964–65, when for a season the unintended consequences of reform permitted the flowering of an affirmative-action era.

Notes

1. *Yick Wo v. Hopkins*, 118 U.S. 356 (1886). Following World War I, the Court upheld state laws barring aliens ineligible for citizenship (Asians) from owning or leasing agricultural lands or practicing certain professions. Following World War II, however, the Court applied strict judicial scrutiny to classifications based on race and ancestry, striking down most state restrictions while leaving Congress wide latitude to shape immigration policy.

2. The chief beneficiaries of soft affirmative action since the 1960s have been women, Asians, and the handicapped. In the U.S. armed forces, for example, soft affirmative action accounts for the rising participation of minorities and women in recruitment and promotion. Hard affirmative action accounts for greater black and Hispanic participation in military procurement contracts, but also for increasing fraud and corruption, as in the Wedtech scandal in the Reagan administration.

3. The Richmond set-aside was challenged in *City of Richmond v. J. A. Croson Co.*, 488 U.S. 469 (1989). Justice Sandra Day O'Connor, speaking for a 6–3 majority, found Richmond's MBE program unconstitutional. The Court ruled that under the equal protection clause of the Fourteenth Amendment, racial classifications by state and local governments triggered strict judicial scrutiny and required compelling government objectives. This was the standard implicit in *Brown v. Board of Education* and elaborated in the racial desegregation decisions of the 1960s. In 1995 in *Adarand Constructors, Inc. v. Pena*, 515 U.S. 200, the strict scrutiny test was applied to federal programs as well, overturning the *Fullilove* decision of 1980 (*Fullilove v. Klutznick*, 448 U.S. 448).

4. Of the 6,002 firms in the section 8(a) program in fiscal 1995, 17 percent were owned by women. Disadvantaged whites were ineligible for the program's sole-source and limited-competition contracts ($5.3 billion) and subsidized loans ($63 billion).

References

Beck, Roy. 1996. *The case against immigration*. New York: Norton.
Berger, Morroe. 1978. *Equality by statute*. Garden City, N.Y.: Doubleday.

Borjas, Georges. 1994. The economics of immigration. *Journal of Economic Literature* 32: 1667–1717.

Briggs, Vernon. 1993. *Immigration policy: A tool of labor economics?* Annandale-on-Hudson, N.Y.: Jerome Levy Economics Institute of Bard College.

Brimelow, Peter. 1995. *Alien nation: Common sense about America's immigration disaster.* New York: Random House.

Cannon, Lou. 1997. *Official negligence.* New York: Times Books.

Cheshire, William. 1995. Set-asides: How millionaires milk today's programs. *Orange County Register,* 7 April.

Congressional Record. 1977. 95th Cong., 1st sess. Vol. 123, pt. 4: 5098, 42 U.S.C. 6705(f)(2).

Fuchs, Lawrence. 1995. What do immigrants deserve? *The Washington Post,* 29 January, C2.

General Accounting Office. 1981. *The SBA 8(a) procurement program.* Washington, D.C.: Government Printing Office.

———. 1993. *Hispanic employment at the United States Postal Service.* Washington, D.C.: Government Printing Office.

Graham, Hugh D. 1990. *The civil rights era: Origins and development of national policy, 1960–1972.* New York: Oxford University Press.

———. 1992. *Civil rights and the presidency.* New York: Oxford University Press.

———. 1994. Race, history, and policy: African American civil rights since 1964. *Journal of Policy History* 6:12–39.

———. 1997. The politics of clientele capture: Civil rights policy in the Reagan administration. In *Redefining equality,* edited by Neal Devins and Davison Douglas, 103–19. New York: Oxford University Press.

Johnson, Alan. 1994. Asian-Indian companies win minority status appeal. *Columbus Dispatch,* 8 July.

Krikorian, Mark. 1994. Affirmative action and immigration. In *Debating affirmative action,* edited by Nicholas Mills, 300–313. New York: Dell.

La Noue, George, and John Sullivan. 1994. Presumptions for preferences: The Small Business Administration's decisions on groups entitled to affirmative action. *Journal of Policy History* 6:439–67.

———. 1998. Deconstructing the affirmative action categories. *American Behavioral Scientist* 41:913–26.

Lowi, Theodore. 1969. *The end of liberalism.* New York: Norton.

McCarthy, Kevin, and Georges Vernez. 1997. *Immigration in a changing economy: The California experience.* Santa Monica, Calif.: RAND.

Miles, Jack. 1992. Blacks vs. browns. *Atlantic* 270:41–68.

National Research Council. 1997. *The new Americans: Economic, demographic, and fiscal effects of immigration.* Washington, D.C.: National Academy Press.

Noiriel, Gerard. 1994. "Civil rights" policy in the United States and the policy of "integration" in Europe. In *Civil rights in the United States,* edited by Hugh D. Graham, 120–39. University Park: Pennsylvania State University Press.

North, David. 1995. *Soothing the establishment: The impact of foreign-born scientists and engineers in America.* Lanham, Md.: University Press of America.

Reimers, David. 1992. *Still the golden door*. New York: Columbia University Press.

Robb, James. 1995. *Affirmative action for immigrants: The entitlement nobody wanted*. Petoskey, Mich.: Social Contract Press.

Schneider, Howard, and James Ragland. 1992. Four dominated D.C. minority contracting. *The Washington Post*, 1 June, A1, A8.

Schuck, Peter. 1992. The politics of rapid legal change: Immigration policy in the 1880s. *Studies in American Political Development* 6:37–92.

Schuck, Peter, and Rogers Smith. 1985. *Citizenship without consent*. New Haven: Yale University Press.

Shull, Steven. 1993. *A kinder, gentler racism? The Reagan-Bush civil rights legacy*. Armonk, N.Y.: M. E. Sharpe.

Skerry, Peter. 1989. Borders and quotas: Immigration and the affirmative-action state. *The Public Interest* 96:94–97.

———. 1993. *Mexican Americans: The ambivalent minority*. New York: Basic Books.

Skrentny, John D. 1996. *The ironies of affirmative action*. Chicago: University of Chicago Press.

Smith, Rogers. 1997. *Civic ideals: Conflicting visions of citizenship in U.S. history*. New Haven: Yale University Press.

Sowell, Thomas. 1983. *The economics and politics of race*. New York: Morrow.

Soysal, Yasemin. 1994. *The limits of citizenship*. Chicago: University of Chicago Press.

Stephanopoulos, George, and Christopher Edley. 1995. *Affirmative action review: Report to the president*. Washington, D.C.: Government Printing Office.

Tilove, Jonathan. 1994. Newhouse news service. *Raleigh News & Observer*, 9 January.

U.S. Bureau of the Census. 1969. *Current population report on ethnic origin: November 1969*. Washington, D.C.: Government Printing Office.

———. 1997. *The foreign-born population: 1996*. Washington, D.C.: Journey to Work and Migration Statistics Branch.

U.S. Commission on Immigration Reform. 1997. *Becoming an American: Immigration and immigrant policy*. Washington, D.C.: Government Printing Office.

U.S. House. 1973. 93d Cong., 2d Sess., 13 C.F.R. 124.8-(c). H.R. Rep. 1178.

U.S. Small Business Administration. 1995. *Report to the U.S. Congress on minority small business and capital ownership development for fiscal year 1995*. Washington, D.C.: U.S. Small Business Administration.

Wagner, Stephen. 1986. *The lingering death of the national origins quota system: A political history of United States immigration policy, 1952–1965*. Ph.D. diss., Harvard University.

Waldinger, Roger. 1996. *Still the promised city? African-Americans and new immigrants in postindustrial New York*. Cambridge: Harvard University Press.

Wilson, James Q. 1989. *Bureaucracy*. New York: Basic Books.

Wilson, William J. 1996. *When work disappears*. New York: Knopf.

3

Deconstructing Affirmative Action Categories

. . .

GEORGE R. LA NOUE AND JOHN C. SULLIVAN

As the debate over the types of affirmative action that include preferences intensifies, there is increased attention to the issue of which groups should be the beneficiaries of those preferences. Whereas preferences are most often defended for African Americans, whose moral and political claims are the most compelling, many affirmative action programs also include women, Hispanics, Asian Americans, Native Americans, Eskimos and Aleuts. For the latter groups, the claims for preferences are more complex (Glazer 1988, 108). Examining the history of decisions about which groups to prefer and the socioeconomic status of these groups suggests that the current affirmative action categories are overinclusive and not based on empirical analysis.

Bureaucratic Initiatives

The original construction of the affirmative action group categories is not a subject for which the research is complete. Most often the decisions took place in the recesses of federal bureaucracies when regulations and reporting forms were developed. Public records of these decisions are limited. Choosing which racial and ethnic groups would receive affirmative action recognition and benefits and which would be excluded was not a decision Congress wanted to confront publicly.

Once the bureaucracies had fixed the group categories, however, these categories were not only replicated in all federal affirmative action programs, but the same categories appeared in hundreds of state and local and even private programs as well. There was almost never any independent examination of whether the federally defined groups fit any theory of social justice or equity. Changes in immigration patterns and in the socioeconomic status of groups, as well as particular local conditions, often made national generalizations about groups that should benefit from affirmative action incorrect or irrelevant. For example, affirmative action plans in Dade County, Florida, were used to advantage Hispanics, often in ways that disadvantaged the older, less prosperous black population, even though many Hispanics were middle-class Cuban political refugees who had no history of disadvantage in the United States (Grenier and Stepnik 1992, 14; see also *Engineering Contractors Association of South Florida v. Metropolitan Dade County*, 943 F. Supp. 1546 (S.D. Fla. 1996), *aff'd*, 122 F.3d 895 (11th Cir. 1997)). Imitating the federal section 8(a) program, the minority business enterprise (MBE) program in Richmond, Virginia, included Hispanics, Asian Americans, Native Americans, Eskimos, and Aleuts, although the 1987 census recorded no firms owned by Eskimos and Aleuts in the Richmond Metropolitan Statistical Area and very few firms owned by Asian Americans and Hispanics.

The affirmative action categories designated by the federal bureaucracies established far-reaching patterns, regardless of whether they were objectively or carefully created. Herbert Hammerman was chief of the reports unit at the U.S. Equal Employment Opportunity Commission (EEOC) when various reporting forms, including EEO-1 (the standard federal affirmative action employment form), were developed. He recalls arguing against inclusion of Asian Americans and Native Americans in the forms because there was no statistical evidence of discrimination against Asian Americans as a group and because Native Americans living on reservations were excluded from Title VII of the Civil Rights Act. Although the EEOC chairman agreed, "he was unwilling to take the political heat that the removal would generate" (Hammerman 1988, 131).

Many of the decisions to include or exclude groups from affirmative action categories were made by the Small Business Administration (SBA), which administers the section 8(a) program, which sets aside billions of federal contract dollars annually for the benefit of businesses owned by economically and socially disadvantaged persons. Economic disadvantage can be defined objectively, but social disadvantage is relative. Screening millions of business owners to determine if their personal histories indicated they were socially disadvantaged would have been a huge bureaucratic task. Moreover, Congressman Parren Mitchell, the head of the Congressional Black Caucus and the Small Business Committee overseeing the section 8(a) program, wanted to limit it to racial and ethnic minorities. Consequently, the SBA decided that any owner identifying with certain racial and ethnic groups was "presumptively" disadvantaged. African Americans, Hispanics, and Native Americans were included from the beginning. Asians and Pacific Americans were added in 1979.

Still, given the enormous demographic variety in the United States, there was controversy over who was to be included in the affirmative action categories and the rich prize of favored access to public contracts. Between 1980 and 1989, the SBA accepted the claims of Asian Indians, Sri Lankans, Indonesians, and Tongans for inclusion, while rejecting Hasidic Jews, women, disabled veterans, and Iranians. Examining SBA files on these decisions, which were obtained through a Freedom of Information Act request, La Noue and Sullivan (1994) concluded that the SBA ignored readily available census socioeconomic data and other empirical sources in determining social disadvantage. After inclusion of Hispanics, many of whom are white, the SBA drew a "people of color" line to include or exclude groups from the 8(a) program (La Noue and Sullivan 1994, 460–63; see also chapter 2, this volume).

Sometimes the decision to include a group was made for more overtly political reasons. When the Nixon administration revised the Johnson administration's EEO reporting rules, it added Cuban Americans to the list of covered groups. Hugh Davis Graham (1990, 328) comments in his monumental book *The Civil Rights Era*, "Adding Cubans made some immediate political sense for a Republican administration, in that the large bloc of Cuban Americans who fled Castro's revolution was overwhelmingly Republican." A reprise of this type of decision occurred in 1991 in Ohio when the Republican governor, George Voinovich, added Asian Indians to the affirmative action categories. That immediately provoked the opposition of Ohio's legislative black caucus, which accused the governor of diluting the affirmative action pool and of favoring Asian Indians who had contributed to his election campaign (Goel 1996, 8).

Judicial Response

The decision about which groups, if any, to prefer has long concerned the courts. As Justice Powell pointed out in the *Bakke* decision (*Regents of the University of California v. Bakke*, 438 U.S. 265, 295 (1978)), which overturned the admissions quotas at the University of California, Davis Medical School:

> The concepts of "majority" and "minority" necessarily reflect temporary arrangements and political judgments. . . . There is no principled basis for deciding which groups would merit "heightened judicial solicitude" and which would not. Courts would be asked to evaluate the extent of the prejudice and consequent harm suffered

by various minority groups. Those whose societal injury is thought to exceed some arbitrary level of tolerability then would be entitled to preferential classifications at the expense of individuals belonging to other groups. Those classifications would be free from exacting judicial scrutiny. As these preferences began to have their desired effect, and the consequences of past discrimination were undone, new judicial rankings would be necessary. The kind of variable sociological and political analysis necessary to produce such rankings simply does not lie within the judicial competence—even if they otherwise were politically feasible and socially desirable. (438 U.S. at 295–97)

Powell went on to comment that "the University is unable to explain its selection of only four favored groups—Negroes, Mexican-Americans, American Indians, and Asians—for preferential treatment. The inclusion of the last group is especially curious in the light of the substantial numbers of Asians admitted through the regular admissions process" (438 U.S. at 309). In fact, the 63 applicants who were successful in the special Medical School admissions process were 33 percent black, 48 percent Hispanic, and 19 percent Asian, whereas, as Powell noted, 37 Asians were also admitted in the regular process (438 U.S. at 276).

Despite Powell's otherwise influential opinion, few lawsuits challenged the validity of preferring specific groups in affirmative action programs. Instead, when plaintiffs managed to get into court, they attacked the plans in general rather than focusing on the fairness of including or excluding specific groups.

Nevertheless, two years after the *Bakke* decision, the issue surfaced again in *Fullilove v. Klutznick* (448 U.S. 448 (1980)). Although the Supreme Court split 6 to 3, upholding the 10 percent MBE set-aside in the $4 billion Public Works Employment Act of 1977, Justice Stevens, in dissent, reopened the question of which groups should be included in affirmative action programs. He wrote:

> The statutory definition of the preferred class includes "citizens of the United States who are Negroes, Spanish-speaking, Orientals, Indians, Eskimos and Aleuts." All aliens and all nonmembers of the racial class are excluded. No economic, social, geographical or historical criteria are relevant for exclusion or inclusion. There is not one word in the remainder of the Act or in the legislative history that explains why any Congressman or Senator favored this particular definition over any other or that identifies the common characteristics that every member of the preferred class was believed to share. (448 U.S. at 535)

In 1989, however, in *City of Richmond v. Croson* (488 U.S. 469 (1989)), the need to justify the inclusion of particular groups in affirmative action programs became constitutionally mandated. One of the arguments Justice O'Connor made in striking down the Richmond MBE program was that

> There is *absolutely no evidence* of past discrimination against Spanish-speaking, Oriental Indian, Eskimos, or Aleut persons in any aspect of the Richmond construction industry. . . . It may well be that Richmond has never had an Aleut or Eskimo citizen. The random inclusion of racial groups that, as a practical matter, may never have suffered from discrimination in the construction industry in Richmond suggests that perhaps the city's purpose was not in fact to remedy past discrimination. (488 U.S. at 506, emphasis in original)

The *Croson* case requires that a jurisdiction's definition of the groups eligible for preferences have a proper evidentiary basis and that the affirmative action program be narrowly tailored. The law is now settled: there has to be an empirical basis proving the existence of discrimination against each preferred group. Consequently, in some jurisdictions, for reason of law or politics, the preference programs have been pared down by eliminating particular groups. Although the pre-*Croson* MBE program in Richmond included all the federally defined groups, the post-*Croson* program includes only African Americans. Native American–owned firms have been dropped from MBE programs all over the country because their numbers are too small for statistical analysis and for garnering political support. The combination of low numbers and limited political power has proved fatal in most places (see Soussan 1997, 1; Sundman 1993, 3–5).

In other jurisdictions, the issue of group inclusion has been decided through litigation. Thus the Third Circuit upheld a district court's ruling on a summary judgment motion that Philadelphia did not have sufficient evidence to include construction firms owned by women, Hispanics, and Asian Americans in its goals program but remanded the issue of the inclusion of African American–owned firms (*Contractors Association of Eastern Pennsylvania v. City of Philadelphia*, 6 F.3d 990 (3d Cir. 1993)). On remand, the district court found the evidence supporting inclusion of African American–owned construction firms flawed and enjoined the whole program (*Contractors Association of Eastern Pennsylvania v. City of Philadelphia*, 893 F. Supp. 419 (E.D. Pa. 1995), *aff'd*, 91 F.3d 586 (3d Cir. 1996)).

Other courts have been critical of the concept of including every minority group in a preference program. As one judge noted, there is no consistency in the way the groups are defined: "one group is defined by race [African American], another by culture [Hispanic], another by country of origin [Asian American], and another by blood [Native American]" (*Concrete Works of Colorado v. City and County of Denver*, 86 F. Supp. 2d 1042 (D. Colo. 2000)). Several courts have been concerned that groups suffering minor discrimination would receive substantial preferential benefits while more seriously harmed groups would received little when the program covers the usual laundry list of minority groups (*Association for Fairness in Business v. State of New Jersey*, 82 F. Supp. 2d, 353, 360, 362, and *Associated General Contractors v. Drabik*, 2000 F. App. 018P, 6 (6th Cir. 2000)).

Consequently, it is now well established that a preference program may not be overinclusive in terms of the groups benefited. Hispanics, for example, cannot be included in a preference program if there is only evidence of discrimination against African Americans (Schmidt 1996, 17).

But what if the affirmative action group categories themselves are overinclusive, masking important differences within a category? This is an issue particularly for the Hispanic and Asian American categories, which include numerous national origin groups that have immigrated to the United States from many different parts of the globe, at different times, under very different circumstances. Are these categories merely bureaucratic conveniences around which political constituencies have been constructed but which do not reflect socioeconomic realities?

So far the courts have not directly addressed this problem. In 1991, a white firefighter challenged a Dade County preference for Hispanics on the grounds that that category was overinclusive because it covered white European Spanish persons and excluded "Greeks, Italians, Portuguese Jews, Israelis, Iranians, and others." The Eleventh Circuit responded, "In adopting an affirmative action plan an employer may rationally limit its application to those minority groups most in need of affirmative action" and upheld the plan. As the force of the strict scrutiny test the Supreme Court has articulated takes hold, it is not clear that future courts will apply a rational basis test to the inclusion-exclusion issue as this court did. Furthermore, the plaintiff's cause was hurt because he apparently relied on no statistical data and was not himself in any of the groups he claimed should be included. The court did concede, however, that if a "light-skinned Castillian with no discernible cultural or linguistic Hispanic characteristics" had been favored, then the plaintiff's claim "would have had more force" (*Peightal v. Metropolitan Dade County*, 940 F.2d 1394, 1409n. 38 (11th Cir. 1991)).

More recently, a lower state court in Ohio (*Associated General Contractors of Ohio v. Drabik*, 50 F. Supp. 2d 741 (1999)) found the state's MBE statute unconstitutional as applied for excluding a firm owned by a Lebanese man. The state had decided that Lebanese persons should not be defined as "Orientals," which was the permissible statutory category. But the court found that because Asian Indians were eligible as Orientals, then,

> Working our way north and west from India we first come to Pakistan, then Iran, then Iraq, then Syria, and finally Lebanon. If Asian Indians are "Oriental," shall we exclude Pakistanis separated from India only by the Great Indian Desert? And if Pakistanis are "Oriental," shall we exclude Iranians who share a common border with Pakistan? And if Iran is "Oriental," shall we exclude Iraq, separated from Iran only by the Zagros Mountains? And if Iraq is "Oriental," shall we exclude Syria, for the Euphrates River flows through both countries? And finally if Syria is "Oriental," how can its contiguous neighbor Lebanon be anything but "Oriental"?
>
> This Court can think of few things more repugnant to our constitutional system of government than the construction of a statute that would exclude a group of United States' citizens and residents of Ohio from a State program, the sole criteria for exclusion being the side of a river, a mountain range, or a desert their ancestor decided to settle. (50 F. Supp. 2d at 770)

Disparity Studies

The problem of overinclusiveness within affirmative action group categories is now directly implicated by a form of research being introduced to defend MBE programs. Under current law, a preference program for minority- and women-owned businesses will not meet *Croson*'s test that the jurisdiction have a compelling interest for the preferences unless the program is supported by research that identifies the discrimination being remedied. Such research is usually compiled in what has come to be called a disparity study because of *Croson*'s instruction that a disparity between the number of "qualified," "willing and able" MBEs and their use might permit an inference of discrimination (La Noue 1993).

More than $55 million has been spent for these studies, most often by state and local governments hoping to maintain or expand MBE programs (La Noue 1993). This research has almost never turned up specific instances of discrimination in the awarding of prime contracts, let alone the "patterns of deliberate exclusion" *Croson* requires if race-conscious remedies are to be employed. Nor have many examples of discrimination in the awarding of subcontracts by prime contractors been discovered. Therefore, disparity studies are increasingly attempting to demonstrate that discrimination in the broader economic environment keeps minorities and women from forming businesses in the first place. On this premise, it is argued, governments should create preference programs for minority- or women-owned business enterprises (MWBEs) to avoid being "passive participants" in that marketplace discrimination.

Croson provides a slender reed of support for this line of inquiry. Justice O'Connor wrote the following:

> As a matter of state law, the City of Richmond has legislative authority over its procurement policies, and can use its spending powers to remedy private discrimination, if it identifies that discrimination with the particularity required by the Fourteenth Amendment. . . . Thus, if the City could show that it had essentially become a "passive participant" in a system of racial exclusion practiced by elements of the local construction industry, we think it clear that the city could take affirmative steps to dismantle such a system. (488 U.S. at 492)

It is probable that too much emphasis is being placed on the passive participation theory in disparity studies. No court has ever upheld an MBE program based on it. But the theory continues to surface in disparity studies to justify MBE preference programs. If the number of MBE businesses that might exist "but for" discrimination can be estimated, goals can be set higher than actual availability.

Variations of the passive participation and "but for" theories appear in many disparity studies, but they occur most often in those conducted by the National Economics Research Association (NERA) (1992) and Browne, Bortz, and Coddington (BBC) (1995). Together these firms have completed about 35 of the existing 130 disparity studies. Browne, Bortz, and Coddington uses logit models based on the Census Bureau's Public Use Micro Survey (PUMS) data to estimate whether (after controlling for variables drawn from the literature that predict business ownership, such as education and years of work experience) group characteristics measured by ethnicity, race, and gender still account for significant differences (BBC 1995, pt. 4 39–51).

The initial assumption in NERA's work on business formation is that but for discrimination "the probability of self-employment depends on demographic characteristics such as family status [and] human and financial capital" and that all persons with certain similar demographic characteristics would form businesses at the same rate regardless of their group identities (NERA 1992, 65). Consequently, NERA also uses census data to create logit models to determine the probabilities of self-employment for whites and then compares the self-employment rates of similarly situated minorities.

Typically, the studies find that the business formation rates of women and minorities are below that of white males. The usual conclusion is the justification of preference programs, sometimes by setting goals at the rate at which the group might have formed businesses but for discrimination. In some of its studies, however, NERA expressed doubt about whether this conclusion is valid for women, arguing that female labor force participation varies over time, making it difficult to attribute female underrepresentation to either discrimination or changing female workforce roles (NERA 1992, 63, n. 91).

But, of course, cultural factors or voluntary decisions about participation in the labor force may have caused differences in business formation rates among different racial and ethnic groups as well. Although disparity studies frequently use differences in business formation rates to justify MWBE goals, NERA concedes several limitations. For example, "if there are any personal characteristics associated with the choice of self employment that we are unable to include, and if whites tend to have relatively more of these characteristics than minorities, then the differences between the estimated minority self-employment rates could be due to these characteristics rather than discrimination." In addition, "it is impossible to determine whether the underrepresentation of minorities in self-employment is due to contemporary discrimination, the effects of past social discrimination or cultural differences between groups" (Evans 1996, 20).

The hypothesis that discrimination rather than other factors causes differences in the business formation rates would be more plausible if those rates were consistent within the affirmative action–designated groups and within the non-MBEs excluded from that category. The business formation argument is based on the theory that the affirmative action group categories represent a commonality of experiences, so that if disparities exist they can best be explained by that group's encounters with discrimination. Thus, if Hispanics or Asian Americans as categories are below the business formation mean, the assumption is that all subgroups in those categories have suffered from a common problem of discrimination.

However, the categories themselves might be overinclusive and calculations based on the mean legally irrelevant. What if some Hispanic and some Asian American groups are above and some below the mean? What if some white ethnic groups are below some Hispanic or some Asian groups? Both possibilities would suggest that there was no commonality in the experiences of the affirmative action categories and that racial or ethnic discrimination was not the most probable cause of the differences that exist. It would further suggest that the affirmative action categories are themselves overinclusive and therefore constitutionally suspect.

It is now possible to test such theories by analysis of the 1990 PUMS database. This sample is based on approximately 12.5 million responses and permits the classification of individuals into sixty ancestry or racial and ethnic groups. The data can also be used to examine self-employment or business formation, as well as other topics. A comprehensive analysis of this database as it relates to business formation has been completed by Robert Fairlie and Bruce Meyer (1996). The authors not only report raw self-employment rates for each ethnic group but display the results of a regression analysis in which education, time of immigration, age, marital status, physical disability, and language proficiency are variables. Other important variables, such as a person's access to capital, possession of relevant licenses or professional certifications, or attitude about the desirability of business ownership, are not included in the database. Nor do these data reflect information about the size or market niches of businesses, which may be relevant to their availability for public procurement, for example. Most MBEs are smaller than non-MBEs, in part because they are newer businesses. For example, in the area of construction, so often the focus of litigation over government procurement programs that are race-conscious, the number of black-owned firms with employees grew by 112 percent between 1982 and 1992, Hispanic-owned firms by 292 percent, and firms owned by Asian American and others by 225 percent, compared to 36 percent for firms owned white males (U.S. Bureau of the Census, 1982, 1992).

The results of the Fairlie and Meyer (1996) regression analysis are shown in table 1. About half of the sixty ancestry groups in the analysis are of European origin, so these groups create the mean. Nevertheless, it is interesting to examine which groups cluster at the top (23 to 20 businesses per hundred workers), the middle, (12 to 9) and the bottom (5 to 2).

As the Fairlie and Meyer data show, there are differences between the affirmative action–designated groups and the others, so the broad generalizations in the disparity studies are likely correct. Groups in the affirmative action categories generally have formed fewer businesses than groups excluded from those categories. But the affirmative action

TABLE 1
Regression-Adjusted Business Formation Rates by Ethnicity and Race (Males), 1990 Census

Top		Middle		Bottom	
Korean	23.7	**White S. American**	12.6	**Spanish C. American**	5.9
Israeli	23.5	Canadian	12.6	**Black Caribbean**	5.7
Russian	21.4	Czech	12.4	**Pacific Islander**	5.0
Greek	20.9	Dutch	12.4	**Other S. Asian**	4.8
Middle Eastern	20.3	Hungarian	12.3	**African American**	4.5
Armenian	20.1	White British	12.1	**Black C. American**	4.5
		White German	12.0	**Black S. American**	4.3
		Ukrainian	12.0	**Puerto Rican**	4.0
		Yugoslav	12.0	**Laotian**	2.6
		Cuban	12.0		
		Finnish	11.2		
		Scottish	11.2		
		Southwest Asian	11.1		
		Belgian	11.0		
		White Nat. Am.	10.9		
		Chinese	10.6		
		Slovak	10.6		
		Spanish S. American	10.6		
		Irish	10.5		
		French Canadian	10.3		
		Polish	10.3		
		Japanese	10.1		
		Thai	9.6		
		Spaniard	9.6		
		Portuguese	9.5*		
		Asian Indian	9.3		

*Portuguese-owned firms are in some affirmative action programs and not others.
Affirmative action groups are in **boldface**.

categories are not homogeneous. Although all African American groups are below the mean for all groups of 10.8 self-employed persons per 100 adult male workers, several important Asian American groups (Chinese and Japanese) are just below the mean, Koreans are substantially above it, and Laotians are at the bottom. In fact, Korean Americans have formed relatively more businesses than any other group. Treating "Asian American" as a single category in analyzing business formation is clearly overinclusive. Among Hispanics, Cubans are above the mean, whereas Central Americans and Mexicans are considerably below it. Nevertheless, there are no MBE programs that include firms owned by Asian Americans or Hispanics as general categories but exclude those owned by Koreans, Chinese, Japanese, and Cuban Americans specifically. Politically, that would be a difficult result to achieve, regardless of what the data said.

Within the category of groups not eligible for affirmative action, Armenians, Israelis, Russians, and Greeks are considerably above the mean, whereas Poles and Portuguese are below it. Between 1980 and 1990, the largest growth in self-employment for men occurred among Vietnamese (148 percent, to 7.3 self-employed per 100 males), Caribbean Spanish (88 percent, to 8.7), Slovaks (70 percent, included in table 1), and Laotians (67 percent, also included in table 1). If these trends continue, the 2000 census will make the affirmative action categories even less a predictor of business disadvantage.

The overinclusive nature of affirmative action categories can be illustrated by examining areas other than business formation. For example, among Asian Americans, who are sometimes included in higher education affirmative action programs and sometimes excluded as an overrepresented group, there are several different patterns. Although the proportion of whites ages eighteen to twenty-four attending college was 43 percent in 1995, compared to 35 percent for black and Hispanics, the percentages for Asian Americans ranged from 66.5 percent for Chinese, 63.5 percent for Japanese, 61.9 percent for Asian Indians, and 60.3 percent for Koreans to 29.7 percent for Samoans, 28.9 percent for Hawaiians, and 26.5 percent for Laotians (Gose 1997, 38). When 1990 census data on the percentage of college graduates or on median family income of native-born Americans is analyzed, the data show wide variations within the affirmative action categories and within white ethnic groups as well. If people are identified by religion, the variations within groups may be even larger (Thernstrom and Thernstrom 1997, 541–42).

Theories of discrimination do not satisfactorily explain many of the business formation, education, or income results described above. Perhaps different sociological research provides a better insight. Thomas Sowell (1994) and others who have examined the role of ethnicity in vocational selection from an international perspective have found that parity in vocational distribution almost never exists. Sowell has written that "[t]he even distribution or proportional representation of groups in occupations or institutions remains an intellectual construct defied by reality in society after society." Further, this cannot all be the result of "exclusions or discrimination, for often some powerless or even persecuted minorities predominate in prosperous professions" (2).

Conclusion

The affirmative action categories are often more bureaucratic conveniences than demographic realities. Enormous economic and cultural differences exist, for example, between Asian Americans of Laotian, Indian, Japanese, and Pacific Islander ancestry. It is certainly an anomaly that many affirmative action programs create separate categories of analysis for Native Americans and for Eskimos and Aleuts because the latter groups argued in 1980 that they did not share "the same history, customs, language, and traditions as American Indians" (Yanow 1996, 490), but at the same time these programs place all Asian Americans in a single group. The Asian American category contains persons who have immigrated from twenty-five different countries covering six thousand miles (Yanow 1996, 494). These peoples reflect many different languages, religions, traditions, and physical characteristics. But for the peculiarities of American affirmative action politics, the very idea of a single Asian American category, seeing these diverse peoples through a single lens, might be considered a Eurocentric bias.

Persons from Spain, Argentina, Cuba, and Mexico are perhaps more similar than those in the disparate groups in the Asian American category, but there are still important differences between Hispanic persons whose culture is essentially European and those who identify themselves as South or Central American or Caribbean Indian. Furthermore, Cuban Americans, Mexican Americans, and Puerto Ricans, the three largest Hispanic groups, often differ as much from each other as they do from non-Hispanic whites (Coughlin 1991, A12). Generalizations based on the large affirmative action categories may frequently be overinclusive and may create misleading conclusions about the causes of disparate social and economic outcomes. So far, even without reconsidering the construction of the affirmative action categories, courts have been unwilling to accept the business formation argument's central proposition: that discrimination creates group variations. In *Croson*, the Supreme Court restated its previous admonition from *Sheet Metal Workers v. EEOC* (1986) that the assumption that "minorities will choose a particular trade in lockstep proportion to their representation to the local population" was "completely unrealistic" (488 U.S. at 507) The Court also pointed out that "Blacks may be disproportionately attracted to other industries than construction" (503). In many cities, blacks, for example, are relatively more often found in public than in private employment.

Several recent judicial decisions that have examined the conclusions of disparity studies on business formation rates have been unpersuaded by them. In *Engineering Contractors Association of South Florida v. Metropolitan Dade County* (943 F. Supp. 1546 (S.D. Fla. 1996), *aff'd*, 1997 WL 535626 (11th Cir.)), the court rejected a business formation analysis in a disparity study because it did not include all the necessary variables. Furthermore, the evidence showed that MBEs were now forming businesses at a faster rate than non-MBEs, which suggested that the barriers that existed in the past no longer existed (943 F. Supp. at 1574). The Eleventh Circuit, in affirming the district court, was also persuaded by current data about the faster growth rate of MWBE businesses and commented on the importance of cultural variables. It stated that

> [i]n a pluralistic and diverse society, it is unreasonable to assume
> that equality of opportunity will inevitably lead different groups
> with similar human and capital characteristics to make similar ca-
> reer choices. . . . "Similarly situated" women, men, blacks, whites,
> Native Americans, Italian-Americans, and every other group that
> might be listed all bring their own values and traditions to the
> socio-economic table, and may reasonably be expected to make
> voluntary choices that give effect to those values and traditions.
> As the Supreme Court recognized in *Croson*, the disproportionate
> attraction of a minority group to non-construction industries does
> not mean that discrimination in the construction industry is the rea-
> son. *See* 488 U.S. at 503. (122 F.3d at 922)

In *Middleton v. City of Flint*, 92 F.3d 396 (6th Cir. 1996), the Sixth Circuit also quoted Thomas Sowell, stating that "it is common for different groups to rely on different mobility ladders" (408), and overturned an affirmative action plan requiring that 50 percent of all police sergeants be members of designated minority groups. Finally, the court in *Associated General Contractors of Ohio v. Columbus*, 936 F. Supp. 1361 (S.D. Ohio 1995), declared that there was no basis for a disparity study's assumption of group parity in business ownership and self-employment rates in the absence of discrimination, and quoted Sowell in stating, "The idea that large statistical disparities between groups are unusual— and therefore suspicious--is commonplace, but only among those who have not bothered to study the history of racial, ethnic, and other groups in countries around the world" (936 F. Supp. at 1411).

If Sowell is right, and the data of Fairlie and Meyer (1996) suggest that he is, at least as business formation rates are concerned, then the disparity studies that *Croson* requires to justify racial and ethnic remedies should consider the possibility that the traditional affirmative action group definitions create overinclusive categories for analysis and that there are many other possible explanations of differences in business formation rates other than discrimination.

This issue cannot be deferred, because it is now the centerpiece of litigation over the constitutionality of federal MBE programs. They make business owners who are members of or who identify with the traditional affirmative action groups presumptively eligible for procurement preferences. When that concept was before the district court on the remand of *Adarand v. Pena*, 515 U.S. 200, on remand (June 2, 1997), the court stated the following:

> I find it difficult to envisage a race based classification that is narrowly tailored. By its very nature, such a program is both underinclusive and overinclusive. This seemingly contradictory result suggests that the criteria are lacking in substance as well as in reason.
>
> The statutes and regulations governing the SCC [subcontracting compensation clause] program are overinclusive in that they presume that all those in the named minority groups are economically and in, some acts and regulations, socially disadvantaged. The presumption is false, as is its corollary, namely that the majority (caucasians) as well as members of other (unlisted) minority groups are not socially and/or economically disadvantaged. By excluding certain minority groups whose members are economically and socially disadvantaged due to past and present discrimination, the SCC program is underinclusive. (*Adarand v. Pena*, 1997, 1580)

If the courts are going to reexamine the composition of the affirmative action categories, it will be important for social scientists to produce better data than currently exist.

References

Browne, Bortz, and Coddington. 1995. The disparity study: Women/minority business enterprises. Report for the city of Minneapolis.

Coughlin, E. K. 1991. Political survey notes differences among Latinos. *Chronicle of Higher Education*, 11 September, A12.

Evans, David. 1996. Expert report, *Houston Contractors Association v. Metropolitan Transit Authority*, June 7.

Fairlie, Robert W., and Bruce D. Meyer. 1996. Ethnic and racial self-employment differences and possible explanations. *Journal of Human Resources* 31 (4): 757–91.

Glazer, Nathan. 1988. The affirmative action stalemate. *The Public Interest* (winter): 99–114.

Goel, Vindu. 1996. The rise of Asian Indians, *The Cleveland Plain Dealer*, 28 July, 8.

Gose, Ben. 1997. Minority enrollments rose in 1995, a study finds. *Chronicle of Higher Education*, 23 May, 38.

Graham, Hugh. 1990. *The civil rights era*. New York: Oxford University Press.

Grenier, Guerillmo, and Alex Stepnik III. 1992. *Miami now*. Gainesville: University of Florida Press.

Hammerman, Herbert. 1988. "Affirmative action stalemate": A second perspective. *The Public Interest* (fall): 130–34.

La Noue, George R. 1993. Social science and minority set-asides. *The Public Interest* (winter): 49–62.

La Noue, George R., and John C. Sullivan. 1994. Presumptions for preferences: The Small Business Administration's decisions on groups entitled to affirmative action. *Journal of Policy History* 6 (4): 439–67.

National Economic Research Associates. 1992. The utilization of minority and woman-owned business enterprises by the city of New York. January.

Schmidt, John R. 1996. Post-*Adarand* guidance on affirmative action in federal employment. U. S. Department of Justice, 29 February.

Soussan, Tania. 1997. Disparity study attacked. *Albuquerque Journal*, 3 March, 1-D2.

Sowell, Thomas. 1994. *Race and culture: A world view*. New York: Basic Books.

Sundman, Helena. 1993. City, Indians clash on contracts. *Chicago Reporter*, July–August, 3–5.

Thernstrom, Stephan, and Abigail Thernstrom.1997. *America in white and black*. New York: Simon and Schuster.

U.S. Bureau of the Census. 1982. Survey of minority and women owned business enterprises and County Business Patterns—United States. Washington, D.C.: Bureau of the Census.

———. 1992. Survey of minority and women owned business enterprises and County Business Patterns—United States. Washington, D.C.: Bureau of the Census.

Yanow, Dvora. 1996. American ethnogenesis and public administration. *Administration and Society* 27 (4) (February): 483–509.

4

How Affirmative Action Became Diversity
Management: Employer Response
to Antidiscrimination Law, 1961–1996

. . .

ERIN KELLY AND FRANK DOBBIN

How did corporate affirmative action programs segue into diversity programs? During the 1970s, active federal enforcement of equal employment opportunity (EEO) and affirmative action (AA) law, coupled with ambiguity about the terms of compliance, stimulated employers to hire antidiscrimination specialists to fashion EEO and AA programs. In the early 1980s, the Reagan administration curtailed enforcement, but as early institutionalists such as Philip Selznick might have predicted, EEO and AA programs had developed an organizational constituency among the specialists and thus survived Reagan's enforcement cutbacks. As new institutionalists such as John Meyer might have predicted, that constituency survived by collectively retheorizing antidiscrimination practices, in terms of efficiency and "diversity management," through their professional networks. By 1997, many U.S. organizations had added diversity management practices while maintaining basic EEO and AA programs.

The Rise and Decline of Antidiscrimination Enforcement

The federal effort to redress employment discrimination that emerged from the civil rights movement was founded on two cornerstones. Title VII of the Civil Rights Act of 1964 required all employers to halt employment discrimination. President Lyndon Johnson's Executive Order 11246 of 1965 required federal contractors to take "affirmative action" to end discrimination. At the beginning of the 1970s, increased enforcement in both realms stimulated employers to search for compliance mechanisms, but the ambiguity of compliance made that task difficult. Uncertain of how best to comply, employers hired EEO and AA specialists to design compliance programs that would shield them from litiga-tion (Edelman 1992; Dobbin et al. 1993).

When Ronald Reagan won the White House in 1980 on a platform of regulatory retrenchment, many observers foresaw the demise of affirmative action. Reagan carried out his pledge to cut enforcement of affirmative action, but employers did not follow suit by cutting their compliance programs. Most continued to support the positions and offices they had created to manage compliance and kept equal employment opportunity mechanisms in place, and cut only their most active affirmative action practices from fear of reverse discrimina-tion suits.

Many EEO and AA offices and activities survived, we argue, because EEO and AA specialists did not respond passively to Reagan's cutbacks in enforcement. At first they touted the efficiency of formalizing "hu-man resources" management through such antidiscrimination measures as grievance procedures, formal hiring and promotion systems, and sys-tematic recruitment schemes. Later they invented the discipline of "di-versity management," arguing that the capacity to manage a diverse workforce well would be the key to business success in the future. Over the space of a quarter of a century, efforts to integrate the workforce were transformed, in management rhetoric, from an onerous require-ment of federal law to a valuable means to increasing organizational effectiveness. The new employment practices that survived the waxing and waning of EEO and AA law, however, have not been those that have done the most to change employment patterns.

The Two Institutionalisms and Antidiscrimination Law

The history of employer response to equal employment and affirmative action law fits well the images of organizational change described by Selznick's early school of "institutionalist sociology" and Meyer's later school of institutionalists. Selznick argued that organizational structures and practices (institutions) develop inertia when members of the organi-zation come to accept them as necessary and useful. As Selznick puts it, practices and routines become institutionalized when they are "in-fused with value beyond the technical requirements at hand" (1957, 17). Selznick and his students observed individual organizations over time and discovered that structures and practices survived even when they no longer achieved the goals for which they had been designed. Studies showed that rather than changing their structures, organizations adopted new goals suited to existing structures. Thus an adult education program's goal of feeding students into four-year colleges gave way to the goal of maintaining enrollment (Clark 1956), and the YMCA's rehabilitation and welfare goals gave way to the goal of providing recreation (Zald and Denton 1963). Selznick observed that once institutionalized, organizational practices gain inertia in part by developing organizational constituencies.

We find a similar pattern. When Reagan curtailed federal enforcement, EEO and AA managers constructed new goals for the practices they shepherded. They downplayed legal compliance and emphasized first the goal of rationalizing human resources and later the goal of increasing profits by expanding diversity in the workforce and the customer base.

We find that this process occurred not merely at the organizational level, as Selznick and his followers find, but at the interorganizational level, as Meyer and his colleagues find. Meyer and Rowan (1977) first observed that organizational practices are socially constructed as useful among groups of organizations (see also DiMaggio and Powell 1983, 1991). Strang and Meyer (1993) have argued that professional networks play a key role in theorizing, and thereby constructing meaning for, organizational practices. They may also retheorize old practices as means to achieving new ends (Baron et al. 1986; Baron et al. 1988). Indeed, in the 1970s managers retheorized internal labor market practices as EEO and AA compliance mechanisms (Dobbin et al. 1993). In the 1980s and 1990s, we argue, human resources managers used their professional networks to collectively construct antidiscrimination practices as means to improving efficiency, at first by touting the gains associated with formalizing hiring and promotion and later by touting the gains associated with utilizing a diverse workforce to serve a diverse customer base. The practices of EEO and AA were soon recast as the "diversity management" component of the new "human resource management" paradigm. In short, practices designed to achieve legal compliance were retheorized as efficient when the original impetus for adopting them was all but withdrawn, just as Selznick might predict, but the process occurred at the interorganizational level, just as Meyer might predict.

Not all antidiscrimination practices fared equally well. Neutral equal employment opportunity practices fared better than did proactive affirmative action practices. Here we take a page from Christine Oliver (1992), who notes that intense political pressure can cause deinstitutionalization of organizational practices. In this case, political pressure came in the form of reverse-discrimination suits, criticism from the administration, employee backlash, and state-level anti–affirmative action movements (see chapters 2 and 5 in this volume). The decline of AA practices did not, however, undermine the roles of EEO and AA specialists, because the ambiguity of the law had caused organizations to adopt a wide range of antidiscrimination practices, some of which continued to thrive.

In the sections that follow we outline four stages in employer response to AA and EEO law, the first two of which have been well documented in the neoinstitutional literature (Dobbin et al. 1988; Edelman 1990, 1992; Abzug and Mezias 1993; Dobbin et al. 1993; Sutton et al. 1994; Sutton and Dobbin 1996). First, in the 1960s, the ambiguity and weak enforcement of these laws led to few changes in employment practice. Second, between 1970 and 1980, increased federal enforcement led employers to pay closer attention to antidiscrimination law, and the continuing ambiguity of compliance led them to hire EEO and AA specialists to devise compliance strategies. In so doing, employers created internal constituencies that championed EEO and AA measures.

Third, when Reagan curtailed enforcement in the early 1980s, EEO and AA specialists began to tout the efficiency gains that had followed adoption of EEO and AA practices: these practices rationalized the allocation of personnel. Fourth, after 1987 the legal future of affirmative action was uncertain. The courts chipped away at the law, and neither Bush nor Clinton offered unqualified support. In response, EEO and AA specialists transformed themselves into "diversity managers" and promoted a range of human resource practices aimed at maintaining and managing diversity in the workforce. Below we focus on the last two periods, which have been little studied (Dobbin and Sutton 1998). For each period, we chronicle public policy shifts and the management rhetoric and practice that resulted.

Affirmative Action and the Civil Rights Act: 1961–1969

Affirmative action and equal employment law emerged at the height of the civil rights movement to rectify past discrimination and preclude future discrimination in employment. "Affirmative action" to end discrimination on the basis of "race, color, creed, or national origin" was required of federal contractors in 1961 under Kennedy's Executive Order (EO) 10925. Johnson's Executive Order 11246 of 1965 extended coverage to *all* work done by contractors and subcontractors (not merely contracted work), and his EO 11375 of 1967 added sex to the list of protected categories (Gutman 1993; Burstein 1985). As John Skrentny discusses in his introduction to this volume, "affirmative action" was not clearly defined in either executive order, and even in the government, policy makers were not sure what it meant. It vaguely encouraged employers to take positive steps to end discrimination, including active programs to hire, train, and promote people from disadvantaged groups. Both orders established regulatory agencies to oversee compliance (EO 10925 created the President's Committee on Equal Employment Opportunity [PCEEO], superseded by EO 11246's Office of Federal Contract Compliance [OFCC]), and both stipulated penalties for noncompliance, including termination of contracts and debarment from future contracts (Hammerman 1984).

Title VII of the Civil Rights Act of 1964 outlawed discrimination in employment not only for federal contractors but for employers at large. Title VII enabled individuals to sue employers for discrimination in hiring or promotion and established the Equal Employment Opportunity Commission to adjudicate claims and oversee compliance.

Between 1961 and 1969, the ambiguity of these laws in the context of weak enforcement produced little change in employment practices (Edelman 1990; Shaeffer 1980). Executive Orders 10925 and 11246 required federal contractors to take "affirmative action" without defining the term or establishing compliance guidelines (Bureau of National Affairs 1967). The Civil Rights Act outlawed discrimination without defining the term or establishing criteria for compliance (Shaeffer 1973, 11; Stryker 1996, 5). Few employers made significant changes in employment practices or structures. Two studies found that by about 1970, only 4 percent of employers had established affirmative action or equal employment offices and less than 20 percent had established EEO and AA rules or policies (see fig. 1; Edelman 1992).

Expanded Enforcement and Employer Response: 1970–1980

From the early 1970s, the scope of both AA and EEO law expanded and enforcement stepped up (Edelman 1992; Dobbin et al. 1993). The scope of AA law expanded through the OFCC's Order 4 in early 1970, which required employers to submit detailed reports on their employment patterns and explicit plans to remedy inequality (Shaeffer

FIGURE 1   Proportion of Employers with EEO and AA Structures

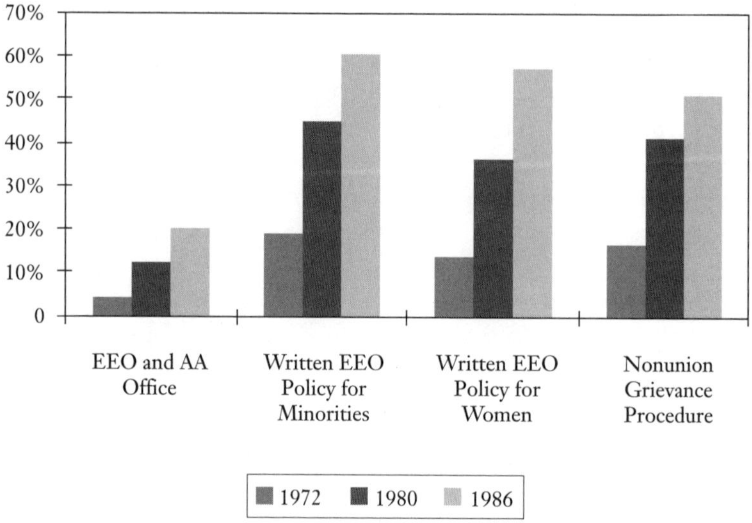

Source: Unpublished data from the study reported in Dobbin et al. 1993.

1973). Order 4 required affirmative action programs from government contractors based on analyses of "underutilization" of blacks, Spanish-surnamed Americans, American Indians, and Orientals in major job categories. This required comparisons between numbers of minorities available in the relevant labor market and the numbers the contractor had already hired. Acceptable affirmative action plans had to include "goals and timetables," specifying a range of how many minorities the contractor would attempt to hire in each category and in what time period (Graham 1990, 343). The following year, a Revised Order 4 added women to the goals and timetables requirement.

The Equal Employment Opportunity Act of 1972 expanded EEOC enforcement, most notably by enabling the EEOC, as well as individuals, to sue employers. The scope of EEO law was also significantly expanded in 1971, with the critical Supreme Court decision in *Griggs v. Duke Power Company* enabling plaintiffs to win suits based not only on *intentional discrimination* but on proof of *disparate impact* of employment practices across groups. Now employment practices that had the *unintentional* effect of disadvantaging women and minorities put employers at risk of litigation.

Expanded enforcement in both areas caused anxiety among employers, for compliance criteria remained ambiguous (Edelman 1990). Employers expressed much concern about litigation, experimenting with a range of compliance measures and establishing new personnel and antidiscrimination offices to carry out these measures. Edelman (1992) found that the prevalence of EEO and AA offices and personnel rules rose slowly before 1970 but quite rapidly during the 1970s. Similarly, Dobbin et al. (1993) found that the prevalence of EEO and AA offices, policies protecting women, policies protecting minorities, and the nonunion grievance systems associated with EEO law rose slowly before 1972 but quite rapidly between 1972 and 1980 (see fig. 1). The Bureau of National Affairs found that by 1976, large numbers of employers had adopted EEO policies or programs, follow-up of hiring and promotion decisions by EEO and AA specialists, and EEO training for supervisors (see fig. 2). Smaller but significant numbers had proactive affirmative action measures designed to increase representation of women and minorities, including targeted recruiting programs, EEO

FIGURE 2   Proportion of Employers with EEO Practices

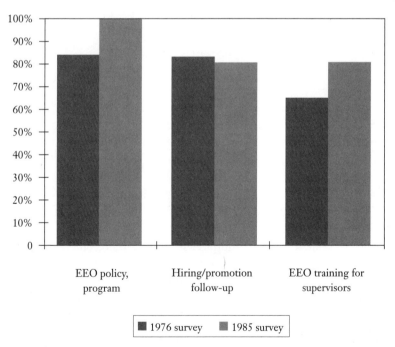

Sources: Bureau of National Affairs 1976, 1985.

FIGURE 3 Proportion of Large Employers with Affirmative Action Practices

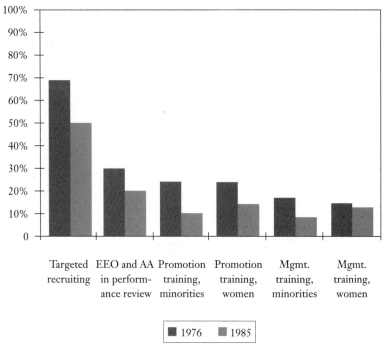

Sources: Bureau of National Affairs 1976, 1985.

and AA records included in managers performance reviews, special promotion training for women and minorities, and special management training for women and minorities (see fig. 3). Voluntary quotas had been prohibited by federal regulation in the early 1970s, but more than 80 percent of employers reported writing affirmative action plans, which included employment goals for women and minorities, by 1976 (fig. 4).

The Bureau of National Affairs study showed that among a sample of large firms, more than 80 percent had EEO policies by 1976. The other two studies, based on samples with higher representations of small employers, showed that more than 40 percent of employers had EEO policies by 1980. In the process of establishing these EEO and AA programs, employers created internal constituencies of EEO and AA specialists who would fight for the maintenance of antidiscrimination measures even after Regain reduced enforcement in the early 1980s (Edelman 1992; Sutton and Dobbin 1996).

FIGURE 4 Proportion of Large Employers with Reporting and Compliance Practices

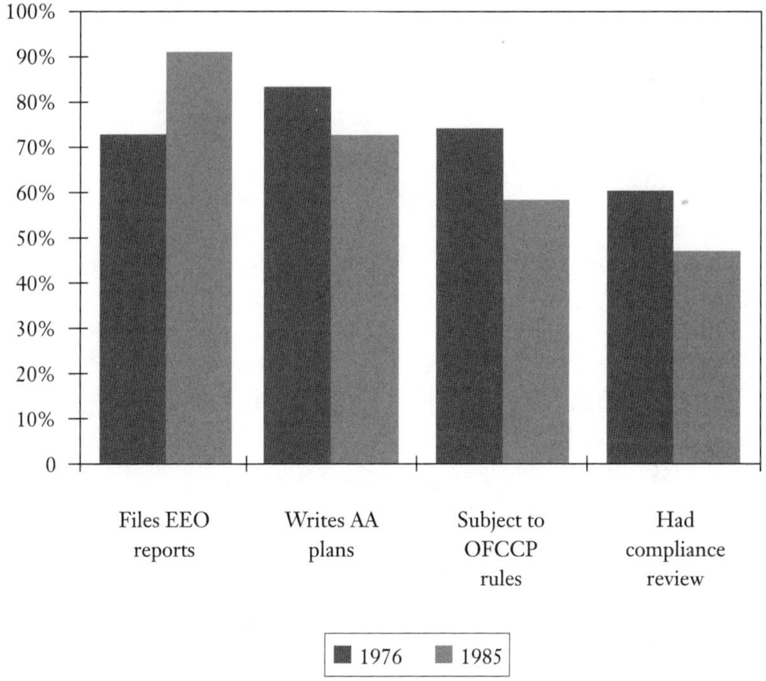

Sources: Bureau of National Affairs 1976, 1985.

Threats to Affirmative Action and Employer Response in the Reagan Years: 1981–1987

In his 1980 campaign, Reagan made clear his opposition to affirmative action, especially "bureaucratic regulations which rely on quotas, ratios, and numerical requirements" (quoted in McDowell 1989; see also Blumrosen 1993; Skrentny 1996). Once in office, Reagan curtailed administrative enforcement of EEO and AA dramatically and appointed federal judges opposed to regulation in general and affirmative action in particular. These changes appeared to threaten the EEO and AA systems hashed out in the 1970s. Specialists in these areas responded by developing efficiency arguments for their programs.

The Reagan administration cut both staffing and funding at the EEOC and OFCCP (the OFCC was renamed the Office of Federal Contract Compliance *Programs* during the Carter administration), reducing the resources for monitoring employment practices (Leonard 1985; Burstein and Monaghan 1986; Gutman 1993). Administrative changes further reduced the pressure on employers. Clarence Thomas, as chair of the EEOC, told the general counsel of his agency not to approve conciliation agreements that included employment goals and timetables (Blumrosen 1993, 270; Skrentny 1996). The EEOC sponsored fewer conciliation agreements and delayed decisions about pending cases (Blumrosen 1993; Yakura 1995). At the OFCCP, procedural changes increased the number of reviews but significantly reduced the sanctions imposed on violating employers (Leonard 1989). For example, the number of workers receiving back pay because of affirmative action violations fell from more than 4,000 in 1980 to 499 in 1986 (Blumrosen 1993, 274). These changes in enforcement led Leonard (1989, 74) to conclude that "[a]n administration lacking the will to enforce affirmative action beyond rubber-stamped compliance reviews has resulted in an affirmative action program without practical effects since 1980."

In addition to reducing affirmative action enforcement, Reagan administration officials proposed regulatory changes that would have dismantled the existing system. For example, proposed changes to the OFCCP's Revised Order 4 would have reduced the number of companies required to submit affirmative action plans by three-quarters, "from about 16,767 to about 4,143" (U.S. Department of Labor, 47 FR 17770, 23 April 1982). Reagan's cabinet also debated revising Johnson's Executive Order 11246 to stipulate that contractors were not required to develop numerical goals and timetables (Detlefsen 1991, 151; see also McDowell 1989; Belz 1991). Although they ultimately failed, these proposals sent a strong signal that the Reagan administration opposed affirmative action.

The legal foundation of affirmative action seemed even shakier once Reagan's Department of Justice began to file amicus briefs supporting the challengers of affirmative action plans. In two of those cases, *Firefighters Local Union No. 1784 v. Stotts* (467 U.S. 445 (1984)) and *Wygant v. Jackson Board of Education* (476 U.S. 267 (1986)), the Court found against AA plans that suspended seniority rules to retain minority workers during layoffs. The Court ruled that a court-ordered recruitment quota was legal, in *Local 28 (Sheet Metal Workers) v. EEOC* (478 U.S. 421 (1986)), but in other cases it discouraged quotas (see *Johnson v. Transportation Agency, Santa Clara County, Calif.* (480 U.S. 616 (1987)).

Corporate Support for Affirmative Action, on New Terms

As federal enforcement waned, human resources managers and EEO and AA specialists developed new arguments to promote antidiscrimination practices. In Selznick's (1949, 1957) terms, an internal constituency reinforced an organizational program that seemed to have outlived its original purpose—in this case of ensuring legal compliance—by developing a new goal for the program. Staff members whose positions, paychecks, and professional identities depended on the continuation of antidiscrimination practices worked to retheorize those practices in terms of efficiency.

Human resources managers responded first by promoting EEO and AA practices as ways to formalize, and rationalize, personnel decisions. Later they developed arguments about how a diverse workforce could improve the bottom line. As early as 1974, Froehlich and Hawyer argued in *Personnel*, a human resources professional magazine, that EEO law had spawned performance-based personnel systems. They went on to underscore the business necessity of such systems: "A performance-based personnel system for selecting, utilizing, and developing corporate human assets should be—but rarely is—as much a component of sound business planning as financial, manufacturing, and market planning are" (62–63). Equal employment opportunity procedures, including formal job postings, interview rules, formal evaluations, and other practices, were thought to help managers choose candidates "objectively" (Harvard Law Review 1989, 669). These practices forced managers to justify their hiring and promotion decisions and thus contributed to the rationalization of personnel allocation (Dobbin et al. 1993).

Affirmative action practices, in particular, were couched as mechanisms to undermine discrimination by middle managers and thereby attract a wider pool of job applicants. As an EEO/AA manager explained it: "Our affirmative action programs are now self-driven. Although we want to avoid EEO liability, we conduct affirmative action because we think it makes good sense to do so. We have no intention of abandoning the use of goals" (quoted in Bureau of National Affairs 1986b, 93). Affirmative action practices, such as personnel department reviews of hiring decisions, were described as an "essential management tool which reinforces accountability and maximizes the utilization of the talents of [the firm's] entire work force" (Feild 1984, 49).

Some business arguments for affirmative action prefigured the diversity management discourse of the late 1980s and early 1990s. For example, in a brief filed in the 1986 *Sheet Metal Workers* case, the National Association of Manufacturers described affirmative action as a "business policy which has allowed industry to benefit from new ideas, opinions and perspectives generated by greater workforce diversity" (quoted in Harvard Law Review 1989, 669, n. 61). A human resources executive explained the principles behind diversity when asked about the business case for affirmative action:

> We have learned that cultivating differences in our work force is a key competitive advantage for our company. The differences among people of various racial, ethnic, and cultural backgrounds generate creativity and innovation as well as energy in our work force. Differences between men and women, managed well, have similar benefits. We are therefore pursuing "Multiculturalism," which is a quantum leap beyond affirmative action. We are doing that not only for ethical reasons, but also because we are confident that it makes good business sense to maximize the unique contribution of individuals to our collective success. (Quoted in Bureau of National Affairs 1986b, 93)

In addition to championing antidiscrimination measures, EEO and AA specialists encouraged their top executives to speak out publicly in support of affirmative action. Major employers filed amicus briefs supporting affirmative action in key court cases, sent telegrams to the White House arguing against the proposed changes to EO 11246, and testified before congressional committees about the benefits of mandated affirmative action (Harvard Law Review 1989, 662). In these expressions of support, executives began to describe affirmative action measures as good business, rather than as responses to antidiscrimination laws or norms (see Donohue 1986).

Prominent employers claimed that they would continue their EEO and AA programs, regardless of whether government policy changed. A 1985 study of Fortune 500 companies, prompted by the proposed changes to EO 11246, found that more than 95 percent intended to "continue to use numerical objectives to track the progress of women and minorities in [their] corporation[s], regardless of government requirements" (Fisher 1994, 270). A 1986 survey of Fortune 500 companies found that 88 percent planned to make no changes to their affirmative action plans and 12 percent planned to increase their affirmative action efforts in 1987 (Bureau of National Affairs 1986b, 90).

Top executives resisted the dismantling of EEO and AA programs in part because the specialists and departments that administered them had become indispensable to the management team. After surveying fifty major federal contractors in 1983, Feild (1984, 49) concluded that "the affirmative action concept has become an integral part of today's corporate personnel management philosophy and practice . . . [with] a highly professionalized specialty" overseeing those programs.

Growth of EEO Practices and Decline of AA Measures

During the Reagan years employers continued to adopt procedural safeguards against discrimination and to hire EEO and AA specialists. The Bureau of National Affairs asked employers in surveys in 1976 and again in 1985 whether they had formal EEO policies, whether supervisors' hiring and promotion decisions were reviewed for compliance with EEO policies, and whether supervisors were trained in EEO laws and company policies regarding hiring and promotion.[1] These EEO policies and practices were very common by 1985 (see fig. 4). A survey that included more small employers (see Dobbin et al. 1993) found lower prevalence but likewise found that employers continued to adopt new EEO and AA practices during the 1980s (see fig. 2).[2]

Many organizations adopted nonunion grievance systems, which were widely advocated as a means to intercept discrimination complaints before they reached the courts. Both Dobbin et al. (1988) and Edelman (1990) found that grievance procedures continued to spread in the early 1980s (see fig. 2). Also, the 1985 BNA survey found that 75 percent of surveyed employers had internal dispute resolution systems, which they reported having adopted to prevent litigation (Bureau of National Affairs 1986a).

Employers also continued to add EEO and AA offices and staff positions during the 1980s. Dobbin et al. (1988) found that by 1983, 18 percent of responding employers had affirmative action offices and 48 percent had designated affirmative action officers (but no distinct office). Other studies show that EEO and AA offices grew steadily during the 1980s (see figs. 1 and 2).

Although employers maintained their procedural safeguards against discrimination and maintained EEO and AA staff, they curtailed their most proactive affirmative action measures. The Bureau of National Affairs studies found that fewer employers had special recruiting programs for women and minorities in 1985 than in 1976, fewer had special training programs, fewer based performance evaluations in part on EEO and AA efforts, and fewer had affirmative action plans (see fig. 3). Moreover, fewer were subject to reporting requirements and compliance reviews by the affirmative action oversight agency, the OFCCP (see fig. 4). It is often difficult for employers to discontinue personnel policies and training programs, because both employees and managers quickly come to expect that these programs will be in place. The decline in proactive affirmative action measures thus signals an important shift in employer policy, probably in response to shifts in the federal government's support for affirmative action.

From Affirmative Action to Diversity Management: 1988–1996

Washington Suggests That the End of Affirmative Action Is in Sight

Limited support from the Bush administration, and seemingly tepid support from the Clinton administration, signaled that the days of affirmative action were numbered. The Supreme Court and two successive administrations seemed to be suggesting that it had fulfilled its purpose. A human resources textbook's chapter on EEO and AA law noted that "affirmative action appears to be under increasing attack, so it is important to realize it can change at any time" (Yakura 1995, 29). Specialists in these areas, and their allies, responded by recasting these practices as part of the new diversity management initiative.

The Bush years gave little hope to the proponents of affirmative action. Bush had been a vocal supporter of equal opportunity measures in the 1960s, but once in the White House, he opposed legislation to reverse a key Supreme Court decision that had taken the punch out of EEO law. Bush eventually signed a compromise bill that limited affirmative action in new ways. In *Wards Cove Packing v. Atonio et al.* (490 U.S. 642 (1989)) the Supreme Court had challenged disparate impact law, placing the burden of proof of discrimination back where it had been prior to the 1971 *Griggs* decision: on the plaintiff. A Democratic Congress passed the Civil Rights Act of 1990 to reverse the effects of *Wards Cove*, but Bush vetoed the bill. Bush eventually signed a modified Civil Rights Act in 1991 that codified disparate impact law but outlawed other key affirmative action practices, such as the "race-norming" of employment tests—comparing scores only within groups.

Signals during the Clinton administration were ambiguous, and uncertainty regarding affirmative action's future remained. Clinton's support for affirmative action seemed qualified, and his decision to review the program and rethink racial equality programs more generally led many employers to believe that he would follow the path of his Republican predecessors. He ordered a critical review of affirmative action policies early in his first term and cut staff at both the EEOC and the OFCCP. On the other hand, his appointees pursued enforcement with more vigor than had their predecessors. Clinton's EEOC chair, Gilbert Casellas, announced: "At the end of my term, if you get a call from EEOC, I want you to worry about it" (Lynch 1997, 342). Renewed enforcement at the OFCCP produced record settlements in favor of plaintiffs by 1994 (Lynch 1997, 343).

Even as enforcement efforts increased, the Supreme Court suggested that federal affirmative action be reevaluated. In *Adarand v. Pena* (515 U.S. 200 (1995)), the Supreme Court required "strict scrutiny" of race-conscious policies adopted by the federal government (Bureau of National Affairs 1995, Yakura 1995). The Court found in favor of Adarand, the lowest bidder on a highway project, who had lost out to a Hispanic contractor, agreeing that the assumption that Hispanics are disadvantaged was faulty.

After the *Adarand* ruling, Clinton advised federal department heads to review their race-conscious policies and suggest revisions to uphold the *Adarand* standard. He concluded that affirmative action had not outlived its usefulness, but ordered agencies to eliminate or reform any practice that created quotas, led to the placement of unqualified individuals, discriminated against majority group members, or continued after its goals had been met (Yakura 1995; Bureau of National Affairs 1995, S-45). The *Adarand* ruling and Clinton's qualified acceptance of affirmative action suggested that the legal basis for affirmative action measures might soon disappear.

Specialists Recast EEO and AA Measures as Diversity Initiatives

Edelman et al. (1991, 74; see also Selznick 1949) note that organizational practices may "develop a life of their own" and evolve in ways that have little to do with legal requirements. In this case, we argue, uncertainty about the future of AA law led many human resources managers and EEO and AA specialists to develop new rationales and programs, which were related to—but legally and politically distinct from—the affirmative action policies and practices they had formerly managed. Affirmative action offices and officers were "the beachhead" within organizations for diversity programs (Lynch 1997, 1).

By the late 1980s, these specialists were recasting EEO and AA measures as part of diversity management and touting the competitive advantages offered by these practices. Human resources managers and supportive executives argued that diversity programs—including anti-discrimination policies, training programs, and recruitment practices virtually identical to EEO and AA measures—produced a "strategic advantage by helping members of diverse groups perform to their potential" (Winterle 1992, 11; see also Miller 1994; Kossek and Lobel 1995; Leach et al. 1995). One early diversity consultant to Fortune 500 companies, R. Roosevelt Thomas, coined the term *managing diversity* and in 1983 founded the American Institute for Managing Diversity. In a 1990 *Harvard Business Review* article, later reprinted, he emphasized the business case while acknowledging the connections to earlier EEO and AA efforts:

> A lot of executives are not sure why they should want to learn to manage diversity. Legal compliance seems like a good reason. So does community relations. Many executives believe they have a social and moral responsibility to employ minorities and women. Others want to placate an internal group or pacify an outside organization. None of these are bad reasons, but none of them are business reasons, and given the nature and scope of today's competitive challenges, I believe only business reasons will supply the necessary long-term motivation. . . . Learning to manage diversity will make you more competitive. (R. Thomas 1994, 34)

A few years later, the next major *Harvard Business Review* discussion of diversity management picked up where R. Roosevelt Thomas had left off:

> Why should companies concern themselves with diversity? Until recently, many managers answered this question with the assertion that discrimination is wrong, both legally and morally. But today managers are voicing a second notion as well. A more diverse workforce, they say, will increase organizational effectiveness. It will lift morale, bring greater access to new segments of the marketplace, and enhance productivity. . . . It is our belief that there is a distinct way to unleash the powerful benefits of a diverse workforce. Although these benefits include increased profitability, they go beyond financial measures to encompass learning, creativity, flexibility, organizational and individual growth, and the ability of a company to adjust rapidly and successfully to market changes. (Thomas and Ely 1996)

The discourse stressing a value on diversity in employment was similar to that stressing diversity in higher education (see chapter 5 in this volume). Employment diversity, however, was rarely if ever explicitly linked to educational diversity. One crucial argument for diversity programs was that demographic changes were altering labor markets and consumer markets. Demographic predictions provided "a sense of crisis, urgency, and purpose" for the diversity programs (Lynch 1997, 9). Diversity specialists argued, first, that labor markets were changing: white men were a shrinking proportion of workers. To attract other kinds of workers, organizations would have to become "employers of choice," welcoming people of different cultures, backgrounds, and identity groups (Winterle 1992). When workers from diverse backgrounds felt appreciated and comfortable, the argument went, they would contribute more to the organization and increase productivity, as well as lend cultural expertise. They argued, second, that consumer markets were changing. To reach new immigrants and newly wealthy minority groups, organizations would have to develop new products and marketing approaches. The best way to do this was to attract employees from those groups.

Moreover, the globalization of markets meant that organizations would be doing business in many countries. Being able to understand and deal with business partners from other cultures would become a "core competency" for at least some workers.

Workforce 2000 (Johnston and Packer 1987), a report commissioned by Reagan's Department of Labor and produced by the Hudson Institute, bolstered the case for diversity management. The report outlined anticipated changes in the business environment, such as the globalization of markets, the growth of the service sector, technological advances, and demographic shifts in the labor force. Workforce 2000 projected that minorities and immigrants would become an ever larger share of the labor force. Two of the six "challenges" identified in the report were "reconciling the needs of women, work, and families" and "integrating Blacks and Hispanics fully into the labor market" (Johnston and Packer 1987, ix).

Specialists in EEO, AA, and diversity seized on Workforce 2000, with its pragmatic, future-oriented message, to increase interest in their own programs. Articles on diversity management increased rapidly after the publication of Workforce 2000 (see fig. 5; Edelman et al. 1998), and many emphasized the report's demographic projections. Workforce 2000 was critical to diversity specialists' attempts to retheorize EEO and AA programs, which had been designed to correct for past injustices

FIGURE 5 Human Resources Management Literature on AA and Diversity

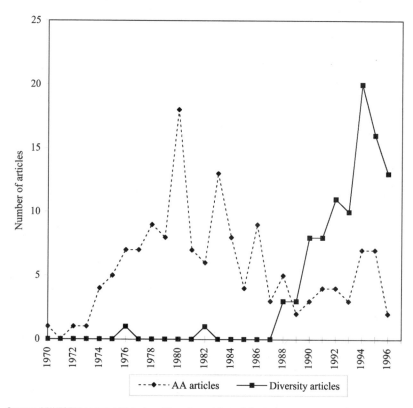

Source: ABINFORM search of American Management Association's human resources journal (*Personnel*, then *HR Focus*) and SHRM's journal (*Personnel Administrator*, then *HRMagazine*).

and discrimination against blacks. Workforce 2000 was self-consciously focused on the future, and its predictions of growing percentages of blacks, Latinos, and Asian Americans in the population lacked the political and historical character of EEO and AA rhetoric.

To emphasize the business case for diversity management, human resources managers and diversity specialists sought to distance it from EEO and AA practices (Edelman et al. 1998; Lynch 1997, 11; Winterle 1992, 14; Yakura 1995, 35). A Fortune 50 manufacturing executive claimed that "the 1960s moral and social arguments have been replaced by tough business issues" (Winterle 1992, 13). In his 1990 *Harvard Business Review* article, R. Roosevelt Thomas argued that employers need to "move beyond affirmative action" while not repudiating the basic effort to create more balanced workplaces. The article opens with the pronouncement that

> Sooner or later, affirmative action will die a natural death. Its achievements have been stupendous but if we look at the premises that underlie it, we find assumptions and priorities that look increasingly shopworn. . . . If affirmative action in upward mobility meant that no person's competence and character would ever be overlooked or undervalued on account of race, sex, ethnicity, origins, or physical disability, affirmative action would be the very thing we need to let every corporate talent find its niche. But what affirmative action means in practice is an unnatural focus on one group, and what it means too often to too many employees is that someone is playing fast and loose with standards in order to favor that group. (Thomas 1994, 29)

Managers distinguished diversity from affirmative action by emphasizing business goals. In convincing employers to initiate diversity programs, managers reported that business-oriented data provided the best ammunition. These data included information on customer or market bases, evidence of globalization, information on how diversity might increase productivity, data on demographic shifts from Workforce 2000, and data on the demographic makeup of the organization itself (Wheeler 1995, 7). Some human resources executives reported that "confusion between diversity and AA/EEO" was a serious barrier to implementing diversity initiatives; this problem was more likely to be mentioned than costs, lack of management support, or fear of white male backlash (Winterle 1992, 15). Yakura (1995), writing in a human resources management textbook, acknowledges that some have a "cynical view" of diversity programs. Some observers might conclude that since "affirmative action has been at the center of a storm of controversy, it has been abandoned in favor of managing diversity. By focusing on managing diversity and its inclusion of all individuals, the tensions created by the affirmative action debates can be ignored" (43). At one conference, Thomas argued that his business-oriented case for diversity helped address accusations that diversity was "just another code word for advancing black issues" (Lynch 1997, 103).

There are important differences between EEO, AA, and diversity management, including different perspectives on the problems facing minorities and women in the workplace (see table 1). As we discuss below, however, there is also significant convergence in the concrete prac-

TABLE 1

Three Perspectives on Diversity in the Workforce

	EEO	AA	Diversity
Source	Statute	Executive order and federal regulations	Human resources specialists in academic and organization settings
Rationale for adoption	Legal compliance	Legal compliance for contractors	Strategic advantages
Implicit cultural values	Egalitarianism, meritocracy	Remedy past wrongs	Inclusiveness, respect for differences
View of the problem	Limited access and individuals' bigotry	Limited access, coupled with limited networks and skills	Organization loses out by asking workers to assimilate to white male system
View of solutions	Formalization of and commitment to nondiscrimination will lead to minorities' and women's advancement	Targeted programs for recruitment, mentoring, training will lead to minorities' and women's advancement	Culture change efforts will remove systemic, institutional barriers to minorities' and women's advancement
Concrete practices	Policies, statements, grievance procedures, internal dispute resolution systems	Affirmative action plans with goals and timetables, revision of performance review criteria, sensitivity and interaction skills training, networking and support groups, targeted recruiting, targeted training	Policies, statements, diversity action plans with goals and timetables, revision of performance review criteria, diversity awareness and skills training, networking and support groups, diversity task forces, culture audits
Concrete effects	Workers have recourse, within organization, for dealing with discrimination	Minorities and women brought into and moved up "the pipeline"	Unclear

Sources: Yakura (1995), Golembiewski (1995), Edelman et al. (1998) and our own observations.

tices adopted under the auspices of EEO, AA, and diversity management.

Specialists and Business Groups Promote
Diversity Management

Who retheorized EEO and AA measures as diversity management? Specialists inside organizations joined with consultants, authors in the business press, and advocates from nonprofit organizations to push this idea. As one critical observer put it, "The key personnel, ideas, and strategies driving this diversity machine come from preexisting, heavily female or minority networks in corporate, government, foundation or university human resources departments, especially in affirmative action offices. Those still inside these institutions have linked up with an army of downsized colleagues-turned-consultants to form the core of the diversity machine" (Lynch 1997, 8).[3] EEO managers often took on the mantle of "diversity manager." A Conference Board survey of organizations committed to diversity programs found that half had lodged diversity and EEO and AA responsibilities in the same position, a quarter had a separate diversity position, and the remainder had no staff dedicated specifically to diversity management (Winterle 1992, 23).

In the 1980s, management consultants first began to push the theory and practices of diversity management (Edelman et al. 1998). Some of the most prominent figures included R. Roosevelt Thomas, Lewis Griggs, Lennie Copeland, and the Kaleel Jamison Consulting Group. Thomas was a Harvard M.B.A. and former professor at Harvard Business School who had developed a training program for supervisors of black managers and, in 1983, founded the American Institute for Managing Diversity at Morehouse College. Lewis Griggs and Lennie Copeland were Stanford M.B.A.s who produced a video, "Going International," for executives doing business in other countries and then, in 1988, followed that with a very successful series of videos, "Valuing Diversity." Copeland published three articles in *Personnel* and *Personnel Administrator* in 1988 that helped bring attention to the video series. In the early 1970s, Kaleel Jamison conducted race relations workshops for Connecticut General Life Insurance Company (now CIGNA). Jamison set up the Kaleel Jamison Consulting Group, which focuses on creating "High Performance Inclusive" organizations, and was soon joined by the former training director at Connecticut General, Frederick A. Miller. This case illustrates two key points. First, like Jamison, many of the early consultants had experience in race relations workshops, which were required components of a number of major EEO consent decrees in antidiscrimination cases from the 1970s, perhaps most notably AT&T's 1972 decree. Second, experts in EEO, AA, and diversity issues move back and forth between corporate management positions and the new consulting and training organizations.

Several leading companies with long records of affirmative action joined the bandwagon early on, including the Digital Equipment Corporation, where EEO and AA director Barbara Walker had developed a "Valuing Differences" training package in the early 1980s; Avon, which brought in R. Roosevelt Thomas for a major overhaul of the corporate culture; Xerox, which had adopted aggressive affirmative action programs in the early 1970s and had a "Balanced Workforce" plan by 1985; and several large defense contractors (Thomas 1994; Bureau of National Affairs 1995; Lynch 1997).[4]

Following the success of Workforce 2000 and the "Valuing Diversity" videos that appeared on its heels, diversity management spread from the pioneering consultants and companies to a wide range of organizations. These organizations had ample guidance, in the forms of articles, books, videos, conferences, newsletters and a growing cadre of consultants, in transforming their EEO and AA activities into diversity programs. One directory of corporate trainers listed fifteen diversity consultants in 1990, eighty-five in 1992, and seventy-three in 1996 (Lynch 1997, 330). By the early 1990s, a "workforce diversity director" of a high technology firm reported that she heard from about twenty consultants per week (Wheeler 1994, 15).

Soon mainstream business organizations accepted diversity management as a legitimate sub-field of human resources management. Beginning in 1991, consultants set up the Annual National Diversity Conferences and promoted diversity management through local branches of the American Society for Training and Development (Lynch 1997). Two major business organizations, the Conference Board and the Society for Human Resource Management (SHRM), developed diversity management programs (Lynch 1997, 9). The SHRM's diversity program began in 1993 and has included publication of a short booklet for human resources generalists, publication of a comprehensive "Diversity Reference Guide," establishment of a newsletter on diversity issues, and certification programs for those completing special SHRM training (Lynch 1997, 176). The Conference Board's program began in 1994 and has included reports on diversity management, co-sponsorship of national diversity conferences, and an ongoing Roundtable of major companies committed to diversity management (Wheeler 1994, 1995; Lynch 1997).

Old Wine in New Wineskins: The Practices Remain the Same

Diversity specialists promoted new management practices for handling workforce diversity during the 1980s and 1990s, but many of these were simply repackaged EEO and AA practices. In 1995, the Conference Board published a list of common diversity practices. It included incorporation of diversity commitment into mission statements, diversity action plans, accountability for meeting diversity goals, employee involvement, career development and planning, diversity education and training, and long-term initiatives directed at culture change (Wheeler 1995, 8). These basic strategies—announcing the organization's commitment to nondiscrimination, training managers and holding them accountable, providing career development advice, encouraging mentors and network contacts, and identifying career paths—were all common to EEO and AA programs. In fact, a 1979 handbook on affirmative action recommends all of the practices on the Conference Board's diversity list but for employee task forces under the mantle of affirmative action (Hall and Albrecht 1979, 28–29, 151, 162–64).

The link between diversity, EEO, and AA measures is confirmed by a study of one of the "new" diversity practices, "diversity training." A Conference Board report concludes that "in its most narrow sense, diversity training is about compliance—equal employment opportunity, affirmative action and sexual harassment. Although there is a strong sentiment that diversity moves far beyond compliance, at this point, practices demonstrate a strong link between the two" (Wheeler 1994, 7).

The most prominent new element introduced by diversity specialists is the workplace "culture audit," in which diversity specialists use surveys, interviews, and focus groups to identify aspects of culture that inhibit diversity (Thomas 1991, 33; Thomas and Ely 1996; Cross 1996). As these audits involve use of diversity consultants, they increase demand for the consultants who promote them (MacDonald 1993; Lynch 1997). These culture change efforts are costly, long-term projects and hence are much less common than the repackaged EEO and AA measures that comprise the core of diversity management.

Prevalence of Diversity Management Measures

In the 1990s, diversity policies and programs became common, first spreading to large organizations and then diffusing more broadly. By the beginning of the decade, about 70 percent of Fortune 50 companies had adopted some type of "diversity initiative" (Wheeler 1994, 9). More than half of the respondents to a Conference Board survey that focused on large companies who participate in this business organization had diversity training for managers and diversity policy statements (Winterle 1992).

Our own study, a more representative survey of 389 employers of various sizes, suggests that some diversity management measures were as common as key EEO and AA structures by 1997.[5] More than half of the responding organizations had diversity training programs, while about the same percentage of organizations had a designated affirmative action officer (see fig. 6). Whereas organizations had added affirmative action officers slowly and steadily from the 1970s on, the growth of diversity training programs skyrocketed from 1988 on. Other diversity programs, including written diversity policies, diversity committees or task forces, and diversity staff, also grew very quickly in the 1990s. In

FIGURE 6   Prevalence of EEO and AA Structures and Diversity Programs

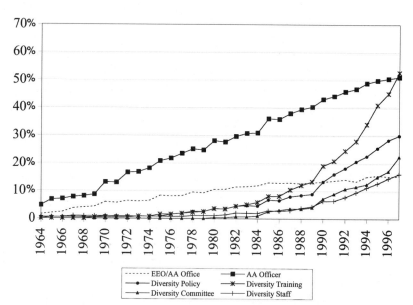

Source: 1997 Human Resources Survey of 389 U.S. worksites with 50 or more employees.

contrast, there were no significant increases in the prevalence of EEO and AA departments during this period.

To summarize, affirmative action seemed to be in trouble by the early 1990s, with the Supreme Court adding restrictions and even a Democratic president vacillating. Few employers put an end to basic EEO and AA programs, but the growth of those programs slowed dramatically. Specialists in these areas responded to these challenges with the rhetoric of diversity management. They repackaged some EEO and AA programs as diversity management measures, while cutting some of the most proactive measures to expand the representation of minorities and women in the workforce. The dramatic growth in diversity programs during the 1990s suggests that personnel managers were aggressively promoting diversity initiatives even as affirmative action per se faced serious challenges.

Conclusion

The federal government's antidiscrimination efforts have waxed and waned since the 1960s, but employers' EEO and AA measures have not simply paralleled enforcement efforts. After an early period of quiet resistance, employers adopted a variety of EEO and AA practices and hired specialists to develop and manage these programs. This expansion came in the 1970s, following an increase in federal powers for enforcing antidiscrimination law.

When federal pressures decreased because of Reagan's opposition, restrictive Supreme Court rulings, and the limited support of both the Bush and Clinton administrations, employers did not abandon their antidiscrimination programs. Instead, EEO and AA specialists who had devised the corporate response to antidiscrimination law retheorized their programs in terms of the business advantages of a diverse workforce. The new diversity management paradigm incorporated many popular EEO and AA practices, but it did not include the most controversial affirmative action measures. With the shift from affirmative action to diversity management, these specialists were able to prevent, or at least to forestall, the deinstitutionalization of their programs and departments.

The history of corporate antidiscrimination efforts reveals the importance of internal constituencies in the institutionalization of corporate practices. In the 1970s, organizations adopted a variety of new practices, but most important, they created a new constituency of EEO and

AA specialists. Philip Selznick (1949, 1957) suggested that organizational practices gain inertia as they develop constituencies of their own. They take on significance even beyond that predicted by their functional utility. Equal employment opportunity and affirmative action measures were first constructed by members of a new management specialty, who ensured that the measures would survive even when affirmative action law was under the gun.

Selznick (1949) and his band of early institutionalists found that individual organizations develop rationales to explain practices that have outlived their original purposes. When affirmative action practices were restyled as "diversity management," however, the process paralleled the initial institutionalization of EEO and AA practices during the 1970s, as John Meyer, W. Richard Scott, and their colleagues depicted it (Meyer and Rowan 1977; Dobbin et al. 1988; Edelman 1992; Sutton and Dobbin 1996). That is, EEO and AA specialists did not develop new rationales for these threatened practices on their own; they developed them collectively through professional networks. Individual specialists learned of new rationales from management consultants, management journals, professional networks, and business associations and articulated these rationales when defending their programs to executives. It was thus that affirmative action offices and practices became "diversity management" departments and programs.

What will the long-term consequences of this change be? It seems clear that employers have reduced their commitment to the targeted recruitment and training programs that they adopted in the 1970s under the OFCCP's guidelines for affirmative action. These were among the most aggressive efforts employers made on the behalf of women and minorities, but they were among the most likely to face legal and political challenges and employee backlash and thus became candidates for deinstitutionalization (Oliver 1992). As chapters 1, 2, and 5 in this volume describe, political backlashes against both immigration and affirmative action have occurred in the past and may occur again. Another threat comes from the courts, which have shown less tolerance in recent years for race-conscious policies. We may see continued dismantling of workplace affirmative action systems. What remains of early EEO and AA systems are the EEO components: formal employment and promotion practices and written affirmative action statements (recast as diversity mission statements).

Will the weakened version of affirmative action found in current "diversity management" practices improve the prospects of women and minorities in the future? One recent study shows that diffuse diversity policies and programs are much less effective than are measures that target women and minority groups (Konrad and Linnehan 1995). Perhaps diversity management will succeed in winning over middle managers because it embraces an economic, rather than a political, rationale (cf. Edelman et al. 1998). But precisely because it is founded on cost-benefit analysis rather than on legal compliance, perhaps diversity management will come under the ax of corporate budget-cutters when America faces its next recession. The results of diversity management will have to be examined as the programs evolve, for as Philip Selznick wrote more than half a century ago, "the meaning of an act may be spelled out in its consequences, and these are not the same as the factors which called it into being" (1949, 253).

Notes

1. The Bureau of National Affairs conducted surveys in 1976 (N = 160) and 1985 (N = 119) of EEO and AA practices (Bureau of National Affairs 1976, 1986a). Respondents were BNA members and thus tended to be large organizations. Changes in geographic representation make trend conclusions tentative.

2. Several studies collected retrospective, longitudinal data on employment practices. Dobbin et al. (1988) (N = 52) surveyed fifty-two northern California employers. In 1985, Sutton et al. (1994) (N = 279) surveyed New Jersey, California, and Virginia employers. Edelman (1992) (N = 346) used a national probability sample.

3. There has been very little research on the development of diversity programs. Most studies are proselytizing tracts written by consultants and human resources experts, hence we rely heavily on Lynch's recent scholarly monograph chronicling the rise of the "diversity machine" as a mini-industry.

4. Walker later became Digital's, and apparently the nation's, first vice president of workforce diversity (Lynch 1997).

5. The survey involved telephone interviews with managers from private, nonprofit, and public employers with fifty or more workers at that location. The interview included questions on the timing of adoption (and dissolution) of a range of antidiscrimination policies and programs. The survey was conducted by the Survey Research Center at the University of Maryland.

Acknowledgments

Thanks to John Skrentny for helpful suggestions. We are grateful to the Alfred P. Sloan Foundation for support.

References

Abzug, Rikki, and Stephen Mezias. 1993. The fragmented state and due process protections in organizations: The case of comparable worth. *Organization Science* 4:433–53.

Baron, James N., Frank R. Dobbin, and P. Devereaux Jennings. 1986. War and peace: The evolution of modern personnel administration in U.S. industry. *American Journal of Sociology* 92:350–83.

Baron, James N., P. Devereaux Jennings, and Frank R. Dobbin. 1988. Mission control? The development of personnel systems in U.S. industry. *American Sociological Review* 53:497–514.

Belz, Herman. 1991. *Equality transformed: A quarter-century of affirmative action.* New Brunswick, N.J.: Transaction Publishers.

Blumrosen, Alfred W. 1993. *Modern law: The law transmission system and equal employment opportunity.* Madison: University of Wisconsin Press.

Bureau of National Affairs. 1967. A current look at: (1) The Negro and Title VII, (2) Sex and Title VII. PPF Survey no. 82. Washington, D.C.: Bureau of National Affairs.

———. 1976. Equal employment opportunity: Programs and results. PPF Survey no. 112. Washington, D.C.: Bureau of National Affairs.

———. 1986a. EEO policies and programs. PFF Survey no. 141. Washington, D.C.: Bureau of National Affairs.

———. 1986b. Affirmative action today: A legal and practical analysis. Washington, D.C.: Bureau of National Affairs.

———. 1995. Affirmative action after *Adarand:* A special report in the Daily Labor Report series, no. 147. Washington, D.C.: Bureau of National Affairs.

Burstein, Paul. 1985. *Discrimination, jobs, and politics: The struggle for equal employment opportunity in the United States since the New Deal.* Chicago: University of Chicago Press.

Burstein, Paul, and Kathleen Monaghan. 1986. Equal employment opportunity and the mobilization of law. *Law and Society Review* 16:355–88.

Clark, Burton R. 1956. *Adult education in transition.* Berkeley: University of California Press.

Cross, Elsie Y. 1996. Managing diversity (letter). *Harvard Business Review* 4 (November–December): 6.

Detlefsen, Robert R. 1991. *Civil rights under Reagan.* San Francisco: ICS Press.

DiMaggio, Paul J., and Walter W. Powell. 1983. The iron cage revisited: Institutional isomorphism and collective rationality in organizational fields. *American Sociological Review* 48:147–60.

———. 1991. Introduction. In *The new institutionalism in organizational analysis*, edited by Walter W. Powell and Paul J. DiMaggio. Chicago: University of Chicago Press.

Dobbin, Frank, Lauren Edelman, John W. Meyer, W. Richard Scott, and Ann Swidler. 1988. The expansion of due process in organizations. In *Institutional patterns and organizations: Culture and environment*, edited by Lynne G. Zucker. Cambridge, Mass.: Ballinger.

Dobbin, Frank, and John R. Sutton. 1998. The strength of a weak state: The employment rights revolution and the rise of human resources management divisions. *American Journal of Sociology* 104:441–76.

Dobbin, Frank, John Sutton, John Meyer, and W. R. Scott. 1993. Equal opportunity law and the construction of internal labor markets. *American Journal of Sociology* 99:396–427.

Donohue, John J. III. 1986. Is Title VII efficient? *University of Pennsylvania Law Review* 134:1411–31.

Edelman, Lauren. 1990. Legal environments and organizational governance: The expansion of due process in the American workplace. *American Journal of Sociology* 95:1401–40.

———. 1992. Legal ambiguity and symbolic structures: Organizational mediation of civil rights law. *American Journal of Sociology* 97:1531–76.

Edelman, Lauren B., Sally Riggs Fuller, and Iona Mara-Drita. 1998. I live for golf while you prefer tennis: The meaning of diversity in the post civil rights era. Paper presented at the American Sociological Association meetings, August 1998.

Edelman, Lauren B., Stephen Petterson, Elizabeth Chambliss, and Howard S. Erlanger. 1991. Legal ambiguity and the politics of compliance: Affirmative action officers' dilemma. *Law and Policy* 13:73–97.

Feild, John. 1984. *Affirmative action: A fresh look at the record twenty-two years after the beginning.* Washington, D.C.: Center for National Policy Review.

Fisher, Anne B. 1994. Businessmen like to hire by the numbers. In *Equal employment opportunity,* edited by Paul Burstein. New York: Aldine de Gruyter. (Reprinted from *Fortune,* 9 September 1985.)

Froehlich, Herbert, and Dennis Hawyer. 1974. Compliance spinoff: Better personnel systems. *Personnel* 51 (1): 62–69.

Golembiewski, Robert T. 1995. Managing diversity in organizations. Tuscaloosa: University of Alabama Press.

Graham, Hugh Davis. 1990. *The civil rights era: Origins and development of national policy, 1960–1972.* New York: Oxford Unviersity Press.

Gutman, Arthur. 1993. *EEO law and personnel practices.* Newbury Park, Calif.: Sage Publications.

Hall, Francine S., and Maryann H. Albrecht. 1979. *The management of affirmative action.* Santa Monica, Calif.: Goodyear Publishing.

Hammerman, Herbert. 1984. *A decade of new opportunity: Affirmative action in the 1970s.* Washington: Potomac Institute.

Harvard Law Review, Editors of. 1989. Rethinking *Weber:* The business response to affirmative action. *Harvard Law Review* 102 (3): 658–71.

Johnston, William B., and Arnold H. Packer. 1987. *Workforce 2000: Work and workers for the twenty-first century.* Indianapolis: Hudston Institute.

Konrad, Alison M., and Frank Linnehan. 1995. Formalized HRM structures: Coordinating equal opportunity or concealing organizational practices? *Academy of Management Journal* 38:787–820.

Kossek, Ellen Ernst, and Sharon A. Lobel. 1995. *Managing diversity: Human resource strategies for transforming the workplace.* Cambridge, Mass.: Blackwell.

Leach, Joy, with Bette George, Tina Jackson, and Arleen LaBella. 1995. *A practical guide to working with diversity: The process, the tools, the resources.* New York: AMACOM.

Leonard, Jonathan S. 1985. What promises are worth: The impact of affirmative action goals. *Journal of Human Resources* 20:3–20.

———. 1989. Women and affirmative action. *Journal of Economic Perspectives* 3 (1): 61–75.

Lynch, Frederick R. 1997. *The diversity machine: The drive to change the "white male workplace."* New York: Free Press.

MacDonald, Heather. 1993. The diversity industry: Cashing in on affirmative action. *The New Republic* 209:22–35.

McDowell, Gary L. 1989. Affirmative inaction: The Brock-Meese standoff on federal racial quotas." *Policy Review* 48:32–50.

Meyer, John W., and Brian Rowan. 1977. Institutionalized organizations: Formal structure as myth and ceremony. *American Journal of Sociology* 83:340–63.

Miller, Joanne. 1994. *Corporate responses to diversity.* New York: Center for the New American Workplace, Queens College.

Oliver, Christine. 1992. The antecedents of deinstitutionalization. *Organization Studies* 13: 563–88.

Rynes, Sara, and Benson Rosen. 1994. What makes diversity programs work? *HR Magazine* 39 (10): 67.

Selznick, Philip. 1949. *TVA and the grass roots.* Berkeley: University of California Press.

———. 1957. *Leadership in administration.* New York: Harper and Row.

Shaeffer, Ruth G. 1973. *Nondiscrimination in employment: Changing perspectives 1963–1972.* New York: Conference Board.

———. 1980. *Nondiscrimination in employment—and beyond.* New York: Conference Board.

Skrentny, John David. 1996. *The ironies of affirmative action: Politics, culture, and justice in America.* Chicago: University of Chicago Press.

Strang, David, and John W. Meyer. 1993. Institutional conditions for diffusion. *Theory and Society* 22:487–511.

Stryker, Robin. 1996. Law, sociology, and public policy issues in equal employment opportunity. Paper presented at the annual meeting of the American Sociological Association, New York.

Sutton, John, and Frank Dobbin. 1996. The two faces of governance: Responses to legal uncertainty in American firms 1955–1985. *American Sociological Review* 61:794–811.

Sutton, John R., Frank Dobbin, John W. Meyer, and Richard Scott. 1994. The legalization of the workplace. *American Journal of Sociology* 99:944–71.

Thomas, David A., and Robin J. Ely. 1996. Making differences matter: A new paradigm for managing diversity. *Harvard Business Review*, September–October 1996, 79–90.

Thomas, R. Roosevelt Jr. 1991. *Beyond race and gender: Unleashing the power of your total work force by managing diversity.* New York: AMACOM.

———. 1994. Foreword: From affirmative action to affirming diversity. In *Differences that work: Organizational excellence through diversity*, edited by Mary C. Gentile. Cambridge: Harvard Business Review Books.

Wheeler, Michael L. 1994. Diversity training (Conference Board Report no. 1083-94-RR). New York: Conference Board.

———. 1995. Diversity: Business rationale and strategies (Conference Board Report no. 1130-95-RR). New York: Conference Board.

Winterle, Mary. 1992. Work force diversity: Corporate challenges, corporate responses (Conference Board Report no. 1013). New York: Conference Board.

Yakura, Elaine K. 1995. EEO law and managing diversity. In *Managing diversity: Human resource strategies for transforming the workplace*, edited by Ellen Ernst Kossek and Sharon A. Lobel. Cambridge, Mass.: Blackwell.

Zald, Mayer, and Patricia Denton. 1963. From evangelism to general service: The transformation of the YMCA. *Administrative Science Quarterly* 8:214–34.

5

Anatomy of Conflict: The Making and Unmaking of Affirmative Action at the University of California

. . .

J OHN A UBREY D OUGLASS

I n the aftermath of the July 1995 decision by the Board of Regents of the University of California to end race- and gender-based prefer-ences in admissions, hiring, and contracting, the ardent liberal Andrew Hacker wrote that "[f]urther efforts to defend affirmative action will be immensely difficult." Among America's electorate, he noted, "its de-fenders are still having difficulty making a convincing case for it" (Hacker 1996, 21). Five months later, Californians passed Proposition 209—a state constitutional amendment barring the use of race- and gender-based decision making in public institutions. Four years later, a similar constitutional proposition passed in the state of Washington.

In both California and Washington, the issue of admissions to the state's highly selective land-grant universities provided a focal point for debating the merits of affirmative action. The controversy over the use of race and gender in admissions decisions is neither the beginning nor the end of a debate over who should have access to universities with selective admissions processes. Particularly in public universities with social and legal obligations that simply do not exist for private institu-tions, there is perhaps no other area of policy as important as deciding who is eligible for admission. Admissions policy is the most visible inter-face between the public institution and one of its primary constituents, the taxpayer.

This chapter has four goals. First, it describes how the University of California has approached the issue of educational opportunity over time, especially in undergraduate admissions. Second, it shows how af-firmative action policies developed, focusing on the difficulties of translating broad institutional goals related to racial diversity into spe-cific policies. Third, it analyzes the regents' decision to end preferences in the early summer of 1995. And fourth, this chapter shows how the debate over affirmative action provides the impetus for a reevaluation of the "social contract" of public universities.

Affirmative action, and specifically the use of race as a factor in admissions, is historically consistent with the larger effort by the University of California (UC) to admit students from a broad range of California society. As in most if not all public universities, admissions policy at UC has been formulated not only to advance the interests of the individual but also to fulfill the university's larger obligations as a force for social and economic change—essentially its *social contract*. To a large extent, the debate over affirmative action revolves around the proper weight a public institution should give to its social contract, and changing notions of what this obligation should include.

Creating the Social Contract

Contemporary admissions policies at the University of California are the result of a long history of defining the categories of persons who should have access to a public higher education. Within the landscape of American higher education, and reflecting the particular circumstances of California's emergence as a state, the University of California has proved a highly progressive institution. Over the span of thirteen decades, a number of principles have shaped admissions policy within what is today a nine-campus system. Each relates to a mix of egalitarian values, the meaning and purpose of the university's social contract, the idea of a meritocracy and, by the early twentieth century, the university's place within one of the nation's first coherent state systems of public higher education.

The first set of principles has their origins in the founding era of the university. The 1868 Organic Act passed by the California legislature provided the charter for the university and directed the regents to, among other things, set the "moral and intellectual qualifications of applicants for admissions" to the state's land-grant university. Reflecting the concerns and values of the Whig-Republican and Unionist Democrat lawmakers then dominating the state legislature, the charter defined four basic principles. The first included the statement that *admission of students should be free of sectarian influences*. Also in the charter was the edict that *admissions, and all other aspects of university management, should be free of political partisanship*. "It is expressly provided," stated the legislative act, "that no sectarian, political or partisan test shall ever be allowed or exercised in the appointment of Regents, or in the election of professors, teachers, or other officers of the University, or in the admission of students" (California State Legislature 1868).

A third principle attempted to open the university to all socioeconomic classes. It was proclaimed that the *University of California should be tuition-free to all residents of the state in order to reduce economic barriers to access.* The no-tuition policy was in marked contrast to virtually all private institutions and most public state universities, which incorporated tuition early as a major funding source. Simply making the institution tuition-free did not make enrolling in Berkeley affordable to all California citizens. However, it did form a meaningful and symbolic statement that economic barriers should not dissuade talented students from furthering their education. A fourth principle required the institution to *draw students from all parts of the state.* "It shall be the duty of the Regents," stated the 1868 act, "according to population, to so apportion the representation of students, when necessary, that all portions of the State shall enjoy equal privilege therein" (California State Legislature 1868). Educational opportunity was thus defined not only in economic terms but also by geographic representation.

Neither gender nor race was mentioned in the Organic Act. In 1870, however, and on the recommendation of the university's faculty, the regents established a fifth principle: *Women should be admitted into the university on equal terms with men.* The egalitarian goals of the new state university, argued a majority of the regents, including Governor Henry Haight, should not, indeed could not, discriminate against women. By 1900, more than 46 percent of the university's total enrollment constituted women in an era when most coeducational colleges and universities had quotas limiting female enrollment and placed women in separate classes. Most eastern colleges and universities remained all-male, and even such progressive universities as the University of Michigan and Stanford maintained quotas limiting female students to approximately 25 percent of all students. But once at Berkeley women faced other obstacles. Social mores of male faculty and students, for example, limited professional training largely to fields such as elementary school teaching, and women tended to major in English, nursing, and similar fields thought gender-appropriate (Gordon 1990; Clifford 1995).

In the early 1870s, the UC faculty and the university's president, Daniel Coit Gilman, embraced a sixth principle. Inspired by the emerging model of the American research university, Gilman in particular articulated the idea that *university admissions should be selective, admitting students who have the ability to successfully complete a university degree.* Unlike most land-grant universities and colleges, particularly those in the Midwest, which were open to virtually anyone who applied, the University of California adopted admissions policies that were relatively selective. Gilman, who would later leave the turbulent politics of California to become the founding president of Johns Hopkins University, argued that a research university was a place for advanced training, research, and public service.

During the Progressive Era, the growing and seemingly insatiable appetite of Californians for public higher education tested the political ability of UC leaders to keep their institution selective. A demand emerged for California's state university to lower its admission standards. In understanding the university's reaction, an important factor must be noted: twenty years earlier, the University of California, and specifically its lay Board of Regents, were given the unusual status of a public trust under the California constitution. The subsequent impact on UC policy making was significant. University officials and faculty could manage the internal affairs of the schools relatively free of legislative forays. Though tied to state budgeting for its operating funds, UC had and has no legal obligation to follow statutory law in areas such as admissions policy. This level of autonomy—one enjoyed to some extent by only five other public universities in the United States—provided a significant ability for the university to both mold its admissions standards and to shape its social contract (Douglass 1992).

Within this policy making context, President Benjamin Ide Wheeler and others in the university appealed to Progressive leaders such as Hiram Johnson, arguing that the university should become, in fact, more selective. To meet both the growing demand for higher education and the desires of the university, Wheeler and others argued for the restructuring of California's public education system. In particular, Alexis Lange, professor of education at Berkeley, suggested that California create the nation's first network of public junior colleges as the primary method to expand access to a postsecondary education. The university might then create matriculation agreements with these two-year colleges, accredit them, and create a flow of students at the junior year to Berkeley. William Rainey Harper at the University of Chicago had earlier advocated a similar model as a natural expansion of America's free public school system, but it was in California that the idea of the junior college as a vital component in expanding educational opportunity was translated into public policy. In 1907, the California legislature passed a bill allowing local high school districts to establish these new institutions.

Establishment of public junior colleges, created by local initiative with state financial support, was accompanied by two other important developments. The first was the conversion in 1921 of the state's set of public normal schools into four-year regional colleges—what became the California state colleges by the 1930s and the California State University (CSU) in the 1960s. The second was the establishment of a southern branch of the University of California in 1919—what became UCLA. The university became the nation's first multicampus university. The result was the creation by 1921 of California's contemporary tripartite structure of public higher education (Douglass 2000).

In no small part, the development of the junior college and the regionally based state colleges helped both protect and further define the purpose of the University of California. Subsequent policy development in admissions was conditioned by the university's place within the tripartite system and its transition to a multicampus framework—essentially allowing for enrollment growth by developing new campuses. This led to another important principle (number seven in our rapid historical tour): that *the University has an obligation to admit students within the selective parameters set by the University* and its corollary, *the University must find a place within one of its campuses for all students deemed "UC eligible" under these standards.*

The ideal of selectivity in University of California admissions gained greater emphasis with the negotiation of the 1960 California Master Plan for Higher Education. Facing projections of a four-fold increase in enrollment demand by the mid-1970s, UC officials engaged in negotiations with other members of the state's higher education community, and with Sacramento lawmakers, on how to maintain California's promise of educational opportunity. The result was the 1960 master plan.

Among the plan's most important recommendations were those regarding admissions policy. Projections showed that California state government could not fully fund the anticipated growth in enrollment demand in the coming two decades. To reduce costs and to provide uniformity in admissions policy, the University of California and the State Colleges (what became CSU) each reduced their eligibility pool of high school graduates. This, in turn, resulted in a shift of prospective university students to the junior colleges, which had lower operating costs. "State-supported institutions," stated the master plan, "have an obligation to adjust their offerings and admissions policies to meet the long-run needs and to fit the fiscal capabilities of the state, as ascertained by constitutional and statutory authorities" (Liaison Committee 1960, 67).

The Emergence of Race-Based Decision-Making

In the 1960s, several factors influenced the creation of affirmative action admissions preferences at UC and eventually established a new principle: *undergraduate admissions of the university should encompass the general ethnic, gender, and economic composition of California high school graduates* (University of California Board of Regents 1988). These factors included the adoption of the master plan in 1960. This new plan rationalized the admissions process and encouraged a new focus on standardized test scores as a tool for reducing enrollment demand. As will be explained, this in turn had a negative impact on future minority enrollments. Another factor was political pressure for increased minority admissions. Within the context of rapid demographic change in California, this pressure came from the minority community, from the state legislature, and increasingly from the admissions officers themselves. These officers became, like the human resources professionals described in chapter 4 in this volume, an important internal constituency for affirmative action. A third factor is the relatively recent imbalance between the demand for access to the university and the limited supply of undergraduate positions, particularly at the campuses of Berkeley and Los Angeles.

Historically, the university has pursued admissions policies intended to be inclusive. Variables such as income, geography, veteran status, and inequities in collegiate preparation have been part of the evolution in the university's social contract. Until 1960, however, the specific issue of enrolling "under-represented minority groups" had not entered the consciousness of California policy makers—at least, not as a stated goal that would receive wide public support. For example, the 1960 master plan, a significant statement of egalitarian ideals and the importance of broad access to postsecondary education, made no mention of the need to address racial or ethnic representation. In the view of those who negotiated the plan, the largest hindrances to access were economic and geographic factors.

Prior to 1960, and under policy set by the Academic Senate of the university, approximately 90 percent of entering freshmen qualified for admission simply by gaining a B average in ten high school subject areas at schools accredited by university faculty—what was termed "regular admissions." The remaining 10 percent were admitted on the basis of "special action," including supplementary criteria such as special talents and a student's socioeconomic background. Although 10 percent was a general goal outlined by the Academic Senate's Board of Admissions and Relations with Schools (BOARS), campuses such as Berkeley and UCLA fluctuated in the percentage of students they admitted under the title of special action. In the immediate post–World War II era, and reflecting the flexibility employed to meet the university's social contract, special action admissions at these two campuses reached nearly 40 percent of all freshman students admitted during the peak year of 1947.

Throughout the 1950s, the percentage of special action students at Berkeley and UCLA fluctuated between 8 and 18 percent. As figure 1 demonstrates, "advanced standing" admissions (junior-year transfers mainly from California's junior colleges) also increased dramatically. The consistently high transfer rates (representing nearly 50 percent of all admissions to these campuses during the 1930s and 1950s) point again to the tremendous importance the university placed on serving a wide spectrum of California society (Academic Senate 1960). These

FIGURE 1   Regular, Advanced Standing (Junior-Year Transfers), and Special Action Admissions at UC Berkeley and UCLA, 1930–1960

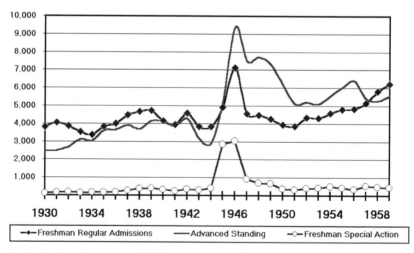

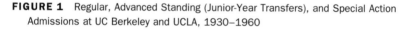

Source: Board of Admissions and Relations with Schools, Representative Assembly Minutes, October 25, 1960.

pre-1960s admissions polices offered a dynamic framework for admitting students, providing a rich mix of traditional meritocratic values such as grades with a range of variables that made the university more inclusive and recognized the varieties of human intelligence and potential.

As noted, the master plan raised admissions standards at both UC and the California State University. It also argued for admissions process mechanics that were much more restrictive. A perception emerged that new methods were needed to evaluate the increasing flood of student applications and to raise admission standards. The 1960 plan called for two major changes: one, the adoption of the SAT, and in turn a lowering of the value placed on grade point averages; and two, the lowering of special action admissions to a mere 2 percent of the total pool of students admitted at the freshman and junior transfer levels. Studies done in the 1950s and 1960s, as today, consistently showed that high school grade point averages provide a more consistent predictor of scholastic success. But the need to reduce the university's admissions pool, and the convenience of adopting what appeared to be a new standard among elite higher education institutions, led to the incorporation of the SAT in 1968 as a requirement in freshman admissions.

The shift in admissions policy induced by the master plan presented, however, a serious dilemma. With the recognition of a growing disparity between the racial mixture of California's population and the university's student enrollment in the mid-1960s, and the creation of a more rigid admissions process, how could the university develop methods to increase minority enrollment? At first, UC adopted two major strategies to increase what became known as "underrepresented groups." The first strategy was to establish new "outreach" programs: counseling and support programs targeted at minority high school students and intended to increase their eligibility for the university. Beginning in 1964, Educational Opportunity Programs (EOPs) were created on each of the UC campuses with the objective of increasing the enrollment of low-income students drawn primarily, but not exclusively, from minority populations (University of California Office of the President 1975, 105). The second strategy was to incorporate race and ethnicity as factors in special action admissions. In 1967, the same year the university adopted the SAT as a requirement for all freshman admissions, the regents agreed to increase the limit for special action admissions from 2 percent to 4 percent, and by 1979 to 6 percent, at both freshman and advanced standing levels. The purpose, stated the regents, was to encourage the enrollment of more students "whose ethnic or economic background had disadvantaged them" (University of California Board of Regents 1968).

Among the leaders of California's growing minority populations, however, and within the halls of the state capitol in Sacramento, there was a pervasive sense in the late 1960s that new approaches were needed to rapidly increase minority enrollment. Some of the UC campuses, including Berkeley and a new campus in San Diego, were sites of protest by black and Latino students who demanded more representation. In 1974, the California legislature passed a statute announcing that the undergraduate student body at UC should "reflect" the general ethnic, gender, and economic composition of the state's high school graduates. This forced university officials to consider new mechanisms that would lead to a representative student body.

As a result, and for the first time, decision-making in regular admissions would include consideration of race. Outside political pressure essentially compelled university officials to significantly expand the effort to diversify the student, faculty, and staff population. In turn, this resulted in an expansion in staff and programs related to affirmative action and the emergence of an internal organizational culture strongly committed to diversity.

Yet the structural changes in admissions pursued by university administrators were not sanctioned by the Board of Regents, nor by the faculty, who historically had purview over admissions. Affirmative action policy was created ad hoc, largely at the campus level, by administrators. Campus officials were under tremendous pressure to diversify their student populations. They quickly sought creative means to help meet this relatively new component of the social contract.

Race as a Criterion for Inclusion and Exclusion

As this quick historical tour of UC admissions policy demonstrates, the notion of using race or gender as one among several criteria for admitting students to California's land-grant university is far from revolutionary. Geographic representation, status as a veteran, family income, status as a foreign or out-of-state student, artistic talent, and a variety of other criteria have been used over time to make the university more inclusive. It was not obvious that race and ethnicity could or should not be included in this list, and until recently, using race and ethnicity in admissions was upheld in the courts.

Yet elevating race to a primary criterion in admissions, essentially co-equal with traditional academic requirements, has proved problematic. In a nation that has spent all of its history struggling over issues of race and equal opportunity, the axiom that we should live in a "colorblind society" has a very distinct meaning for perhaps the majority of Americans. In short, it is an effort to protect the rights of the rugged individual, no matter who that individual is. Thus far, complicated arguments over past discrimination and efforts at amelioration for distinct racial groups have not been persuasive tools for generating public support.

Within the confines of the University of California's campuses, race-based decision-making first proved problematic when it emerged as a perceived method for rejecting applicants seeking enrollment at the most prestigious campuses and who were, on academic criteria alone, officially eligible to enter the university. This phenomenon first occurred at two of the university's most prestigious campuses, Berkeley and UCLA. In the early 1970s, both campuses were accepting virtually all UC-eligible students, redirecting only a small pool of students to other UC campuses with room for enrollment growth—usually students attempting to enter the highly competitive engineering program. By the early 1980s, however, the number of students wanting to attend Berkeley and UCLA increased significantly. For the first time, large numbers of academically eligible students, under UC policy, were rejected at these campuses. While the other campuses of the university were still accepting virtually all UC-eligible students, Berkeley and UCLA were rejecting approximately two out of every three applicants (Academic Senate, 1989a).

Adherence to a strict definition of academic aptitude, as determined by high school GPA and SAT scores, and the selection of students only from the top of this pool, would have resulted in an overwhelmingly Euro-American and Asian American student population. To increase the number of "underrepresented" students, primarily Chicano/Latinos and African Americans, these two campuses employed new methods to alter the composition of their undergraduate populations. The affirmative action programs at both campuses shifted their attention to addressing the problem of underrepresentation and increasingly and myopically away from the concept of serving "disadvantaged" students. These two categories had become, in the view of not just university officials but state lawmakers as well, one and the same. A relatively new concept emerged: to be part of an underrepresented group is to be, in effect, disadvantaged—even if that student is from a second-generation college-educated family with an upper-middle-class or higher income.

In the post-*Bakke* era quotas were to be avoided, but there were other systematic ways to provide access to underrepresented groups. To select a diverse student body out of this large pool of prospective students, both campuses significantly altered their admissions process. Not only did they use special action to expand minority enrollment, which had been limited to 6 percent of all freshman admissions by the Regents, but they also now used the process of regular admissions to meet diversity goals, developing formulas that relied heavily on race to determine admissions. The net affect was that race had become a variable for determining not only inclusion but also exclusion.

The problems of translating broad affirmative action policy goals into practical decision-making are best illustrated by the Berkeley experience. Campus officials decided that their goal was general parity between the racial and ethnic composition of the undergraduate enrollment and that of the state population in general. In the course of attempting to attain this parity, in 1984 the admissions office stopped considering Asian Americans eligible for special consideration outside of academic achievement because, in short, their numbers at Berkeley far exceeded their proportional share of the available undergraduate pie. They had become overrepresented, and hence no longer a "disadvantaged" group.

Berkeley's attempt to redefine who was and who was not a disadvantaged minority had a significant impact on the Asian American community, particularly in the Bay Area. The campus's Asian American undergraduate enrollment declined significantly in a two-year period. Although their numbers would again climb, considerable consternation ensued. "Have Asian American students, known for their impressive grade-point averages and their steadily growing numbers on campus, become victims of their own success?" asked Michael Manzagol in the *California Monthly*. They constituted 16.1 percent of the freshman class at Berkeley in 1975, a figure that climbed to 26.9 percent in 1983 but then dropped to 24.1 percent in 1984 "amid charges that campus administrators have introduced changes in admissions policy criteria . . . in order to place an unofficial quota on Asian Americans" (Manzagol 1988, 20). Berkeley officials were attempting to fulfill the university's social contract as they understood it. But this change quickly aggravated a relatively new and powerful special interest group and heightened a growing public perception: that access to Berkeley should not simply be an internal policy decision of the academy.

Berkeley's choice to add race and ethnicity as determinants for regular admissions raised an important question: had Berkeley set quotas for admission of Asian Americans and for other racial and ethnic groups? "We as a university are against quotas," insisted Bud Travers, the assistant vice chancellor for undergraduate affairs, "and we have never used them against Asian-Americans." But Travers did admit that Berkeley had devised a method to apportion enrollment to targeted groups. "We are playing what is called the least-sum game," noted Travers. "If any ethnic group gains in admissions, then another ethnic group loses. We are supposed to service the top 12.5 percent of high school students *and* have affirmative action programs. Take these two things and add the fact that Asian-Americans are at Berkeley in numbers four times higher than they graduate from high school, and you have a model that is unworkable" (Manzagol 1988, 20).

Reacting to the controversy generated at the Berkeley campus, in 1988 the regents adopted new policies on undergraduate admissions formulated by the president's office. The hope was that this move would clarify admissions policy at the nine-campus university system and provide support for campuses such as Berkeley that faced growing public criticism. Each campus, stated the regents, was to "encompass" the ethnic, racial, cultural, and economic composition of California's population. And for the first time since 1960, the regents formally stated that regular admissions could include supplemental criteria, including race, as factors in the admissions process.

Each campus within the rapidly growing UC system then attempted to articulate how the admissions process would work under the Board of Regents' new policy. An index that mirrored the GPA and the SAT indexes but was composed of supplemental criteria was created on many campuses, including Berkeley and UCLA. Each campus version was different, reflecting the increasingly decentralized mode of policy making in admissions that began in the early 1980s. These inventions were a conscientious effort to detail and quantify the admission process for the California public. Yet at campuses with a significant and growing disjuncture between the demand for access by qualified students and the supply of freshman places, they simply provided fodder for a new round of controversy.

A Regental Debate

What led to the wholesale rejection of race and gender preferences by a majority of regents at their July 1995 meeting? Although their debate included the university's hiring and contracting practices, it was admissions, and in particular undergraduate admissions, that provided the greatest source of questions regarding the purpose of California's public land-grant university—among the regents, the larger university community, and within the media. At no time did the regents reject the long-standing policy that student enrollment at the University of California should reflect the general ethnic and gender composition of the state. That policy remains sanctified in California state law and remains the stated goal of the board. Rather, the focus of the debate was over the method that a public university should use to choose who will and who will not gain entrance to the increasingly valuable commodity of a university education.

The months leading up to the regents' decision captured the volatility of a confrontation that left little room for subtlety or compromise and that was profoundly political in content. As this volume attests, affirmative action is the source of a polarizing national discussion over the best methods to ameliorate racial, gender, and socioeconomic inequities in American society. Discussion within the university community reflected this division but was further complicated by charges that Regent Ward Connerly and Governor and Regent Pete Wilson were using the university for political purposes. Many believed that Connerly and Wilson used the issue as a vehicle to generate publicity and support for a state constitutional amendment to ban race and gender decision making in all public agencies (Proposition 209). And in doing so their efforts might then help launch a national campaign against affirmative action, bolstering Wilson's presidential campaign.

Why should the university engage in a politically divisive debate that was likely to be settled by the California electorate? This question was posed by UC president Jack Peltason but was ignored by the majority of regents. "I believe that in our discussions of the University's programs and policies," Peltason warned, "we need to be careful not to embroil The Regents, and therefore the University, in a debate that is and should be taking place in the state and national arenas. Affirmative action is a volatile issue that generates strong feelings on every side. . . . I hope we can conduct our dialogue on this subject with the clarity, [the] thoughtfulness, and the precision it deserves" (Peltason 1995a).

Regent Connerly, and others, argued that precisely because the university is a public agency, and because of its obligations to the people of California, the board was exactly the type of forum in which such issues should be debated. In virtually all other states, the debate would have occurred in the legislature. Connerly saw the opportunity to confront affirmative action within the more politically favorable confines of the regents. The regents' questions regarding the legitimacy of race-based decision making corresponded with a general shift in the political orientation of the board and in the apparent saliency of the issue among both lawmakers and California's voters. The formal adoption by the regents of race and ethnicity as factors in special action admissions, and the belated and tacit approval of their use in regular admissions, occurred when the board had a significantly larger number of liberal Democrats. In that era, the state legislature, also controlled by the Democratic Party, was a major force in both mandating and funding affirmative action–related programs and goals. By the mid-1990s, the political predilections of the Board of Regents had changed, owing in part to the succession of two conservative Republican governors who made all regental appointments (regents serve twelve-month terms). And the Assembly (one of two houses of the California legislature) had shifted for the first time since 1958 to a majority of Republicans—many with sharply conservative agendas.

In early January 1995, Regent Connerly had told President Peltason that he would formally request a review of the university's affirmative action programs and that he planned to force a vote on the issue in the early part of the summer. At their January 19 meeting the regents supported Connerly's request for information on the extent of race-based preferences in the university and placed the burden on the president and the Academic Senate to develop analyses and to outline possible policy options. Yet the Office of the President either did not fully comprehend the desire of the regents for a serious review of policy options, or it deliberately avoided such a discussion. Whatever the motivation, they vigorously defended the myriad of affirmative action–related programs in the university and provided little analytical information—a strategic approach reinforced and encouraged by the chancellors of the nine UC campuses.

At the outset of the debate, a sense prevailed among university and campus administrators, and not least the chancellors, that any indication that affirmative action policies might require modification would weaken their ability to defend their diversity efforts. Anything but a strong defense of the UC's existing policies and programs would also draw significant criticism by a contingent of activist students, a significant portion of the faculty, and other groups within the university community.

Responding to Regent Connerly's request for a review of affirmative action policies and programs, President Peltason stated that the Office of the President was "preparing an inventory and report on affirmative action programs, not because I intend to make recommendations for change—in my judgment, no changes are needed—but because we want to be prepared to answer any questions about them that may arise as a result of recently proposed legislation and constitutional amendments." Peltason also told the regents that he would "accelerate" the completion of the report. It would be available for the June 1995 meeting of the board—the meeting at which Regent Connerly stated his intention to submit a proposal for a possible change in the university's affirmative action policy. The president concluded that the university's policies derived from a "broad national consensus" and indicated that it would be premature for the regents to act: "If that consensus changes, so will federal and state policy and law. The University, as it is obligated to do, will respond at the appropriate time" (Peltason 1995a).

Subsequent meetings of the board provided public spectacles of the division between regents such as Connerly and the university's administration. Acrimonious debate, fueled by charges of racism, tended to sharpen the differences among regents and solidify what appeared to be a majority opinion: that the university's affirmative action programs had gone too far, possibly violating the *Bakke* decision. And with no solid framework of past regental actions regarding the proper scope and goals of affirmative action policies, a perception arose that racial preferences had no sanction from either present or past members of the board. They were, in essence, the invention of campus administrators and not of a publicly accountable lay board.

The decentralized nature of affirmative action efforts within the nine-campus system also presented significant difficulties for the president and university administrators, eroding their credibility among many regents. The lack of a strong understanding of the numerous affirmative action programs at individual campuses made it virtually impossible to accurately describe the breadth of these programs. President Peltason at one time stated that no campus admitted students solely on the basis of their race—it was simply one factor of many both in special action admissions and in choosing among UC-eligible students. Later, it was admitted that at least two campuses automatically admitted all UC-eligible underrepresented students and that Berkeley and UCLA employed a weighted admission process that heavily favored underrepresented groups. Although such revelations did not directly refute the statements of the president and other university administrators, it provided evidence to many regents that they were not being told the true nature of what was, in fact, a dizzying array of affirmative action programs (Peltason 1995b).

In a press release announcing his intention to propose a resolution to end race-based decision making, Connerly openly pointed to the credibility problem of the administration (Connerly 1995). Governor Wilson also stated that the true extent of race-based decision making, and its consequences, was not being revealed to the regents by the administration. Before the board, the governor insisted that the regents not tolerate university policies and practices that "violate fundamental fairness, trampling individual rights to create and give preference to group rights. It has become clear," he argued, that "despite official claims to the contrary . . . race has played a central role in the admissions practices at many UC campuses" (University of California Board of Regents 1995, 1).

By the time of the fateful July meeting of the regents, there appeared to be no room for compromise. Race-based preferences, a core aspect of affirmative action, would either be embraced or rejected. Connerly, with the clear support of the governor, pursued a remarkably effective campaign to place this issue before the regents and to systematically outline the key weaknesses to the university's approach to diversity. In an effort that encompassed not only admissions policies but extensive outreach efforts to local schools, the university's leadership had created a labyrinth of policies and programs focused on race and gender. Connerly had forced them into the light of day, and he ruthlessly pointed to their inadequacies, real and imagined. And in this political adventure, he tore at not only the credibility of the defenders of affirmative action within the administration but the sense of community within the university itself—a process unintentionally bolstered by the strategic approach employed by the president and the chancellors.

The July meeting was thus more a political event than the final phase of a coherent policy debate. The board would make its judgment in the midst of a cavalcade of both critics and defenders of what Connerly had argued was the status quo—intransigent liberals arguing for affirmative action in seeming perpetuity. Addressing the board and a largely hostile public audience, Governor Wilson reminded the board that it is "the Regents' responsibility, not that of the administration or the faculty, to set policy and to ensure that the university's practices adhere to those policies. . . . The question before the Board is whether the University is going to treat all individuals fairly or continue to divide them by race." Then came a number of state lawmakers along with various representatives from the private sector and from conservative and liberal think tanks who addressed the regents, interrupted only by the vocal outbursts of student protesters and their subsequent removal by university police.

Willie Brown, the former Speaker of the Assembly, stated that the board should take no action until and unless the California Civil Rights Initiative (Proposition 209) was enacted: "To do so [otherwise] would place the members of the Board in the political arena, from which extrication would be impossible." Diane Watson, also an African American and a state senator from Los Angeles, questioned why taxpayers should support the University if it abandons affirmative action. State Assemblyman Bernie Richter argued that affirmative action "has become a code word for preferential policies, quotas and set asides" and that the time had come to end "government-based racism." Nao Takasugi, an assemblyman, explained that he was a former prisoner in the relocation camps of World War II, but he believed the university's admissions policies amounted to unwarranted discrimination. Finally, Jesse Jackson spoke in a measured oratory. The most deceptive element of Regent Connerly's proposal, he stated, was the naive notion of a "bias-free meritocracy." Jackson then forced a moment of prayer—an unusual moment within the secular confines of the board—before leading a march of student protesters to a news conference (University of California Board of Regents 1995, 11).

A total of sixty-five people addressed the regents before Ward Connerly moved his proposal and urged the board to take action. Connerly insisted that affirmative action was an issue that the board could not skirt: "The University has been granting racial preferences to remedy some of the historical unfairness and injustice projected upon many Americans, particularly Black Americans. The assumption has been made, however, that these preferences would be temporary . . . it has now become entrenched as it builds its own constituency to defend and sustain it as a permanent feature of public decision making" (University of California Board of Regents 1995, 13–14).Connerly told the board that he now believed that the obsession with race contributed to a racial divide.

Discussion among the board members was temporarily interrupted by a bomb threat that forced the board into an executive session in a more secure room. Subsequently they voted 14 to 10, with one abstention, to adopt Connerly's proposal, adding a new and final principle for UC admissions: *"Effective January 1, 1997 the University of California shall not use race, religion, sex, color, ethnicity, or national origin as criteria for admissions"* (University of California Board of Regents 1995).

The Future of Diversity and the Paradox
of the Parity Model

During the debate by the regents, proponents of affirmative action predicted dire results in undergraduate admissions, and they continue to do so. And indeed, at the most selective campuses of the University of California—Berkeley, UCLA, and San Diego—the ban on affirmative action has had a significant impact. At Berkeley, the oldest campus, which has garnered the most national attention in the post–Proposition 209 era, freshman enrollment of African Americans and Latinos dropped by 54 percent between 1997 and 1998. Perhaps more important, Latino enrollment alone declined by 30 percent (University of California, Berkeley 1999). California's Latinos make up the fastest-growing segment of the population, followed by Asian Americans, approximately 35 percent and 18 percent of the state's people, respectively. In contrast, African Americans remain approximately 8 percent of California's total population, and will likely decline as a percentage.

A review of 1999 ethnic data at the university level, however, provides a more sanguine glimpse into the impact of Proposition 209. Data on freshman enrollment for fall 1999 show an overall drop in underrepresented minorities (African Americans, Latinos, and American Indians) of only 3 percent since 1997. The initial and significant drop in enrollment of these groups at San Diego, UCLA, Berkeley, Santa Barbara, and Davis have been, in part, offset by gains at Santa Cruz, Irvine, and Riverside—in general, less selective institutions with plans for large-scale enrollment expansion, but also with high quality and nationally ranked academic programs. The decline at the most selective institutions confirms their heavy reliance on race in admissions decisions before Proposition 209 was passed (University of California, Berkeley 1999).

The long-term outcome of the university's change in admissions policy is, thus far, inconclusive. The potential variables in projecting enrollment patterns are multiple and volatile. One study completed by the university administration predicts long-term declines in the number of African American and Latino enrollments. But this study also assumed that college-going rates (the percentage of, for example, Latino students who will meet minimal academic eligibility requirements) among these and other groups will not change significantly in the next fifteen years. A small change in these rates dramatically alters these enrollment projections and the prospective ethnic composition of the student body.

In California, the movement toward a more diverse student population at the university will continue, regardless of the fate of a vast array of programs created under the rubric of affirmative action. This is not to downplay the importance of affirmative action efforts at the university, but simply to point to one of several megatrends in which these programs operate. California is in the midst of a demographic shift of major proportions that each year produces a larger and more diverse pool of high school graduates. Over the past three decades, affirmative action programs at UC have, in effect, bolstered an inevitable and expanding flow of minority students. Between 1980 and 1995, the university's total undergraduate enrollment grew from 97,100 to 124,300 students. In that fifteen-year period, minority enrollment grew from 24 percent to 54 percent of the student population (see fig. 2). At the undergraduate level, the University of California already enrolls more "minorities" than Euro-American students (if we include Asian Americans as minorities). Despite the growing pool of Euro-Americans applying to the UC system, they make up a declining percentage of enrolled students.

FIGURE 2   University of California Euro-American and Minority Undergraduate Enrollment, 1980–1995

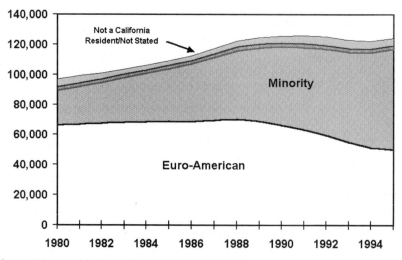

Source: University of California, Office of the President (1995).

Within this larger picture of the shift in minority and Euro-American enrollment, there are important differences in the UC eligibility rates of different groups. With the master plan target of accepting only the top 12.5 percent of California's high school graduates, eligibility is a zero-sum game in which an increase in one ethnic group is offset by a decrease in another group. The first UC eligibility study that included ethnicity was based on 1983 data. Two studies have been completed in the 1990s, one based on 1990 data and one on the 1996 public high school graduating class. Outreach programs—for example, college counseling services, tutorial programs in math and science, and summer programs on UC campuses—were developed to increase participation rates of underrepresented groups. These programs focused on African American and Latino students. Yet these studies have shown no major changes in the eligibility rate of African Americans or Latinos between 1983 and 1996 (as shown in figure 3). The number of Latino high school graduates has actually dropped since the first study was conducted (University of California Office of the President 1995). One reason is the surge of low-income immigrants from Mexico; another is the significant decline in the funding and quality of public schools—particularly in urban areas.

The net result of these varying eligibility rates is that the remarkable growth in minority enrollment has not been equally distributed

FIGURE 3   University of California Freshman Eligibility Rates for High School Graduates by Ethnicity, 1983, 1990, and 1996

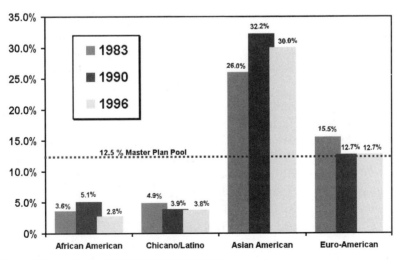

Source: California Postsecondary Education Commission.

among racial and ethnic groups. Though minority undergraduate enrollment grew from 23,000 in 1980 to just over 70,000 in 1995, most of this growth was in the number of Asian American students. In 1980, Asian Americans represented 54 percent of the university's undergraduate minority enrollment; by 1995, they represented 63 percent. Retention rates after enrollment also vary tremendously by ethnic group, with African Americans and Latinos having among the lowest graduation rates.

If the goal of the University of California is to reach parity between the ethnic composition of its total undergraduate population and that of California's high school graduates (the policy goal of the legislature's 1974 statute), there remain substantial difficulties and paradoxes. As noted, a cornerstone of affirmative action programs at UC is to increase the number of underrepresented groups (University of California Board of Regents 1984). Statistics for 1995, the year of the regents' edict on preferences, expose significant disparities among ethnic and racial groups (see fig. 3). No single group shows a strong correlation between the number of public high school graduates and UC enrollment. In 1995, Latinos remained the most underrepresented group: though they represented approximately 30 percent of the state's public high school graduates, they comprised only 14 percent of the university's undergraduate population. In raw numbers, this means that in that year a total of 20,270 additional Latino students would have needed to enroll in UC to reach parity between high school graduates and UC enrollees. This disparity is a major problem for the university, and for the state of California. In total numbers, however, Euro-Americans technically became the second largest "underrepresented" group—larger in number than African Americans (see fig. 4). In 1995, the UC system would have needed to bring in 8,292 Euro-American and 4,556 African American students to achieve UC student parity with the high school graduation class.

It is also important to note that a growing number of UC undergraduate students declined to state their racial or ethnic background. One might conjecture that Euro-Americans make up a significant portion of this category. But there may be another factor. California is also the nation's most ethnically diverse state. The simplistic categorization of ethnicity into five groups reflects a construct of federal legislation in the late 1960s that is antiquated for analyzing the demographic mix of the state and the enrollment of higher education institutions. Given the datedness of these federal categories, the dramatic rise in those who refuse to or cannot readily identify their ethnic identity (for example,

FIGURE 4   California Public High School Graduates and University of California
Undergraduate Enrollment by Ethnicity, 1995

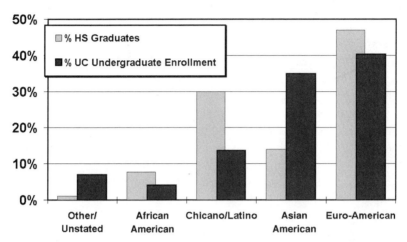

Source: Department of Education, California Basic Educational Data System; University of California,
Office of the President.

mixed-raced students) provides evidence of the restrictive way in which
the university and other public institutions have approached the issue
of race.

Here is a predicament not entirely of the university's making. Like
the debate over racial categorizations in the U.S. Census, any change
in the existing labeling of racial groups is viewed by many interest
groups as a political choice. Altering the gathering of data, including
expanding the number of racial and ethnic categories, might erode the
influence of Latino interest groups, for example, on admissions policy.
The result is that the need to expand our understanding of the great
demographic shifts in California society has thus far, and once again,
run into the cold reality of political interests.

Data on the number of high school graduates and university enrollments demonstrate the complications of setting vague policy goals in an
area as politically volatile as UC admissions policies. Many Californians
perceive UC admissions as a public resource and a determinant of socioeconomic mobility. With the drift toward the notion of underrepresented groups, and the corresponding decline in the concern for geographic and socioeconomic representation, affirmative action became
virtually the sole mechanism for achieving some form of parity. Ironically, under the parity rubric, Euro-Americans became an "underrepresented" group—at least according to the data for 1995. This is not to

argue that Euro-Americans should now become eligible for affirmative action programs. Rather, it points to the paradoxes of a simplistic approach toward diversity.

Within both the university and California society, confronting such paradoxes has proved extremely difficult. Basic questions necessary for formulating coherent policy remained unanswered even in the aftermath of the regents' wholesale rejection of race-based preferences. What does it mean to "encompass" California's population? Is the university's goal to reach parity of the undergraduate population with the ethnic composition of the general population, or only the high school graduating class? In the zero-sum game of admissions, it is impossible to reach some general form of parity (say, within 10 percent) without a significant effort to, in effect, constrain enrollment of one or more groups.

A New Era

Critics of the regents edict have stated that there is no surrogate for race and ethnicity in the admissions process. And indeed, a UC-generated simulation of the undergraduate admissions process that replaced race and ethnicity with economic class as a primary factor showed that certain groups, specifically African Americans and Latinos, would likely drop in enrollment—at least in the short run. Conversely, it was projected that Asian Americans' and Euro-Americans' enrollment would increase, with the former group making the largest gains, further solidifying their position as an "overrepresented" group. And as noted, post–Proposition 209 shifts in enrollment by race have followed this projected pattern. One reason is that race and ethnicity, along with grades and test scores, came to dominate what was once a more dynamic process of admissions. At a campus such as UCLA, which in 1995 rejected approximately 11,000 UC-eligible students, an upper-class African American with a relatively modest high school academic record and a parental income above $100,000 would be admitted because of his or her university-defined status as a "disadvantaged" student. At the same time, a lower-class Asian American of the first generation to attend college, with a stellar grade point average and high SAT scores, might be rejected under the admissions model that emerged in the 1980s. Race had become much more important that economic class.

Evidence of this pattern of decision making eroded support for affirmative action among the Board of Regents, and apparently among a majority of California voters—even though it does not tell the full story of what the university is attempting to achieve, or the fact that UC-eligible students rejected at UCLA have the option of enrolling at one of the less competitive University of California campuses. Although it is conjecture, one might argue that a better understanding of the history and purpose of the university's social contract would have resulted in a more balanced, coherent, and publicly defensible admissions process. Geographic representation and economic class could have been a more integral part of an affirmative action strategy. Not only would it have helped expand the diversity of UC's undergraduate student body; the greater integration of these historical variables into policy would also have more fully articulated the university's social contract.

As this chapter has attempted to portray, there is a logic to the adoption of race- and ethnicity-based preferences in the aftermath of the paradigm shift toward standardized tests. In a pattern reflected in other American universities and colleges, university officials perceived the sledgehammer of race as the only method for a significant effort to provide proportional representation within the context of California's rapidly changing demographic mix. It was a counterbalance to the obsession of the higher education community with a single national test intended to provide scientific evidence of scholastic aptitude. This one-size-fits-all approach to human intelligence appeared more objective than grades and would lessen the dependence on subjective criteria.

Just as the strong reliance on race was perhaps a mistake, its abandonment in the undergraduate and graduate admissions process is also imprudent. All indications are, however, that race- and gender-based preferences will decline as a formal part of policy making in public institutions. The specter of additional state propositions like those in California and Washington offer one determiner of the fate of affirmative action. The judiciary, however, specifically the Supreme Court, may provide the most sweeping declaration regarding the use of race and ethnicity in admissions decision making. What might replace this tool in the admission process?

If there is a positive aspect to the divisive debate over affirmative action, it is that the actions of the regents, the voters, and the courts have forced the higher education community to revisit the question of the purpose of the academy. Both the adoption of standardized tests and the emergence of race-based preferences marked significant shifts in defining access to higher education. One might argue that we are in the midst of another shift that could, for example, include a reappraisal of the modern addiction to standardized testing and a resurgence of traditional criteria such as geographic representation. As William Bowen and Derek Bok persuasively argue in their book *The Shape of the River*, test scores and grades "are far from infallible indicators of other qualities some might regard as intrinsic, such as a deep love of learning or a capacity for high academic achievement" (Bowen and Bok 1999, 277).

Some states, including California, have sought means other than race preferences in the admissions process to create a more representative student body. One option is to guarantee a place in the state university system for students who graduate near the top of their state high school classes (see chapter 13 in this volume). This model was used by UC in one form or another between 1880 and 1960. Given the de facto segregation that exists in the nation's schools, which creates schools that are overwhelmingly Euro-American and schools that are overwhelmingly minority, in some states this technique could bring large numbers of blacks and Latinos into the university system. The University of California is about to reinstitute such a plan, guaranteeing a spot for the top 4 percent of each state high school's graduating class. Texas has recently established a similar plan for the top 10 percent, and Florida governor Jeb Bush proposed guaranteeing admission to Florida state universities to the top 20 percent of each high school's graduates. Though these ideas are promising, concerns remain regarding the preparedness of some of these students for university instruction. The top of the class usually includes hard-working, ambitious students, but many rural and "majority-minority" schools, usually in the poorest sections of the cities and the state, cannot, thus far, simulate the rigors of university education.

The constructs of UC's admissions policy will continue to change. But what is the goal with regard to diversity? The parity model remains the formal policy of the university. Precisely because it is problematic, essentially elevating a larger societal goal over the rights of individuals, it remains a vague doctrine fully understood by neither UC officials nor the pubic. Although it is steeped in the rationale of egalitarianism, the politics of its logical conclusion is substantial: only by limiting the access of one racial group (or one economic category) can another "underrepresented" group gain increased access. This would mean systematically constraining access by "overrepresented" groups, for example, Asian American students. The irony of such a path illustrates the complexity of seeking social redress.

Such conundrums point to the need for a larger policy framework for constructing and managing the process of admissions. As competition for places has increased, the interests of specific groups have tended to drive public discourse, and the mechanics of the admission process has become the target of attention. As noted, it is a political process that can be found in other venues where public resources are allocated in an increasingly competitive environment.

References

Academic Senate, Board of Admissions and Relations with Schools. 1960. Report to the representative assembly: Minutes, October 25.

Academic Senate, University of California at Berkeley. 1989a. Freshman admissions at Berkeley: A policy for the 1990s and beyond.

———. 1989b. Report of the special committee on Asian-American admissions of the Berkeley division of the Academic Senate.

Bergmann, Barbara R. 1996. *In defense of affirmative action.* New York: Basic Books.

Bowen, William G., and Derek Bok. 1998. *The shape of the river: Long-term consequences of considering race in college and university admissions.* Princeton: Princeton University Press, 1998.

Burdman, Pamela. 1997. The long goodbye. *Lingua Franca* 7 (June–July): 28–39.

California State Legislature. 1868. An Act to Create and Organize the University of California.

Clifford, Geraldine Joncich. 1995. Equally in view: The University of California, its women, and the schools. Berkeley: Center for Studies in Higher Education/Institute for Governmental Studies.

Connerly, Ward. 1995. Press release, 5 July.

Douglass, John Aubrey. 1992. Creating a fourth branch of state government: The University of California and the constitutional convention of 1879. *History of Education Quarterly* 32:31–72.

———. 2000. *The California idea and the history of American higher education: 1855 to the 1960 master plan.* Stanford: Stanford University Press.

Dworkin, Ronald. 1998. Is affirmative action doomed? *New York Review of Books,* 5 November, 56–61.

Eastland, Terry. 1996. *Ending affirmative action: The case for colorblind justice.* New York: Basic Books.

Gates, Henry Louis, Jr. 1996.*The future of the race.* New York: Knopf.

Glazer, Nathan. 1975. *Affirmative discrimination: Ethnic inequality and public policy.* New York: Basic Books.

Gordon, Lynn. 1990. *Education and higher education in the Progressive Era.* New Haven: Yale University Press.

Hacker, Andrew. 1996. Good-bye to affirmative action? *New York Review of Books,* 11 July, 21–29.

Hollinger, David. 1995. *Post-ethnic America: Beyond multiculturalism.* New York: Basic Books.

Kinder, Donald R., and Lynn Sanders. 1996 *Divided by color: Racial politics and democratic ideals.* Chicago: University of Chicago Press.

Liaison Committee of the State Board of Education and the Regents of the University of

California. 1960. A master plan for higher education in California, 1960–1975. Sacramento: California State Department of Education.

Manzagol, Michael. 1988. Sins of admissions. *California Monthly*, April, 20–23.

Mills, Nicolaus, ed. 1994. *Debating affirmative action: Race, gender, ethnicity, and the politics of inclusion.* New York: Delta Press.

Peltason, Jack. 1995a. Memo to the UC Board of Regents (January 19). Oakland: Office of the University of California Board of Regents.

———. 1995b. Memo to the UC Board of Regents (July 20). Oakland: Office of the University of California Board of Regents.

Skrentny, John David. 1995.*The ironies of affirmative action: Politics, culture, and justice in America.* Chicago: University of Chicago Press.

Takaki, Ronald. 1993. *A different mirror: A history of multicultural America.* New York: Little, Brown.

Thernstrom, Stephen, and Abigail Thernstrom. 1997. *America in black and white: One nation, indivisible.* New York: Simon and Schuster.

University of California Board of Regents. 1968. Minutes of March 15. Oakland: Office of the University of California Board of Regents.

———. 1984. Policy on undergraduate admissions by special action. Minutes of November 16. Oakland: Office of the University of California Board of Regents.

———. 1988. Policy on undergraduate admissions. Oakland: Office of the University of California Board of Regents.

———. 1995. Minutes of July 20. Oakland: Office of the University of California Board of Regents.

University of California Office of the President. 1975. A report to the president of the University of California from the student affirmative action task groups. Oakland: University of California Office of the President.

———. 1995. Diversity: An introduction to the University of California's policies and programs. Oakland: University of California Office of the President.

———. 1999. Admissions report (fall). Student Academic Services.

University of California, Berkeley. 1999. Admissions and enrollment, University of California-Berkeley. Berkeley: Office of the Associate Vice Chancellor, Admissions and Enrollment.

University of California, Los Angeles. 1990. Report to the regents: UCLA freshman admissions in the 1990s: A decade of rapid change. Oakland: Office of the University of California Board of Regents.

PART II

AFRO-AMERICANS AND IMMIGRANTS

IN THE WORKPLACE

6

Producing Conflict: Immigration and the Management
of Diversity in the Multiethnic Metropolis

. . .

MICHAEL LICHTER AND ROGER WALDINGER

A new ethnic order is emerging in America today. This is due in
part to the civil rights revolution, but it is more directly the result
of the post-1965 emergence of mass immigration at levels not seen since
the turn of the twentieth century. Coming mainly from Latin America
and Asia, the multi-hued millions of newcomers have upset the black-
white paradigm that has long framed American thinking about race and
ethnicity. In addition to their non-European origins, the socioeconomic
diversity of today's immigrants distinguishes them from their predecessors. Still, less-educated labor migrants loom large among the new
foreign-born Americans, and immigrants who do enter at the bottom
of the labor market comprise a group of outsiders who are stigmatized
by foreign tongue, distinctive physical appearance, and, not infrequently, precarious legal status.

With the working class diversifying anew, researchers have begun
to inquire into how employers have adapted to the changing circumstances. Faced with the new immigration, employers have little choice
but to adopt a more complex picture of the world. One might imagine
finding, especially in the immigrant-dense regions of southern California, southern Florida, or New York, that Euro-Americans' apprehen-
sion over the political and demographic consequences of immigration
might lead them to revise their long-held racial antipathy for blacks.
And yet, as Kirschenman and Neckerman (1991), Neckerman and
Kirschenman (1991), Moss and Tilly (1996), and Waldinger (1997) have
shown, there is continuing prejudice against hiring African Americans,
even if the alternative involves recruiting Mexicans and Central Americans, toward whom Euro-American employers often evince considerable aversion.

The aversions and prejudices of employers are not the whole story, however. Though it may seem otherwise, managers cannot always hire just as they please. Managers in large, rule-bound, bureaucratic firms are constrained in their choices, but so too are the freewheeling owners of small businesses. Legal restrictions narrow the scope for the exercise of personal preferences, but only to a limited extent. Decisions regarding hiring and firing rarely eventuate in litigation—especially at the low end of the labor market—and nondiscrimination laws are rarely significant, especially for smaller firms (chapter 13, this volume). A more important source of constraint derives from the preferences of workers and customers, whom managers ignore at their peril; it is these parties on which this chapter focuses. We argue that hiring in America's high-immigration cities involves a process of sorting through a complex, cross-cutting set of preferences and conflicts. We observe that managers, workers, and customers typically have *preferences for* interactions with members of their own social group and *aversions against* dealing with particular sets of outsiders. We refer to these two kinds of dispositions as "own-preferences" and "other-aversions," respectively. The manager who places his or her own-preferences and other-aversions above those of the workers risks rebellion, and the manager who ignores the own-preferences and other-aversions of customers risks the loss of business.

What is potentially most vexing to the manager is the complexity of balancing preferences and aversions when attempting to employ a diverse workforce to serve an equally heterogeneous clientele. Each group of immigrants is likely to arrive with (or quickly form) a full set of own-preferences and other-aversions. In the new ethnic order, each group's hierarchy of other-aversions becomes a matter of import. Of particular concern to us are immigrants' feelings regarding contact with African Americans. Although immigrants surely bring a set of particularized hatreds and dislikes with them, history points to the advantages of adopting the Euro-American prejudice against African Americans (Roediger 1991).[1] African Americans likewise have preferences and aversions, and these are no longer as irrelevant to employers as they were earlier in the century. The greater resources of the expanded African American middle class make the tastes of African Americans less easy to ignore, while the changed ideological climate reduces the scope for open display of distaste for contact with African Americans (Feagin 1991). Notably, as acculturated Americans, African Americans are likely to have some of the same preferences and aversions as their Euro-American counterparts, especially with regard to the linguistic environment of the workplace (as discussed below).

Motivation is one thing, opportunity another. Whatever the sources of groups' own-preferences and other-aversions, it remains the case that the *potential* to act on predispositions will vary. Workers are likely to always have at least *some* leverage, but the weight of their preferences within a firm is likely to depend on specific organizational features. Organizations relying on informal, as opposed to structured and impersonal, recruitment and selection procedures have fewer mechanisms for resisting the demands of incumbent workers who act to assure that outsiders remain a quantitative minority. When the result is unbalanced ("tilted") work settings, incumbents will find it relatively easy to both express hostility and channel it toward specific out-groups (Kanter 1976). By contrast, bureaucratic recruitment and selection procedures are likely to produce work groups characterized by a higher level of ethnic diversity—a context less conducive to targeted hostility, though one in which conflict may nonetheless occur (Waldinger 1999).

Similarly, the nature of the job will affect the degree to which employers prove responsive to workers' views. Some tasks are inherently team efforts. The more social the work activity, the less success the individual worker will have in completing his or her tasks without the cooperation of others. The greater the degree to which productivity is a collective rather than an individual characteristic, the greater the dependence of the employer on the goodwill and cooperation of the workers. The need to elicit the cooperation of the dominant ethnic group in the workforce might well lead management to collaborate in the exclusion of outsiders. Note that a particular ethnic group will often have effective dominance of only a single occupation or a cluster of closely linked occupations within a firm. The group will typically have little influence over hiring for other occupations until it is able to break into them and repeat the process that gained the group its initial niche in the firm.

The characteristics, needs, and preferences of the clientele can either reinforce or cut against workers' preferences. Customer preferences do not always come into play, since customers don't always have contact with the workforce. Some contexts effectively hide the workforce from view. Restaurant or hotel kitchens make for physical invisibility, and one suspects that social distance between hotel guest and housekeeper has a similar effect. Factory workers are also likely to keep a low profile. The typical manufacturer's client will never see the factory floor, much less have an opportunity to interact with the rank-and-file employee. Thus, client preferences are likely to be influential only in those settings in which a public has direct contact with the workforce.

Even under those circumstances, own-preferences may have a strongly practical nature, as when customers need to speak with employees who can converse in their native tongue. We note that own-preferences need not take a purely invidious form. Clients may not be so much concerned with the ethnicity of any particular employee as with ensuring that their group is adequately represented. Signals from the clients become pressures on the organization, and the organization must accommodate them or accept the consequences.

Background

This chapter draws on in-depth interviews, conducted in 1993 with managers and owners in 228 establishments in Los Angeles County, including 44 restaurants, 44 printers, 40 hotels, and 39 furniture manufacturers, 25 department stores, and 36 hospitals.[2] With the exception of the restaurants, which were drawn from the Yellow Pages with an eye toward representing both chains (varying in size from 3 to 55 units) and independent operations, our sample of firms was drawn from business directories using a random selection scheme.[3] The organizations we contacted were located in a variety of areas throughout Los Angeles County, both within the central city and in more suburbanized areas. With few exceptions, our organizations were drawn from the "mainstream economy," and few immigrant-owned firms were included.

The interviews were arranged with the highest-ranking person involved in the hiring process, and they were structured by an instrument involving a mix of closed- and open-ended questions. In the beginning of the interview, we asked the respondent to identify the largest category of "entry level" jobs for which he or she hired and then focused the remainder of our discussion on those jobs and the workers who filled them. The interviews typically lasted ninety minutes but ranged from less than an hour to more than three hours. Most interviews were tape-recorded (with consent) and subsequently transcribed; for the rest, detailed notes were made of interviewees' responses. The open-ended nature of the interview produced both a conversational tone and lengthy, often highly detailed discussions of matters perceived as important by respondents. Consequently, they allow for a quasi-ethnographic investigation, in which the transcripts and detailed notes provide clues to patterns initially unanticipated by the researchers.

We presented our study to employers as an inquiry into the skills and qualities that they were seeking in entry-level workers. Our additional not-so-hidden agenda was to learn about employers' racial and ethnic attitudes and preferences. Consistent with our purpose, our interview protocol did not call for scrutiny of the ethnic preferences of incumbent workers or customers and clients, nor did it direct the interviewer to seek out evidence regarding the existence of ethnic conflict within the workplace. Nevertheless, managers touched on these subjects quite frequently, often spontaneously. Managers' comments were commonly provoked by a query about managing the region's multiethnic workforce. Most employers initially responded to this innocuous-sounding question—"Many people these days say that 'managing diversity' is the human resources challenge of the 1990s. In what way is 'managing diversity' a challenge for you?"–with a laugh or a derisive grunt, followed by either "We've always been diverse; there's no change" or "It is a *big* challenge." *Diversity* was not always understood as intended; that a number of respondents used the dubious phrase "people of diversity" or referred to "diverse people" as a category of human beings reveals that *diverse* has become both a buzzword and a euphemism for *nonwhite*. For some respondents, "We've always been diverse" means only that the firm has always had nonwhite or immigrant employees, not necessarily from heterogeneous backgrounds. Likewise, the comment that diversity is a "big challenge" may mean only that the company's managers don't speak Spanish very well.

Nonetheless, many of our respondents did manage workers from a variety of different backgrounds, and they spoke eloquently about the challenges involved. A typical example follows. Hospitals were, on average, the largest and most diverse organizations we contacted, and many of them gave us highly detailed answers. Asked about the challenge of diversity, a human resources (HR) manager from a large health maintenance organization (HMO) told us:

> As our minority [customer] population grows, we need to employ a
> diverse group of employees. Once you get into the workplace, you
> can't just have an X number of everything to make everybody
> happy. We have to work with the employee groups and have them
> understand each other's cultural differences and learn how to get
> along because there's going to be some inherent conflicts. To me,
> that's really the challenge. The real challenge is how are we going
> to get them to get along and meet the end goal of serving the
> member.

Our "managing diversity" question, as the reply above indicates, generated descriptions both of the diversity and of its correlates. The latter often entailed tension or conflict but sometimes also involved what were, from our respondents' viewpoints, more positive outcomes. The topic of tension or conflict, however, came up frequently enough that interviewers sometimes prodded the respondent if he or she did not mention any difficulties of that sort. For these reasons, answers to the "managing diversity" question constituted a major part of the data analyzed for this chapter. Still, there were a number of other items in the questionnaire—especially those asking for intergroup comparisons on "work ethic" and other characteristics—that also elicited responses highlighting employee and customer preferences.

The fact that our information comes from managers and not from workers or customers has important implications. It means that we only know about conflicts, tensions, and preferences of which the manager was aware, filtered through the manager's ability to comprehend the feelings and motivations of others. In addition, since we did not uniformly ask respondents about customer or worker preferences and conflicts as such, where we did learn about customer or worker preferences, it was invariably a matter of *revealed* preferences, typically presenting themselves in conflictual form. This means that the picture we are able to paint is inevitably partial and skewed toward the negative.

Another source of bias in the information we received has to do with the interests of the firms that were the subjects of our investigation. There are many reasons to expect organizations to seek to quell both incidents of and reports of conflict within their workforce. Many of the organizations that we visited claimed to have a "zero tolerance" policy as regards ethnic conflict. This meant being on constant lookout for problems and maintaining a readiness to intervene. Some managers simply laid down the law to sparring workers—"You're required to get along or you can't stay here," as one printer put it. Other managers took a more nuanced approach. For example, one retailer reported first making an effort to "find out what's causing the friction" and then taking action, "even if it means having to move somebody to another area" or "even if it means we have to terminate somebody" in extreme cases. Moreover, conflict management and reduction was often part of our respondents' job descriptions, especially those of the human resource managers with whom we were particularly likely to speak in hotels, department stores, and hospitals. Consequently, respondents who told us that "we have no conflicts" were telling us that they were doing a good job, while respondents from the more bureaucratic organizations were framing conflict in ways that reflected HR ideology: "there are inevitably culture clashes," but "it all works out though. There are difficulties understanding each other, but no real conflicts." Since conflict was thus inconsistent with the prevailing managerial ideology, and reports of conflict could in some ways be read as indicators of failure, respondents were probably biased to minimize, rather than maximize, the revealed degree of tension among the workers.

Keeping these limitations in mind, we searched our interview transcripts for passages pertaining to ethnic conflict or preferences among *nonsupervisory workers* and between the latter group and customers. These passages were coded as representing either "conflict" or "preference." Initially, we coded based on a "human" reading of all documents. We also made use of the QSR NUD*IST computer program for qualitative data analysis to locate other instances of conflict using keywords—such as *conflict, hate,* or *fight*—generated from our first pass. In our coding, "conflict" and "preference" both entailed some form of overt expression. Among the results of this effort was the identification of 89 instances of ethnic conflict (see table 1). This does not mean that exactly 89 of 208 firms we contacted (41 percent) experienced ethnic conflict;[4] our interpretation is simply that many of the firms hiring less-skilled workers have experienced some level of ethnic conflict. We want to emphasize that the few numbers we present are intended to be understood only in this very general way.

Finally, given the diversity of the workforce—no less impressive in our eyes than in those of our respondents—it was inevitable that our interviews illuminate all sorts of conflicts above and beyond those involved in ethnic tensions. In light of space constraints, we simply note that gender, sexual preference, and occupational privileges were among the issues around which groups contended, and move on.

TABLE 1

Instances of Conflictual Intergroup Relations Reported by Managers

	Black vs. Latino	Intra-Latino	Asians vs. Others	Multi-group	Total
Department stores	1	1	3	11	16
Furniture factories	12	8	1	5	26
Hospitals	2	2	4	10	18
Hotels	4	7	1	3	15
Printers	0	2	0	2	4
Restaurants	3	5	1	1	10
Total	22	25	10	32	89

Source: Authors' tabulation from Skills Survey interviews.

Note: Instances coded as described above.

Workers' Preferences and Workplace Conflict

Since so much of the recent literature on economic aspects of ethnicity emphasizes the positive role of social networks, it tends to either downplay or miss the processes that give rise to ethnic conflicts at work. By their very nature, ethnic networks tend to sort groups into different places in the labor market, evidence of which frequently appeared in our research. To the extent that such networks create segregated *ethnic niches*, they also diminish the likelihood of intergroup conflict. This effect was noted by a fast food manager who, when asked about the consequences of diversity, replied: "In my store, there's no problem. We're all Latinos." The silent exclusion produced through network recruitment is always less than perfect, however; especially when the job has appealing features or when work is scarce, others will try to break in. Furthermore, organizations may actively seek to diversify the workforce. As groups consolidate their ethnic niches, however, they come to regard jobs in their specialization as *property*. The presence of outsiders constitutes a potential challenge to a group's "ownership" of jobs, leading to some of the conflictual outcomes we describe below.

The intergroup tensions highlighted by our data could have arisen from any number of sources. Managers often invoked clashing customs and language or cultural differences for the conflicts that they experienced: "There will always be throwbacks from an age when people believed that they didn't have to work with any other type of employee or any culture or any other language, etc." Sometimes this kind of conflict was neutral in the sense that strife resulted from misunderstanding of a more or less innocent sort; at other times, the causes of conflict were less benign. Often, as suggested by the manager quoted below, the factors making for tension were mixed:

> Semantics is a big problem. Just customs and how people treat each other. I've got people from Thailand, from the Philippines, from Mexico, from, you know, all over, and we've had some very difficult times. How they respect authority, how they don't respect authority, how they respect women, how they don't respect women. [There is] difficulty with being a woman in management when you get some of this going on. And it's enough being in the United States and having people with prejudices against other people. But then I get somebody from Thailand who's prejudiced against someone from the Philippines and I have no idea what's going on there. So [it is difficult] constantly being a mediator for some of those kinds of things.

In other cases, hostilities that were manifest in the workplace reflected antagonisms that developed outside, as when gang loyalties were brought onto the shop floor. Outside events also added to the brew. For example, the multiethnic violence in 1992 following acquittal of the police officers who had beaten African American Rodney King made for work environments where "you could cut the atmosphere with a knife, it was so tense." We also detected hostility rooted in a sense of group position, most evident when groups were trying to exclude others. These were the types of tensions that managers highlighted when they talked—as they often did—about members of two groups "hating" each other.

Although our respondents did not indicate that workplace conflict was pervasive, there did appear to be plenty of it. What was impressive to us and bewildering to managers was the range of groups involved: Mexicans against Puerto Ricans, Filipinos against blacks, Armenians versus Hispanics, Belizeans pitted against Bangladeshis—just about any pairing bore a potential for conflict to the managers with whom we spoke. Though not much meaning should be read into the counts in table 1, our tabulation does indicate that a wide range of conflicts are possible and do occur under some circumstances. Indications are that the number of conflicts increased with the number of groups in the mix, so that navigating a multiethnic workplace was a difficult task for workers and managers alike. All sorts of unknowns and anxieties had the potential for stirring up trouble, meaning that, as one manager said to his workers, open bigotry against *anyone* was a bad idea: "We tell employees that's the workplace now. It isn't all, you know, white Americans, and, you know, it's very different. We have to be careful of the kind of jokes we tell, and how we conduct ourselves, and how we, you know, if we talk about 'the crazy people in the Middle East' and that, you know, and here's an Iranian sitting there. It causes problems."

Black-Latino Conflict

Many people have written about competition between immigrant Latinos and native-born blacks, often assuming that because many blacks lack a college education, and because the same is true of most Latino immigrants, that they must be vying for the same jobs. This ignores the fact that blacks are native English speakers, and even the least educated among them are usually better educated than the average Latino immigrant. These differences, as well as the network processes that we have just described, tend to separate blacks and Latinos and thus reduce the potential for conflict. Nonetheless, there is still plenty of contact, especially in larger organizations, such as hospitals or department stores, that hire on a large scale and therefore rely on bureaucratic recruitment and selection mechanisms. And even the smaller organizations, which are more apt to hire from among referrals made by the existing workforce, will also hire walks-ins or advertise in the newspaper, thereby opening the door for boundary crossing.

There is far more black-Latino contact than there is black-Latino conflict. Although twenty-one of the respondents reporting ethnic conflict made note of tension between African Americans and Latinos, this kind of intergroup tension does not appear in all industries. A variety of groups are at odds in department stores and hospitals, but in those contexts conflicts of blacks against Latinos seem rare. Rather, the locus of conflict is in furniture manufacturing, an industry with many plants in and around the once black, now increasingly Latino, South Central Los Angeles ghetto. This is also an industry where firm size is relatively small and managerial styles tend toward the paternalistic.

None of our interviews suggest that either group is overwhelmed with love for the other. A respondent in a large nonprofit hospital on Los Angeles's West Side told us, "We have Latino and black conflict. The blacks say that the Latinos have a chip on their shoulder. Latinos say that the black supervisors take sides." A restaurant manager reported, "Blacks and whites think they are better than the Latinos because they speak English." A furniture manufacturer indicated that "blacks aren't happy that there are so many Latinos." Latinos and African Americans sometimes entered the workplace with antagonisms that threatened to spill over onto the shop floor. Said a furniture manufacturer: "Some of our younger employees were probably gang members before they came to work, and so we really discourage graffiti inside of the plant and the Hispanics outnumber the blacks and we let them know that if they do it in the property they will be given their checks and be fired."

Any preexisting rivalries were likely to be exacerbated by other differences among the groups. Language is one tension-producing factor: "It's difficult to have a half-Hispanic, half-black housekeeping department because the Hispanic employees generally speak Spanish to each other and the black employees don't understand it. And because the work ethic and job performance [of the Hispanics] outshine [the blacks] it creates animosity between them." As the quotation suggests, and as we have argued elsewhere (Waldinger 1997; Lichter 1999), it is entirely possible that blacks and Hispanics have different expectations about what constitutes a reasonable day's work, in which case the willingness of Hispanics to put in more work than blacks could raise employers' expectations, making black workers understandably upset.

A factor precipitating conflict in the furniture industry may have been that African American workers there tended to find themselves a small minority working alongside a large and growing population of Latino immigrants, expanding primarily through reliance on network recruitment. In these situations, as suggested above, the simple fact of being a minority made African Americans more vulnerable to the views and actions of the numerically dominant Latino workforce. When asked why "the people that are not Hispanic don't last very long," a furniture manufacturer explained, "We have hired a few blacks and they quit on their own. They don't want to be a minority." A black manager who oversaw operations for a company providing janitorial services to hospitals described an instance in which outsourcing prompted the replacement of African American workers by Latinos, further underscoring the difficulties associated with the ethnically tilted situation:

> I see it in hospitals, like in one hospital we have, you see, the
> blacks on one side of the room, the Hispanics are on the other side of
> the room, at one of these general meetings. And you can hear it in
> some of the questions that come up, and some of the answers that
> come up, the representation from the unions. There's a certain
> amount of animosity because the union representative is speaking in
> Spanish. So it comes up, there's an attitudinal thing. I think the blacks
> feel probably threatened because there's so many Hispanics here.

Not only were African Americans likely to be a small minority in these Latino-dominated contexts, but the nature of the work made them highly dependent on their Latino co-workers. Almost all of our respondents rated "ability to work successfully with co-workers" as a key skill expected of any applicant. But interethnic conflict often threatened that cooperation, putting African American workers at risk, precisely because of their status as *numerical* minorities. Cooperation was particularly important in furniture manufacturing, since jobs there are highly interdependent and new workers learn from experienced hands. These conditions made conflict more common than in any of the other industries, shaping the job opportunities available to African American workers, as a furniture manufacturer with a lifetime of experience helpfully explained:

> The shop has always been 98 percent Latino. I have hired some
> blacks. You put two men on a machine, the Mexicans won't work

with a black. They aggravate him 'til he quits. You can't make it inter-racially. I'm not going to be a sociologist and tell them "you're in the same boat, ought to work together." The only place where we have blacks is in the trucks, because they work by themselves. [Though] blacks have been much less stable, that's in the plant. Among the drivers, they've been very good.

Conflict among Latino Immigrant Groups

For the most part, we interviewed a Euro-American population for whom awareness of diversity among Latinos—let alone intra-Latino conflict—was a novel acquisition. A hotel manager told us, "To me, an Anglo, they're all Hispanic. We tend to see them as all alike." Experience, however, taught this manager, and his colleagues, another lesson: "I know that Mexicans don't like Salvadorans."

Indeed, both the intensity of the intra-Latino conflicts and the plethora of ethnic subgroups engulfed by tension often surprised managers. Regional antagonisms transported from the home country threatened to reemerge in southern California: One of our furniture manufacturers, referring to three Mexican states, noted that "you have everybody from the Puebla area or Zacatecas area or something like that and what occurs is that they don't talk to people from Jalisco." Conflicts among nationalities cropped up along with subnational dislikes, as noted by a man who had only recently moved to California: "The thing that surprised me was the prejudices that did exist between the various Hispanic groups. You have the Mexicans from Chihuahua over here and the Mexicans from Guerrero and then the Colombians. They are very cliquish and nationalistic. There has been conflict, because of the nationalities, and among the Mexicans, the particular state. It's not just blacks. That was a surprise to me."

"Not just blacks" was a common refrain, echoed by a hotelier who told us, "I've noticed that more Spanish people will fight among themselves than [with] black people." Despite public and scholarly preoccupation with black-Latino conflict, we heard more frequent reports of intra-Latino conflict. These reports are the all more credible because they were often accompanied by positive assessments of the immigrants' performance, as with a factory manager who thought that Latino immigrants "have fairly decent work ethic" but then told us, "One of my biggest bitches is intragroup conflict." The frequency of these reports may reflect the high levels of Latino representation in both our sample and Los Angeles's workforce and thus imply a lower level of conflict, relatively speaking, than in the case of Latinos and African Americans. Nonetheless, we were impressed by the intensity of the intra-Latino conflicts that management reported. As one hotel manager told us: "The biggest diversity problem is within Hispanic countries. . . . Fights in garage because of insults, Central American and Mexican conflict. There is outward nontolerance. That's where it is. Call each other names. Set each other up. More diversity problems between Hispanic workforce than cross-culturally." As the managers saw it, the widespread and intense antipathy among Latino groups often had to do with imported own-preferences. In general, people prefer to work alongside people like themselves; for Latino immigrants, people from other Latin American countries are *not* like themselves.

Such own-preferences were frequently accompanied by other-aversions. Indeed, some managers suggested that the antipathies expressed in the workplace stemmed from deep-seated rivalries between countries that the immigrants brought with them to the United States, rather than from developments on the job:

> Within their own subcultures, Mexicans think that Salvadorans are quote unquote below them or visa-versa. We have had employee problems with employees from one group or another. We've had employee fights . . . we find out that the Salvadorans want to work together on the same floor, or the Hondurans. If we have pairs they prefer the two women together to be from the same background. . . . We accommodate them but we also want them to learn to work with other people. . . . We have terminated employees for constantly bickering among themselves and it's not work-related. They curse each other: "Hey, you slob! You come from El Salvador."

On the other hand, most of the reports of intra-Latino conflict highlighted the tension deriving from job competition among Latino groups, particularly between Mexicans and Salvadorans. As we noted earlier, once a group establishes a niche in an occupation or industry, it may come to see the relevant jobs as a sort of group property. Promoting hiring through networks helps maintain the niche. But in occupations where there is rapid turnover or where more formal hiring methods predominate, maintaining the niche may require other measures. The isolation of black workers, as described above, is one of the techniques for maintaining control over a niche. The task is not very hard, both because employers often share worker prejudices against black workers and because black workers have difficulty functioning in a predominantly Spanish-speaking environment. Furthermore, African Americans are unable to expand or maintain their footholds as well as immigrants can, because they have smaller families and their personal networks, as far as we can tell, are not as large or as strong as those forged by immigrants in the migration process. By contrast, because Central American workers are more difficult to exclude through informal means and can naturally cope in a monolingual Spanish environment, they are likely to work alongside Mexicans, with contact thus creating the potential for conflict.

Conflict between Whites and Others

As whites have moved up occupationally and out residentially, they have become relatively scarce in the kinds of entry-level jobs that we studied. Furthermore, most of the whites in these jobs were women—sales clerks in department stores, clerical workers of various types in hospitals, wait staff in restaurants. Although one is reluctant to accept stereotyped views that suggest that women are less likely to express conflict overtly than are men, our interviews were certainly consistent with this belief. Factory owners and managers, for example, highlighted conflict among African American and Latino men working on the shop floor but were also quite likely to report, "I've had in the office a couple of black employees at various times, usually a couple of girls in the office who are black," with whom there had apparently been no problem. (Of course, native-born African American women doing office work were less likely to have immigrant competition than their male fellows on the production floor.)

Where white workers do come into contact with minority workers, tensions are more likely to take a racialized form than they do in conflicts between native minorities and immigrants, regardless of the initial source of strife. When members of historically dominant groups come into conflict with those from historically subordinate groups, traditional understandings (and misunderstandings) provide a framework for comprehending the friction. In department stores, for instance, where it was not uncommon for Euro-Americans to be supervising minority workers, managers complained that their sales "associates" were quick to see criticism as a display of racism. As one experienced department store manager lamented, "When we coach an associate who is of an ethnic background, and myself of course being Caucasian, there is that underlying tone in the associate's voice that we're discriminating."

We would expect to see the highest levels of conflict between whites and others in environments where they hold the same or similar jobs. The best example of this kind of contact in our survey was in the hospital industry. In hospitals, whites usually predominate in professional and especially in managerial posts, holding few menial jobs. Blacks, however, are well represented in Los Angeles hospitals at most occupational levels, especially in the public sector. This means considerable contact between blacks and Euro-Americans in similar positions, and a higher than average incidence of African Americans overseeing Euro-Americans. The managers we interviewed, however, did not report much conflict arising out of this contact. The lack of data is probably more a result of our focus on entry-level jobs than an indication of cozy relations between white and black workers in local hospitals.

Customers: Own-Preferences and Other-Aversions

For many of the organizations providing services or goods in multiethnic Los Angeles, the reality is one of a workforce far less diverse than the clientele. The region's new demographics are largely irrelevant to manufacturers and impinge only mildly on the restaurants, which mainly service a neighborhood clientele and maintain kitchens that are largely hidden. The same is true of the hotels, where the immigrant workforce is concentrated in positions with limited guest contact. But retailers and hospitals are in constant contact with the new ethnic mix of Los Angeles, and the own-preferences of the region's new inhabitants lead organizations in these industries to attempt to change their workforce to mirror their customer base.

Both retail establishments and hospitals sought to serve a diverse clientele, and that imperative pushed them toward outreach while also breeding an aversion to reliance on hiring through workers' contacts. "Diversity is in our customer [base] and we want to bring it in to our workforce," explained a department store manager. A unit of one of the region's most important HMOs saw diversity "as a reality based, from the personnel standpoint, on our applicant pool, [and] from a business standpoint, [on] our membership. You want to have a workforce that's representative and can respond to the needs of our members." A department store manager told us that clientele and employees "parallel each other steadily. You need to truly understand that you have a melting pot in your workforce and you have to look at your workforce and clientele objectively as a marketing group." And for these reasons, employees should "reflect the cultural diversity of your clientele. If I could hire

10 percent black, 10 percent Filipino, 8 percent white, 7 percent Hispanic, and really get it in line with what's really going on, as far as how people live in this area . . . what more could you ask for?"

Although the clientele can vary—yielding, in one case, a workforce that is "white, because it matches the demographics of the area"—the quest "to match our store to the people who come to the store" motivates managers to "try hard to have Spanish speaking people, and the Middle Eastern language group (Iranians, Afghans, Armenians)." Similar factors shaped personnel policies among the hospitals.

But one should not think that hospitals or department stores had been bitten by the multicultural bug. Although many managers sounded like the diversity consultants described in chapter 4, most claimed to be simply listening to the marketplace, which told them that sensitivity to ethnic matters counted and that they should respond in appropriate ways. Customers "don't just notice the merchandise," explained a manager at an old-line department store, "they look at the people who are working there." Consequently, both retailers and hospitals were likely to have concluded, "The employee base has to reflect the customer base."

We found that the goal of satisfying the own-preferences of Los Angeles's multiethnic consumer market made ethnicity-conscious hiring desirable in a more general way than that described in chapter 7. One manager reported following these informal guidelines: "When [we] are out hiring folks . . . [we] consciously make sure that we have a wide variety of people working at the store, so many Blacks, so many Hispanics, and that seems to help business a lot." Customers pay attention to the composition of the people trying to service their needs and are willing to complain when not happy about the faces they see. A top-of-the-line department store in the South Bay received "letters from African American customers asking, where are the African American employees?" The firm is "now training to focus on an African American base." Noting that "the biggest challenge I have is getting the right candidate into the store," a manager underlined the impact of customers' ethnic preferences: "I have customers in Huntington Beach who do not want someone who is Korean and Vietnamese waiting on them . . . conversely I have a customer in West Covina who is East Asian or Hispanic and sometimes they are extremely uncomfortable in being waited on by someone who is Caucasian." Considerations such as these led stores not only to recruit from a diverse pool but also to engage in monitoring practices that would ensure adequate representation of the different components of the customer base. "I like to have a balanced workforce," explained a department store manager. "It's always on our mind."

Language—Symbolic and Practical Locus of Conflict

Whether resulting from passive adaptation to the environment or from the deliberate recruitment efforts described above, the advent of a large foreign-born labor force in Los Angeles introduced foreign languages into the workplace. In such immigrant-dense industries as hospitality and furniture manufacturing, reliance on network recruitment has produced a monolingual work world in which Spanish, not English, is the lingua franca. This development impedes access to anyone who doesn't speak Spanish—a group including most whites, Asians, and, most important, blacks.

Department stores and hospitals recruited more bureaucratically than did hotels and furniture manufacturers. By reducing the hold maintained by the social networks of employees while also seeking diversity in its own right, as noted above, they secured a more diverse workforce. But the infiltration of an ethnically mixed group also transformed many of these organizations into towers of Babel, where linguistic differences highlighted boundaries and reminded workers and customers of both own-preferences and other-aversions.

Consequently, public use of "foreign" tongues served as a catalyst for customer and worker conflict, yielding pressures to suppress linguistic differences and exclude certain workers. Though department stores tried to accommodate the linguistic needs of their immigrant workforce, managers also insisted, "We need them to speak English. We have a very diverse ethnic population in our company and in the stores." Clearly, the mix of languages among workers and customers was a source of tension, one that many managers wanted to alleviate. "We have customers complaining [using a whining voice] that '[the workers] can't speak English and [yet] they live in California.'" Similarly, our hospital respondents reported that English-speaking patients and visitors evince "a lot of dissatisfaction with people who speak another language" on the job.

Use of unfamiliar languages arouses unhappiness for a variety of reasons, some of which are purely practical in nature. In a hospital environment, for example, "Patients . . . will ask you things, and . . . if you don't understand them, you know, they get very apprehensive and they get upset." When immigrant salespeople or service providers speak

Spanish, Farsi, or Tagalog, adverse reactions arise for reasons that have nothing to do with foreigners or foreignness as such. For example, there is "the American customer who . . . hears associates speaking in another language and gets offended, thinking they're talking or laughing about them."

But customer dissatisfaction is also related to own-preferences and other-aversions, and not just among Anglos. "The Baldwin Hills store is definitely an African-American population," noted a regional personnel manager. "From a language standpoint, there have been situations when I've had to tell workers to speak English on the floor." Moreover, the adverse reaction goes beyond an allergy to Spanish. One manager fretted about customer complaints she had received about "the downtown stores, [where] the Filipino workers would speak to each other in Tagalog," while another described "the Middle Eastern, who is intent upon using their native language instead of English." As an overt indicator of change, language crystallizes resentment and anxiety: "The Filipino workers that work here are, I would consider them rude, because they get in a group, and they speak their language, and no one else around can understand. And I've heard that throughout the hospital. They just find that to be rude. They're saying it's just part of their culture."

Conclusion

The multiethnic workplace of early twenty-first-century Los Angeles is a conflicted but far from Hobbesian world. We have put the spotlight on interethnic tensions at work, but we need to remind the reader that only one-third of the 230 firms we visited made mention of ethnic conflicts or reported preferences on the part of customers and workers. It is not entirely clear whether this indicates that the level of conflict is high, low, or where one would expect it to be. Immigration, the fundamental transforming factor, is a network-driven process, and the prominent role played by ethnic networks in the labor market makes for ethnic separation, not generally considered an optimal outcome. High levels of interethnic conflict cause firms to be dysfunctional, which is why many of the organizations we contacted try hard to keep peace, defusing conflict whenever possible and removing the troublemakers when necessary.

Contact is usually thought preferable to separation, but it is also what makes for conflict. The conditions under which contact occurs vary in ways that structure and crystallize the intergroup tensions that we have reviewed. One axis of variation involves the nature of the recruitment process. Some of the industries we studied—most notably furniture, restaurants, and hotels—rely heavily on network recruitment, yielding an ethnically tilted situation in which one group predominates heavily. Outsiders inevitably leak in, but they find themselves highly vulnerable to the views and actions of the numerically dominant group. Moreover, the latter are relatively free to act on their preferences whenever interdependency within the workplace is high, and management has few incentives to resist. These situations impinge with particular force on African Americans, who often comprise a small proportion of the workforce, lack the community resources of immigrant groups, and are frequently disliked by employers as well.

The conditions of conflict are quite different in larger organizations that connect with a mass public. In this case, both bureaucracy *and* the market promote diversity, with a multiethnic clientele seeking familiar-looking faces and familiar-sounding voices among those who serve them. As we've noted, own-preferences in the service interaction yield exclusionary effects along with integrating impacts, though we put the emphasis on the latter.

Where bureaucratic mechanisms of recruitment and selection prevail—as in hospitals and department stores—they also weaken the grip of network-based processes of social reproduction, increasing the degree of ethnic heterogeneity. Under these circumstances, tilted groups of the type found in restaurant kitchens or furniture factories appear less often. Ethnic majorities are therefore less common, and where found are not so dominant numerically. Sales workers are less interdependent than workers in manufacturing, which means that they are less exposed to the views, and possible coercive actions, of their colleagues. Lower-level hospital employees work more closely together, but since they are also dependent on higher-level workers, themselves often of different ethnic origins, they have less leverage to act on their own group's preferences and aversions. Thus, whereas a high level of ethnic diversity in the workplace sets the stage for conflict, it can also diffuse the tension by forestalling the emergence of a clear target.

Before concluding, we must note that our chapter looks at the face of ethnic conflict at the very bottom of the economy, and for that reason probably understates the level and intensity of intergroup tensions in American workplaces as a whole. After all, our study focused on the least skilled jobs, which as our respondents reminded us, "nobody wants." At this level, ethnic succession and network-based processes of ethnic segregation are two forces keeping insider and outsider groups apart. The situation is likely to be different higher up the occupational hierarchy, where there seems to be a perpetual scarcity of "good jobs" and an oversupply of workers looking for them. When jobs are both scarce and *good*, the incentives are much stronger for insiders to hold on to what they have and for outsiders to do everything they can to break in. As newcomers acclimate to American conditions and gain skills and experience, and as their native-born children enter the workforce, the good jobs will find more and more claimants. For that reason, all is not likely to be quiet on the multiethnic labor front.

Notes

1. To be sure, joining that bandwagon may be harder today than it was earlier in the century, when the "swarthy" immigrants from southern and eastern Europe succeeded in making themselves "white."

2. Three-fourths of the interviews took place between July 1, 1993, and September 30, 1993. The remainder were spread out over a period stretching from December 1992 to March 1994. All respondents were counted only once, even if they were owners or managers of multi-unit operations. Three of the hospital interviews involved persons not directly employed by hospitals; these were with the vice president of a company supplying contract housekeeping services to hospitals, an official in a large public sector hospital workers' union, and two personnel officials in a local government department responsible for general healthcare services.

3. Our list of acute care medical hospitals in Los Angeles County was taken primarily from a local street guide, supplemented by a regional business directory.

4. Note that if there were multiple reports of conflict for a single firm each would be counted separately, so the number of firms represented here is probably a bit smaller than 89.

References

Feagin, Joe. 1991. The continuing significance of race. *American Sociological Review* 56:101–6.

Kanter, Rosabeth Moss. 1976. *Men and women of the corporation.* New York: Basic Books.

Kirschenman, Joleen, and Kathryn Neckerman. 1991. "We'd love to hire them, but . . .": The meaning of race for employers. In *The urban underclass,* edited by Christopher Jencks and Paul Peterson. Washington, D.C.: Brookings Institution.

Lichter, Michael. 1999. "Black/immigrant labor market competition: New insights from a case study of the hospital industry in Los Angeles county." Working Paper 30. Lewis Center for Regional Policy Studies, University of California, Los Angeles.

Lieberson, Stanley. 1980. *A piece of the pie: Blacks and white immigrants since 1880.* Berkeley: University of California Press.

Moss, Philip, and Chris Tilly. 1996. "'Soft' skills and race: An investigation of black men's employment problems." *Work and Occupations* 23:252–76.

Neckerman, Kathryn, and Joleen Kirschenman. 1991. "Hiring strategies, racial bias, and inner city workers." *Social Problems* 38:433–37.

Roediger, David. 1991. *The wages of whiteness: Race and the making of the American working class.* New York: Verso.

Waldinger, Roger. 1997. Black/immigrant competition re-assessed: New evidence from Los Angeles. *Sociological Perspectives* 40:365–86.

―――. 1999. Network, bureaucracy, and exclusion: Recruitment and selection in an immigrant metropolis. In *Immigration and opportunity: Race, ethnicity, and employment in the United States,* edited by Frank Bean and Stephanie Bell-Rose. New York: Russell Sage Foundation.

7

The Racial and Ethnic Meaning behind *Black:*
Retailers' Hiring Practices in Inner-City Neighborhoods

. . .

J ENNIFER L EE

How does race affect hiring in today's inner-city neighborhoods? If we look at retail businesses, we find that it matters in surprising ways. On one hand, old-styled discrimination against black Americans is alive and well. Some small business owners avoid hiring African Americans because they believe they do not work hard and complain about the long hours and low wages in most retail jobs. On the other hand, race can also work in favor of blacks.[1] Though technically illegal to do so, employers use race as a type of "bona fide occupational qualification" (BFOQ). This is the term used in Title VII of the Civil Rights Act of 1964, which legally exempted some, but not all, types of difference-conscious hiring.

Inner-city retailers prefer hiring blacks for reasons that have nothing to do with Title VII or government pressure for affirmative action.[2] Small business owners prefer hiring blacks because of their perceived utility as "cultural brokers" in dealing with a predominately black clientele. Blackness, however, carries both ethnic and racial meanings, and native-born blacks may find black immigrants being chosen ahead of them. The overinclusiveness of the racial preferences practiced by these retailers parallels the ways affirmative programs may reach beyond their original beneficiaries, as described in chapters 2 and 3, to include minority immigrants.

Research Design and Methods

This paper is based on my research on Jewish, Korean, and black merchants in New York City and Philadelphia. Between March 1996 and May 1997 I conducted in-depth interviews of fifteen merchants in each of five research sites, totaling seventy-five merchant interviews. Although most of the businesses had fewer than fifteen employees, a few had as many as forty. I inquired about the merchants' hiring practices in their stores, why they hired members of certain groups, and whether they favored some groups over others. I also did a great deal of nonparticipant observation in these stores, since I visited each store at least twice. In addition, I benefited from participant observation while working as a bag checker in a store on 125th Street in West Harlem and as a cashier in a store on 52d Street in West Philadelphia. These positions were invaluable to my research since I was able to observe the daily activities of the merchants and their interactions with customers.

The neighborhoods in New York City are East Harlem, West Harlem, and Jamaica, Queens. In Philadelphia, the neighborhoods include West Philadelphia and East Mount Airy. Each of these neighborhoods has major commercial strips lined with a variety of small retail businesses, and since each site is easily accessible by public transportation, the avenues are well traveled. In these neighborhoods, the customers are primarily black, and the merchants are a mixed lot: Jews, Koreans, Arabs, Asian Indians, Latinos, African Americans, West Indians, and Africans.

New York City and Philadelphia provide a useful comparison because both are large eastern cities, and even though New York is significantly larger than Philadelphia, these cities are similar on a number of key dimensions such as the self-employment rate, the proportion of service-sector employment, the rate of unemployment, and the percentage living below the poverty line (Carpenter 1992). But the one key dimension on which these two cities differ remarkably is the rate of immigration. New York City has one of the highest percentages of foreign-born residents in the country; in 1990, 28.4 percent of its residents were foreign-born. By contrast, Philadelphia ranked thirty-seventh in the United States for foreign-born residents, having only 6.6 percent of its residents born outside the country (U.S. Department of Commerce 1991). In this context, my research design allows for a comparative analysis of Jewish, Korean, and black entrepreneurs and their effect on the employment opportunity structure for African Americans in inner cities.

The Resentments of Race and Class

Merchants in poor black neighborhoods must sometimes deal with the resentments of race and class that are present in low-income black communities such as Harlem or West Philadelphia. Seemingly trivial arguments—for instance, over exchanges without receipts or exchanges of used or damaged merchandise—can quickly become racially charged when the merchants are Korean, Jewish, or for that matter, members of any nonblack racial group. In this tricky area of merchant-customer conflict, Robert K. Merton's concept of "in-group virtues" and "out-group vices" is particularly useful. Merton (1968) demonstrates that similar patterns of behavior by in-group and out-group members are differently perceived and evaluated. Throughout my nonparticipant observation, I examined the extent to which Jewish, Korean, and black store owners behave differently toward their black customers and the extent to which similar patterns of behavior are defined and differently perceived by their customers.

For example, a Haitian manager of a large inner-city chain sportswear store in East Harlem explained to me why the owners of this store, who happen to be Jewish, always have black store managers instead of white managers. He illustrated the following scenario: if a customer comes in and wants to return a pair of sneakers that he bought, and for some reason the black manager does not take them back, then the customer might get upset, but then that is the end of it. But if the store owner is white and does not take the sneakers back, then the customer could immediately assume that it is because he is white that he will not take the sneakers back. And similarly, if the store owner is Korean and he refuses, the customer could assume that it is because he is Korean.

Hence, the same behavior by black, Jewish, and Korean store owners can be differently perceived and evaluated by the black customer because he sees the Jewish and Korean merchants as part of the out-group, or as outsiders, and the black merchant as the in-group, or as an insider.[3] As Merton explains, "the very same behavior undergoes a complete change of evaluation in its transition from the in-group [black merchants] to the out-group [Jewish and Korean merchants]" (1968, 482). Therefore, what is not a racial argument can begin to take on a racial tone or become racially coded when the store owner is racially distinct from the customer. Likewise, a Puerto Rican employee of a Jewish-owned electronic store in West Harlem observed that "it only comes up when you don't give them proper service or they think they're getting ripped off. . . . If someone wants to bring something back after four or five months because it doesn't work anymore and they don't have their receipt, we don't replace it. Then they'll say something stupid, something racial." Recalling a former black employee at the same store, he explained how customers didn't "say anything racial to him because he was black. They [black customers] tend to separate us. It's harder for us to calm down someone who [is not] of the same race or color."

Similarly, a Jewish merchant in a furniture store in East Harlem complained of racialization of issues when he brings delinquent customers to whom he has extended credit to court: "They say to me, 'You're doing this because I'm black.' And I say to them, 'I don't care if you're yellow, white, green, purple or whatever. I'm taking you to court because you haven't paid your bill.' " Even long-time Jewish store owners admitted to being the recipients of racial and ethnic slurs by angry customers, including "damn whitey," "Jew bastard," "cheap Jew," or "We can Jew him down." They claimed that regardless of how long they have been in the community, customers sometimes make sly remarks about their race, ethnicity, or religion when they are dissatisfied with the store's policies, as a second-generation Jewish store owner on Jamaica Avenue admitted: "I've had incidences in the past where I've heard some racial mumblings coming from their ignorant breaths, but I live with it. Like a black guy says, 'You white mother fucker,' or something like that, but I don't let it bother me."

As racially distinct newcomers who are not part of the dominant white hierarchy, Korean merchants are most vulnerable to racial and ethnic taunts by angry customers. For example, a furniture store owner in West Philadelphia explained that when customers become very angry over an economic dispute, "the argument always does come down to race." Accusations that Asians—and Koreans specifically—are taking over black business communities are not uncommon in low-income communities when merchants and customers disagree over exchanges of merchandise or refunds. When the Korean store owner refused to take back the floor display furniture model that he had recently sold to a woman at a discount, she immediately muttered to her mother, "He's just a chink and a gook." Incensed by the racial insult, the merchant retorted, "Now wait a minute, what would happen if I called you a nigger? What would happen then? You're sitting here calling me these names, what if I did that to you?" Infuriated by the hint of a racial innuendo, the woman threatened to start picketing outside his store, but ultimately she did not follow through on her threat. The owner commented about the matter, pointing to a system of "reverse racism" in which blacks now play the "race card":

> It just shows that it's totally backwards. It's reverse racism is what it
> is. And anytime there's an argument about anything, it always
> comes down to, "You damn Orientals are taking over all the busi-
> nesses in the neighborhood!" or "You Koreans are doing it!"
>
> This isn't all the time, but every once in a while you get a cus-
> tomer who's totally unreasonable, and if things don't go their way,

they pull that old card out of their pocket, the race card, and throw it down. And it's a shame that they got to stoop to that level just to get what they want. I mean if they were to talk to me reasonable, without yelling and ranting and raving, we probably would have got things worked out more to their liking. But you can't come in here and yell at somebody and expect to get what you want.

Simple economic arguments can become loaded with symbolism— with customers and merchants responding not only to the objective features of the argument at hand but also, and at times primarily, to the *meaning* that the argument has for them. When tensions run high, customers and merchants alike battle over far more than the intricacies of the economic exchange. Imported into merchant-customer altercations are the ideologies of race and opportunity in a system of racial and ethnic stratification. When Jewish or Korean merchants refuse to take back merchandise from blacks, the customers may perceive out-group merchants *not* as individuals who make business decisions but as outsiders who enter and exploit the community at large. These simple economic disputes can stir collective ideologies and identities, becoming symbolic of the apparent power, class, and status distinctions between two racially and ethnically distinct groups—a mere commercial exchange becoming symbolic of America's racial and ethnic order.

By stark contrast, black store owners are often shielded against the resentments of race and class because black customers perceive black merchants as part of the in-group, thereby giving them a "co-ethnic advantage" over their Jewish and Korean counterparts in business. For instance, when asked whether merchant-customer disputes ever take on racial overtones, an African American furniture store owner in West Philadelphia laughed and replied, "They don't say that to me. Well they can't because I'm black and they're black!" Because both are black, when customers become irate toward black merchants, race has no place in the argument.

Race and BFOQs: Blacks as Cultural Brokers

Section 703(e)(1) of Title VII of the Civil Rights Act of 1964 allows employers to make distinctions "in those certain instances where religion, sex, or national origin is a bona fide occupational qualification reasonably necessary to the normal operation of that particular business or enterprise." Race is not included in this title. The practice of race-based hiring, however, has been perceived as reasonable under certain conditions, following a logic similar to that for BFOQs. For example, John Skrentny (1996) shows that federal officials promoted the hiring of blacks in city police departments because they believed that an all-white police force used to control black rioting during the 1960s in urban neighborhoods exacerbated racial tensions.[4]

Today, race is an increasingly important factor in hiring in the inner-city job market, especially when the business owners are not black. Jewish and Korean merchants in New York City and Philadelphia hire blacks as "cultural brokers" who mediate between them and their predominantly black clientele. Black employees and managers serve this function in a variety of ways: as linguistic links, as cultural links, as symbols that they are "giving something back to the community" in which they serve, and, most important, as conflict-resolvers. Therefore, it is not affirmative action but the logic of the market and the culture that call for color-coded hiring. For many Jewish and Korean merchants in the inner-city market, race has become a bona fide occupational qualification in hiring.

For Korean immigrant merchants, hiring black employees is particularly instrumental since blacks are able to communicate with their customers in English. A Jewish merchant in West Philadelphia said of the role of black employees in Korean-owned stores, "It's a way for them to deal with their language barrier. Korean merchants who don't speak English can hire blacks to talk to their customers." Black employees serve as interpreters not only for Korean immigrant store owners but also for native-born Jewish merchants, who affirm that black employees have a certain way of "talking" and "dealing" with their clientele. Consequently, even though Jewish merchants are fluent in English, they too benefit from hiring black employees because blacks have distinct cultural styles, tastes, and modes of communication, often drawing on the black English vernacular in their interactions (Labov 1972). The use of cultural brokers by American-born Jewish business owners points to how different the black inner-city cultural style has become from that of nonblack outsiders. For example, a Jewish retailer in Mount Airy frankly revealed,

> It does help when you have an African American employee in an African American neighborhood. It creates a good atmosphere, rather than let's say an all Jewish or all white, Anglo Saxon staff in a neighborhood that is opposite of you, or all Koreans for that matter. It makes good communications, and he can talk to the customers in many ways I cannot relate to, just by him being a man of the neighborhood. And that helps a lot in many ways.

Black employees also have the culturally specific knowledge needed to sell to a black clientele. When asked whether she felt she needed black employees in her grocery store, a Korean merchant on Jamaica Avenue replied in her very limited English, "Sure I need. When black worker is here, they [are able to get] through together [with the] customer. When they explain, customers understand more than when I explain. They through together I feel. So language, customs, everything the same." This Korean merchant admitted that the black employees she hired in the past were more familiar with the specialty products and therefore they were able to bridge the cultural gap between the owners and their ethnic clientele. In addition, a Korean woman who sells inner-city sportswear in West Harlem commented that her black employees know how to sell to her black customers. She explained, "Black people say each other, 'Oh you look good. This look good.' They know everything, they know." Her son, who works part-time, commented, "African American employees respond better to the customers, talk to them better, and they're better salesmen." And a Jewish store owner in West Harlem added that African American customers prefer dealing with each other: "If you have African Americans working in the stores, the customers feel more comfortable. If all of my employees were white, then people probably wouldn't want to shop here."

Apart from bridging linguistic and cultural barriers, black employees are also visible symbols that merchants are giving something back to the community in which they serve. Jewish, Korean, and black merchants generally agree that if they profit from the community, it is important to hire its members—virtually reciting the rhetoric of the media and of black nationalist leaders. In fact, when there are no black employees in nonblack-owned businesses, especially in the larger stores, merchants sense pressure to hire community members. For example, a Jewish store owner on Jamaica Avenue in Queens sensed the subtle disapproval when his black employees were not present in his store:

> The argument in these neighborhoods is if you don't have blacks employed for you, they object to that. They feel as though you come in and you take money out of the community, but you don't give anything back. I've had times where it was just Eric [my cousin] and myself here, and people would come in and they would look, and I know what they're looking at.

For some residents, the number of black employees in nonblack-owned businesses is an indicator of the extent to which Jewish and Korean merchants give back to the community in which they make their living.

In addition to acting as cultural brokers and symbols of giving back, black employees serve most critically as arbitrators who can defuse and deracialize anger. To capture his relationship with his Korean employer, an African American employee in East Harlem asked me, "Did you see the movie with Whitney Houston and Kevin Costner? That's me. I'm her bodyguard, her protection, her interpreter."

While working as a bag checker on 125th Street in West Harlem, I observed the cooling-off process in action as a Korean merchant was explaining his reliance on black employees to smooth out incidents. He said to me, "If you have black management, no problem, but if you have a Korean manager or whatever, you can get into trouble." On the heels of this logical explanation, a black customer tried to exchange the dirty pants he was wearing for a new pair. The Korean store owner handed him off to the black manager, who told the man, "I'm not disputing that you bought the pants here, sir, but we wouldn't have sold them to you like that. Look at all our pants here, none of them look like that. That's your hand that made them like that. Here, look at my pocket. If I'm reaching in there all the time and my hand is dirty, then they're going to get dirty. It's your hand." The owner, visibly nervous that the man refused the manager's explanation, said, "Call the police." But the black manager reassured him, "We don't need to call the police. He's just drunk. When he comes around tomorrow, he'll come back and apologize." The owner then turned to me and said, "If that was a Korean manager, there would have been a little bit of commotion."

As new immigrants who do not have a firm grasp of the English language or its nuances, Korean merchants agree that black employees are notably better at understanding grievances and calming down irate customers. Jewish merchants have also adopted this strategy of using black employees to defuse racial arguments with their customers. For example, a Greek salesman in a Jewish-owned furniture store on Jamaica Avenue illustrated how easily the racial element can disappear from merchant-customer arguments:

> I'm white, and I deal with the black customers. Sometimes you have problems, but 99% of the time you never have problems because we always try to deal with the customer. We always have the philosophy that they're right, that's the way that we try to deal with it. But always, you're going to have problems that we're not able to solve, but you see that if it gets to a racial point, or if the customer feels that it's racial, then you give him to somebody of his own race, and he cannot say that anymore.

Black customers undoubtedly protect nonblack merchants, often preventing economic arguments from erupting into racially charged anger. The 1992 Los Angeles riots proved to be pivotal for Korean merchants in South Central Los Angeles, whose number of black hires nearly doubled after this massive uprising (Park 1998). And Jewish merchants reacted similarly after riots swept the nation's major cities in the 1930s and 1960s; they too began hiring black sales associates and managers to alleviate tensions.

From the perspective of black managers and sales associates, mediating heated arguments between the customers and their nonblack employers is just part of the job. And even when customers accuse black managers and workers of "taking the other side" and acting like Uncle Toms, black employees firmly hold their ground, recognizing that succumbing to peer pressure is not worth their job. Fully cognizant that their presence alone defuses rising tensions, black employees realize all too well that there would be far more racial animosity between the black customers and nonblack store owners if they were not present to handle customer gripes. For example, a black manager of a clothing store in Harlem candidly maintained,

> When I'm here, 99% of the time, everything comes through that door [exchanges or returns], I gotta look at it. And I have gotten some things that are worn, chopped off. It's an absolute fact that if I weren't the manager, they would have more problems with exchanges. It's a fact because the customers always think, "Whitey's trying to get over them." They use that expression. So they will get hostile very fast. The owners would have to change their way of talking very much or . . . take back a lot of stuff they don't want to take back just to keep the peace because there really would be a hostile situation. All you have to do is see it once.

In a racialized society with a system of ethnic stratification, black customers can easily interpret the refusal to exchange merchandise within a racial framework, and the refusal becomes symbolic of the power relations between two ethnic groups. Statements such as "Whitey's trying to get over on me" and "You damn Orientals are coming into our neighborhoods taking over every store" are symbolic expressions of how black customers construct race, opportunity, and historic exploitation. Implicit is the sense that blacks question and challenge the racial hierarchy in which they find themselves, once again, at the bottom. Jewish and Korean merchants are acutely aware that black employees bridge the racial, class, and status gaps between cus-

TABLE 1

Employers and Percentage of Foreign-Born and Native-Born Black Employees
in New York

	Jewish Merchants	Korean Merchants	Black Merchants
Foreign-born black employees	69%	76%	55%
Native-born black employees	31	24	45
Total N	45	43	22

tomers and nonblack business owners. Their in-group status often protects merchants, keeping day-to-day merchant-customer tensions under control.

A Preference for Immigrants

To simply describe these employees as black obscures the way *black* carries both ethnic and racial meanings, and on this point the comparison between New York City and Philadelphia is most illuminating. The pattern of hiring in New York City reveals an ethnic preference for Caribbean and West African blacks rather than African Americans. By contrast, the blacks who work in Philadelphia are largely African American. Therefore, what is construed as an ethnic preference reveals a preference for immigrants. Table 1 illustrates that in New York City, foreign-born blacks are significantly more likely to be hired than native-born blacks in these retail businesses, accounting for 69 percent of the black hires in Jewish-owned stores and 76 percent of the black employees in Korean-owned stores. Even black-owned stores in New York City reveal a higher proportion of foreign-born hires (largely accounted for by black immigrant merchants and managers who prefer hiring co-ethnics). Table 2 shows that, by contrast, in Philadelphia, virtually all of the black hires are African American.

TABLE 2

Employers and Percentage of Foreign-Born and Native-Born Black Employees
in Philadelphia

	Jewish Merchants	Korean Merchants	Black Merchants
Foreign-born black employees	0%	7%	0%
Native-born black employees	100	93	100
Total N	9	14	15

In New York City, where store owners have a choice between native- and foreign-born black employees, Korean, Jewish, and black immigrant merchants and managers are more likely to hire the foreign-born. For example, the Jewish store owner in West Harlem who underscored the need for hiring African Americans has three black employees who are African, Haitian, and Colombian. Merchants generally agree that native-born Americans of any kind, not just African Americans but also whites and even the merchants' American-born children, are unwilling to work in small business and put in the long hours and the physically exhausting labor for so little pay. Small retailers in inner cities are not the first to admit their preference for immigrants. Studies of employers' hiring preferences (Holzer 1996; Kasinitz and Rosenberg 1996; Neckerman and Kirschenman 1991; Newman 1999; Waldinger 1997) and the high employment rates of immigrant groups (Aponte 1996; Grasmuck and Grosfuguel 1997) reveal that in industries across the spectrum, employers choose immigrants over African Americans.

Many immigrant merchants, especially those who have "made it," do not understand why native-born Americans would not take advantage of the business opportunities before them. Immigrants—whether Korean, Jewish, or black—are extremely critical of the American-born, especially African Americans in low-income neighborhoods, who, they feel, lack the drive to take advantage of the opportunities open to all, using past oppression as a crutch. An immigrant from Spain—who worked his way up from janitor to sales manager in charge of hiring for a large Jewish-owned furniture store on Jamaica Avenue—spoke candidly of his disdain for the work ethic of native-born Americans, defending his preference for immigrants and scoffing at race-based affirmative action policies in hiring:

> It has a lot to do with the culture. See, I also come from outside. The reason why I became the Vice President of the previous company is because of my background. Hard work. It's like your background. We were taught that nothing is going to be given to us from this world. You got to be respectful of your elders and the company that you work for, and you have to be dedicated and prove to yourself that you're better than the rest. And don't look at your limitations but your potential, and don't come up with excuses.
>
> Unfortunately in America because of the social and political up-

heaval in the '60s, early '70s, everything changed and everybody
thought that we had to give our kids everything for free. People
that are born here don't have the drive. They don't have the values
and the principles that are going to make them successful because
this is unfortunately a society that's a welfare society. They give
you a job because you're a minority. They're going to give you a
job because you are Asian American, because you're black, because
you speak Spanish, and that is the wrong way to assess the workforce. You give the job, in my book, to the one who deserves it the
most, even if they're pink, as long as they show proficiency in what
they do.

Unfortunately, society is trying to come up with excuses to promote people without capabilities, without knowledge, based on
color, based on appearance, based on limitations. They're not trying to get the most capable people; those are the ones you help, if
you give them a chance, but they're not doing it.

You, me, and people who come from outside because our way
of living is so hard, we were taught that we have to work hard for
what we want. Don't wait for handouts. That's a big difference. It's
very simple. Everybody knows it, but only a few want to admit it because it's not politically correct.

Another Jewish store owner in Queens shared a similar view that affirmative action should not apply in the hiring process:

That's why I'm not a believer in affirmative action because affirmative action is not based on your qualifications, it's based on whether
you're a man, whether you're a woman, whether you're black,
whether you're white, whether you're yellow. That doesn't qualify
for me. If you were here, and there's a polka dotted person, and
that person had more knowledge about my business than you do,
I'd hire them, not because they're polka dotted, but because they
have knowledge. That's the way jobs were based on, not on anything else. And that's why I think affirmative action is a bunch of
baloney, it really is.

Small business owners believe that they should be able to hire those
who are most qualified for the position, but the most important qualification seems to be a willingness to work long hours for little pay with
few, if any, benefits. Retailers largely prefer immigrants to the native-
born because they believe that the latter are socialized to expect decent

working conditions, no less than the minimum wage, and certain benefits that many small retail businesses do not offer. Compared to the native-born, immigrants are a more docile workforce and are far less likely to complain about the low hourly wage, the six-day work week, and the lack of health or material benefits to which many native-born Americans have become accustomed. Their tractability places immigrants higher in the labor queue. Waldinger's research (1996) confirms that because African Americans' aspirations and expectations have changed, they are more likely to reject low-paying jobs than are immigrants. Not only retailers but also employers in a wide range of industries agree that a sense of entitlement epitomizes much of the difference in work ethic between African Americans and the foreign-born.

A second-generation Jewish merchant in West Harlem who employs between forty and fifty mostly foreign-born employees asserted that African Americans are less willing to work in retail than are black immigrants. He explains that

> native African Americans tend not to like to work in a retail store. It's not our choice, it's their choice. They feel that they're at a different level for the most part, so you don't get them applying as much. The retail level is an entry level position, it's a little bit above minimum wage, but it's not a great wage. Somebody comes in and the color of their skin is black but their heritage is not American, they're willing more to start at a lower pay and hopefully get a little bit ahead. You don't have to stay here your entire life, but it's a nice place to start.

But the wariness about African Americans is, in part, a preference for immigrants. For example, when asked whether he noticed a difference between West Indian and African American employees, a Korean store owner in West Harlem pointed to the poor work ethic of the American-born, which results largely from the crutch of a generous welfare system:

> There's a big difference. The worst employees that you can hire are those employees that have lived especially in the City all their lives, people from Harlem. My best workers are college students that live outside of Harlem, and people that are from the West Indies. And from what I can tell, especially those people from Harlem, the entire welfare system, it created a generation where they have no work ethic. They won't come to work on time, and when they're here, they're here to waste time away, not do any work. I mean a paper can fall right in front of your face, and they'll just walk by

without picking it up. If they see clothes all in shambles, they won't
fix it unless they're told to do so. And when they're told to do so, it
takes them a long time to do what they're supposed to do. It's like
a different work ethic.

People from the West Indies, I mean you can see the hunger
in their eyes. They want to work! They want to make more money.
They want to work harder, but people on welfare, there is no incentive for them to work harder.

Not only do merchants and managers favor the foreign-born, they
also express a bias against inner-city fashions and culture, ascribing negative values to these class and ethnic markers and using them as a proxy
to measure the work ethic of those who exhibit them. Inner-city-style
clothing, the use of nonstandard English, the manner in which applicants walk and carry themselves, and fashion accessories such as large
gold jewelry signal to employers that these applicants have a poor work
ethic, a bad attitude, and a propensity toward absenteeism (Newman
1999; Wilson 1996). A West Indian manager of a Jewish-owned store
in West Harlem revealed how he scrutinizes an applicant's personal
style when he chooses which applicants he will hire: "I look at their
dress. I don't like them to be too flashy. I don't like it when they have
the gold teeth or big earrings or if they wear their pants down low like
this. That looks delinquent to me." Merchants and managers discriminate against applicants whose style of dress or demeanor connotes an
inner-city culture, which they perceive as threatening and indicative of
delinquency and a poor work ethic (Jencks 1992).

Korean and Jewish store owners are not the only ones who demonstrate a preference for immigrants; black immigrant entrepreneurs and
managers in these neighborhoods also favor the foreign-born. For example, a black store owner in West Harlem who is American-born but
whose parents are of Caribbean descent and who self-identifies as West
Indian has three employees, all of whom are immigrants: one from St.
Martin, one from Trinidad, and another from Africa. She expresses the
same preference for immigrants shown by her Jewish and Korean counterparts.

Furthermore, West Indian and African-born employees generally
share their employers' views that they work harder than African Americans. One Trinidadian-born employee in a Korean-owned clothing
store in West Harlem stated:

I think West Indians generally work harder than Americans. I'm
not saying that to put Americans down, but I find that in my opin-

ion that I observe that most West Indians when they come to America, they work very hard for their money. It's just the maturity of West Indians, they work very hard for their money. We show up on time. We do what we're supposed to do without having the manager tell us what to do.

I just like watch, I just observe Robert [the manager]. I just observe his behavior, how he goes about folding his stuff, knowing what items to put on the racks, knowing what the sizes are that are needed on the racks, where the merchandise [is] located in the basement, so I can bring it out without following his direct orders. I just go automatically and locate it in the basement, bring it up, and put it on the racks. I won't like to say the names, but some people, Robert has to beg behind them to make sure that they're doing stuff.

And when asked why there are no African American employees in this large Jewish-owned clothing store in East Harlem, an African security guard replied frankly, "They [African Americans] don't want to work for $4.25. They think it's an insult to work for only $4.25. They go on welfare, they don't want to work."

Because hiring in these retail businesses is most frequently done by word of mouth or through employee referrals, these networks are a crucial means of securing employment, especially for the least educated (Aponte 1996; Holzer 1996). As these employment networks become embedded in immigrant communities, African Americans who apply for these retail jobs find themselves increasingly excluded, even in their own neighborhoods. Immigrants—*including* black immigrants—are favored over the native-born, and even in an all "black" labor market, African Americans are losing out.

From an African American perspective, however, it is not that immigrants work harder; they are just more willing to work for less, consequently undermining what African Americans have achieved with the civil rights movement. An African American merchant explained his disdain for immigrants, particularly black immigrants:

Someone that comes from the West Indies has not lived through the '60s as a black man who lived here. So he has to understand the racial thing like going to segregated bathrooms and stuff. So for someone to come after the fact, after things have changed and make these comments, is insulting to a black person. Yeah that's why you have these divisions, these racial divisions among them because how can you say that? You haven't lived here.

> I shouldn't have to work for less than minimum wage when I
> know what we struggled for. You might come here and take that
> dollar, but I'm not supposed to. It's not a sign of laziness, it's about
> understanding the history why. It's not that they're desperate. I
> think sometimes it's a lack of not really knowing what goes on and
> how those people [whites] have treated you.

Likewise, an African American beauty salon owner in Harlem complained that the Korean owners of the fruit and vegetable store adjacent
to her business hire very few blacks, preferring to hire Latinos who
work for less than the minimum wage. She asserted that if merchants
were to pay a decent wage, many African Americans would be willing
to work in immigrant-owned retail businesses. However, because these
business owners pay so little, African Americans may shun these jobs
altogether:

> They hire Mexicans for minimum wage, less than minimum wage,
> and they don't hire any blacks. I asked them why they don't hire
> any blacks, and they said it's because they don't want to work.
> These people want to work, but they won't work for nothing. If
> they told me they wanted to hire someone and I made an announce-
> ment in my church, there would be lots of people interested. Now
> they have one black guy sitting outside watching the store, looking
> in. That's an insult. That's insulting.

Very seldom was this point mentioned among Jewish, Korean, and
black immigrant store owners and managers. Few merchants felt that
as native-born Americans, African Americans should expect more than
new immigrants in terms of wages, working conditions, or opportunities for mobility. Instead, the majority pointed to what they perceive
as cultural and behavioral differences between African Americans and
immigrants. Interestingly, only one Korean merchant remarked that as
native-born Americans, African Americans should be paid a decent wage
if store owners expect them to work in these retail businesses. She at-
tributed the relatively low percentage of African American employees
in these neighborhoods to the merchants' unwillingness to pay them
appropriately:

> You go into a Korean store, you see not many black people [Afri-
> can Americans] work. But Korean people they try not to pay right
> way. They keep long hours and they try to give them hundred
> something [dollars]. That's not right. So a decent black guy, they
> want to work for Korean, and when they get a check, they don't

want to work. I pay that guy [the manager] over $500 a week plus bonus. You have to pay right. If you want right guy, you have to pay right. And Korean people, mostly they hire Spanish, they got cheap labor. They not residents, they illegal, so they can give $100, $150, it don't matter. If you looking for nice black worker, you got to pay decent. Korean people have to realize why they cannot hire blacks. Because black is lazy? No, not that. Because they don't pay right.

Because this study looks solely at employers' attitudes, it cannot address the question of whether American-born blacks want these retail jobs. However, the hiring of American-born blacks in Philadelphia stores, as well as other research in Harlem (Newman 1999), suggests that they do want some of these jobs. This indicates the problem is the preferences of employers, not of American-born blacks.

Conclusion

The shop floor has become a site where Jewish, Korean, and black store owners, along with their black customers, construct and negotiate race, ethnicity, and opportunity. As nonblack merchants doing business in predominantly black neighborhoods, Jews and Koreans fully recognize that their out-group status can easily make them targets of racially charged arguments, or even more, overt incidences of conflict such as boycotts and riots. As visible racial and ethnic outsiders, Jewish and Korean merchants hire black employees to serve as "cultural brokers" who bridge the linguistic, cultural, racial, and class gaps between the owners and their predominantly black clientele. Cultural brokers mediate, defuse, and deracialize arguments, maintaining the day-to-day routine and order in these communities.

"Black," however, is a flexible category—connoting race, ethnicity, and nativity. In the city that leads the country in the percentage of foreign-born residents, New York's merchants overwhelmingly choose black immigrants over African Americans. Immigration from the Caribbean and Africa is redefining the meaning of the category "black." On one hand, from the customers' perspective, because the merchant-customer dichotomy often falls between the black-nonblack racial divide, African American customers are pleased to find black employees at all, regardless of ethnicity or nativity. Race is constructed and negotiated dialectically, that is, according to who the "other" is. If the "other" happens to be nonblack merchants such as Jews and Koreans, West Indians and Africans are "black" to the customers.

It is clear that retailers' hiring practices are a significant part of the inner-city and national labor markets. In the United States in 1992, nearly 45 million people worked in small businesses, 27 million of whom were paid employees. The retail trade accounted for 21 percent of small business workers, second only to the service industry (Rauch 1996; U.S. Department of Commerce 1996), and perhaps more important, retailing accounts for 40 percent of Americans' first jobs (Moss 1995). Therefore, the retail sector is a vital source of early job experience for all Americans, particularly youth. In northeastern cities such as New York City and Philadelphia, where manufacturing jobs have declined in the past thirty years (Bluestone and Harrison 1982; Holzer 1991; Portes and Sassen-Koob 1987), service-sector and retailing jobs are increasingly important sources of employment.[5] If African Americans are disfavored in comparison to other groups, *including* black immigrants, this has significant consequences for the employment opportunity structures for African Americans, particularly the youth.

And last, because hiring in these retail businesses is often done through existing employee networks, African Americans are becoming increasingly excluded, even in their own neighborhoods. At the same time, the larger employers, subject to Equal Employment Opportunity Commission regulations that require periodic reports of the numbers of blacks and members of other groups that are hired, can present to the government data showing that they may indeed employ many blacks. Affirmative action regulations do not distinguish between American-born and foreign-born blacks. Race-based hiring, therefore, does not necessarily mean that African Americans will benefit; the overinclusiveness of the racial category "black" can undermine the goal of giving opportunity to the original intended beneficiaries of affirmative action policies.

Notes

1. *Black* refers to a generic category that includes African Americans, West Indians, and Africans.

2. Title VII applies only to firms with fifteen or more employees. Some firms are under obligation to have an affirmative action program only if they have a government contract. A court may also order a firm to implement an affirmative action plan to compensate for past discrimination.

3. This differential in perception and evaluation among black customers suggests a follow-up study to see whether Jewish and Korean customers also exhibit a similar pattern in relations with in-group and out-group merchants.

4. Although this reasoning justified increased black hiring in some municipal police forces, this hiring was necessarily undertaken as affirmative action, not as BFOQ-related.

5. Portes and Sassen-Koob (1987, 46) estimate that between 1970 and 1980, New York City lost nearly half a million jobs, and in manufacturing alone, there was a 35 percent decline.

Acknowledgments

The author wishes to thank the International Migration Program of the Social Science Research Council, the Andrew W. Mellon Foundation, and the National Science Foundation, SBR-9633345, for generous research support on which this chapter is based. The author also thanks the University of California's President's Office for support during the writing of this chapter. For comments and suggestions on an earlier version of this paper, thanks are due to Herbert Gans, John Skrentny, and Roger Waldinger.

References

Aponte, Robert. 1996. Urban employment and the mismatch dilemma: Accounting for the immigration exception. *Social Problems* 43:268–82.

Bluestone, Barry, and Bennett Harrison. 1982. *The deindustrialization of America: Plant closing, community abandonment, and the dismantling of basic industry.* New York: Basic Books.

Carpenter, Allan. 1992. *Facts about cities.* New York: H. W. Wilson.

Grasmuck, Sherri, and Ramon Grosfoguel. 1997. Geopolitics, economic niches, and gendered social capital among recent Caribbean immigrants in New York City. *Sociological Perspectives* 40:339–63.

Holzer, Harry J. 1991. The spatial mismatch hypothesis: What has the evidence shown? *Urban Studies* 28:105–122.

———. 1996. *What employers want: Job prospects for less-educated workers.* New York: Russell Sage Foundation.

Jencks, Christopher. 1992. *Rethinking social policy: Race, class, and underclass.* Cambridge: Harvard University Press.

Kasinitz, Philip, and Jan Rosenberg. 1996. Missing the connection: Social isolation and employment on the Brooklyn waterfront. *Social Problems* 43:180–96.

Labov, William. 1972. *Language in the inner-city: Studies in the black English vernacular.* Philadelphia: University of Pennsylvania Press.

Merton, Robert K. 1968. Self-fulfilling prophecy. In *Social theory and social structure.* New York: Free Press.

Moss, Mitchell L. 1995. Harlem's economic paradox. *New York Times,* 13 December, 23.

Neckerman, Kathryn M., and Joleen Kirschenman. 1991. Hiring strategies, racial bias, and inner-city workers. *Social Problems* 38:433–47.

Newman, Katherine S. 1999. *No shame in my game.* New York: Knopf and Russell Sage Foundation.

Park, Kyeyoung. 1998. "No tension, but . . .": Latino commentary on Koreans and the South Central aftermath. Paper presented at the Paul F. Lazarsfeld Center for the Social Sciences, Columbia University.

Portes, Alejandro, and Saskia Sassen-Koob. 1987. Making it underground: Comparative material on the informal sector in the Western market economies. *American Journal of Sociology* 93:30–61.

Rauch, James E. 1996. Trade and networks: An application to minority retail entrepreneurship. Working paper, Russell Sage Foundation, New York.

Skrentny, John D. 1996. *The ironies of affirmative action.* Chicago: University of Chicago Press.

U.S. Department of Commerce. 1996. *1992 survey of minority-owned business enterprises.* Washington, D.C.: U.S. Government Printing Office.

U.S. Department of Commerce, Bureau of the Census. 1991. *County and city data book.* Washington, D.C.: Government Printing Office.

Waldinger, Roger. 1996. *Still the promised city? African Americans and new immigrants in postindustrial New York.* Cambridge: Harvard University Press.

———. 1997. Black/immigrant competition re-assessed: New evidence from Los Angeles. *Sociological Perspectives* 40:365–86.

Wilson, William J. 1996. *When work disappears.* New York: Alfred A. Knopf.

PART III

THE VIEWS OF MULTIETHNIC AMERICA

8

Race, Interests, and Beliefs about Affirmative Action:

Unanswered Questions and New Directions

. . .

Lawrence D. Bobo

The debate over affirmative action often seems to involve two warring camps, each of which stakes a mutually exclusive claim to moral virtue (Edley 1996). Defenders of affirmative action cast themselves as the champions of racial justice and the keepers of Dr. King's dream. Opponents of affirmative action cast themselves as champions of the true color-blind intent of cherished American values. In the eyes of the defenders of affirmative action, the latter are, at best, apologists for racism. Opponents see their antagonists as advancing a morally bankrupt claim to victim status and the spoils of racial privilege for African Americans and other racial minorities. Advocates within both camps increasingly turn to research on public opinion to validate their assertions. Yet both the morally judgmental character of advocacy and the extant body of research on public opinion are problematical. Both misread the meaning of race in the American experience and the role of group interests intrinsically raised by affirmative action politics.

Two sharply opposed views of public opinion on affirmative action dominate research. In one account, the controversy and often the intense opposition to affirmative action among white Americans are centrally rooted in antiblack racism (Kinder and Sanders 1996; Sears et al. 1997). In the opposing account, whites' deep discomfort with affirmative action is said to reflect high-minded value commitments and little if any antiblack animus (Lipset and Schneider 1978; Sniderman and Piazza 1993). In either view, ironically, affirmative action policies are seen as unlikely to fare well at the bar of white public opinion.

Although there is a debate here of serious scholarly moment, I wish to bring into critical focus three features or presumptions shared by both the racism school and the values and ideology (read: principled objections) school of thought about public opinion. First, both approaches contribute to the distorted view that opposition to affirmative action among whites is monolithic. It is not (Steeh and Krysan 1996). Affirmative action policies span a range of policy goals and strategies (Chermerinsky 1997; introduction and chapter 4, this volume), some formulations of which (for example, race-targeted scholarships or special job outreach and training efforts) can be quite popular (Bobo and Kluegel 1993; Bobo and Smith 1994). Second, the racism and the principled objections arguments focus on one element of public opinion: policy preferences themselves. Perceptions and beliefs about the possible benefits and costs of affirmative action are almost never explored. From the vantage point of those wishing to make a constructive contribution to the policy process, this is disappointing. It is much easier to envision changing such beliefs than to hope of ending racism or of fundamentally reshaping values and ideological identities. Although what one believes about the effects of affirmative action does not singularly determine policy views in this arena, such beliefs surely are an important element in the larger politics of affirmative action.

Third, scholars advancing both types of accounts share an emphasis that has thoroughly marginalized the opinions of African Americans and other racial minorities. This has had unfortunate consequences for theory development and for the capacity of public opinion analysts to make useful contributions to the larger public discourse. Ignoring the voices of people of color results, chiefly, in a severe underestimation of the role of group interests in the politics of affirmative action and facilitates the stalemate of opposing claims of moral virtue on the Left (the valorous nonracists) and the Right (the valorous color-blind). Ironically, a focus on interests might better facilitate constructive dialogue and compromise. Interests can be understood in both a short-term and a long-term sense. Whereas the short-term interests of racial groups in affirmative action may seem zero-sum in character, the long-term interests surely are not. What is more, our legal and political system routinely grapples with how to reconcile conflicting interests and arrive at sustainable compromises. Such compromises are, after all, the art of politics. Our institutions have a much harder time adjudicating opposing claims of rights and of moral virtue than those based on interests. Left at this level of discourse, a sort of self-righteous tyranny of the majority is ultimately to prevail.

Thus, in this chapter I examine beliefs about the costs and benefits of affirmative action. I pursue a multiracial analysis, assessing the views of black, white, Latino, and Asian respondents to a set of questions contained in the 1992 Los Angeles County Social Survey. And I expressly examine the effects of perceived group competition and threat on beliefs about the effects of affirmative action. All of this is done while taking seriously the ideas advanced in the racism and principled objection schools of thought about public opinion on affirmative action.

Background

General assessments of public opinion on affirmative action point to three noteworthy patterns. First, there has been considerable stability in basic policy views. Contrary to the tenor of media framing, which both claims and, in its own portrayal, embodies a more sharply negative trend in recent years (Entman 1997), the general trend has been for stability (Steeh and Krysan, 1996). Second, the exact wording of questions heavily influences the observed level of support for affirmative action. This pattern is unlikely to involve a simple methodological artifact. It appears to reflect substantively important differences in the character of the policy goal and strategy used. Elsewhere, I have discussed this as a difference between opportunity-enhancing forms of affirmative action and outcome-directed forms of affirmative action (Bobo and Kluegel 1993; Bobo and Smith 1994; see also Lipset and Schneider 1978). Programs with the goal of improving the human capital attributes of minorities tend to be far more popular than those aimed at equalizing outcomes. And programs that call for the application of quotas and clear-cut racial preferences are highly unpopular, even among blacks (Schuman et al. 1997). Third, opinions on affirmative action usually differ by race, with blacks a good deal more supportive than whites (Kluegel and Smith 1986). Indeed, depending on the exact question and policy, the situation is often one of majority black support for a specified form of affirmative action and majority white opposition, although neither group is univocal in outlook (Jaynes and Williams 1989).

There are few scholars who would dissent from this summary. The debate is joined, however, over the question of the social wellsprings of white opposition to affirmative action. Here the research literature divides between those arguing for the importance of racism and those arguing for the importance of cherished values and ideological commitments.

The Racism Hypothesis

The large body of work on symbolic racism (Sears 1988; Sears et al. 1997) and isomorphic arguments about abstract racial resentments

(Kinder and Sanders 1996) posits that a new form of antiblack racism has risen. This racism is more subtle than the coarse racism of the Jim Crow era that bluntly advocated racial segregation, discrimination, and the inherent inferiority of blacks to whites. It involves a blend of early learned antiblack feelings and beliefs with traditional American values of hard work and self-reliance. It is expressed in resentment and hostility toward blacks' demands for special treatment and toward government recognition of blacks' demands, and in unreasoned denial of the modern potency of racial discrimination or bias. It has no meaningful dependence on material contingencies in the private lives of individual whites: It is a learned attitude, rather than a reflection of socially rooted instrumentalities.

This new attitude is elicited when political leaders or discourse invokes issues or labels that call to mind blacks. Whites respond in terms of this underlying psychological animus against African Americans. One effect of symbolic racism is a rejection of policies such as affirmative action. Research has shown that measures of such attitudes are the central factor—more important than ideology, values, personal risk of loss, and perceived group threat—in determining whether whites support or oppose affirmative action–type policies (Kinder and Sanders 1996; Sears et al. 1997).

It is quite important in this research that specific types of attitudes and their effects on policy views be understood as racism. These outlooks are held to rest heavily on fundamentally irrational antiblack feelings and fears rather than objective, realistic conflicts of interest (Sears 1988). The symbolic racism researchers are quite explicit in the judgment that such attitudes and their political effects are morally wrong and deserving of disapprobation, no matter the exact terminology. As Sears (1998) argued, "There is no doubt that *racism* is pejorative, but so is *prejudice*; none of us like to think we are either racist or prejudiced" (79, emphasis in original). This point is pressed further by Kinder and Sanders (1996), who claim that most other prominent analysts of white racial attitudes have "white-washed racial prejudice" (269–72).

The Principled Objections Hypothesis

The symbolic racism research has been criticized on a remarkably wide variety of grounds. The most widely discussed and accepted alternative theoretical account of views of affirmative action posits that important values and ideological outlooks, thoroughly devoid of antiblack animus, prompt many whites to reject affirmative action. As Sniderman and Piazza (1993) argue, "At the deepest level though, racial politics owes its shape not to beliefs or stereotypes distinctly about blacks but to the broader set of convictions about fairness and fair play that make up the American Creed" (176).

This hypothesis about principled bases of objections to affirmative action has a special twist. To wit, not only is racism a small part of the modern politics of race, but it is only among the politically unsophisticated that racism carries force. Among politically sophisticated individuals who understand what it means to hold a conservative identity and values, it is these high-minded and race-neutral considerations that motivate opposition to affirmative action.

Accordingly, the influence of racism has been vastly exaggerated by the symbolic racism researchers (indeed in a manner and to a degree that has led to a harmful politicization of social science scholarship) (see Sniderman and Tetlock 1986; Tetlock 1994). Furthermore, as the larger civil rights movement shifted its focus from fundamental civic equality and a rhetoric of color-blindness to a focus on equal social rewards and a rhetoric of race-based entitlements, it lost the moral high ground. Blacks and their allies placed themselves, in fact, at odds with the values embodied in the American Creed (Sniderman and Piazza 1993).

The Group Position and Perceived Threat Hypothesis

This approach springs from the sociologist Herbert Blumer's (1958) theory of race prejudice as a sense of group position. He argued that critical elements of prejudice were feelings of entitlement to social resources, status, and privileges, and perceived threats to those entitlements posed by members of other groups. In this view, any social system with long-standing racial identities and institutionalized racial inequality in life chances sets the stage for realistic or meaningful struggle over group interests defined along racial lines (Bobo 1997).

The core argument here is that racial politics unavoidably involves a nettlesome fusion of racial identities and attitudes with racial group interests. It suggests that many whites will oppose affirmative action, not so much because they see a race-based policy as contravening their highest values or because they have learned a new, politically relevant set of resentments of blacks, but rather because they perceive blacks as competitive threats for valued social resources, status, and privileges.

Although it would be appropriate to interpret an explicitly racialized motive for opposition to policies aimed at racial equality as an aspect of racism, doing so is not essential to the group position and perceived threat argument.[1] Indeed, because racial identities and racial group interests are seen as historically emergent and contingent, the crucial implication is that it is the understanding of group interests and what affects those understandings that is analytically and politically most important. With respect to the rhetoric of racial politics, the group position and perceived threat argument stands in sharp contradistinction to both the symbolic racism and the principled objections arguments. One can judge the moral worth of the sources of affirmative action beliefs, but at some level, interests and perceived threats are simply that: interests and perceived threats.

Data and Measures

The data come from the 1992 Los Angeles County Social Survey (LACSS), a countywide, random-digit-dialed, computer-assisted telephone survey of adults living in households. The survey oversampled telephone numbers in zip code areas with high concentrations of blacks (65 percent or more) or Asians (30 percent or more) to generate larger numbers of black and Asian respondents. To capture Los Angeles's large Latino population, the survey developed a Spanish version of the questionnaire. A total of 1,869 respondents were interviewed: 625 whites, 483 blacks, 477 Latinos, and 284 Asians. Owing to a split-ballot design, this analysis is based on a randomly selected one-third of respondents who were given the questions on affirmative action for blacks.[2]

Symbolic racism was measured with a scale based on three Likert-type response format items asking the following: "Most blacks who receive money from welfare programs could get along without it if they tried"; "Government officials usually pay less attention to a request or complaint from a black person than from a white person"; and "Irish, Italian, Jewish, and many other minorities overcame prejudice and worked their way up. Blacks should do the same without any special favors." Scale scores range from 0 to 1, with higher scores reflecting higher levels of symbolic racism.

The principled objections hypothesis was tapped with three different measures concerning political ideology, inegalitarian outlooks, and commitment to the work ethic or individualism. *Political ideology* was measured by self-identification on a 1-to-7 point scale ranging from extremely liberal to extremely conservative. Inegalitarianism was measured by using responses to two Likert-type items asking the following:

"Some people are just better cut out than others for important positions in society" and "Some people are better at running things and should be allowed to do so." Individualism was measured using responses to two Likert-type items asking, "If people work hard they almost always get what they want," and "Most people who don't get ahead should not blame the system: they really have only themselves to blame." Both sets of measures are drawn from the measures of core American values developed for the National Election Study surveys by Feldman (1988).

Perceived threat was measured with responses to four Likert-type items asking the following: "More good jobs for blacks means fewer good jobs for members of other groups"; "The more influence blacks have in local politics the less influence members of other groups will have in local politics"; "As more good housing and neighborhoods go to blacks, the fewer good houses and neighborhoods there will be for members of other groups"; and "Many blacks have been trying to get ahead economically at the expense of other groups." These items and their properties are discussed in fuller detail elsewhere (Bobo and Hutchings 1996). It is worth noting here that these items constitute a conservative approach to tapping perceived threat. The items always expressly invoke at least two groups, speak to relatively concrete resources, specify a zero-sum relationship, and use neutral language. All of these steps are taken in order to avoid the type of conceptual ambiguity and confusion that still surround the notion of symbolic racism.

I also introduced controls for two other aspects of racial attitudes that tap important dimensions of antiblack attitudes. Intergroup *affect* is measured with a feeling thermometer score ranging from 0 to 100, with high scores indicating more positive affect. Racial *stereotypes* are measured with an index composed of three items that used 7-point bipolar trait ratings. Respondents rated blacks on the trait dimensions of intelligent/unintelligent, prefer to be self-supporting/prefer to live on welfare, and easy to get along with/hard to get along with.

Results and Analysis

Race and Beliefs about Affirmative Action

Are beliefs about the effects of affirmative action sharply divided by race, with racial minorities perceiving overwhelmingly positive outcomes and whites perceiving overwhelmingly negative outcomes? Responses to the four questions on the impact of affirmative action, shown in table 1, present a somewhat more complicated pattern. To be sure,

TABLE 1

Race/Ethnicity and Beliefs about the Impact of Affirmative Action for Blacks

	Strongly Agree (%)	Agree (%)	Neither (%)	Disagree (%)	Strongly Disagree (%)	Total (%)	N
Affirmative action for blacks is unfair to whites.							
White	11	34	24	23	8	100	216
Black	5	13	17	45	20	100	173
Latino	5	25	32	35	2	99	160
Asian	4	30	35	25	6	100	88
Affirmative action in education gives an opportunity to qualified blacks who might not have had a chance without it.							
White	9	50	22	16	3	100	217
Black	29	55	5	10	1	100	172
Latino	8	58	22	11	2	101	161
Asian	8	46	29	16	1	100	87
Affirmative action for blacks may force employers to hire unqualified people.							
White	13	47	13	21	6	100	217
Black	5	22	10	44	19	100	173
Latino	3	36	20	38	3	100	161
Asian	7	32	20	37	5	101	87
Affirmative action in the workplace for blacks helps make sure that the American workforce and economy remain competitive.							
White	2	27	24	39	8	100	216
Black	17	43	17	18	4	99	173
Latino	2	53	24	18	4	101	160
Asian	5	32	28	31	5	101	87

there is a large and significant racial group difference in response to each item, with blacks (especially) and Latinos usually more likely to adopt favorable views of affirmative action than are whites. However, Asians' views are typically closer to those of whites than to those of blacks or Latinos. And in no instance does even the black-white difference reflect diametrically opposite views. Indeed, to a degree that should discomfit both the racism school and the principled objection school, white opinion is neither monolithic nor uniformly negative. Nearly one-third of whites (29 percent) perceive affirmative action for blacks as helpful to American economic competitiveness, one-third reject the idea that affirmative action is unfair to whites, and nearly 60 percent agree that affirmative action provides educational opportunities for qualified blacks who might not otherwise get a chance. The point where affirmative action encounters the most negative perceptions among whites was acceptance of the idea that it leads to hiring unqualified blacks (60 percent gave agreeing responses).

This picture of quite real but muted racial differences in perceptions of the effects of affirmative action is more readily appreciated by examining results for a simple summary scale based on the four items (alpha reliability = .66), as shown in figure 1. Scores of 0 on the scale indicate maximally favorable perceptions of affirmative action, and scores of 5 indicate maximally negative views of affirmative action. First, there are highly reliable race differences in the likelihood of perceiving affirmative action to have negative effects; $F (3, 625) = 18.09$, $p < .00001$. Second, even among whites, the mean score on the Perceived Negative Effects of Affirmative Action scale rises just above the mid-

FIGURE 1 Race and Mean Perceived Negative Effects of Affirmative Action

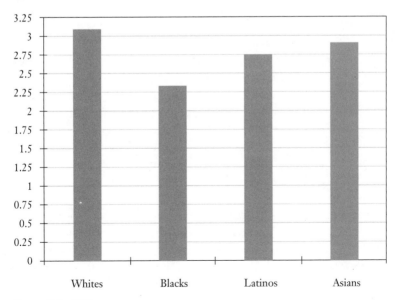

Source: Bobo 1992.

point of 3.0. Third, the figure highlights what some would interpret as an American racial hierarchy in views of affirmative action (Jankowski 1995). At the bottom of the racial hierarchy, and thus least likely to hold negative perceptions of affirmative action, are African Americans, followed by Latinos, then Asians, and finally whites, at the top of the hierarchy and most inclined to hold negative perceptions.

To this point, the results provide at least some initial suggestive evidence for a more interest-group-based understanding of views of affirmative action. Views are differentiated by race in predictable ways. Blacks, whose historical experiences in the United States have most consistently embodied a lower-castelike status, are the least willing to embrace negative views of affirmative action.

It is entirely possible, however, that what appear to be race-based differences in opinion really reflect differences in socioeconomic background or other demographic composition characteristics (for example, native-born status) that we should be cautious to interpret as reflecting racial group interests. To address this issue, table 2 estimates a series of regression equations for which the Perceived Negative Effects of Affirmative Action is the dependent measure. Model 1, which includes only a set of dummy variables identifying black, Latino, and Asian respondents (with white respondents as the omitted or contract group), reiterates the results of figure 1. There are significant differences between blacks and whites and between Latinos and whites. However, there is no statistically discernible difference in the likelihood that Asians and whites view affirmative action as having negative effects. Overall, a simple control for race explains about 12 percent of the variation in beliefs about the effects of affirmative action. Does the impact of race on views of affirmative action diminish on introducing controls for social class characteristics, such as education and income, and other demographic factors, such as age, sex, and native-born status? No. Indeed, if anything, the black-white and the Latino-white differences grow larger after introducing social class and demographic characteristics controls (compare model 2 to model 1 in table 2). The black-white gap widens by about 10 percent, and the Latino-white gap widens by about 8 percent.

Those arguing from the principled opposition point of view might reasonably conjecture, however, that much of what appears to be a racial difference is actually a difference in ideology and values that, primarily for historical and political reasons, overlap with race. If this is true, we should find that controlling for ideological conservatism, inegalitarian values, and individualism should considerably diminish racial group dif-

TABLE 2

Ordinary Least Squares Regression Models of Perceived Negative Effects of Affirmative Action for Blacks ($N = 497$)

	Model 1	Model 2	Model 3	Model 4
Race/ethnicity				
White (omitted)				
Black	−0.127***	−0.134****	−0.123****	−0.092****
	0.015	0.016	0.015	0.015
Latino	−0.048***	−0.052***	−0.051***	−0.056***
	0.016	0.049	0.018	0.017
Asian	−0.024	−0.008	−0.001	−0.015
	0.020	0.022	0.022	0.0020
Social background				
Education		−0.0060	−0.006	−0.000
		0.004	0.004	0.004
Age		0.000	0.000	0.000
		0.000	0.000	0.000
Male		0.019	0.016	0.013
		0.012	0.012	0.011
U.S. native		0.029*	0.030*	0.042***
		0.017	0.016	0.015
Family income ($10,000s)		−0.007**	−0.007**	−0.003
		0.003	0.003	0.003
Ideology and values				
Conservatism			0.020***	0.015****
			0.004	0.003
Inegalitarianism			0.040	0.004
			0.033	0.031
Individualism			0.047	−0.028
			0.032	0.031
Racial attitudes				
Affect				0.000
				0.000
Stereotypes				−0.006
				0.035
Perceived threat				0.235****
				0.041
Constant	0.602****	0.677****	0.541****	0.255***
	0.011	0.060	0.065	0.071
Adjusted R^2	0.121	0.132	0.190	0.316

Figures listed are unstandardized coefficients and standard errors.

*p < .10   **p < .05   ***p < .001   ****p < .0001

ferences. As model 3 in table 2 shows, controlling for ideology and values slightly reduces the black-white (9 percent) and the Latino-white difference (2 percent) but still leaves highly reliable racial group differences in each case. It should be noted that in this race-pooled model, there are no significant effects of inegalitarianism or individualism on

perceived negative effects of affirmative action. Only ideological identification itself appears to matter.

For the sake of completeness, we take the further step of introducing a battery of explicit racial attitude measures (see table 2, model 4).
Even this, however, fails to eliminate significant race effects. Most dramatically, once we remove the impact of several types of arguably antiblack attitudes, the Latino-white difference actually grows larger. To
be sure, the black-white difference narrows nontrivially (about 25 percent), but it remains sizable.

To borrow Cornel West's (1993) pithy observation, race matters.
Beliefs about the consequences of affirmative action are shaped in important ways by racial group membership and therefore, we would infer,
by the differential short-term stake or interest that racial groups have
in affirmative action policies (see Jackman 1994 for a similar argument).

Whites' Beliefs about the Negative Effects
of Affirmative Action

It could be argued that by pooling the responses of blacks, whites,
Latinos, and Asians, we are masking potentially important distinctive
patterns in the views of white respondents. In particular, both the principled objection school and the racism school arguments were formulated initially as accounts of the attitudes of white Americans. To this
end, table 3 reports regression models of the determinants of the Perceived Negative Effects of Discrimination measure among white respondents only. This part of the analysis also considers the claim of
the principled objections theorists that the views of the highly educated
exhibit less dependence on racial attitudes and a greater influence of
ideological and value-based reasoning. We do so by specifying interactions between level of education and each of the values and ideology
measures and the two theoretically central racial attitude measures: perceived threat and symbolic racism. For this part of the analysis, level
of education is treated as a dummy variable distinguishing college graduates from those without college degrees. Among whites, virtually no
LACSS respondents had fewer than eleven years of schooling, and a
very high fraction, fully 40 percent, had completed college. Thus, this
is an admittedly truncated examination of the education interaction hypothesis, but a truncation that reflects the real distribution of education
levels among white adults in Los Angeles County.

Consistent with the results from the pooled race models (see table
2), the only element of the values and ideology argument to exhibit a

TABLE 3
Ordinary Least Squares Regression Models of Perceived Negative Effects of Affirmative
Action for Blacks (White Respondents Only, $N = 163$)

	Model 1	Model 2
Constant	.178 (.080)**	.127 (.091)
Social background		
College degree	−.002 (.021)	.128 (.123)
Age	.001 (.001)	.001 (.001)
Male	.028 (.021)	.030 (.021)
Family income ($10,000s)	.008 (.005)	.008 (.005)
Values and ideology		
Conservatism	.020 (.006)***	.022 (.009)**
Inegalitarianism	.119 (0.12)*	.116 (.028)*
Individualism	−.122 (.062)*	−.151 (.080)*
Racial attitudes		
Affect	−.000 (.001)	−.000 (.001)
Stereotypes	−.109 (.080)	−.115 (.082)
Perceived threat	.218 (.089)**	.084 (.111)
Symbolic racism	.380 (.081)***	.498 (.107)****
Interactions		
College × conservatism	—	−.003 (.013)
College × inegalitarianism	—	.013 (.121)
College × individualism	—	.052 (.127)
College × perceived threat	—	−.007 (.179)
College × symbolic racism	—	−.264 (.156)*
Adjusted R^2	.332	.327

Cell entries are unstandardized regression coefficients. Figures in parentheses are standard errors.
*$p < .10$ **$p < .05$ ***$p < .01$ ****$p < .001$

significant relation (at conventional levels of statistical discernability, $p < .05$) to perceived negative effects of affirmative action is conservative self-identification. If a more generous criterion for statistical discernability is applied ($p < .10$), which may be justifiable in this instance given the overall small number of cases and the arbitrariness of the conventional standard, then both inegalitarianism and individualism influence beliefs about affirmative action. The effect of individualism, however, is in the opposite direction of that expected under the principled objections hypothesis: The more whites are committed to notions of reward for hard work, the less likely they are to hold negative beliefs about the effects of affirmative action for blacks.

The effects for perceived threat and symbolic racism are more straightforward. Both significantly enhance whites' perception of negative impacts of affirmative action, particularly so for symbolic racism. And these two variables contribute the lion's share to the overall 33.2

percent of the variance explained in perceptions of the negative effects of affirmative action under model 1 in table 3.

Model 2 (see table 3) allows for possible interactions between level of education and the values and ideology measures, as well as the perceived threat and symbolic racism measures. None of the interaction terms meet conventional criteria of significance. Given the small Ns, however, it is worth noting that the effect of symbolic racism does appear to be smaller among the college-educated (p < .10). However, there is no evidence of a heightened effect of ideology or for either of the value and ideology measures among the better educated. There is no sign that the effect of perceived threat is contingent on level of education. The model including the interaction terms, furthermore, does not yield a meaningful improvement in variance explained over the model specifying no interactions. On the whole, the education-interaction hypothesis is not borne out. The relatively limited capacity of education to reduce the level or impact of some forms of intergroup negativism has, of course, been anticipated by Jackman's ideological refinement thesis (Jackman and Muha 1984).

Conclusion

Our results support several conclusions. First, whites and racial minority group members do not hold diametrically opposed views of the costs and benefits of affirmative action for blacks. Although much of the media discourse about affirmative action highlights intense group conflict, especially between blacks and whites, there is far more overlap in outlooks than such packaging recognizes (Entman 1997). Whereas the results point in manifold ways to the central importance of race to affirmative action politics, the arena for potential common ground is larger than the general discourse or the tenor of recent scholarship on public opinion about affirmative action has properly acknowledged. To be sure, beliefs about the effects of affirmative action do not foreordain specific policy positions. Yet, much of the politics of affirmative action is a discourse about the effects of such a policy. These results point to some useful wellsprings of favorable and potentially more consensual views of affirmative action.

Second, much of the reason race matters would appear to reflect group-based interests. This is, we submit, the only reasonable interpretation of the powerfully robust racial difference in opinion that separates the views of blacks and of Latinos from those of whites and Asians. Certainly this is not a context where one would argue for a heritable proclivity to favor affirmative action. Yet, group differences are just one possible indication of an interest basis to public opinion. But even in terms of understanding the effects of perceived group threat and, to a degree, of symbolic racism on whites' beliefs, what appears to be at stake is something about how individuals understand their place in the American racial order. That is, it would be a mistake to interpret these results as simply confirming the advocacy of those on the Left, who wish to don the armor of moral superiority and classify opponents of affirmative action as transparent racists. These are racial attitudes as situated in a powerfully racialized economic and political context where there is a meaningful and indisputable short-term difference in group interests (Bobo 1997).

It might be argued that group differences in opinion are to be expected under both symbolic racism theory and group position theory. After all, symbolic racism is a theory about the ideas and, if you will, "group cultures," enveloping race relations. Perhaps. Such a claim is convincing if and only if it can be fashioned without reference to the social structural conditions, such as persistent segregation and deep economic inequality, that are the fundamental basis for objectively different racial group interests in a policy such as affirmative action. If the nature of differences in group cultures is bound up with differences in the structural conditions of group life, then culture, ideology, and interests cannot be neatly separated. More to the point, if the nature of group differences in opinion aligns with underlying objective interests of the groups at stake, then symbolic racism's emphasis on the core non-rational—indeed, purely ideational and irrational (Kinder and Sears 1981; Sears 1988)—basis of racial attitudes is immediately called into question. Given the inability to explain away these differences on the basis of other individual-level factors, it seems reasonable to hold that there is some pull, influence, or effect on public opinion of the real-world contingencies extant in a racially stratified society. At a minimum, once social structural conditions are invoked, whether the influence of these conditions is seen as proximal or distal, as an element of group differences in opinion, then the strong version of the symbolic racism argument fails.

The failure of symbolic racism in this regard, however, does not automatically make the group position argument persuasive. If the group position interpretation were correct, some might argue, wouldn't there be stronger evidence of overtly racialized claims by whites against affirmative action than we actually observe? Not necessarily. Intensely felt in-group identity and expressly articulated racial group interests among dominant group members are not necessary to the group position argument in this instance. To be sure, group position theory is directly concerned with hierarchical social arrangements: systematic and long-standing advantage and disadvantage, privilege and disprivilege allocated along racial lines. Yet, group position theory is also expressly historicized. The moment of greatest overt and intense concern with the group boundaries arises at the point of origin of a system of racialized inequality. Once a set of arrangements and practices is well institutionalized and rationalized, the dominant groups' privilege is readily maintained by defending "the system" and reacting against threats to it posed by members of the subordinate groups (Blumer 1958; Jackman 1994). This is precisely why group position theory emphasizes the critical importance of perceptions of threat, not merely group identity and differentiation or other intergroup orientations such as racial stereotypes (see Bobo 1999 for a fuller discussion).

William Julius Wilson (1987) convincingly argued that liberals lost their hegemonic position in the discourse on social welfare and poverty policy because they failed to acknowledge important, if often unsettling, realities about the nature of life in poor ghetto communities. Liberal analysts of public opinion on affirmative action have effectively committed the same error by ignoring or disparaging the all-too-transparent social reality of the differing stakes that blacks and Latinos, on one hand, and whites and Asians, on the other, have in the preservation and implementation of affirmative action. By not addressing the role of interest groups and perceived group interests and by stressing instead moralistic judgments of who is and who is not a racist, they opened the door to a conservative response that cast opponents of affirmative action as the truly moral figures in the debate. Thus, the transparent fact that political advocacy for affirmative action has come principally (although far from exclusively) from the traditional civil rights community, especially from black organizations explicitly seeking to advance the interests of the black community, is not addressed at all by liberal analysts of racial attitudes. The extent of this error remains so great that even the most recent efforts to revive symbolic racism theory commit again the grave error (for example, Sears et al. 1997) of classifying attitudes toward civil rights leaders and black political activism as an abstract racial resentment, namely symbolic racism (see Bobo 1988a, 1988b; Hughes 1997; Tuch and Hughes 1996 for a critique). By having legitimated and made central a discourse of values and morality, liberal analysts made it easy for conservative analysts to cast the demands made by blacks and other minorities as morally corrupt self-aggrandizement.

Third, and perhaps above all else, the talk of values and ideology—of a putatively principled basis of objection to affirmative action—is largely discredited by this analysis. Ideological identification has a real net effect on beliefs about the impact of affirmative action among whites. However, part of the gross effect of ideology stems from its correlation with explicitly racial attitudes and, what is more, the effects of perceived threat and of symbolic racism are a good deal more consequential.

Of course, it has been easy to overplay the argument from principles. Those on the Right who wish to don the armor of moral innocence in their war against affirmative action are ready to accept this view. Certainly, seminal elite treatises (Glazer 1975) and media discourse (Entman 1997) have placed such exaggerated emphasis on the word *preferences* and so routinely packaged affirmative action as a profound break with an American tradition of resisting government recognition of groups that the real historical record is easily misunderstood. Explicitly race-based policies, usually actively antiminority in design, have characterized major social policies in the United States almost from the very founding of the nation (Takaki 1994), so much so that the logic of affirmative action policies, rather than contradicting the American historical pattern, is actually entirely consistent with it (Skrentny 1996). As the eminent historian John Higham explained,

> There was nothing novel or constitutionally irregular about governments or private bureaucracies favoring a class of citizens who need special help. Consider, for example, the Freedman's Bureau, which Congress created in 1866 to assist newly freed former slaves in the conquered South, or the long history of federal water policy, tax laws, and veterans legislation—all of which singled out a particular group for government benefits. (1997, 20)

Indeed, given the historic intertwining of race and the understanding of values in the United States, it is somewhat paradoxical, if not Orwellian, that an argument concerning values and ideology is ever credibly positioned as completely race-neutral. Race has long been the axis along which full and genuine membership in the polity was established and which set the boundaries for determining what constituted appropriate or inappropriate treatment of individuals (Bobo 1988b; Prager 1987; Steinberg 1995). Race has been so profoundly implicated in American politics that it played the central role in reshaping partisan identities and party alignments in the post–World War II period (Carmines and Stimson 1989; Edsall and Edsall 1992).

In sum, neither U.S. history nor the wellsprings of public opinion provide much support for the values and ideology position. Given the resounding rejection of this theory in a range of studies using different samples and with finality (see Bobo 1991; Kinder and Sanders 1996; Meertens and Pettigrew 1997; Sears et al. 1997; Sidanius, Pratto, and Bobo 1996), absent some powerful new evidence, the principled objections hypothesis stands as a plausible but repeatedly disconfirmed hypothesis.

Students of public opinion on affirmative action will better understand the social phenomenon they study and make more useful contributions to the national dialogue on race if (a) research reaches beyond policy preferences to include beliefs about the effects of affirmative action, (b) the importance of race and racial group interests is repositioned to a more central analytical place, and (c) multiracial analyses and comparisons become more commonplace. Without denying that racism remains a problem or that ideological conservatism matters for white attitudes, affirmative action is about the place racial groups should occupy in American society.[3]

Although sometimes differing in degrees and forms, the economic disadvantages and modern-day racial discrimination faced by blacks and Latinos are tangible. These groups are more likely to live below the poverty line, indeed far below it as compared to whites (Harrison and Bennett 1995); they are far less likely to complete college degrees (Hauser 1993), a form of certification that increasingly draws the line between a middle-class standard of living and a life of constant economic hardship (Danziger and Gottshalk 1996); and they will almost certainly face discrimination in searching for a place to live (Massey and Denton 1993) or for employment (Holzer 1996; Kirschenman and Neckerman 1991; Turner, Fix, and Struyk 1991). The removal of affirmative action in higher education has immediate and potentially disastrous effects on the positions of blacks and Latinos (Weiss 1997). It is increasingly clear that loosening the pressure brought by government for affirmative action and for activist civil rights enforcement produces real and often drastic declines in the economic and educational fortunes of blacks and Latinos (Carnoy 1994). Despite all the high, abstract, and moralizing rhetoric, affirmative action is about concrete matters of who gets what.

A rhetoric centered around a mutual recognition and accommodation of legitimate interests is a far more promising basis for racial progress than are the brickbats of moral superiority now wielded so vigorously by those on the Left and those on the Right. Furthermore, advocates of affirmative action would do well, first, to shed the perception that white public opinion is monolithic on this question and, second, to set about the eminently political task of promoting ideas and values consistent with affirmative action. Such framing of issues by elites is a critical factor shaping public opinion. The far-from-overwhelming vote in California in favor of Proposition 209 and, more recently, the defeat of an anti–affirmative action measure in Houston suggest that there is more promise of an effective pro–affirmative action strategy than the current air of liberal defeat recognizes. As I have argued elsewhere (Bobo and Smith 1994, 395), assuming that public opinion on an issue is fixed can be more constraining than the public opinion itself.

Notes

1. Group position theory holds that it is essential to understand individual level attitudes as centrally concerned with relative group positions. At a macro social, historical, and cultural level, it is surely legitimate to understand group position theory as speaking to the dynamics of racism (Bobo, Kluegel, and Smith 1997). Unlike symbolic racism theory, however, the group position argument does not hinge on the existence of a singular, individual-level, attitudinal dimension best conceptualized as running from tolerance at one end to racism at the other. Instead, consistent with See and Wilson 1989, racism is best conceptualized as a property of social systems and prejudiced attitudes as a property of individuals.

2. A fuller discussion of the survey sample can be found in Bobo and Hutchings 1996 and Bobo and Zubrinsky 1996. The "Ethnic Antagonism in LA" survey had multiple objectives and piloted many new items. To accomplish this multipurpose agenda, it had a split-ballot structure. One-third of the sample received questions on attitudes toward Asians and immigration involving Asians. One-third of the sample received questions on attitudes toward Latinos and immigration involving Latinos. This analysis centers on the one-third of the sample that received questions concerning blacks and affirmative action for blacks in particular. The basic patterns of group differences reported below for the LACSS 1992 data are consistent with those found in household surveys with much larger samples (see Bobo and Johnson 2000).

3. There may be other principled grounds of objection to affirmative action. These would include concern over limiting the coercive power of government, especially the federal government (Schuman and Bobo 1988), and an aversion to governmental policy recognition of "racial" distinctions among the citizenry (Patterson 1997). Neither position, however, has been central to the public discourse on affirmative action or to empirical examinations of public opinion.

Acknowledgments

I wish to thank Edward Carmines, Jack Citrin, Donald Kinder, David Sears, and Paul Sniderman for their comments on an earlier draft of this chapter. This research was partly supported by National Science Foundation grant SBR-9515183.

References

Blumer, Herbert. 1958. Race prejudices as a sense of group position. *Pacific Sociological Review* 1:3–7.

Bobo, Lawrence. 1988a. Attitudes toward the black political movement: Trends, meaning, and effects on racial policy preferences. *Social Psychology Quarterly* 51:287–302.

———. 1988b. Group conflict, prejudice, and the paradox of racial attitudes. In *Eliminating racism: Profiles in controversy*, edited by Phyllis A. Katz and Dalamas A. Taylor. New York: Plenum.

———. 1991. Social responsibility, individualism, and redistributive policies. *Sociological Forum* 6:71–92.

———. 1992. *Los Angeles County social survey: Ethnic antagonism in LA* (machine readable data file and codebook). Los Angeles: Institute for Social Science Research, University of California.

———. 1997. The color line, the dilemma, and the dream: Race relations in America at the close of the twentieth century. In *Civil rights and social wrongs: Black-white relations since World War 11*, edited by John Higham. University Park: Pennsylvania State University Press.

———. 1999. Prejudice as group position: Microfoundations of a sociological approach to racism and race relations. *Journal of Social Issues* 55:445–72.

Bobo, Lawrence, and Vincent L. Hutchings. 1996. Perceptions of racial group competition: Extending Blumer's theory of group position to a multiracial social context. *American Sociological Review* 61:951–72.

Bobo, Lawrence, and Devon Johnson. 2000. Racial attitudes in a prismatic metropolis: Mapping identity, stereotypes. Competition and views on affirmative action. In *Prismatic metropolis: Inequality in Los Angeles*, edited by Lawrence Bobo, Melvin L. Oliver, James H. Johnson, and Abel Valenzuela. New York: Russell Sage Foundation.

Bobo, Lawrence, and James R. Kluegel. 1993. Opposition to race-targeting: Self-interest, stratification ideology, or racial attitudes? *American Sociological Review* 58:443–64.

Bobo, Lawrence, James R. Kluegel, and Ryan A. Smith. 1997. Laissez-faire racism: The crystallization of a kinder, gentler antiblack ideology. In *Racial attitudes in the 1990s: Continuity and change*, edited by Stanley A. Tuch and Jack K. Martin. Westport, Conn.: Praeger.

Bobo, Lawrence, and Ryan A. Smith. 1994. Antipoverty policy, affirmative action, and racial attitudes. In *Confronting poverty: Prescriptions for change*, edited by Sheldon Danziger, Gary Sandefur, and Daniel H. Weinberg. Cambridge: Harvard University Press.

Bobo, Lawrence, and Camille L. Zubrinsky. 1996. Attitudes on residential integration: Perceived status differences, mere in-group preference, or racial prejudice? *Social Forces* 74:883–909.

Carmines, Edward G., and James A. Stimson. 1989. *Issue evolution: Race and the transformation of American politics.* Princeton: Princeton University Press.

Carnoy, Martin L. 1994. *Faded dreams: The politics and economics of race in America.* New York: Cambridge University Press.

Chermerinsky, Edwin. 1997. Making sense of the affirmative action debate. In *Civil rights and social wrongs: Black-white relations since World War II*, edited by John Higham. University Park: Pennsylvania State University Press.

Danziger, Stanley, and Peter Gottshalk. 1996. *America unequal.* New York: Russell Sage Foundation.

Edley, Christopher. 1996. *Not all black and white: Affirmative action and American values.* New York: Hill and Wang.

Edsall, Thomas B., and Mary D. Edsall. 1992. *Chain reaction: The impact of race, rights, and taxes on American politics.* New York: Norton.

Entman, Robert M. 1997. Manufacturing discord: Media in the affirmative action debate. *Press/Politics* 2:32–51.

Feldman, Stanley. 1988. Structure and consistency in public opinion: The role of core beliefs and values. *American Journal of Political Science* 82:773–87.

Glazer, Nathan 1975. *Affirmative discrimination.* New York: Basic Books.

Harrison, Robert J., and Charlotte E. Bennett. 1995. Racial and ethnic diversity. In *State of the union: America in the 1990s*, vol. 2, *Social trends*, edited by Reynolds Farley. New York: Russell Sage Foundation.

Hauser, Robert M. 1993. Trends in college entry among whites, blacks, and Hispanics. In *Studies of supply and demand in higher education*, edited by Charles T. Clotfelter and Michael Rothschild. Chicago: University of Chicago Press.

Higham, John. 1997. Introduction: A historical perspective. In *Civil rights and social wrongs: Black-white relations since World War 11*, edited by John Higham. University Park: Pennsylvania State University Press.

Holzer, Harry J. 1996. *What employers want: Job prospects for less-educated workers.* New York: Russell Sage Foundation.

Hughes, M. 1997. Symbolic racism, old-fashioned racism, and whites' opposition to affirmative action. In *Racial attitudes in the 1990s: Continuity and change*, edited by Stanley Tuch and Jack K. Martin. Westport, Conn.: Praeger.

Jackman, Mary R. 1994. *The velvet glove: Paternalism and conflict in gender, class, and race relations.* Berkeley: University of California Press.

Jackman, Mary R., and Michael J. Muha. 1984. Education and intergroup attitudes: Moral enlightenment, superficial democratic commitment, or ideological refinement? *American Sociological Review* 49:751–69.

Jankowski, Martin S. 1995. The rising significance of status in U.S. race relations. In *The bubbling cauldron: Race, ethnicity, and the urban crisis*, edited by Michael P. Smith and Joe R. Feagin. Minneapolis: University of Minnesota Press.

Jaynes, Gerald D., and Robin M. Williams Jr. 1989. *A common destiny: Blacks and American society.* Washington, D.C.: National Academy Press.

Kinder, Donald R., and Lynn M. Sanders. 1996. *Divided by color: Racial politics and democratic ideals.* Chicago: University of Chicago Press.

Kinder, Donald R., and David O. Sears. 1981. Prejudice and politics: Symbolic racism versus racial threats to the good life. *Journal of Personality and Social Psychology* 40:414–31.

Kirschenman, Joleen, and Kathryn Neckerman. 1991. "We'd love to hire them, but . . .": The meaning of race for employers. In *The urban underclass,* edited by Christopher Jencks and Paul E. Peterson. Washington, D.C.: Brookings Institution.

Kluegel, James R., and Eliot R. Smith. 1986. *Beliefs about inequality: Americans' views of what is and what ought to be.* New York: Aldine.

Lipset, Seymour M., and William Schneider. 1978. The *Bakke* case: How would it be decided at the bar of public opinion? *Public Opinion* 1:38–48.

Massey, Douglas S., and Nancy A. Denton. 1993. *American apartheid: Segregation and the making of the underclass.* Cambridge: Harvard University Press.

Meertens, Roel W., and Thomas F. Pettigrew. 1997. Is subtle prejudice really prejudice? *Public Opinion Quarterly* 61:54–71.

Patterson, Orlando. 1997. *The ordeal of integration: Progress and resentment in America's "racial" crisis.* Washington, D.C.: Civitas.

Prager, J. 1987. American political culture and the shifting meaning of race. *Ethnic and Racial Studies* 10:62–81.

Schuman, Howard, and Lawrence Bobo. 1988. Survey-based experiments on white racial attitudes toward residential integration. *American Journal of Sociology* 94:273–99.

Schuman, Howard, Charlotte Steeh, Lawrence Bobo, and Maria Krysan. 1997. *Racial attitudes in America: Trends and interpretations.* Cambridge: Harvard University Press.

Sears, David O. 1988. Symbolic racism. In *Eliminating racism: Profiles in controversy,* edited by Phyllis A. Katz and Dalamas A. Taylor. New York: Plenum.

Sears, David O., Colette Van Larr, Mary Carrillo, and Rick Kosterman. 1997. Is it really racism? The origins of white Americans' opposition to race-targeted policies. *Public Opinion Quarterly* 61:16–53.

See, Kathleen O'Sullivan, and William J. Wilson. 1989. *Race and ethnicity.* In *Handbook of sociology,* edited by Neil Smelser. Newbury Park, Calif.: Sage.

Sidanius, James, Felicia Pratto, and Lawrence. Bobo. 1996. Racism, conservatism, affirmative action, and intellectual sophistication: A matter of principled conservatism or group dominance? *Journal of Personality and Social Psychology* 70:476–90.

Skrentny, John D. 1996. *The ironies of affirmative action.* Chicago: University of Chicago Press.

Sniderman, Paul M., and Thomas Piazza. 1993. *The scar of race.* Cambridge: Harvard University Press.

Sniderman, Paul M., and Phillip E. Tetlock. 1986. Symbolic racism: Problems of political motive attribution. *Journal of Social Issues* 42:441–55.

Steeh, Charlotte, and Maria Krysan. 1996. The polls—trends: Affirmative action and the public. *Public Opinion Quarterly* 60:128–58.

Steinberg, Stephen. 1995. *Turning back: The retreat from racial justice in American thought and policy.* Boston: Beacon.

Takaki, Ronald T. 1994. Reflections on racial patterns in America. In *From different shores: Perspectives on race and ethnicity in America,* edited by Ronald T. Takaki. New York: Oxford University Press.

Tetlock, Phillip E. 1994. Political psychology or politicized psychology: Is the road to scientific hell paved with good moral intentions? Political Psychology 15:509–29.

Tuch, Stanley A., and M. Hughes. 1996. Whites' racial policy views. *Social Science Quarterly* 77: 710–29.

Turner, Margery A., Michael Fix, and Raymond J. Struyk. 1991. *Opportunities denied, opportunities diminished: Racial discrimination in hiring.* Washington, D.C.: Urban Institute.

Weiss, Kenneth. 1997. UC law schools' new rules cost minorities spots. *Los Angeles Times,* 15 May, A1.

West, Cornel 1993. *Race matters.* Boston: Beacon.

Wilson, William J. 1987. *The truly disadvantaged.* Chicago: University of Chicago Press.

9

Understanding Racial Polarization on Affirmative Action: The View from Focus Groups

. . .

Carol M. Swain, Kyra R. Greene, and Christine Min Wotipka

Understanding public opinion on socially divisive issues such as affirmative action is of utmost importance in twenty-first-century America. Unfortunately, most of what we know about affirmative action comes only from research on the attitudes of Euro-Americans and to a much lesser extent African Americans. Other groups, such as Asian Americans and Latino Americans, have generally been excluded from analysis because the typical national survey has too few respondents from each of these categories to compute meaningful statistics.[1]

The dearth of information about Asian Americans and Latinos is especially problematic given the increasing diversity of the United States. Already minorities constitute majorities in cities such as Los Angeles, Houston, Miami, New York, and San Francisco. By the year 2050, racial and ethnic minorities are expected to constitute at least 47 percent of the U.S. population. Asian, Latino, and African Americans will all experience population growth, with Latinos growing the fastest, surpassing blacks by the year 2010. By then, it is expected that blacks and Hispanics will compose about one-fourth of the national population (Bositis 1998, 5).

This chapter takes a first step to fill this gap in our knowledge of public opinion on affirmative action. By studying conversations of different racial and ethnic groups that were conducted in controlled settings, we can learn much about American attitudes and views on affirmative action. Using data from focus groups, this chapter explores the beliefs of Asian, Latino, African, and Euro-Americans.

Overview of Survey Research

Beginning in the mid-1970s, social scientists accumulated a large body of public opinion data on American attitudes regarding affirmative action. After analyzing the universe of affirmative action–related questions from polls taken between 1977 and 1995, Steeh and Krysan (1996) concluded that the structure of public attitudes on the subject defines acceptable affirmative action policy as falling somewhere between color-blindness and desire for preferences. An overwhelming majority of Americans support outreach programs to locate qualified women and minorities for employment opportunities, a form of soft affirmative action. Most other forms of preferential treatment of minorities, however, including the use of quota programs and set-asides, garner much less support. Programs geared specifically for African Americans are the least popular among Euro-Americans, whereas those that benefit women are most popular (Moore 1995).

Before publication of this volume, very little systematic research existed on how the attitudes of Asian Americans and Latinos compare with those of Euro-Americans and African Americans. Moreover, the multiethnic studies that have been conducted have tended to focus on the attitudes of elite subgroups found in privileged settings such as colleges and universities (Bell et al. 1997; Fukurai et al. 1994; Kravitz and Platania 1993; Niemann and Dovidio 1998). One study that assessed the attitudes of university students and managers towards affirmative action in employment found similar levels of support for the policy among Asian Americans and Latino Americans (Bell et al. 1997). These groups were more supportive of employment preferences than were Euro-Americans, but they lagged behind African Americans in their enthusiasm for the policy. In a similar study using a sample of academicians in psychology departments in the United States, Niemann and Dovidio (1998) found that African Americans held the most favorable view of affirmative action, followed by Latinos, Asian Americans, and whites. Bobo's more representative survey research (chapter 8) finds a similar ethnic ordering of support for affirmative action.

How a given person responds to survey questions about affirmative action, however, depends to a considerable extent on how the items are framed, the answer choices available to the respondents, and the context of the questions (Adkins 1996; Fine 1992; Gamson and Modigliani 1987; Kinder and Sanders 1990, 1996; Schuman et al. 1997; Sigelman and Welch 1991; Steeh and Krysan 1996; Stoker 1997; Swain, Rodgers, and Silverman 2000). For example, affirmative action questions that ask about quotas and preferential treatment of minorities, especially blacks, garner less support than those that address support for equal opportunity measures and job training programs for disadvantaged Americans

(Lipset and Schneider 1978; Lipset 1992; Norman 1995; Sniderman and Piazza 1993; Sniderman and Carmines 1997). Steeh and Krysan (1996) found that several cross-cutting dimensions influence how respondents answer survey questions about affirmative action. Among these are cognitive considerations, that is, whether the person understood the question enough to give an informed answer, the type of policy asked about, and its stated beneficiaries. Because of the complicated problems of context and question framing, the survey data on attitudes toward affirmative action are often difficult to interpret. Greater awareness of the sensitivity of affirmative action questions to framing and contextual problems has led some researchers to conclude that validity could be greatly improved if we abandoned the use of the actual phrase "affirmative action," as well as other confusing and imprecise terms such as "quota," "special consideration," "preference," and "preferential treatment," and instead describe the actual content of specific policies (Adkins 1996; Steeh and Krysan 1996).[2]

Given the dominance of survey research on affirmative action, the shortcomings common to all surveys, and especially the problems regarding surveys of opinion on affirmative action, we felt that much could be gained by conducting several well-structured focus groups. In the sections to follow, we present data from the conversations of relatively well-educated Americans discussing their views of what affirmative action policy is, how the policy works, the nature of its goals, and its intended beneficiaries. We show that widespread misunderstandings about the inner workings of affirmative action characterize public opinion even among educated people. Consequently, we question whether researchers can say with any degree of certainty how to interpret data from different racial and ethnic groups.

Refocusing on Focus Groups

Focus groups consist of small numbers of people brought together to discuss an assigned topic. Although political scientists today rarely use focus groups, the methodology has been used in scholarly research since the early 1940s, when Paul Lazarsfeld and Robert K. Merton pioneered their use in the Office for Radio Research at Columbia University. Today, commercial marketing groups, professional psychologists and sociologists, U.S. military officials, and political campaign consultants frequently use focus groups to test products and ideas (Stewart and Shamdasani 1990; Kolbert 1992).

Focus groups have an advantage over conventional public opinion polls because they allow researchers to interact directly with respondents, thus giving them opportunities to probe deeper and ask for clarifications of the kinds of attitudes revealed in standard surveys. Morgan (1997, 2) states that "the hallmark of focus groups is their explicit use of group interaction to produce data and insights that would be less accessible without the interaction found in the group." Focus groups allow researchers to capture discussions in a special setting where strangers converse among themselves knowing that there is little likelihood of ever encountering their fellow discussants again—perhaps alleviating concerns about violating norms or practical sensibilities.

Nevertheless, as with all types of research methods, focus groups have their limitations. Focus group results, for instance, are not generalizable to a larger population, and the interactions between the participants and the moderator can affect what people say. Moreover, some individuals will undoubtedly continue to give socially desirable responses rather than actual opinions. Conover et al. (1991, 805) point out, however, that "focus groups mirror the social context within which many people actually experience citizenship." Since we always have leaders and followers in this society, we should not be overly concerned if some groups have dominant members who emerge as opinion leaders, while other members take a back seat. Because so much of what we know about American attitudes toward affirmative action comes from national surveys, we made a conscious decision to sacrifice greater generalizability for greater specificity about what some Americans living in the Northeast were thinking about the issue.

To conduct our focus groups, the lead author commissioned Focus Plus of New York City and Schlesinger Associates of Edison, New Jersey, to recruit and organize participants for a total of six focus groups. Between May 8 and May 11, 1995, a group of African Americans, a group of Euro-Americans, and a group of Latinos met in Edison, while a second group of African Americans, a second group of Euro-Americans, and a group of Asian Americans met in New York City. Our groups ranged in size from ten to twelve members, most of whom had some college education and many of whom were college graduates. A moderator of the same race or ethnicity as the members of the group led each group in a loose, semi-structured questioning format for a two-hour session (see Anderson et al. 1988).

Perceptions of Affirmative Action by Race:
The Dominance of Quotas

Using a stratified random sample of Chicago residents, Crosby and Cordova (1996, 641) found that "people who understand affirmative action in its traditional or classical sense endorse the policy much more strongly than do people who believe that affirmative action means quotas." By "traditional view of affirmative action," Crosby and Cordova meant a soft affirmative action that offers equal opportunity and outreach to the disadvantaged. Affirmative action viewed as a quota program carries with it the notion of unqualified minorities being unfairly advanced through the use of racial preferences (see also Hochschild 1999).

Our focus groups show that each group, including African Americans, has internalized the idea that affirmative action is about quotas. There were differences, however, in the way in which racial groups think quotas operate. Whereas most groups describe quotas as the forced selection of fixed numbers of minorities for jobs and other societal goods, African Americans view quotas as restrictions used to limit the number of blacks in a given setting. None of the participants in our study seemed to be aware that the widely shared perception that affirmative action involves quotas is factually incorrect—quotas are illegal unless imposed by a court as a remedy for past discrimination.

The fact that so many people associate affirmative action with quotas demonstrates how well the Republican Party has framed the issue. When President Bush vetoed the proposed Civil Rights Act of 1990, he stated that the bill was not about civil rights protections but about "quotas, quotas, quotas" (Kinder and Sanders 1996, 163). Media reports of dual admissions standards and questionable forms of affirmative action have no doubt fueled this perception of the policy.

The comments below are illustrative of what some of our participants were thinking and saying about the relation between affirmative action and quotas.

Asian Americans' Perceptions of Affirmative Action

Asian Americans described affirmative action quotas as a means to equalize opportunities and diversify workplaces and educational institutions. For a few Asian Americans, quotas meant that less-qualified minorities were being hired for some jobs. Others argued that the main objective of affirmative action was to ensure the hiring of minorities when they were qualified, and they believed that instances of unqualified minorities being hired to fill quotas were "rare." Regardless of whether they felt that minorities were being hired with lesser qualifications, most of the Asian Americans were not convinced that race was enough to keep someone in a job once hired. They believed that the minority employee, like any other employee, needed to have or develop job skills in order to retain a position. One middle-aged woman remarked, "Affirmative action will work up to a certain point, if you want to get the job. But there's also performance. You also have to prove yourself. You can't stay in a company just because of your color."

One Asian American male stated a view, common among blacks, that racial quotas are used by companies to restrict rather than to expand the number of minorities. Using the Adolph Coors Company as his example, he explained how the company was reluctant to hire minorities until a group of homosexuals in San Francisco was able to get the bars in that city to stop selling Coors beer until the company changed its employment practices. "The point is," he explained, "[quotas] were good, but not good. Because now . . . different people work for [the company]," but he stated, "Do you know what? They're still just meeting their quota. They're still just hiring just enough [minorities] to meet their quota." Although no one in the Asian American group made the connection, this participant's example of the negative uses of quotas coincides with the claim by many Asian Americans that since the early 1980s ceilings have been placed on the number of Asians admitted to top universities (Takagi 1992).

Latinos' Perceptions of Affirmative Action

Unlike the respondents in the study by Bell et al. (1997), Latinos in our focus groups were less supportive of affirmative action than were the Asian Americans. Like all other groups, Latinos described affirmative action programs as involving quotas and set-asides for minorities. The majority believed that lower standards were being unfairly used to select minorities for employment and for admissions to higher education. One Latino man gave an example of the use of racial preferences that other members of his group agreed was unfair. In his fictitious example of race norming, two candidates applied for a job and took an examination. Even though the white applicant scored a 90 on the exam, the Latino with a score of 75 was offered the job. Latinos opposed affirmative action that operated in this manner. One woman declared, "I don't think quotas should be [used] or standards . . . lowered. It should be the same for everybody whether you're black, white, green, or yellow. There should be one level [for everyone to reach]." Another woman stated that the use of job-related quotas by employers to lower the standards for minorities when they compete against white people is racism.

Unbeknown to this participant, and most of the others in our groups, race norming, in which the scores of minority candidates are grouped and compared only with the scores of other members of their group, has been illegal in the employment context since the passage of the 1991 Civil Rights Act. The focus group members were generally unaware of this and, perhaps because of media depictions of affirmative action programs that appear to openly use dual standards in higher education, focus group members almost invariably assumed that race norming and quotas are core elements of affirmative action programs.

Latinos felt that affirmative action preferences harmed minorities by labeling them as less competent than Euro-Americans. Many articulated some of the same concerns of black conservatives as they discussed the stereotypes and stigmas attached to the beneficiaries of affirmative action programs. A foreign-born man gave an example that he offered as proof of the negative assumptions that whites made about successful minorities:

> The messenger comes in the morning; he's American, Anglo-Saxon. He comes and he says to me, "What are you doing here?" [I say,] "I work here. I work in the computer room." He says, "I don't understand. They give the better jobs to people who come from other countries." I got very upset. I said, "Look. I went to school. I educated myself and I'm working here. You can do the same thing if you want to. [But] if you want to stay down and be a messenger all your life, it's your problem."

Of course, what is occurring in the above exchange is that two people are talking past each other. The Anglo is aware that the newly arrived Latino is possibly a beneficiary of racial preferences, whereas the Latino's image of himself is of a person who worked hard to earn his job. As Graham has pointed out in chapter 2, the convergence of immigration policy and affirmative action is partially responsible for the hostility towards the policy.

African Americans' Perceptions of Affirmative Action

African Americans never defined affirmative action in terms of preferential treatment, and they used the concept of quotas differently from most whites and members of other groups. They saw quotas as potentially harmful restrictions used to limit the number of minorities in a given setting. Indeed, quotas were the means that institutions used to discriminate against them. An African American male commented that employment quotas ensure that "only a certain number of blacks can succeed, or benefit from affirmative action, when maybe there's a whole cluster of people that are qualified. Maybe affirmative action says . . . you have to have three . . . [blacks]. What about the rest of those people?" In other words, they felt that affirmative action quotas could harm blacks overall by limiting the numbers of offered positions. To them, the possibility existed that qualified African Americans are being overlooked once a certain threshold has been reached by a given institution.

Regardless of the general unconstitutionality of racial quotas in most cases, a majority of African Americans seems to believe that quotas exist and are reflected in the makeup of institutions. Although African Americans saw quotas as potentially harmful restrictions, they did not oppose their use and saw them, in fact, as assuring a minimal level of protection against discrimination. If anything, blacks wanted employment quotas increased so that more than a token number of minorities would be hired, and they displayed little interest in whether there might be times when there were not enough qualified minorities to meet the demands of increased quotas. African Americans' acceptance of quotas follows from their fear of leaving their fate to the goodwill of Euro-Americans. Just as with many Jews, African Americans see the potential harm that quotas can pose for their group.

African Americans were the only group to state that racism can operate in the selection of minority applicants for affirmative action positions. One man stated, "If you have a quota to hire four blacks, white employers may [run out and] just grab four blacks who may not be qualified for the job." In essence, African Americans thought that affirmative action may require employers to hire a fixed number of applicants of a certain race but that this did not insure that employers will seek the best-qualified of the minorities. According to this view, some Euro-Americans treat African Americans as though they were interchangeable. Therefore, some employers will not consider the differential qualifications of blacks in the same manner as they would for white applicants.

Euro-Americans' Perceptions of Affirmative Action

Euro-Americans in the New York City group were the most negative about affirmative action and blamed the policy for allowing unqualified minority applicants to obtain positions while excluding more-qualified whites. One woman complained: "It's an unfair system. . . . Why should someone get into Harvard with lower grades than . . . a white male. . .? Just because they're filling quotas, they're letting them go to Yale. That's not the way this country was built. This country is [one where] you're recognized for your ability, not your sex, not your color, and not your religion and that's the way it should be." A young college-educated white teacher explained affirmative action by stating that it operates so that "if you are the hiring boss and one applicant is white and the other black, you have to select the quota. . . . You have to fill the quota and hire the black." An older white man agreed: "Employers will not take white males when they have to take blacks, Hispanic, and Chinese. . . . Otherwise, they are going to be called racist. The government has put this policy in place and rammed it down our throats—this affirmative action."

When Euro-Americans discussed affirmative action, they usually spoke as if it were a relief program that required people to go in and sign up. For example, some whites prefaced their comments with statements such as, "when people are in this affirmative action . . ." Their comments suggested a belief that most, if not all, minority hires or college admittees are unqualified beneficiaries. However, a few Euro-Americans expressed concern that affirmative action unfairly maligned qualified blacks by detracting from their achievements.

In short, Euro-Americans do not associate affirmative action with equal opportunities for all. One white male viewed quotas as a form of restriction in a way many African Americans do. He stated:

> I think that affirmative action gives a person the right to be choosy in discrimination. [In other words,] I filled my quota, so now I don't have to hire any more blacks, Latinos or Asians. . . . Now I can hire whoever I want, because my quota's already been met. . . . [Once quotas are met] somebody can come to the office who is a qualified black or Latino or Asian or whatever, and they could say, "Well . . . we don't have to [hire this person]."

More typically, whites believed that affirmative action gives African Americans better opportunities than Euro-Americans in both employment and education. Although the Euro-Americans in Edison were less hostile than the New Yorkers, one woman nevertheless complained to the nods of others that having African Americans in her work group meant that she had to perform her duties and theirs too. There was a general belief among whites that once blacks were hired under affirmative action they knew that they could not easily be fired and often neglected their duties.

The Goals of Affirmative Action through Different Eyes

People confuse the procedures used in affirmative action programs with the stated goals of programs. The confusion of goals with methods has implications for survey research, since researchers often ask respondents whether they think affirmative action programs have been successful in accomplishing their goals. The survey responses leave us with more questions than answers because we found that racial groups shared neither a common definition of affirmative action nor a uniform idea of its goals. Our data suggest that respondents' opinions are influenced by vastly different conceptual understandings of the policy.

The perceived goals of affirmative action varied across the groups. In all, the most commonly stated goals were (1) promoting equal opportunity in employment and education; (2) eradicating racial discrimination; (3) diversifying workplaces and other institutions; (4) maintaining quotas; (5) assisting the poor; and (6) assisting people with disabilities.

Asian Americans discussed affirmative action in terms of its equal opportunity and diversification goals. They believed the policy has been instrumental in increasing the numbers of African Americans in a workforce traditionally dominated by Euro-Americans. In addition, the majority stated that affirmative action programs are still needed because of the discrimination that blacks continue to face. One woman said, "If I were a black person and if I [went] to an interview, even if I [had] the educational background, I think I'd have to work harder to reach or to meet their expectation, because of what . . . employers are thinking, expecting [of] black people." One Asian American man saw the issue purely in numerical terms. He stated, "I think equalization or parity is the key word in affirmative action in that the government looks at the ratios of people [who are] minorities . . . as well as the majority, and then by that they set their quotas."

Despite their stated misgivings about the policy, many Latinos spoke in terms of its being a vehicle for increasing opportunities in education, employment, and minority-owned businesses. One man stated that "a lot of people have gotten to go to school that wouldn't be able to. A lot of people have gotten jobs based on their knowledge, and their standing, that before [affirmative action] they might have never been able to." Significantly, however, no one in this group mentioned diversity enhancement or the remediation of past and present discrimination as either a justification or a goal of affirmative action. Also, unlike other groups, Latinos believed that affirmative action should address issues relating to bilingual education and discrimination against people with Spanish surnames.

African Americans mostly described affirmative action programs as a means to combat racial discrimination in employment. One black man stated: "[Affirmative action] is mostly based on federal positions, and it mostly looked to education. And it looked at ways to remedy past discrimination and ways to recruit more African Americans and bring more African Americans into the work force and into the mainstream." Blacks described affirmative action policy as being beneficial for getting interviews and entry-level jobs, but like many other focus group members they believed that promotions were based on merit. Although blacks acknowledged enhanced opportunities in education brought about by race-specific grants and scholarships, unlike other groups, they did not seem to consider such programs to be affirmative action.

One elderly black man said that affirmative action was established to pacify blacks. He stated, "It says if we hire three whites, we should hire two blacks, because we don't want blacks to overrun the place. We don't want them in charge, so we have to have some whites in there to keep it balanced." Similarly, a Jamaican male commented, "What I see in offices in corporate America is one African American receptionist or secretary at the front desk, an African American supply manager who fixes the copy machine, and that is the structure of corporate America." However, a more favorable assessment of corporate affirmative action policies came from a young black female who stated, "I see affirmative action as positive, because black people who are qualified get a chance. Otherwise, they would not be seen. Equally qualified or not," she said, "affirmative action allows for an opportunity that otherwise would not have been had."

Euro-Americans generally believed that affirmative action programs are used to give preferences to less qualified minorities. They saw affirmative action as covering a denser network and wider scope of activities than members of our other groups thought. Their examples, for instance, frequently mentioned affirmative action policies not only in hiring decisions but in promotion decisions as well. They believed that affirmative action programs were common in higher education both in admissions to colleges and universities and in the granting of scholarships, and they drew attention to affirmative action programs in government contracting and loans. Although they mentioned several types of affirmative action programs, whites made no real distinction between quotas, goals, and special efforts at recruitment and outreach.

It seems likely that part of the racial polarization in public opinion on affirmative action issues comes about because groups possess different understandings about affirmative action and its goals. The framing of the issue in the media, especially by political entities, may have contributed to their confusion, but the differences are entrenched. Whites clearly believe that a major goal of affirmative action is to give preference to less-qualified minorities who cannot compete on their own merits, whereas many blacks believe that the primary goal of the policy is to eradicate otherwise intractable discrimination through the use of numerical goals that they too call quotas. African Americans see attacks on affirmative action as attacks on their lifeblood because to them affirmative action is the only policy that addresses the effects of persistent and ongoing white discrimination against blacks. For many African Americans the alternative is seen as either mandatory numerical goals or quotas, or continued racial discrimination against them that will deny blacks jobs and promotions in businesses and governmental agencies.

Between these poles are Asian Americans and Latinos. Like African Americans, both Latinos and Asian Americans see affirmative action as necessary. However, Asian Americans see the program as one that benefits blacks and angers whites. They were unclear as to the impact of affirmative action on their own life chances and opportunities. Latinos, on the other hand, see affirmative action as having a direct impact on their lives, but as a group they are ambivalent about whether the programs affect them in a positive or a negative way. Latinos more than African Americans are concerned that affirmative action stigmatized them by casting doubt on their achievement.

The Beneficiaries of Affirmative Action: Who Does and Who Should Benefit?

African Americans and at least one Latino argued that whites benefit from affirmative action because companies that comply with the policy gain advantages in loans and government contracts. One New Yorker stated that her employer "got extra money and they got grants that came in because they had me there." Using very different reasoning, Derrick Bell (1995) arrived at a similar view. White women in particular, Bell has argued, have benefited from affirmative action and have often received a greater percentage of affirmative action jobs than have African Americans. Similarly, he contends that white men have benefited from the widespread advertising of jobs done pursuant to the requirements of affirmative action programs. Were it not for affirmative action, he argues, these jobs would be filled by the "Old Boys Network," which restricted the opportunities of some white males.

African Americans addressed some of the issues raised by Graham (chapter 2) regarding immigrant beneficiaries of affirmative action and the evolution of hostility toward the program. More than other groups, African Americans rejected the view that all minority groups in the United States should be beneficiaries of affirmative action. They were also the only group to differentiate between native-born blacks and black immigrants. The majority of African Americans did not think that newly arrived immigrant groups should be allowed to benefit from affirmative action policies; rather, they believed that these policies should be reserved for members of historically disadvantaged groups in America. One woman stated that a "woman from India came in and took advantage of [affirmative action] and is making millions and millions of dollars. She's not the only one, it's people that are coming in from other countries and they're taking advantage of all that is here."

As Graham (chapter 2) and La Noue and Sullivan (chapter 3) point out, Asian Americans, though usually not included in university admissions affirmative action, are among the groups protected under federal affirmative action regulations. Nevertheless, our Asian focus group members expressed innocence concerning how their group benefits from the policy. Most Asian Americans, they argued, are uninformed about their eligibility for affirmative action. The group blamed a number of factors for this, including a lack of outreach into Asian American communities, complacency, citizenship status, and the poor language skills of some Asian immigrants.

Latinos spoke mostly of African Americans as being the beneficiaries of the policy, although they understand that they too are a protected group. Latinos favored class-based affirmative action because they thought that such a policy would reduce the stigmatization of beneficiary groups. Some Latinos stated that affirmative action was responsible for increased hostilities between racial and ethnic groups, especially between Euro-Americans and Latinos and between Latinos and blacks. Latinos expressed some concern that affirmative action was harmful to some minorities because it caused them to feel privileged and, as a consequence, not to work as hard as they might.

Euro-Americans saw the beneficiaries of affirmative action as being mostly undeserving African Americans. When they discussed other racial groups, their tone was less hostile. Two older white women in the New York group acknowledged gender discrimination, but argued that they had risen in their jobs without any assistance from affirmative action. White women oppose the preferential treatment of racial minorities as much as white men (Moore 1995; Ladd 1995; *Gallup Poll Monthly* 1989; *Gallup Poll Monthly* 1977). Perhaps this is because white women believe that preferential treatment of minorities lessens the opportunities of their husbands, sons and daughters. They are somewhat more supportive of affirmative action for women, as is the general population, but they oppose preferences for racial minorities (Moore 1995).

When it comes to determining who should benefit from affirmative action policies, there is substantially more consensus that the disabled and the poor are deserving. Affirmative action for the disabled was not a major area of contention for any group. Focus group participants appeared to suggest that the disabled were not responsible for their condition, and that as a consequence the discrimination against them was unfair (see also Sniderman and Carmines 1997). The apparent implication of this argument—that racial minorities *are* somehow responsible for their condition—was not explored by group members opposed to affirmative action. Although many of the focus group members stated the general proposition that individual merit should be used to judge applicants for jobs, when they discussed the disabled, a majority held that people should be hired for jobs that they are physically capable of performing. They did not add the qualification that the disabled applicant should be the most qualified for the position. One man saw helping people with disabilities as a positive kind of affirmative action. He stated, "As far as disabled people went, when a potential employer wants to discriminate against a disabled person because he is disabled, there are affirmative action laws to combat that and to make sure that the disabled person gets a fair shake." The moderator then asked, "So you think that the affirmative action program for disabled people is a positive program?" The man responded, "Somewhat positive, yeah . . . but, you've got to use it. . . . You've got to understand your rights and you have to use it."

A majority of members in each group seemed to concur with the general public that poor people, regardless of race or ethnicity, should be among the beneficiaries of affirmative action. Those who believed that strong individuals lead to stronger communities were more likely to favor programs that benefited people in need. A Latino male stated:

> There [are] so many people that before a lot of these [affirmative action programs] were implemented never had a chance to get an education because of their class or economic standings or their race, though people will deny that, but, yeah, that's the truth and the fact of the matter is that without an education, you're never going to get that economic growth that you need in those communities and you're always going to have—it's just a circle.

While supporting some class-based affirmative action, Euro-Americans were more ambivalent about need-based scholarships than were members of our other groups. They were concerned about persons who would be excluded from participation. To the agreement of others in her group, one woman stated that "a child should be able, based on his ability, how smart he is, what he's learned in his elementary years, that if he is deserving to go to a better school, whether his parents can afford to send him to a city university or private institution, that he deserves [a scholarship] on his own merit." A Latina expressed the opposite view when she argued that the "cruel reality" is that children who go to good high schools receive a better education and have superior opportunities for going to good universities. Consequently, scholarships based solely on merit are unfair. Another participant agreed:

> I think having a scholarship just open to everyone is probably not a good idea. There should be some other merits besides [academic achievement] because . . . if people anywhere are going to get at the scholarships, the majority of them are going to be . . . upper class kids, regardless of their race, because they get the better education. They get the better schools and everything else.

African Americans were mostly in favor of group-based affirmative action that takes race into consideration. The majority of whites opposed such programs. Some Latino Americans were concerned that race-based affirmative action programs spoil minorities, making them believe that they deserve special treatment because of their minority status. To them, all people should be treated equally as individuals without regard to race and without any preferential treatment. The majority of Asian Americans saw a need to consider the needs of both individuals and groups. However, they too expressed concerns about the abuse of some of the programs; these references were directed mostly at blacks.

Just as with the goals and the definition of affirmative action, our focus groups could not agree on who the beneficiaries of affirmative action are or should be. Not only were there different ideas relating to which specific racial and or ethnic groups have benefited and should benefit from affirmative action programs, there were also disagreements as to whether emphasis should be given to groups who suffer from past and present discrimination or just individuals in financial need. Group differences about the beneficiaries and goals of affirmative action highlight the difficulty of interpreting previously acquired data on affirmative action.

Perceptions of Discrimination by Race and Ethnicity

The most crucial explanatory factor for understanding differences between the racial and ethnic groups' views of affirmative action programs is their disparate perceptions of the existence of discrimination in American society today. Consistent with much survey research, we found our groups divided over whether racial discrimination against blacks and other people of color is a common occurrence (Schuman et al. 1997; Kinder and Sanders 1996). On this issue, Euro-Americans and African Americans saw different realities as whites minimized the extent of discrimination against blacks, while blacks asserted its prevalence. Asian Americans and Latinos expressed an awareness of continued discrimination against minorities, although these groups did not explicitly agree with blacks that affirmative action is the most appropriate remedy for discrimination. Only in one instance did a Latina express the belief that present-day discrimination justified the need for affirmative action programs. She frequently faced discrimination because of her physical appearance as someone of Latin descent. She stated, "It might not be all the time, but it's there, a little bit. So once you go into the job market from school, I think that [minorities] can still need that help from affirmative action."

Euro-Americans, for their part, believed that racial discrimination against minorities was largely a thing of the past. Many, however, viewed themselves as victims of "reverse discrimination." Given the media attention given to Euro-Americans' claims of reverse discrimination, it was not startling that many whites saw themselves as its unprotected victims. In each of our minority groups, a few Asian Americans, Latinos, and African Americans acknowledged the possibility of reverse discrimination against whites. Several Asian Americans stated that if they were Euro-Americans, they would be resentful of affirmative action because it seems to deny white people jobs for which they are qualified. In this context, one person observed that there is a growing "reactionary move-ment in this country, the angry white male."

Using focus group material on a number of diverse topics including affirmative action, Gamson (1992) identified this same sort of equivoca-tion in his groups. Gamson developed the concept of "moral indigna-tion" to explain their ambivalence. According to Gamson, racial groups may express moral outrage at perceived injustice against their group, a concept he calls "single indignation." A more complex version of this concept is the existence of "double indignation," in which a person may express outrage at how her group is being treated and frustration and anger at how other groups are affected. With affirmative action, double indignation can occur when individuals, such as African Americans, ac-knowledge that their own group is discriminated against while also ad-mitting that attempts to rectify the injury can have adverse impacts on others. In each ethnic group, at least one person expressed sensitivity to members of other groups. A black advocate of quotas in employment worried that unqualified minorities will sometimes be hired for jobs that more qualified individuals deserve. Another woman talked about the benefits that diversity can bring to institutions, but she nevertheless ex-pressed fears that in some instances people are being selected because of their skin color and not their ability—a development that she thought was detrimental. Similarly, an older Asian American woman reported feeling "divided on the issue" of affirmative action. She stated, "[I] wouldn't feel good about taking [a] job if I knew that I [received] it because of [my] origins."

Asian Americans and Discrimination

Members of this group did not feel that they faced much discrimination in their everyday lives as they discussed the benefits of being perceived as a "model minority." One man said that Asian-Americans may experi-ence some prejudice directed toward them but they are not discrimi-nated against outright. A middle-aged Asian American woman said, "Maybe [discrimination] has been directed towards me; I've never felt it." Other research suggests, however, that Asian Americans continue to face forms of public and private discrimination (Wang and Wu 1996; Narasaki 1995; Takagi 1992). Bell et al. (1997) contend that Asian Americans experience workplace discrimination that surpasses that of Euro-Americans but is less than that of Latinos and African Americans. In his discussion of discrimination, Skerry (1993) cites a 1989 *Los Angeles*

Times poll of southern California which found that nearly half of all blacks, 29 percent of Latinos, and 41 percent of Asian Americans in the survey reported having experienced some discrimination in their lifetimes.

Unlike our other groups, Asian American participants openly discussed the fact that their co-ethnics might be perpetrators of discrimination. One young man said that Asians themselves are a very discriminatory people and that they are responsible for discriminating against others, including other Asian American subgroups. He used as his example a company for which he works, a Japanese company in New York City that is 85 percent Japanese, the other employees being mostly whites and Hispanics. "We have only one black [employee]," he complained. "[The company has 80 employees] and only one black. . . . Proportion-wise it's really strange; it's not right." Another Asian American stated that "affirmative action helps in that it forces those who cannot see beyond what they've grown up with, to take a step [forward] and hire a person that might be different from what they've been used to."

The fact that our Asian Americans participants did not feel that they had been victims of discrimination, but had witnessed discrimination against other groups, especially African Americans, is very important. This perception may explain, in part, why Asian Americans in our study, while not seeing affirmative action as beneficial to their group, nevertheless supported the policy.

Latino Americans and Discrimination

The Latino group provided a number of examples from their own lives that showed experiences with discrimination. Some expressed the view that the job experiences of Latinos differed significantly from those of their Euro-American counterparts. For one bank teller, it meant that she had to stay in a particular branch location in order to accommodate the bank's Latino customers despite her request for a transfer and desire for a promotion (see chapter 6 for the employers' perspective on this practice). Others talked about subtle and not-so-subtle reactions to their Spanish surnames. For example, one woman explained that since she married and began using her husband's Anglo last name, she has been treated more positively by society. Not only did Latinos encounter discrimination resulting from surnames, but they also suffered from stereotypes about their countries of origin. Much as some Italian Americans are sensitive about Mafia stereotypes, the natives of Colombia in our focus groups felt that they were looked on by American society as drug dealers.

African Americans and Discrimination

As would be expected given their history in the United States, African Americans expressed the strongest emotions about the impact of discrimination in their everyday lives. Overall, blacks seemed supportive of affirmative action more because of their concerns about current discrimination than about discrimination in the past. In fact, concerns about current discrimination seemed to dominate blacks' conversations about affirmative action.

African Americans support affirmative action largely because they view its programs as their only protection against continued racial discrimination, and they looked toward it rather than civil rights legislation to provide them with a measure of relief. Yet, many blacks were extremely cynical about actual affirmative action programs. One young black male complained that even with affirmative action blacks have fewer opportunities to get ahead in business than do whites. He asked, "[Why] do blacks have to work twice as hard as whites? Why can't we all work at the same pace and get the same benefits?" Similarly, a middle-aged black male commented that "affirmative action is a buzzword defined by the media to suggest that we're getting remedies for past discrimination, which means that somehow a black person must take a job from a white person, which suggests that white people are foreordained to have the jobs." As long as blacks see affirmative action as their only line of defense against rampant societal discrimination, they will, of course, express strong support for the policy and view any attempts to modify affirmative action programs as a threat to their well-being.

Euro-Americans and Discrimination

Other than their fears of "reverse discrimination," most whites did not express concern that racial discrimination has had any serious impact on their lives. Some of the participants in our New York group felt that whites in the city had experienced discrimination under the Dinkins administration. One man stated that when the African American David Dinkins was mayor, the city government did not hire white people for construction jobs. He stated: "[A person] had to be black to get the job. They didn't have to do the job right, they didn't have to know anything, but they had to be black. Now, all these unions were protesting this. . . . Men that had experience that [could do] the job . . . couldn't get the job because they weren't black. So there it is. Reverse discrimination." In the less racially hostile New Jersey group, a man who otherwise seemed sympathetic toward blacks commented that "a white man is the last one hired. And in my opinion, that's the only negative thing to affirmative action." Therefore, even among whites who view the policy favorably, there is some agreement with the sentiment that affirmative action had gone too far in helping minorities.

The fact that African Americans and Euro-Americans have had very different experiences with discrimination helps explain some of the divergent views that they hold about the need for continuing affirmative action. The middling degree of discrimination experienced or acknowledged by Latino Americans and Asian Americans leads these groups not to enthusiastically declare a need for continuing affirmative action policies. The intensity of experiences with discrimination, however, is not the only source of polarization on the issue. Groups express different opinions about affirmative action policies because they have varying amounts of information about the need for the programs, how they work, and the problems that they are designed to address.

Concluding Observations

Our study offers some interesting contrasts to the extant work on affirmative action. In our study, the most striking difference is the greater support of affirmative action by Asian Americans than by Latinos. Previous studies have consistently found that Asian Americans and Latinos fall somewhere between whites and blacks in their overall support for affirmative action. Usually, Latinos are closer to blacks and Asian Americans nearer to whites in terms of support for these programs. One reason that our study may have elicited different results is the way the racial groups framed the issues early on in their discussions, and how this may have shaped their subsequent opinions. Asian Americans started their discussion with a general agreement that affirmative action had little to do with them, and they quickly expressed a belief that members of their group were rarely victims of discrimination. Latinos, on the other hand, adamantly disapproved of the way that affirmative action policies harmed minorities *including themselves*. They believed that

the lowered standards for minorities endorsed by affirmative action programs resulted in the labeling of nonwhites as less competent than
whites.

While not refuting a straight group interest theory (as proposed by
Lawrence Bobo in chapter 8), these data provide an interesting alternative. As Gamson suggests, some groups that might be expected to be
strong supporters of the policy are attentive to negative implications
that can dampen their enthusiasm. This makes the Asian Americans
especially puzzling, because as a group they failed to recognize any obvious benefits of affirmative action; in addition they were the only group
to discuss the ways in which members of their group might discriminate
against others. Thus, affirmative action may provide a different type of
benefit to the Asian Americans in our study, who may have supported
affirmative action because they think that the policy is fair. Such an
explanation is also consistent with the significantly lower levels of support by Euro-Americans who fail to acknowledge lingering racial discrimination while seeing affirmative action as reverse discrimination.

In sum, our focus groups have provided us with a rare opportunity
to gather insights from beneficiaries of affirmative action rarely heard
from—Asian Americans and Latinos—and for exploring those views in-
depth and in comparative context. Listening to the discourse of different groups is useful for sorting out what people mean when they tell a
pollster that they support or oppose "affirmative action." Much of the
national debate about affirmative action consists of little more than people talking past one another about a concept that could not be more
ambiguous in their minds.

Despite their willingness to express their opinions, Americans lack
a shared vocabulary and a shared perceptual basis for evaluating affirmative action policies. As one of our participants noted: "[Y]ou have to
educate the people that are going to use [affirmative action] from the
managerial standpoint. . . . What is the plan? . . . What actually [should
affirmative action programs] do? Spell it out. . . . [T]he majority of
Americans [don't] understand affirmative action." If our focus groups
are indicative of how racial subgroups think about affirmative action
policy, then the participant quoted above is quite correct. Within and
across groups, discussions were confused, suggesting that Americans
lack a common understanding of affirmative action and its goals.

Gallie (1962) referred to "essentially contested concepts" in which
discrepant and partially shared meanings lead to empty debates, devoid
of meaning. Affirmative action is a highly charged abstraction that
evokes very different emotions in the minds of individuals depending

on their group affiliations and degree of exposure to the subject or its beneficiaries. Because we speak different languages and we see different realities, we are yet to have a serious discussion about affirmative action policies. Presently, too, many of our opinion leaders are talking about substantively different phenomena when they enter the debate on behalf of their perceived group interest. If we are ever to reach consensus on affirmative action policies in this country, we must first take steps to ensure that we are using a shared language and understanding to discuss matters of common concern.

Notes

1. For an exception see Bositis 1997.
2. An overview of public opinion on affirmative action can be found in Swain 2000.

Acknowledgments

I would like to thank the focus group moderators: Herb Abelson, Joanne Mitchell, Jill Nishi, and Mark Lopez of Princeton University, as well as the National Science Foundation (SBR-9357951) for its generous funding.

References

Adkins, R. 1996. Affirmative action and public opinion polls. In *Race versus class: The new affirmative action debate*, edited by Carol M. Swain. Baltimore: University Press of America.

Anderson, B. A., B. D. Silver, and P. R. Abramson. 1988. The effects of the race of the interviewer on race-related attitudes of black respondents in SRC/CPS National Election Studies. *Public Opinion Quarterly* 52:289–324.

Bell, Derrick. 1995. The mystique of affirmative action. Public address, Princeton University, April 24.

Bell, Myrtle P., David A. Harrison, and Mary E. McLaughlin. 1997. Asian American attitudes toward affirmative action in employment: Implications for the model minority myth. *Journal of Applied Behavioral Science* 33:356–77.

Bositis, David A. 1997. National opinion poll on children's issues. Washington, D.C.: Joint Center for Political and Economic Issues.

———, ed. 1998. *Redistricting and minority representation*. Washington, D.C.: Joint Center for Political and Economic Studies.

Conover, P. J., I. M. Crewe, and D. Searing. 1991. The nature of citizenship in the United States and Great Britain: Empirical comments on theoretical concerns. *Journal of Politics* 53 (3): 800–32.

Crosby, F. J., and D. I. Cordova. 1996. Words worth of wisdom: Towards an understanding of affirmative action. *Journal of Social Issues* 52 (4): 633–49.

Fine, T. 1992. The impact of issue framing on public opinion toward affirmative action programs. *Social Science Journal* 29 (3): 323–34.

Fukurai, Hiroshi, Darryl Davies, Anne Shin, Dionelle Fletcher, Belinda Lum, Khanh Ngo, Lauren Pieter, Bhavani Parsons, Michael Shin, and Kara Sloman. 1994. The ironies of affirmative action: Empirical analyses of UC students' views on fallacies and problems of affirmative action. *California Sociologist* 17–18 (1–2): 91–128.

Gallie, W. B. 1962. Essentially contested concepts. In *The importance of language*, edited by Max Black. Englewood Cliffs, N.J.: Prentice-Hall.

Gallup Poll Monthly. 1977. Affirmative action programs, March 25–28.

———. 1989. Preferential treatment for women and minorities, December 7–10.

Gamson, William A. 1992. *Talking politics.* New York: Cambridge University Press.

Gamson, William A., and A. Modigliani. 1987. The changing culture of affirmative action. *Research in Political Sociology* 3:137–77.

Hochschild, J. 1999. Affirmative action as culture warfare. In *The cultural territories of race: White and black boundaries*, edited by M. Lamont. Chicago: University of Chicago Press.

Kinder, D. R., and L. Sanders. 1996. *Divided by color: Racial politics and democratic ideals.* Chicago: University of Chicago Press.

———. 1990. Mimicking political debate with survey questions: The case of affirmative action for blacks. *Social Cognition* 8:73–103.

Kolbert, E. 1992. Test marketing a president: How focus groups pervade campaign politics. *New York Times Magazine*, 30 August.

Kravitz, David A., and Judith Platania. 1993. Attitudes and beliefs about affirmative action: Effects of targets and respondent sex and ethnicity. *Journal of Applied Psychology* 78:928–38.

Ladd, Everett C. 1995. Affirmative action: Welfare and the individual. *Public Opinion and Polls*, April–May.

Lipset, S. M. 1992. Affirmative action and the American Creed. *The Wilson Quarterly* 16: 52–62.

Lipset, S. M., and W. Schneider. 1978. The *Bakke* case: How would it be decided in the court of public opinion? *Public Opinion* 1:38–44.

Moore, David W. 1995. Americans today are dubious about affirmative action, *Gallup Poll Monthly*, March.

Morgan, D. L. 1997. *Focus groups as qualitative research.* 2d ed. Thousand Oaks, Calif.: Sage Publications.

Narasaki, K. K. 1995. Separate but equal? Discrimination and the need for affirmative action legislation. In *Perspectives on affirmative action.* Los Angeles: Asian Pacific American Public Policy Forum.

Niemann, Yolanda Flores, and John F. Dovidio. 1998. Tenure, race/ethnicity, and attitudes toward affirmative action: A matter of self-interest? *Sociological Perspectives* 41 (4): 783–96.

Norman, J. 1995. America's verdict on affirmative action is decidedly mixed. *Public Perspective* 6 (June–July): 49–52.

Schuman, Howard, Charlotte Steeh , Lawrence Bobo, and M. Krysan. 1997. *Racial attitudes in America: Trends and interpretations.* 2d ed. Cambridge: Harvard University Press.

Sigelman, L., and S. Welch. 1991. *Black American views of inequality: The dream deferred.* New York: Cambridge University Press.

Skerry, Peter. 1993. *Mexican Americans: The ambivalent minority.* New York: Free Press.

Sniderman, P. M., and E. G. Carmines. 1997. *Reaching beyond race.* Cambridge: Harvard University Press.

Sniderman, P. M., and T. Piazza. 1993. *The scar of race.* Cambridge: Harvard University Press.

Steeh, Charlotte, and M. Krysan. 1996. The polls—trends: Affirmative action and the public, 1970–1995. *Public Opinion Quarterly* 60:128–58.

Stewart, D. W., and P. Shamdasani. 1990. *Focus groups: Theory and practice.* Newbury Park, Calif.: Sage Publications.

Stoker, L. 1997. Understanding whites' resistance to affirmative action: The role of principled commitments and racial prejudice. In *Perception and prejudice: Race and politics in the United States,* edited by J. Hurwitz and M. Peffley. Chicago: University of Chicago Press.

Swain, Carol M. 2000. Affirmative action: Areas of consensus and agreement among Americans. In *America becoming: Racial trends and their consequences,* edited by Neil Smelser, William J. Wilson, and Faith Mitchell. Washington, D.C.: National Research Council.

Swain, C., R. Rodgers, and B. Silverman. 2000. Life after *Bakke* where whites and blacks agree: Public support for fairness in educational opportunities. *Harvard BlackLetter Law Journal* 16:147.

Takagi, Dana Y. 1992. *The retreat from race: Asian American admissions and racial politics.* New Brunswick, N.J.: Rutgers University Press.

Wang, Theodore Hsein, and Frank Wu. 1996. Beyond the model minority myth: Why Asian Americans support affirmative action. *Guild Practitioner* 53 (winter): 35–47.

PART IV

CIVIL RIGHTS AND AFFIRMATIVE ACTION

BEYOND AMERICA

10

Positive Action or Affirmative Action? The Persistence

of Britain's Antidiscrimination Regime

. . .

S TEVEN M . T ELES

The most fundamental thing to understand about affirmative action in Britain is that there is none.[1] Or, rather, that there is no "hard" affirmative action as we understand it in the United States: minority group hiring goals and timetables required of government contractors, accepted in consent decrees or ordered by courts, and often involving the deliberate adjustment of standards or ability tests in employment and education to permit racial minorities to be more proportionately represented in those fields.[2] In Britain, using differential standards to benefit minority groups is called positive discrimination and is forbidden by the Race Relations Act of 1976 (RRA). Of course, under a reasonable interpretation of the Civil Rights Act (CRA), affirmative action is also illegal (Gold 1985). In fact, the CRA makes no provision for any exceptions to race neutrality, whereas the RRA does, permitting special recruitment and targeted training for underrepresented racial minorities (RRA, 1976, pt. 6, secs. 35–38).

Why, despite these similarities in their civil rights law, has Great Britain failed to develop affirmative action along the lines of the United States? I have been unsatisfied with all of the single-factor explanations that one might apply to this question. Instead, my examination of the subject will show how demographic, institutional, historical, and cultural factors have interacted to create a very different—and apparently durable—"antidiscrimination regime" in Great Britain. I will begin by examining the state of affirmative action in Britain, then proceed to suggest a number of the formative elements of the British antidiscrimination regime (and with it the reasons for the absence of U.S.-style affirmative action within that regime), and conclude by suggesting what this analysis says about the future of British equal opportunity policy and what lessons it might have for the United States.

The State of Affirmative Action in Britain

Affirmative Action or Positive Action?

The keystones of British civil rights law are the Race Relations, Sex Discrimination, and Fair Employment Acts (the latter covering religious discrimination in Northern Ireland). The RRA, passed in 1976, expanded on previous laws passed in 1965 and 1968 by broadening the scope of discrimination to include indirect discrimination (that is, rules that are neutral on the surface yet have an indefensibly discriminatory effect), and created a new body, the Commission for Racial Equality (CRE), to undertake formal investigations under the law and to encourage equality of opportunity more broadly. The core of the law, its definition of racial discrimination, is race-neutral: "A person discriminates against another . . . if on racial grounds he treats that other less favourably than he treats or would treat other persons" (RRA, pt. 1, sec. 1).

Britain is not like the France that Erik Bleich describes in chapter 11, however. A number of exceptions to Britain's basic nondiscrimination rule recognize racial difference. One is an exception for genuine occupational qualifications, which permits the use of race when it can be shown to be necessary for the performance of a particular job, for example, "when the holder of the job provides persons of that racial group with personal services promoting their welfare, and those services can most effectively be provided by a person of that racial group" (RRA, pt. 2, sec. 5).

The other exception, of central relevance to this chapter, is for what the law calls positive action.[3] Unlike Executive Order 11246, the British law permits, but does not require, special actions to aid minority group members. Employers may grant "persons of a particular racial group access to facilities or services to meet the special needs of persons of that group in regard to their education, training or welfare, or any ancillary benefits" (RRA, pt. 6, sec. 35). It also permits employers to specially encourage racial minorities to apply when they are below their proportion in the community (RRA, pt. 6, sec. 38).[4] Most important, the law permits employers to grant "only those . . . employees working at that establishment who are of a particular racial group access to facilities for training which would help to fit them for that work" (RRA, sec. 35, pt. 38). There are no positive action requirements for government contractors' employment in Britain, no quota set-asides for government to do business with set percentages of minority-owned businesses, and in fact, no required record keeping of a firm's employment of minorities, as there are in the United States. Controversies of seniority rights and especially employers' use of ability tests (as opposed to the narrower issue of their content) that have been frequent in the United States (Belz 1991) have not occurred in Britain. In university hiring and admissions, in which the preferential policies in the United States clearly affect outcomes, Britain has barely embraced soft practices such as outreach and encouragement.

How Is Equal Opportunity Protected in Britain?

In the United States, small provisions like those in the RRA could quite easily be stretched by judicial-bureaucratic cooperation to permit, or even require, affirmative action. For reasons particular to British law and culture, they have not been. The genuine occupational qualification provision could have opened the door to affirmative action in pursuit of diversity, on the argument that across the boards, greater minority representation is needed in all types of organizations. The courts have not looked kindly on this argument. For example, in *Lambeth London Borough Council v. CRE* (1990 I.C.R. 768, (1990) I.R.C.R. 231 (C.A.)), the Court of Appeal looked at the case of an advertisement for two jobs in the council's housing benefits department, which stated that "in view of the personal services the postholder will provide the members of the black community," race was a genuine occupational qualification (the majority of the department's clients are racial minorities). According to Mary Coussey (personal communication, 29 April 1997), the former director of employment at the CRE, the commission brought suit against Lambeth because it was openly flouting the RRA. The CRE argued that if Lambeth wished to have more ethnic minority staff, it should make sure they were recruited through mainstream schemes, not by labeling them as "special needs" recruits, which would restrict their subsequent careers and trap them in "race specific" work. The court agreed. It stated, "Promoting positive action is not one of the main purposes of the Act. The substance of the Act is to render acts of racial discrimination unlawful." Essentially, the court drew a line between positive action and Genuine Occupational Qualification (GOQ), emphasizing the narrowness of the RRA's provisions rather than attempting to make them more capacious.

The consequence of both the law and its interpretation by courts and administrative bodies is that there is little if any hard affirmative action in Great Britain. This is clear both from what official bodies say and by what employers (including the government) do. For example, official documents from Her Majesty's Civil Service (1996) state that The Sex Discrimination and Race Relations Acts do not permit "positive discrimination." They do, however, permit positive action in connection with training for particular work where women, men, or people of a particular racial group are not represented or are underrepresented in relation to their numbers in the workforce or the relevant population (6).

This understanding of the line between permissible and impermissible behavior is repeated again and again in official documents. The Employment Department Group's "Ten Point Plan for Employers" makes a point of noting that "selections for interviews and jobs must be based on merit alone" and suggests that "because positive action measures involve singling out a particular racial group or one sex for special attention, it is very important that you ensure that the action you propose is within the law" (Employment Department Group 1996). The Race Relations Employment Advisory Service observes that "[p]ositive action does not allow racial discrimination in recruiting, selecting, or promoting" (Race Relations Employment Advisory Service n.d.). Finally, "Race for Opportunity," a business-led campaign to encourage greater positive action, states clearly that "[p]ositive discrimination is not only illegal, but in our view, unhelpful. Yes we do want to see a more diverse workforce, but one that is created through equality of opportunity" (Business in the Community n.d.).

Studies of the implementation of positive action in the United Kingdom show that the line on paper is held in practice. Jonathan Edwards, who closely studied the practice of a number of companies in Britain with positive action programs, concluded, "It would be naive to assume that preferential treatment does not happen in Great Britain, though its extent is impossible to judge. . . . What can be said with certainty is that the magnitude of preferential treatment in Great Britain is infinitesimal compared with the United States" (1995, 165). The four employers he studied all had something called positive action on their books, but none appeared to change traditional standards to employ more minority applicants. Rather, all used a fairly standard core group of methods, such as targeted job advertisements, outreach to schools, and in some cases targeted training. In most of Edwards's jurisdictions, positive action meant little more than effectively administering a policy of nondiscrimination.

Of substantial interest for Americans is the absence of affirmative action in higher education. As John Douglass demonstrates in chapter

5, preferential policies in higher education have clearly affected outcomes and not just added procedures, as they sometimes appear to have done in private employment. In addition to the cultural reasons for an absence of affirmative action, some of which will be discussed below, the institutional structure of British higher education acts as a brake against granting admissions on a racial basis. British universities admit students to specific programs, such as medicine, politics, and literature, rather than to the university as a whole, and the critical admissions decisions are made at the departmental level, not by a university-wide admissions department. As a result, admissions decisions are highly decentralized and, therefore, difficult to influence from the top. At Oxford and Cambridge, the pinnacle of the university system, the decentralization by department is further complicated by the enormous power of the individual colleges. A professor of political science at Oxford (personal communication, 17 February 1997) suggested to me that "the extreme federalism and fragmentation of authority of Oxford prevents any central accountability." This decentralization has limited efforts to expand the representation at Oxford and Cambridge from state secondary schools, which has been a major area of contention, and would stymie any effort to implement affirmative action as well.

All of this said, it should be emphasized that the absence of U.S.-style affirmative action does not mean the absence of action. The difference is that whereas the United States, roughly speaking, often emphasizes changing selection and meritocratic standards while doing very little to help underprivileged groups meet the original standards, British-style positive action works in the opposite manner. Britain's positive action keeps selection and meritocratic standards clear while providing opportunities within the education and work environment. This is, at least, the theory. The implementation of this theory has been very gradual in Britain, in part because there are no mechanisms to force employers to adopt positive action programs, such as government contract compliance rules (as in the United States) or a straight legal requirement. The RRA merely allows positive action.

Even so, there are reasons to believe that more aggressive forms of positive action are growing. Of the organizations studied by the Capita Management Consultancy report, 33 percent had adopted in-service training, and 41 percent had some form of pre-entry training for ethnic minorities (Welsh et al., 1994, chap. 4, fig. 4). These numbers compare favorably with soft affirmative action as practiced in the United States, as is shown in chapter 4.

Although employers that have positive action are not merely implementing the least controversial forms, such as targeted outreach, it must be said that the breadth of application of positive action still is fairly limited, being quite strong in some urban councils and increasingly popular among stakeholding and large firms but quite a bit less the smaller the company or the more conservative the local government.[5] Also, although the CRE does not advertise its equal opportunities policy aggressively, present and former officials at the CRE pointed to the civil service as having a strong positive action program. The difference in policy between small and large firms was underlined in a survey of Britain's largest companies by the CRE, which found that 29 percent used positive action encouragement, 12 percent used positive action training, and 24 percent used access training (which is provided to all underrepresented groups; Commission for Racial Equality 1995, 14).

Positive action is clearly more prevalent among government agencies. A survey of police forces commissioned by the Home Office (Britain's government department in charge of police, prisons, fire departments and emergency services) found that twenty-nine of the forty-three forces surveyed had some form of active recruitment of ethnic minorities and that forces serving larger jurisdictions, which typically have higher concentrations of minorities, engage in more active and encompassing methods (Holdaway 1991, 47). The Civil Service actively recruits minorities for its "high flyers" track, and officials of the CRE repeatedly have emphasized its quiet model equal opportunities policy, including positive action.

Why Britain Doesn't Have Preferential Treatment

The Brixton Riots and the Scarman Report

Violence is often a spur to governmental action, and government officials in the United States developed affirmative action in part as a response to riots in the black sections of a number of American cities (Skrentny 1996). President Lyndon Johnson created the National Advisory Commission on Civil Disorders (also known as the Kerner Commission, after chairman Otto Kerner, governor of Illinois), whose report called for massive government action, including preferential treatment for residents of ghettos, to confront what its members saw as the real causes of the riots. Johnson also personally urged employers in the cities to relax and reevaluate old selection standards for employment.

In 1981, Britain was faced with riots that, if not as severe as those that rocked the United States in the 1960s, were equally as shocking to the nation. In Brixton from April 10 to 12 and later in other British cities, there was collective violence on a scale that exceeded that of any in living memory. In response, the Home Office requested that the distinguished jurist Lord Scarman inquire into the causes of the riots and suggest remedies. Scarman (1981) argued that, despite the need to attach individual responsibility to the participants, the riots were a symptom of a widespread racial problem in the United Kingdom, one that required a much more focused solution than had hitherto been applied. "It is clear from the evidence of ethnic minority deprivation I have received that, if the balance of racial disadvantage is to be redressed, as it must be, positive action is required. I mean by this more than the admirable approach adopted by at least some central and local government agencies at present, which is intended chiefly to persuade the ethnic minorities to take up more of their share of general social provisions. Important as this is, it is not, in my view, a sufficient answer. Given the special problems of the ethnic minorities . . . justice requires that special programmes be adopted in areas of acute deprivation" (109).

Scarman argued that, despite the fact that targeted programs for minorities could cause a backlash from the majority, a program of positive action was necessary nonetheless. In the report, Scarman only referred to positive action, suggesting that the principle on which the necessary action would be based was already in the RRA. However, Scarman later used the term *positive discrimination* to describe the measures he desired (Scarman, cited in Benyon 1984, 261), and a number of news reports at the time suggested as much (Prashar, cited in Benyon 1984, 210–11). In all likelihood, Scarman did not adequately appreciate the distinction between the two terms, and the media preferred the more extreme interpretation (Benyon 1984, 167).

In another context, Scarman's call for an extension of the principle of positive action could have led to American-style affirmative action. It did not. It failed to do so for a variety of reasons, primarily to do with the political tone of the times: Uprisings that in the 1960s would have led to new social programs or the transgressing of old taboos on positive discrimination led instead to more aggressive police powers and greater suspicion of immigration. This, at least, was the national government response. Some local governments attempted to respond to the riots in a much more opportunity-increasing manner. The "City of A" metropolitan district, in Jonathan Edwards's (1995) *When Race Counts*, "first declared itself an equal opportunities employer in 1982 in the wake of the civil unrest of 1981 and a growing concern on the part of the ruling Labour Party that insufficient attention was being paid to the needs and level of representation in the district council of the large minority population. The district introduced a Race Equality and Employment policy in February 1982, and this saw the beginning of an annual headcount of minority employees of the council" (46–47).

The Greater London Council (GLC) and a handful of other local councils also took substantial action in response to the riots, but the increasing centralization of the British regime served to brake much of this activity. The most important responses to the riots were completely race-neutral, especially projects to encourage more private development in distressed urban areas and a number of youth training schemes.

The fact that the riots did not lead, as they did in the United States, to the creation of hard affirmative action is all the more puzzling when set beside the experience of Northern Ireland. There, continued violence and persistent discrimination on a religious basis led to the Fair Employment Act, which was consciously modeled, in a way that the RRA and Sex Discrimination Act were not, on some aspects of contemporary U.S. practice. In Northern Ireland, employers must collect information on the religion of their employees, and large employers are required to collect similar information on applicants as well (McCrudden 1992, 171). When the workforce is unbalanced, the employer is under an obligation to implement a program of positive action, and the Fair Employment Commission can require an employer to do this when it is not undertaken voluntarily. Standard mechanisms of U.S. affirmative action, such as race-based hiring goals and timetables, the use of government contracts to ensure that employers are meeting goals, and administrative supervision of the balance of a firm's employees, are all used in Northern Ireland (McCrudden 1992, 171–72). Although the types of action that are permitted are not dramatically different in Northern Ireland from those permitted in Britain for race and sex discrimination, the *obligation* to use them and the administrative apparatus and collection of data are. When a condition is considered severe enough, the United Kingdom is capable of moving closer to U.S.-style affirmative action.

The Numbers and Economic Status of Minorities

One obvious explanation for the absence of preferential treatment in the United Kingdom is raw demographics: Britain is still an overwhelmingly white country. As of 1994, 93 percent of those in the General Household Survey identified themselves as white, down from the 95 percent of Britons who so identified a decade earlier (Office of Population Censuses and Surveys 1996, table 2.34). The minority population of Britain has no single, overwhelming group. Indians are the largest group, followed by (in descending order) Afro-Caribbeans, Pakistanis, African Asians (largely refugees from Uganda and Kenya), Africans, Chinese, and Bangladeshis (Jones 1996, 23; Modood and Berthoud 1997, 13).[6] This compares to the United States, where more than one-quarter of the population identify themselves as members of racial minorities (U.S. Bureau of the Census 1996, table 13).

Many British citizens, and even a few scholars, are surprised when they discover the relatively small ethnic population of the country. This may be because of the extreme concentration of racial minorities in the southeast of England and especially in London. Whereas ethnic minorities are 7 percent of the population of Britain, racial minorities make up 20.2 percent of the population of Greater London (Wrench and Hassan 1996, 8). Of all African Caribbeans in Britain, 41.3 percent reside in just ten local authorities (Wrench and Hassan 1996, 10; Modood and Berthoud 1997, 184–90).

The smaller size of the minority population of the United Kingdom is significant for the politics of affirmative action in Britain compared to the United States, but it is possible to overemphasize demography. First, though Britain's minorities are concentrated in the political and economic center of the nation—London—organized advocates for nonwhites have not made U.S.-style affirmative action a priority. In other words, the minorities that *are* in Britain have not demanded affirmative action. Second, Britain does not have affirmative action for women either, and women are, obviously, approximately 50 percent of the population.

One of the most important reasons for the lack of support for affirmative action in Britain is the great diversity of economic circumstances that characterize the various ethnic minorities, and just as important, the trajectory of their economic improvement. Unlike France (see chapter 11), Britain does allow the collection of statistics on the basis of race. Some groups, in particular ethnic Chinese and African Asians, are approaching parity, followed closely by Indians and Africans. Pakistanis and Bangladeshis, on the other hand, form a severely underprivileged underclass, with chronic and severe levels of unemployment, low earnings, and residence in very poor housing. In the middle are the Afro-Caribbeans, the group of longest residence in Britain.

Because they are the two largest minority groups in Britain, the situation of African Caribbeans and Indians is worth examining a bit more closely. The African Caribbean story is one highly divided by gender. Although black male hourly pay was far below that of whites (£7.01 per hour versus £8.34 per hour), black female earnings were higher than white female earnings (£6.71 per hour versus £6.59 per hour). Unemployment levels for Afro-Caribbeans are very high. Thirty-one percent of Afro-Caribbean males were unemployed in 1996 (the figure for females was 18 percent; Modood and Berthoud 1997, 89). Even more disturbing, young Afro-Caribbean males had an unemployment rate of 39 percent versus 14 percent for whites (Office of National Statistics 1996, table 4.15). Unemployment is very high even for those with a higher qualification (A Level Equivalent or above):[7] 16 percent for blacks, 7 percent for whites (Modood and Berthoud 1997, 92; Office of National Statistics 1996, table 4.16). Qualifications that are a guarantee of well-being for whites are no such thing for blacks. These numbers are especially distressing given that unlike the rest of the ethnic minority population, Afro-Caribbeans have been in Britain for some time: their relative deprivation cannot be blamed on their recent arrival. This is most clearly proved by the depressing economic straits of young Afro-Caribbean men, who are "disproportionately without qualifications, without work, without a stable family life and . . . disproportionately in trouble with the police and in prison" (Modood and Berthoud 1997, 350).

That said, there are reasons for optimism about the state of blacks in the United Kingdom, the most important being education and integration. Afro-Caribbeans have higher qualifications at almost the rate of whites, and Afro-Caribbean women actually outstrip white women in this area.[8] In addition, in contrast to the situation in the United States, Afro-Caribbeans are not a socially isolated minority: "Four in ten Black Caribbean men aged 16 to 34 were living with a White female partner in 1991" (Office of National Statistics 1996, 23), whereas somewhat lower rates of mixed partnerships were found among black women. In comparison, only around 5 percent of black men in the United States are married to white women. Although the figures for live-in partners are undoubtedly higher, it is unlikely they are as high as in Britain. What is more, the level of residential segregation of all ethnic minorities, but especially Afro-Caribbeans, is very low, especially when compared to the "hyper-segregation" of American blacks. (Peach 1996, 1998; Massey and Denton 1993). If such a pattern persisted, it would lead to the gradual melting of most of the Afro-Caribbean population into British society. This is, to say the very least, not a prospect on the horizon in the United States. This social integration of Afro-

Caribbeans, which makes them far from the "discrete and insular minority" that blacks were once (and to some degree still are) in the United States, complicates their political situation and makes them more likely to organize on a nonracial basis, despite their economic troubles.[9]

Finally, there are the Indians, who are in some ways the most complicated group. They have very high labor force participation levels, approaching the level of whites, and their unemployment rates are much lower than those of blacks, Pakistanis, and Bangladeshis (Jones 1996, table 5.1). Hourly earnings of Indian men, at £8.01 per hour, compare favorably to those of whites at £8.34 per hour (Jones 1996, table 4.17).[10] Of even greater significance is the outstanding educational performance of Indian men: 38 percent of Indian men aged twenty to twenty-four were in full-time education, compared to 7 percent of white men (Modood and Berthoud 1997, 76). But as suggested before, these economic factors are complicated by the attitudes of whites toward Indians: "While the over 34 years old are only slightly more likely to say they are prejudiced against Asians and Muslims than Caribbeans, the under 35 years old are half as likely again to say they are prejudiced against Asians and Muslims than Caribbeans" (Modood and Berthoud 1997, 16). This cultural isolation is mirrored in rates of mixed partnerships: Only 9 percent of Indian males and 5 percent of Indian females had partners from other ethnic groups, about one-quarter of the black rate (Office of National Statistics 1996, table 2.8). Indians look more like whites at work, but Afro-Caribbeans look more like whites at home.[11]

It may be that, combined with the economic success of African Asians and Chinese in Britain, the mixed integration of the two largest groups, Indians and African Caribbeans, makes claims for specifically race-based entitlements very difficult to muster. The cultural, and especially religious, differences that separate the Indian groups from whites also create tensions with Afro-Caribbeans, a fact reflected by recent surveys showing high levels of animus among Britain's ethnic minority groups (Institute for Public Policy Research 1997).[12] This suggests that whatever racism the ethnic minorities face as a whole, this experience has not created a sense of solidarity, and it probably explains why activists' efforts to popularize the term *black* as an umbrella for Africans, African Caribbeans, and Indians has failed.

The Relevance of Immigration

The fact and the social meaning of immigration is of the greatest significance for the politics of positive action in Britain. Briefly put, the control of immigration and measures to alleviate racial discrimination have always gone hand in hand in Britain, and the very identity of the nation as multiethnic has always been a controversial one. Decent treatment of racial minorities once in the country has gone hand in hand with efforts to control further immigration. As Bob Hepple observes, "The price for the Race Relations Act of 1968 was the Commonwealth Immigration Acts of 1962 and 1968 and the price for the Race Relations Act 1976 was the Immigration Act of 1971 and the British Nationality Act 1981" (Hepple and Szyszczak 1992, 28). Colin Brown further observes that "[p]oliticians felt that the base on which the Race Relations Acts rested was the end of immigration; they believed public support for (or, more accurately, public acquiescence to) legal measures to promote racial justice could only be maintained by assuring white people that "coloured immigration would be firmly controlled" (Brown 1992, 56).

This argument is bolstered by even a cursory reading of the debates on the Race Relations Bill 1976. In introducing the bill to the House of Commons, Home Secretary Roy Jenkins, known as a great liberal, observed right after suggesting the need for the bill that "[t]he third principle of Government [race relations] policy is that there is a clear limit to the amount of immigration which this country can absorb, and that it is in the interests of racial minorities themselves to maintain a strict control over immigration" (Hansard 1976b). Earlier he put the point even more clearly: "Together with that strong control over immigration, we must have a most determined and liberal policy of complete equality for those settled in this country. I regard these matters as two sides of the same coin" (Hansard 1976a).

This attitude was necessitated by the extremely strong opposition of the entire Conservative Party and many elements of the Labour Party to even the level of immigration that had already occurred as of 1976. Enoch Powell, who had previously been Secretary for Health and had a disturbing degree of popular support, had called for outright expulsion of British citizens of New Commonwealth origin. Despite the fact that the RRA was passed with cross-party support, the voices of Powell and those who echoed him were strongly felt in the debate on the Race Relations Act of 1976, many questioning the principle of nondiscrimination itself and suggesting that the basic problem was the presence of those of foreign origin.

This background is necessary to understand why even a liberal like Jenkins would say that immigration control was in the interest of immigrants themselves. Substantial immigration into England and Wales is a quite recent phenomenon in the nation's history. From 1891 to 1951, the number of people born in the New Commonwealth increased only from 112,000 to 202,000, just slightly ahead of the increase in the British population on the whole. Then, from 1951 to 1971, the New Commonwealth population skyrocketed, increasing more than fivefold (Coleman and Salt 1992, 482). This increase did not go unnoticed by the British population: Between 1951 and 1961, support for "free entry for immigrant workers from the colonies" went from being evenly split to being almost wholly opposed (21 percent positive to 73 percent negative) (Banton 1983, 292). This change led to the rise of Powell, and mainstream political figures were forced into more extreme positions on immigration to limit his appeal.

British and, more particularly, English nationality is not connected, as it is in the United States, to a universal set of principles but to a shared history connected to specific institutions and ways of life. As a result, immigration has often been perceived as a threat to the solidity of the nation, and the rapid increase of ethnic minorities as something of an inadvertent mistake that a decent society has to make the best of but, if possible, avoid extending any further. This tie between policy on discrimination and immigration is still clear, for example, in the Conservative Party Manifesto of 1997, which states that "[f]irm, but fair, immigration controls underpin good race relations" (Conservative Party 1997, 43).

As a result of this weaving together of immigration and nondiscrimination policy, and of the uncertain place of racial minorities in British nationhood, claims for special protection are on very uncertain ground. The first objective of racial minorities was, and continues to be, an assurance that they are considered citizens both in form and in substance.[13] Especially where ethnic minorities from the Indian subcontinent are concerned, many whites harbor grave suspicions of their Britishness, even as their economic status increases, due much less to race than to religion and culture, especially where Muslims are concerned. Attempts to even further restrict immigration are seen by representatives of the minority communities as direct attacks on their presence in British society,[14] an argument that they are unwanted and that Britain would be better off without them. The rhetoric of public argument, therefore, is often one that puts racial minorities on their heels, forced to argue for the maintenance of their status rather than for any extension to or expansion of that status, such as affirmative action.

Acceptance of immigration by the mass of British society has been premised on the idea that, at least in public, ethnic minorities would absorb the formal, political aspects of Britishness and not hold any group status superior to British citizenship. To organize for rights that would be distributed on a racial basis would be to open oneself up to the claim of holding a group membership above British citizenship. Immigration is a touchy subject in Britain because the mass of British citizens have little desire to form a multicultural state, even if they approve of a multiethnic one. The maintenance of their status in British society, therefore, is premised on a low level of ethnic political organization, for this would be interpreted as a rejection of British citizenship. Combined with their relatively recent arrival in the United Kingdom, their low numbers, and their distribution across a number of groups that do not see themselves as having much in common, the continuing presence of the immigration debate helps dampen ethnic political organization, which in turn prevents the creation of programs, such as affirmative action, that distribute goods on a racial basis.

Finally, and most simply, the fact that virtually all ethnic minorities entered Britain by their own free choice means that claims for extraordinary treatment lack the same kind of sting that those of American blacks have. White Britons can claim that by letting ethnic minorities into the country and granting them citizenship, they have already done much more than their European counterparts would, and that to ask that meritocratic standards be modified to accommodate minorities on top of that would be asking far too much. Unlike America, where whites can (and should) feel guilty for the nation's history of slavery and segregation, Britain, quite simply, has less to feel guilty about, and thus less for which to offer reparations. Because permitting immigration in the first place is viewed by many Britons as more than doing their part for members of the commonwealth, it is difficult to squeeze into popular discourse an argument for granting rights in addition to citizenship.

The Difficulty of Hiring by the Numbers without the Numbers

An important element of systematic, governmentally enforced affirmative action is the collection of racial data at the firm and the national levels, the former for administrative surveillance, the latter for agenda setting. Central administrative oversight requires that racial data be available for all firms in a relatively homogeneous form so that comparisons may be made to determine where lower levels of minority hiring occur. As Kelly and Dobbin argue in chapter 4, employers' fear that they would be sued based on proof of "disparate impact" rather than simple intentional discrimination acted as a powerful spur to the creation of equal opportunity and affirmative action policies. Fear of lawsuits based on firm-level data, therefore, helped induce the firms to create affirmative action offices. There is no mandatory collection of racial data on employees in the United Kingdom. What is more, firms have incentives not to collect this sort of data voluntarily, because it may be used against them to prove discrimination. In Britain, an employer who counts minorities is behaving suspiciously.

Beyond the level of the firm, the collection of racial data in general is sparse in the United Kingdom. Compare the basic abstract of statistics of the United Kingdom and the United States. Whereas hundreds of tables in the United States' Statistical Abstract break down data by race, in the United Kingdom's, only a handful do. Racial data in other official publications are sparse as well, and it is only recently that a separate publication has summarized the available data on racial minorities. It was only in 1991, after years of heated conflict, that the British Census surveyed for ethnic background (Coleman and Salt 1992, 477–78). The collection of racial data used for university admissions shows a similar pattern. All university applicants are requested to select an ethnic category on their initial, centralized application form. This part of the form is torn off and used for monitoring purposes, but it is never seen by the admissions tutors who make the relevant decisions. And universities do not widely advertise their racial balance. In Oxford's prospectus, for example, there is a complete breakdown of applications and acceptances by type of school (state or public) and region, but not by ethnicity. This reflects the inequalities that are thought politically and socially relevant and those that are not.

Social statistics are rarely collected simply because they are interesting. Rather, they both reflect political concerns and drive them as well. The limited collection of racial data in the United Kingdom is a reflection of the low status that peculiarly minority concerns have in the United Kingdom. But the sparseness of data also serve to dampen the issue as a concern for the larger public and for researchers in particular (who, having few data to deal with, choose other issues).

Centralization

The centralization of the British state has been one of the main obstacles to the evolution of U.S.-style affirmative action in the United Kingdom. To understand why, it is necessary to appreciate the special role the RRA gave to local government in the administration of the act and the attitude toward local government that has been popular at the national level for most of the act's history.

Section 71 of the RRA gives local authorities a central role in advancing good race relations (pt. 10, sec. 71). Although the Commission for Racial Equality was given the statutory duty to assist in the enforcement of the RRA, local government was expected to bring attention to racial justice into the ordinary operation of government. As a significant employer, consumer, and force setting the overall tone of social conduct, local government had a number of important resources it could bring to bear against the problem of racial discrimination. Furthermore, given its mandate to promote equality of opportunity, some room for pushing toward affirmative action could have been justified by the language of the RRA.

Some local councils took the act's encouragement more seriously than others and continue to do so. The most significant, at least in symbolic terms, was the GLC. The 1960s and 1970s had been the high tide in Britain of municipal socialism and of the march through local government of the Labour Party's hard Left, which had become just as concerned with issues of gender, sexuality, and race as the old Labour Party had been with class. The most prominent hard Left council was, undoubtedly, the GLC under "Red" Ken Livingstone. From the moment it was elected in 1979, the Conservative Party found itself hounded and annoyed by Livingstone's GLC, just across the Thames from the Houses of Parliament. For their trouble, Thatcher abolished the GLC in 1985, leaving London the largest city in the world without a municipal government. The GLC building is now an aquarium.

If these were the real reasons Thatcher eliminated the GLC, perhaps the reason she got away with it was the council's reputation as "loony Left," a position symbolized by the GLC's aggressive action on race, gender, and sexuality. The GLC gave substantial grants to ethnic organizations in the London area (creating a financial incentive to organize on such a basis), began to put pressure on the organization's bureaucrats to hire more women and minorities, and established requirements that companies supplying the GLC implement equal opportunity policies that included the area of race. Given the mixture of a citywide government creating financial incentives for an ethnicity-based organization, a commitment to antidiscrimination policy, and the very radical tenor of London's left wing at the time, the best opportunity in Britain's history existed for the creation of affirmative action policies.

Some observers, such as Herman Ouseley, now the chair of the CRE, believe that the GLC's activities with respect to race were the main reason for the council's abolishment, but it is unlikely that this was more than a pretext for a decision the government made for other reasons. However, eliminating it certainly had an impact, closing off yet another path that could have led to affirmative action. Furthermore, the abolishment of the GLC made local councils cautious. "No longer wishing to be dubbed by the mass media as 'loony left,' . . . these authorities have cut the programmes and commitment to race equality, if not the 'equal opportunity employer' slogans appearing on their job vacancy announcements" (Ouseley, cited in Ball and Solomos 1990, 150).

Whether or not the actual effect has been this dramatic, local councils have found it to be in their interest to downplay what they are doing to reduce racial discrimination. There are no political points to be made by breaking through existing taboos, and creating U.S.-style affirmative action would require taboo-breaking. Some councils are doing more than others to push for positive action under the RRA, but few are pushing its boundaries, and those that have tried, such as the London Borough of Lambeth, have found themselves rebuffed in the courts.

Finally, the changes that have been made in the political structure of Britain by the Conservatives since 1979 have made the task of enforcing, or expanding, discrimination law more difficult. Mary Coussey (personal communication, 29 April 1997) argues that "[p]aradoxically, centralisation was done by devolving decisions to local units, as in local government, NHS [National Health Service,] and education. Middle tiers were removed. Centralised units for race equality went too. I did a study of four devolved organisations. . . . I found that devolved decision making had led to fragmentation of resources. It was difficult to get positive action schemes off the ground because budgets were fragmented, and managers became more territorial. Competitive tendering also led to functions being defined narrowly to cut costs . . . and long term activities such as training and positive action could no longer be justified because they were not market related."

This restructuring of the British state, done for reasons having little to do with race relations, has nonetheless substantially limited the avenues through which an expansion of positive action could occur. What is more, by injecting the market into the delivery of services, subnational governments have been gradually leached of their ideological enthusiasm, as an ethos of value for money and administrative efficiency has taken over.

Absence of a Leading Group

In the United States, affirmative action spread from one unquestionably oppressed group (native-born blacks) outward to other groups with a lesser claim to exceptional treatment, including other racial minorities, most of whom were recent immigrants, and women. It was the exceptional experience of American blacks and the urgently felt need to correct it that permitted the principle of affirmative action to be legitimated in the first place and subsequently to be picked up by other groups who would not have been able to make the original claim.

Britain, quite simply, lacks this vanguard group. As discussed earlier, none of the racial minorities can make a claim to exceptional oppression, and whatever claim they can make is largely obliterated by their status as immigrants or the offspring of immigrants. But what of other groups that could possibly have legitimated the principle of affirmative action? One group could have, but so far has not, sought affirmative action on the basis of a great historical wrong: women.

To understand why British feminists have not sought affirmative action, and correspondingly, why they have not legitimated the principle such that ethnic minorities could draw on it, one must examine the very different content of British feminism. In the area of workplace discrimination, British feminists generally seek comparable worth or pay equity and welfare-type social programs and workplace rights, rather than affirmative action. British feminists typically argue that traditionally female occupations should be given a higher status in British society, and this includes motherhood. Comparable worth, by raising the wages of "women's jobs," is based on the idea that women should not necessarily aspire to be like men in male occupations. As Sandra Fredman (personal communication, 7 March 1997), tutor at Exeter College, Oxford, argues, most British feminists have a "skepticism of fitting in with the white male world. We want to change it. . . . It is not good enough just to let women conform to men's roles." A result of this attitude is that British feminists typically push for welfare-state interventions, such as paid family leave, that challenge the hegemony of the market over the sphere of the family and caregiving. Affirmative action would go in the opposite direction from the interventions that British feminists want, drawing women away from traditional occupations and caregiving, rather than drawing the public sphere and the lives of men closer to traditionally female concerns. As a result, affirmative action has never received the initial support it needs from the most plausible beneficiary in British society and, correspondingly, ethnic minorities have not been able to draw on women's legitimate claims in order to make their own.

Furthermore, even if British feminists were to make affirmative action an important part of their political agenda, it is likely that they would find their way blocked by the law, if not in Britain, than in the European community. Women-only short lists, which were used to increase the representation of women among Labour members of Parliament (MPs), were struck down by the British courts. A recent decision by the European Court of Justice, *Kalanke v. Freie Hansestadt Bremen*, held that "A national rule that, where men and women who are candidates for the same promotion are equally qualified, women are automatically to be given priority in sectors where they are under-represented, involves discrimination on grounds of sex" (Schick 1996, 241). Whereas pay equity legislation passes muster in the European community, and in fact has been pushed by Brussels (Rhoads 1994), the European Court of Justice looks quite unfavorably at preferential treatment. This should act as a critical brake on the development of affirmative action for women in the United Kingdom, and thereby for racial minorities as well.

The Logic of the Welfare State

Despite the partial retrenchment of the welfare state in Britain during the Thatcher years (Pierson 1994), Britain still has more extensive public provision in most areas than the United States, though considerably less than is common in western Europe. More important than the numbers, however, is what we might call the logic of the welfare state: the rhetorical claims that are considered legitimate within it. The postwar settlement that created the British welfare state incorporates a notion of social citizenship—a set of rights to provision that are determined by membership in the collectivity rather than by personal identity. This understanding, which has been eroded on the conservative side of the spectrum, is still quite strong within the Labour Party. Unlike that of the United States, Britain's Left still remains a strongly class-based party rather than a collection of identity-based groups, and this organizational basis, combined with the language of social citizenship, strongly constrains the sorts of claims that are generally taken as legitimate. As Sewell (1993) puts it, "[The Labour Party] has the difficult task of retaining its working class support whilst trying to deny that it is a class party. Part of the solution is to replace class with a notion of an appeal to 'the people.' But conceptions of 'the people' remain homogenous. 'The people' or 'working people' are not broken down into different constituencies, with possible conflicting interests. It is this self-defined image which inhibits it from acknowledging distinctions along racial lines" (26).

For this reason, claims to special dispensation on the basis of race or any other sort of identity, are extremely difficult to squeeze into mainstream discourse. The problems of racial minorities are typically understood to be derivative of their standing in the class system, rather than intrinsic to their place in some sort of racial hierarchy. In the United States, the absence of a language of social citizenship or of a broadly legitimate welfare state in a peculiar way plays into the hands of those who want to justify affirmative action. Blacks, and by extension other identity-based groups, can claim to be aberrant, to exist outside of a widely legitimate individualist system, and thus can claim special dispensation on this basis. Affirmative action, far from being an extension of the welfare state, is in large measure dependent for its justification on the absence of a hegemonic discourse of social citizenship. In combination with other factors discussed in this chapter, the larger ideological structure of British politics, especially left of center, mitigates against the kind of identity-based claims that support affirmative action in the United States.

The Structure of the Labour Party and the Electoral System

One important factor that perpetuates affirmative action in the United States is the political organization of minorities on the basis of race, in the Democratic Party and elsewhere. The Congressional Black Caucus (CBC) is a strong influence on the Democratic Party and a focal point for organizing within Congress on an explicitly racial basis. Until recently, the Democratic Party itself maintained standing racial caucuses, which had the same impact on the party as the CBC. This organizational structure provides a mechanism through which the interests of black voters can be channeled into the political process on a racial basis, rather than processed through mechanisms that would structure their claims on a class or other basis.

Few such mechanisms exist in British politics. Although there was movement for organized black sections within the Labour Party in the early 1980s, it was not rousingly successful outside of London, where "by October 1984, 25 constituency parties in the London area had allowed formation of black sections, despite their unconstitutional nature." Interestingly, and connected to arguments made elsewhere in this chapter, "[i]n cities with large Asian populations, such as Leicester and Bradford, it was difficult to establish black sections because a politics of ethnicity based on religion prevented establishment of a black organisation attempting to unite diverse ethnic minority groups" (Geddes 1996, 77). Party conferences in 1984 and 1985 decisively defeated resolutions calling for the creation of black sections. Members of the party's elite, such as Deputy Leader Roy Hattersley, reflected polls of minority voters (Geddes 1996, 108) in considering them "deeply patronising, a retrograde step" (Sewell 1993, 103). A watered-down form of representation, the Black and Asian Socialist Society, was eventually created in 1990, though it is not officially recognized by the Labour Party.

There are no ethnic caucuses within the House of Commons, nor does there seem great pressure to create them. Although ethnic minorities provide overwhelming support to the Labour Party, this support has been for reasons of class, rather than in response to the specifically racial policies of the party. In a 1983 poll, 78 percent of African Caribbean Labour supporters said they would vote for the party because "they support the working class," whereas only 7 percent said they would do so because "they support blacks and Asians." The comparable numbers for Asians were 65 percent and 34 percent, respectively. Other polls report similar findings (Sewell 1993, 83, 84).

Finally, the larger structure of the British electoral system is a brake on the expression of peculiarly ethnic minority concerns. Britain has a system of single-member districts, and though Britain's ethnic minorities are concentrated in the cities, their concentrations in the districts are too low to make them "majority-minority" districts (Glazer and Young 1983, 260). Were ethnic minorities concentrated in the same way the Scots or the Welsh are, they might have been able to create nationalistic parties like the Scottish National Party or Plaid Cwynd. This might change if Britain adopts a system of proportional representation, which would allow relatively small groups such as ethnic minorities to organize and gain representation disassociated from the major parties or to threaten to leave the major parties and thereby force them to create internal representation. But full-blown proportional representation seems unlikely, and it is unclear that Britain's ethnic minorities would take advantage of the opportunity for narrow representation if it were available.

Conclusion: The Future

Ultimately, it may be that affirmative action is off the agenda in Britain for a much simpler reason than any I have suggested so far: optimism. Britain does not have a long history of settlement by nonwhites, and for that reason there is not the weariness with persistent inequality that affects the United States. Black and white Britons are early enough in the experience of a multiethnic society to believe that reasonable parity between groups can be established on the basis of individualism, backed by the rule of law. As Herman Ouseley, chair of the CRE and a long-time advocate of positive action, puts it, "You don't build good race relations if you create resentment. You can't give people an additional advantage, because you are then denying others who may on merit be getting jobs or access to services. We believe that black and ethnic minorities in Britain have the talent and the ability, and if you removed discrimination they could compete equally" (Wavell 1995).

Although many of the cultural forces that have kept affirmative action off the agenda in Britain are likely to persist for some time to come, there are signals that the institutional obstacles discussed earlier may not be so imposing in the future. Under the New Labour government of Prime Minister Tony Blair, the institutional landscape of Britain is in a process of wholesale change, with consequences that are, at this point, difficult to predict. There are reasons to suspect that, given this uncertainty, these institutional changes will transform the political status of Britain's ethnic minorities.

The first significant change is Blair's reshaping of the Labour Party. Although Labour was never a wholly class-based party, it is the case that this was a critical element of its public face and of the way it conceptualized disadvantage. In a strategy that was one part electoral strategy, and one part reasonable attempt to update social democracy to new conditions, Labour has largely dropped the language of "equality" and substituted the concept of "social exclusion." The upper reaches of the Labour intelligentsia now understand disadvantage to be a function of forces much more wide-ranging than labor market position, including gender, education level, region, and ethnicity. This new approach has become institutionalized in the prime minister's Social Exclusion Unit, as well as in prestigious university-based research centers such as the Center for the Analysis of Social Exclusion at the London School of Economics. Anthony Giddens, who has emerged as the central ideologist of the prime minister's "Third Way," sums up the shift: "There is no future for the egalitarianism-at-all-costs that absorbed leftists for so long. Modernising social democrats have to find an approach that reconciles equality with pluralism and life-style diversity" (Giddens 1999).

The language of social exclusion provides an opening for ethnic minorities to express their disadvantage in terms other than class, given that New Labour's self-definition is no longer challenged by identity-specific claims. Interestingly, the same classless dynamic that has allowed the Labour Party to reach out to middle-class voters in the suburbs may also open the door to a more whole-hearted Labour Party multiculturalism.

The second and perhaps even more important change is the Labour government's program of political decentralization. As I argued earlier, the dramatic centralization of politics in the 1980s, along with the strict constructionist interpretation of the English courts, short-circuited local movements, turning them away from the fairly limited forms of positive action and toward something more ambitious. The Labour government is now in the process of returning a certain amount of power to local government, quite ambitiously where Scotland and Wales are concerned and to a somewhat more limited degree in English local government. Although minorities make up a relatively small percentage of Britain's overall population, they constitute an impressive percentage of the population in London, Birmingham, Bradford, Leeds, and other major cities. If a large degree of power is devolved to local government, ethnic minorities will have a serious incentive to mobilize politically at the urban level, to use their political power strategically, and to push—if they choose—for more aggressive efforts toward social inclusion on a proportional basis.

Third, and potentially of the greatest importance, is the impact of the Stephen Lawrence inquiry on police personnel systems. To make a very long story very short, the racially motivated murder of a young Afro-Caribbean man, Stephen Lawrence, in 1993, compounded by the incompetence and probable malfeasance of the police in investigating his killers, set off a major bout of institutional soul-searching among the British political elite. To clear up the facts around the Lawrence murder investigation, the government established the first major government inquiry on race-related issues since the Scarman report. Sir William MacPherson's government-mandated report, "The Steven Lawrence Inquiry," called for a major overhaul of the English police force, especially personnel systems, declaring that they were influenced by "institutionalized racism." Among other things, the report recommended that "policing plans should include targets for recruitment, progression and retention of minority ethnic staff" (Home Office 1999a, 32). The Home Office has accepted this recommendation and has published employment targets for ethnic minorities in the Home Office itself and in the prison, police, probation, and fire services (Home Office 1999b). In addition, the government, to some degree propelled by the Lawrence inquiry, is crafting a new Race Relations Act that will increase the enforcement powers of the CRE, including (despite initial resistance) strengthened provisions concerning "indirect discrimination." (Travis 2000).

These moves do not necessarily suggest that Britain is moving to full-scale, U.S.-style affirmative action—even where the police are concerned. The government's recent moves in response to the Lawrence inquiry notwithstanding, it seems unlikely that Britain would break through the wall that divides "soft" from "hard" affirmative action. All of these moves would lead, in all likelihood, only to perfection of the regime of positive action described earlier, rather than a dramatic move toward the American regime of affirmative action. Unless the institutional changes wrought by the new identity of the Labour Party and devolution turn out to be much more powerful than they appear, Britain will end up with a much better implemented, but fundamentally stable, regime of race relations.

In short, Britain has deeply institutionalized a different model of equal opportunity policy, an evolutionary groove that it will continue, in its own way, rather than mimicking American practice. That model is similar to what Glenn Loury has suggested as an alternative to preferential treatment in the United States: "Instead of using different criteria of selection, the employers and schools in question . . . [should seek] to meet their desired level of black participation through a concerted effort to enhance performance, while maintaining common standards of evaluation. Call it 'developmental,' as opposed to 'preferential,' affirmative action" (Loury 1997, 40–41). This is, in theory, what the British already have on the books, and this is the approach they are in the process of strengthening.

This suggests a paradox: The British have a model of affirmative action that conforms well to shared Anglo-American meritocratic principles, but they are only gradually enforcing it as strongly as they might. On the other hand, America has a model of affirmative action that, at least procedurally and in some cases practically, undermines universal meritocratic standards and that as a result is highly controversial, but it is backed by a large (if not always effectual) enforcement structure.

Perhaps the more interesting question is whether America, with a major commitment of time, resources, and people, will be able to adopt at least part of the British model of affirmative or positive action. The political environment in the United States is slowly turning against preferential treatment, and commentators across the political spectrum are grasping for an alternative that strives for universal standards but does not passively accept the fact of racial inequality. The death of affirmative action could lead to the rise of another, superior tool for tackling racial disadvantage. Moreover, the recent welfare debate also suggests that the public's desire for change, if not satisfied in a more egalitarian direction, could lead to something much less attractive (Teles 1996, chap. 8). With affirmative action as we have known it under continuing political pressure, the British approach to antidiscrimination policy (if not its practice) provides at least one model of how the liberal principle of meritocracy and a commitment to combating discrimination may be reconciled.

Notes

1. A brief note on terms: In this article, when I use the terms *positive discrimination* or *affirmative action*, I intend the terms to be equivalent. The term *positive action* is different and means only those methods permitted by the Race Relations Act 1976.

2. Affirmative action, of course, is as much if not more widely applied to women in the United States but, with few exceptions, I will only be discussing the policy as it relates to ethnic or racial minorities.

3. It is, in fact, an accident that the United States and Great Britain do not both use the term *positive action*. Nicholas Lemann reports that Hobart Taylor Jr., the young lawyer who wrote Executive Order 10925, "was searching for something that would give a sense of positiveness to performance under the Executive Order and I was torn between the words 'positive action' and the words 'affirmative action.' . . . And I took 'affirmative' because it was alliterative" (Lemann 1999, 162).

4. By *recruitment*, I mean encouragement to apply rather than a direct attempt to hire, which would be impermissible under the RRA.

5. The term *stakeholding firm* means, in the British context, a company that takes a broader view of its constituency than simply its stockholders, including suppliers, employees, and the communities in which it operates. Many companies have included positive race relations as an important part of their stakeholding principles.

6. I must caution that the term *black* can be highly misleading in the British context, since it covers both Africans and Afro-Caribbeans, who have very different positions in British society. Where possible, I have used statistics that break these ethnic categories down, so as to avoid the use of the term *black*. Unfortunately, many sources of data, especially official government sources, use the term *black*. Whether I use *black* or *Afro-Caribbean* is wholly determined by the source I am using. Whenever possible, I use

the Policy Studies Institute's Fourth National Survey of Ethnic Minorities, edited by Tariq Modood and others, which is the gold standard of British data on ethnic minorities.

7. Forty-six percent of white men attained this level of educational qualification, as compared with 38 percent of Caribbean men and 46 percent of Indian men (Modood and Berthoud 1997, 73).

8. It must be noted that although the numbers of African Caribbeans holding qualifications is higher than the figure for whites, the prestige of these qualifications is, on average, not as high as the average for whites. Even so, the possession of any qualification is a major distinguishing factor in British society, and the difference in quality of qualification should not be permitted to overshadow this fact.

9. That said, data on residential segregation and on concentration of minority students in majority-minority schools are not as positive as those for interracial relationships. However, even these measures are much less negative than in the United States.

10. Average earnings, when not broken down by gender, are not so favorable: 7.12 per hour versus 7.73 per hour for whites. This is due to Indian women's much lower earnings.

11. This statement should be qualified somewhat, in that Indians actually have a higher rate of male self-employment than whites—25 percent versus 18 percent. Even so, both the white and Indian rates are much higher than those for Caribbeans, suggesting that my generalization holds true. (Modood and Berthoud 1997, 122).

12. For example, far more Asians stated that they would mind if one of their close relatives were to marry an African Caribbean (Question 16).

13. On this mark, Britain does quite well compared to its continental counterparts. In Britain, "most of the visible minorities have a form of British citizenship or residency status and all categories enjoy the full protection of industrial and anti-discrimination law" (Forbes and Mead 1992, 25). By contrast, in Germany "citizenship has never been afforded as a matter of course to people who have a non-German origin. . . . Turks, for example, who have been in Germany for thirty years, are still seen and categorised as foreigners" (ibid., 38).

14. But not, perhaps surprisingly, among the mass of racial minorities. In the Institute for Public Policy Research survey of racial minorities, more Asians than whites agreed that there is "too much Asian immigration to Britain" (Question 9), whereas fewer Asians than whites agreed that "most refugees in Britain are in need of our help and support," or that "most people claiming to be refugees are not real refugees" (Question 7). On the other hand, fewer Asians than whites are concerned about illegal immigration (Question 8). On almost all these indexes, African Caribbeans are the most supportive of immigration and immigrants (Institute for Public Policy Research, 1997).

Acknowledgments

I would like to thank all of the people whom I interviewed in the conduct of this quite unplanned research project, in particular Mary Coussey and Tariq Modood. The latter deserves special thanks for the enormous amount of time he spent making sure I got the story right—if I didn't, it isn't for his lack of effort.

References

Ball, Wendy, and John Solomos, eds. 1990. *Race and local politics.* London: Macmillan.

Banton, Michael. 1983. *Racial and ethnic competition.* Cambridge: Cambridge University Press.

Belz, Herman. 1991. *Equality transformed.* New Brunswick, N.J.: Transaction Publishers.

Benyon, John, ed. 1984. *Scarman and after.* Oxford: Pergamon.

Braham, Peter, Ali Rattansi, and Richard Skellington. 1992. *Racism and anti-racism.* London: Sage.

Brown, Colin. 1992. Same difference: The persistence of racial disadvantage in the British employment market. In *Racism and anti-racism,* edited by Peter Braham, Ali Rattansi, and Richard Skellington. London: Sage.

Business in the Community. n.d. Race for opportunity: Questions and answers [online]. Available from http://www.blink.org.uk/reports2/oppques.htm.

Coleman, David, and John Salt. 1992. *The British population: Patterns, trends, and processes.* Oxford: Oxford University Press.

Commission for Racial Equality. 1995. Large companies and racial equality. London: Commission for Racial Equality.

———. 1999. Race Relations (Amendment) Bill: House of Lords Briefing for Second Reading. London: Her Majesty's Stationery Office.

Conservative Party. 1997. *Conservative Party manifesto.* London: Conservative Party.

Edwards, Jonathan. 1995. *When race counts: The morality of racial preference in Britain and America.* London: Routledge.

Employment Department Group. 1996. Ten point plan for employers. London: Her Majesty's Stationery Office.

Forbes, Ian, and Geoffrey Mead. 1992. *Measure for measure: A comparative analysis of measures to combat racial discrimination in the member countries of the European community.* London: Equal Opportunities Study Group, University of Southampton.

Geddes, Andrew. 1996. *The politics of immigration and race.* Manchester: Baseline.

Giddens, Anthony. 1999. Social change in Britain: Inequality and social democracy, ESRC Lecture, 21 October.

Glazer, Nathan, and Ken Young. 1983. *Ethnic pluralism and public policy.* Lexington, Mass.: Lexington Books.

Gold, Michael. 1985. Griggs' folly: An essay on the theory, problems, and origins of the adverse impact definition of employment discrimination and a recommendation for reform. *Industrial Relations Law Journal* 7:429–598.

Hansard. 1976a. 905, c. 596. Proceedings of the British Parliament, 21 February.

Hansard. 1976b. 906, c. 1547. Proceedings of the British Parliament, 4 March.

Hepple, Bob, and Erika Szyszczak. 1992. *Discrimination: The limits of the law.* London: Mansell.

Her Majesty's Civil Service. 1996. Good practice for equal opportunities staff complaints procedures. London: Her Majesty's Civil Service.

Holdaway, Simon. 1991. Recruiting a multiracial police force. London: Her Majesty's Stationery Office.

Home Office. 1999a. Steven Lawrence inquiry: Home Secretary's action plan. London: Her Majesty's Stationery Office.

———. 1999b. Race equality: The Home Secretary's employment targets. London: Her Majesty's Stationery Office.

Institute for Public Policy Research. 1997. IPPR attitudes to race survey. London: Institute for Public Policy Research.

Jones, Trevor. 1996. *Britain's ethnic minorities.* London: Policy Studies Institute.

Lemann, Nicholas. 1999. *The big test.* New York: Farrar, Straus and Giroux.

London Borough of Lambeth v. Commission for Racial Equality. 1990. *Industrial Relations Law Review,* 231–36.

Loury, Glenn. 1997. How to mend affirmative action. *The Public Interest* 127:33–43.

Massey, Douglas, and Nancy Denton. 1993. *American apartheid.* London: Harvard University Press.

McCrudden, Christopher. 1992. Affirmative action and fair participation: Interpreting the fair employment act 1989. *Industrial Law Journal* 21 (3) (September): 170–98.

Modood, Tariq, and Richard Berthoud, eds. 1997. *Ethnic minorities in Britain.* London: Policy Studies Institute.

Office of National Statistics. 1996. Social focus on ethnic minorities. London: Her Majesty's Stationery Office.

Office of Populations Censuses and Surveys (Social Survey Division). 1996. Living in Britain: Results from the 1994 General Household Survey. London: Her Majesty's Stationery Office.

Peach, Ceri. 1996. Does Britain have ghettos? *Transactions of the Institute of British Geographers* 21:216–35.

———. 1998. South Asian and Caribbean ethnic minority housing choice in Britain. *Urban Studies* 35 (October): 1657–80.

Pierson, Paul. 1994. *Dismantling the welfare state?* Cambridge: Cambridge University Press.

Race Relations Employment Advisory Service. n.d. Positive action: Promoting racial equality in employment. London: Race Relations Employment Advisory Service.

Rhoads, Steven. 1981. *Incomparable worth: Pay equity meets the market.* Cambridge: Cambridge University Press.

Scarman, Lord. 1981. The Brixton disorders, 10–12 April 1981. (Cmnd. 8427). London: Her Majesty's Stationery Office.

Schick, D. 1996. Positive action in community law. *Industrial Law Journal* 25 (3): 241.

Sewell, Terri. 1993. *Black tribunes: Black political participation in Britain.* London: Lawrence and Wishart.

Skrentny, John D. 1996. *The ironies of affirmative action.* Chicago: University of Chicago Press.

Sowell, Thomas. 1990. *Preferential policies.* New York: William Morrow.

Teles, Steven M. 1996. *Whose welfare? AFDC and elite politics.* Lawrence: University Press of Kansas.

Travis, Alan. 2000. Straw extends race bill. *Guardian Unlimited,* 27 January.

U.S. Bureau of the Census. 1996. Statistical abstract of the United States: 1996. 116th ed. Washington, D.C.: Government Printing Office.

Wavell, S. 1995. Wrestling for an equal share. *Sunday Times,* 26 March, 9–12.

Welsh, Colin, James Knox, and Mark Brett. 1994. Acting positively: Positive actions under the race relations act 1976, employment department group (Research Series No. 31).

Wrench, John, and Edgar Hassan. 1996. Ambition and marginalisation: A qualitative study of underachieving young men of Afro-Caribbean origin. London: Her Majesty's Stationery Office.

11

The French Model: Color-Blind Integration

. . .

ERIK BLEICH

In explicit opposition to the United States, France maintains a firm "color-blind" approach to policy making. France has roundly rejected all elements of race-based affirmative action,[1] both hard and soft.[2] Although it passed antidiscrimination laws as early as 1972, France targets no social policies specifically to benefit groups defined by race or ethnicity, nor does it collect census, employment, or other forms of data that reveal a citizen's race or ethnicity. French political elites, left-leaning interest groups, and even minorities themselves have overwhelmingly opted for a color-blind approach to policy making.

France has upheld and reaffirmed this formula in the decades since World War II, even in the face of a substantial influx of ethnic minority immigrants. Of the countries in Europe that have been the primary recipients of migration since the war, Britain, France, and the Netherlands are most closely comparable to the United States and to other immigration targets in that they have transformed relatively high percentages of first- and second-generation immigrants into citizens. Yet unlike France, both Britain and the Netherlands have adopted some elements of affirmative action policies. Each country is "race-conscious" to the extent that it collects systematic ethnic data and tailors particular policies to benefit specific ethnic or racial groups, even if not to an extent comparable with American policies (Rath and Saggar 1992; chapter 10 in this volume). Although it has percentages of immigrants and minorities equivalent to those found in Britain and the Netherlands, France has chosen to anchor the color-blind end of the international policy spectrum. Understanding how and why it developed its policies and how they are sustained may shed light on the potential for a similar approach in other countries.

Before accounting for the French model, it is necessary to understand its contours and contents. Even though French policy is officially color-blind, France's leaders are not blind to the challenges of diversity.

In the first section of this chapter, I demonstrate that the French approach is rooted in an understanding of identity differences that diverges substantially from that which prevails in the United States. The source of ethnic and "racial" diversity in metropolitan France has been postwar voluntary migration.[3] Whereas in the United States many immigrants benefit from affirmative action because they are categorized as minorities (chapters 2 and 3 in this volume), in France, ethnic minorities (even citizens) are typically defined as "immigrants" or as "second-generation immigrants." Social tensions or problems that are associated with these populations are typically interpreted as problems of immigrant integration rather than as ethnic or "race" relations problems, the lens through which much American social policy is viewed (Noiriel 1994; Williams 1998). This path was, of course, far from preordained. Britain, for example, while also acknowledging immigration as a pressing social and political issue, has tended to focus greater attention on "race relations" concerns and has developed policies that directly target ethnic minorities (Favell 1998; Lapeyronnie 1993).

How did it come to pass that France, confronted with an economically disadvantaged ethnic minority population, chose to reject the path of affirmative action and to opt for a race-neutral model? The next three sections of the chapter attempt to answer this question, exploring three factors that are central to understanding. First, as reflected in much American public debate about affirmative action and most other social policies, there is a *normative* or *moral* element invoked when policy making turns to race. Scholars, political leaders, and average citizens make principled arguments about the value of meritocracy, color-blindness, diversity, or proportional equality. These principles and values can sway people's opinions about a policy, adding or detracting from its perceived legitimacy. I argue that there is a normative consensus in France that affirmative action or any race-conscious policy is anathema to French values. Lessons drawn from the Revolutionary and Vichy eras and use of the United States as an "anti-model" underpin this consensus. In particular, there is a connection between race categorizations and the horrors of Nazism that is much stronger in France than in the United States.

Another factor is the power and strategy of purely *interest-based* lobbying for or against affirmative action. Quotas, goals, and timetables, targeted training programs, and other exceptions to color-blind policies have tangible economic and political consequences. Some people benefit while others lose from affirmative action. As a result, in the United States, groups lobby for its maintenance or dissolution. A similar pattern holds in France, although affirmative action advocates are much weaker there than in the United States. I examine French interest group politics on equal rights and opportunities issues, focusing on the anti-racism movement. Although this movement briefly opened a window of opportunity for affirmative action policies in the early to mid-1980s, this window closed quickly because the movement fragmented and the threat from the far Right increased.[4]

Finally, affirmative action can be justified or rebuffed on the basis of its *policy effectiveness* in achieving concrete goals. A polity may aim for a measure of proportional equality among its citizens, or more simply for social peace. From this perspective, the core issue at stake is not whether affirmative action is *right or wrong*, nor whether social groups lobby *for or against* it, but rather whether it is *effective or not* in solving problems of discrimination, social order, and unequal group representation.[5] This chapter shows how these problems are either difficult to perceive in France given existing institutional practices and prevailing beliefs, or are differently interpreted given the dominant French approach of color-blind integration.

In practice, all of these factors—morality issues, interest group lobbying, and assessments of policy effectiveness—may operate simultaneously; nevertheless, by distinguishing them analytically and examining each in turn, it is possible to understand why France has eschewed policies of affirmative action. I conclude by reflecting on the lessons that the French experience may afford those interested in the applicability of the color-blind model to the United States.

Immigration and Color-Blind Integration

Contrary to popular perception, France has long been a country of immigration (see Horowitz and Noiriel 1992; Noiriel 1988). During the decades following World War II, immigrants from non-European regions began arriving on French shores in substantial numbers. By 1975 there were almost three and a half million foreigners living in France, of whom almost 1.3 million originated from Africa or Asia (Weil 1995a, annex VI).[6] The 1990 census showed foreign Africans and Asians in France numbering 2,069,890, or 3.7 percent of the total population of 56,634,299 (see Weil 1995a, annex VI).[7] Because only non-French are enumerated (and then only by country of origin, not by ethnicity or race), it is impossible to gauge precisely the number of ethnic minorities in France. Nevertheless, its relatively inclusive citizenship and naturalization laws (Brubaker 1992) and the presence of citizens from former

French colonies,[8] combined with the official numbers of non-French Africans and Asians, implies that the visible minority population may be close to 5 percent of the total population. With millions of ethnic minority citizens and long-term settled residents, France has clearly entered an era of demographic multiracialism.

In contrast to the United States and to Britain, however, France has not viewed its new demography and "ethnic dilemmas" through a multicultural or race relations prism. Although it has not pursued difference-blindness to its logical extreme, France has developed a model of color-blind immigrant integration that closely parallels the chimerical American ideal of the melting pot.[9] During the 1980s and 1990s—as immigration became a contentious issue in France—politicians, policy makers, experts, intellectuals, and the public engaged a high-profile and protracted debate over how to cope with the "problems" of immigration (see, for example, Commission de la Nationalité 1988). Perhaps the most prominent issue considered was the mode of interaction between immigrants and the host society. The options revolved around three potential models—assimilation, insertion, and integration (see Haut Conseil à l'Intégration 1991). Whereas *assimilation* was ultimately judged too stringent because it required immigrants to forego their native cultures and group-based identities in public and private life, *insertion* was judged too lax because it allowed minority cultures and groups to claim rights and recognition in the public sphere.[10] Instead, France opted for a middle ground of *integration*, which permits immigrants and minorities to retain their religion, culture, and identities in the private sphere, while disallowing any group-based claims on the state.

Attempting to strike the delicate balance between unity and diversity, the High Council on Integration (1991, 18)[11] described the French philosophy: "it is a question of evoking the active participation of different and various elements in the national society, while at the same time accepting the maintenance of cultural, social and moral specificities and taking for granted that the whole is enriched by this variety, this complexity. Without denying differences, knowing how to take them into account without exalting them, a policy of integration accents similarities and convergence." As Silverman (1992) warns, it is tempting to overstate and to oversimplify the French model as a coherent alternative to the more communitarian approaches favored elsewhere. Without falling into this trap, it is nevertheless correct to perceive a certain level of national policy coherence.

The color-blind element of the French model has two aspects. First, organizing social inquiry or targeting social policy based on group markers of "race" or skin color is strictly taboo. There is not a single policy in France that targets individuals or groups by race or by skin color. Avoidance of race as a meaningful social variable is sometimes by design and sometimes unselfconscious. Whereas in the United States, armadas of scholars, journalists, and policy makers have contributed to the formation of a "racial state" (Omi and Winant 1994) by collecting, analyzing, and often anguishing over race-based group differentials, France pays scant attention to such concerns and downplays their significance. Moreover, there is no census question on race or ethnic origins. Collecting data on potentially vulnerable minorities is so anathematized in France that a 1978 law (78-17) rendered computerized storage of information on race illegal, except with express consent of the individual or after obtaining formal approval from a national commission. French elites, of course, recognize that social and political tensions may arise in a multiracial society. The cornerstone French antiracism law, passed in 1972 (72-546), banned discrimination and racist acts in private and public life, punishing perpetrators in criminal courts with stiff fines and jail sentences. Yet the logic of French law is precisely opposed to that of affirmative action. Its aim is to punish racists committing bigoted acts motivated by racist intent, not to foster numerical racial equality nor to compensate a class of victims defined by race.[12]

Second, issues that would be interpreted in the United States as containing a racial dimension are typically viewed through a different lens in France. The integration model focuses attention on problems and social divides associated with culture, class, geography, and citizenship status rather than race or skin color. To be sure, discussions of significant differences between immigrants and native French easily become elided with distinctions based on skin color (Silverman 1992, 3–5). Nevertheless, formal research and policies track foreign residents—subdivided by country of origin—rather than racial or ethnic minorities (such as Afro-Americans or Latinos) when calculating social mobility and acculturation (see Favell 1998, 72–73; Hargreaves 1995). Because immigrants rather than minorities are the salient out-group, much emphasis is placed on acquisition of French citizenship as the crucial step to attaining equality within the polity (Brubaker 1992; Commission de la Nationalité 1988; Favell 1998). Once within the formal bounds of the nation, all categorization by the previous nationality ceases, as citizens are regarded as equal, irrespective of origin, race, or religion. By consequence, French institutions focus on immigrant problems of poor housing, low skills, and educational difficulties as problems potentially faced by all residents. As one cabinet minister declared at the end of the 1980s, "integration policies for immigrants and their children (*populations issues de l'immigration*) have to be seen as part of a global policy undertaken by the Government with respect to disadvantaged groups" (cited in Lapeyronnie 1993, 161).

To the extent that there is any special consideration given on the basis of ethnicity, it is targeted at "immigrants" rather than "minorities" and formally takes place through nonracialized avenues. The principal government institution for integrating immigrants (the Social Action Fund for Immigrant Workers and Their Families, or FAS) allocates a portion of its resources to intercultural studies and to programs focused on groups such as North Africans, West Africans, and Southeast Asians. Its primary goal, however, is to foster integration by overcoming problems of cultural misunderstanding rather than to promote diversity or group equality (Fonds d'Action Sociale 1996), marking a critical difference from affirmative action for immigrants in the United States (see chapters 2, 4, and 5 in this volume). At its most multicultural, the FAS may grant funds to a group of Algerians for an ethnic festival. Yet from the state's point of view, money is given to a local association, not to a minority group seeking to promote its community's identity (confidential interview, Paris, 17 March 1997). Of course in practice, this money also serves both to promote an ethnic identity and (perhaps more important) to placate and to co-opt a potentially active ethnic organization—but these are never admitted as the primary functions of the funding. As Soysal (1994, 61) stresses, even these "'multiculturalist' tendencies in policy remain within the bounds of 'republican citizenship,' deemphasizing collective incorporation and reifying individual membership."

The closest the French come to redistributive policies based on ethnic identity markers is through informal, soft quotas in public housing. In lieu of ethnic data, ethnicity is judged based on last names on applications or discerned from face-to-face applicant interviews. These quotas, however, operate in reverse, limiting immigrants' access to buildings and encouraging native French to occupy publicly financed apartments (Hargreaves 1995, 198–99; Lapeyronnie 1993, 244–45; Schain 1993, 61–63).[13] Such actions are justified as preventing ghettoization of ethnic groups.[14] As Weil (1995a, 399) explains, "between quotas and ghettos, the public powers very clearly chose quotas." The means may be distasteful to liberal Anglo-Americans, yet the results are clear: local concentrations of foreigners, immigrants, and minorities in France are less dramatic than those in Britain or in the United States (Lapeyronnie 1993, 236–45; Weir 1995).[15]

French policies, though race- and color-blind, are not wholly differ-ence-blind. Beyond immigrants, at least four other identity groups ben-efit from varying levels of recognition and unequal treatment before the law: overseas French citizens, regions, religious groups, and women. French citizens from the four overseas *départements*—almost exclusively individuals of color—have received special administrative attention once in metropolitan France. In the 1980s, a state agency (the National Agency for the Insertion and Promotion of Overseas Workers, or ANT) began providing assistance aimed solely at these citizens, such as loans and direct financial aid, as well as interventions made on their behalf to the state or to welfare organizations (Domenach and Picouet 1992, 96–99). Regions, too, have taken advantage of the more relaxed attitude toward minority cultural claims of the once-Jacobin state. Languages such as Basque and Breton have seen a recent revival with support from successive governments in Paris. And Corsica, like the overseas depart-ments, now enjoys a modicum of regional autonomy from the central-ized state (Safran 1989).[16]

Counting and labeling citizens by their religious affiliation remains taboo (and prohibited by the 1978 law); yet bargaining between the state and religious elites is not uncommon.[17] Not only have French poli-ticians met with Catholic, Protestant, and Jewish organizations, but they have also actively sought to create a formal Muslim structure.[18] Finally, difference-blindness is least applicable to women, who are not only enumerated in censuses, but who have been the objects of what little formal affirmative action France has implemented. After arriving in office in 1981, the Socialist party established a Ministry of the Rights of Women, which developed and supported training programs designed to encourage women to move into more high-tech occupations (Jenson 1988, 160–64). The impact of such programs was extremely circum-scribed, however, and provoked reservations among some legal experts (Dekeuwer-Defossez 1985, 137–41; Jenson 1988). Moreover, once the Socialist government tightened its belt in 1983 the policy momentum was largely lost (Jenson and Sineau 1995). Viewed from an international perspective, affirmative action policies for women have found only lim-ited purchase in France. (Recent decisions about political "parity" for women—discussed below—are an important exception to this rule.)

But even if France may flirt with the logic of affirmative action by providing goods or recognition to various groups, these exceptions never break the color-blind rule. Even the exceptions must be recog-nized as minor and marginal, relative to the dominant mode of interac-tion with most minorities—as immigrants to be integrated. The French model is therefore very different on the ground from the American model. If racial or ethnic minorities benefit from government policies, it is indirectly as immigrants, natives of overseas departments, or through their religious affiliations. Not all minorities are eligible for benefits, and the policies in place also benefit nonminorities. Moreover, since these policies rarely have a strong redistributive intention, what benefits are available typically pale in comparison to those afforded by affirmative action programs. The avowed goal of French policy is to minimize friction and competition between groups defined by ethnicity or race and to maximize national social cohesion. As one well-placed interviewee proclaimed, the French approach is not the easy solution, it is the hard one.[19] The color-blind integration model thus stands in self-conscious contrast to the logic of affirmative action, representing the road not taken by the United States.

Cultural Barriers to Affirmative Action

Although several types of factors serve to reinforce the color-blind model in France, perhaps the most visible and potentially the most influential are those embedded in French political culture. Race-based affirmative action policies are not *legitimate* in France because they immediately and consistently evoke cultural repertoires that condemn them as inappropriate. Of course, that French political culture would be interpreted as insurmountably hostile toward preferences was not inevitable. Many liberals in the United States argue that affirmative action can be morally justified on the ground that it fosters substantive equality (equality of outcome), even if it is at the expense of procedural equality (equality before the law). France has a strong penchant for substantive equality, plainly visible in its progressive welfare state. This strand of French thinking could have been deployed to argue for policies that benefit disadvantaged ethnic minorities. Yet these themes have been overshadowed and overpowered by others with more specific prescriptions for interethnic relations. When contemplating actions vis-à-vis minorities, French leaders instinctively refer to two sets of historical reference points: the integrative Republican tradition of the Revolution, and the anti-Semitism that culminated in the Vichy regime.

As Brubaker (1992) has demonstrated, discussions of immigration and citizenship in France virtually always activate memories of the nation's Revolutionary and Republican history. These epochs are complex and multifaceted, and therefore no simple line can be drawn between them and France's present-day integration model (Brubaker 1992, 98–

102; Noiriel 1988, 339). Nevertheless, casting an eye back to the Revolution and the Third Republic, modern-day political and intellectual elites have focused on elements seen as "naturally" supporting the color-blind integration paradigm. Most centrally, they evoke the principle of equality before the law and the ideal of the indivisible nation.[20] Grounded in the Declaration of the Rights of Man and of the Citizen, Sieyès' pamphlet "What Is the Third Estate?," and the emancipation of slaves,[21] these values forcefully shape attitudes toward immigrants and minorities. The principles of formal, procedural equality and unmediated relations between individuals and the state serve forcefully to delegitimize affirmative action. As the HCI (1991, 19) spelled out the French logic, "the identitarian and egalitarian principles which stretch back to the Revolution and to the Declaration of the Rights of Man and of the Citizen impregnate our conception, founded thus on the equality of individuals before the law, whatever their origins, their race, their religion . . . to the exclusion of an institutional recognition of minorities."

If memories of the Revolutionary and Republican traditions help shore up the egalitarian aspect of the color-blind integration model, rejection of the collaborationist regime of World War II has also influenced French thinking on the evils of ethnic and racial distinctions. Memories of mass arrests and deportation of Jews during the Vichy era have deeply delegitimized any policy that singles out ethnic groups for categorization. This link was evident in 1978 during passage of the law against collection of ethnic or racial data.[22] Even today, a cold sweat runs down many French backs when talk turns to categorizing minorities. Although leading demographer Michèle Tribalat recently obtained permission to conduct large-scale research based on ethnic variables, her project was placed in jeopardy for precisely this reason (Tribalat 1995, 14–17).[23] Speaking about the process of classifying immigrant minorities, one well-placed and powerful observer reflected:

> What would we have to have? Legislation which says that one is recognized as being an immigrant, in order to have special rights, if one has parents of foreign origin or has at least two grand-parents of foreign origin. That would be an acceptable definition. Do you know what that is? That is the ordinance of 18 November 1940 which defines the Jew according to the Vichy regime, which says that one is a Jew if one has one Jewish parent or two Jewish grandparents. It is impossible to imagine a French law which uses this formulation. It would have a frightening effect. It is absolute evil.[24]

These factors help create an especially strong stigma against unequal treatment on the basis of race or ethnicity. French national elites are typically unwilling to turn a blind eye to programs that explicitly violate the color-blind principle.[25]

Beyond historical memories that delegitimize affirmative action lies one final cultural factor that undergirds France's integration policies: the American anti-model. French intellectuals and policy elites typically use the United States (and sometimes Germany, Britain, and the Netherlands) as a "reverse exemplar" (Bennett 1991) to legitimate the color-blind model (see Fassin 1999; Haut Conseil à l'Intégration 1991; Schnapper 1992; Todd 1994). Drawing on American writers' own discourse, they associate the U.S. model with ethnic politics, ghettos, tribalism, balkanization, segregation, and apartheid (Granjon 1994; Massey and Denton 1993). The U.S. and French models are often cast as binary opposites serving to reinforce pride in and attachment to the assimilationist flavor of France's melting pot. On other occasions the American anti-model is used not as a foil for France's approach but rather to draw attention to aspects of domestic society that come dangerously close to an American "negative utopia," or to threaten a similarly ominous future should France let down its guard (Wacquant 1993). Moreover, even when analysis of the United States is subtle, it is rarely positive (Granjon 1994). General agreement reigns on both the Left and the Right that the French color-blind model of integration has distinct advantages over rivals that recognize minorities. The HCI (1991, 19) argues that the French conception of integration must obey a "logic of equality," not a "logic of minorities." The combination of such anti-modeling with the incantatory references to deeply embedded French national values creates powerful rhetorical disincentives to adopting affirmative action policies.

The Politics of Antiracism

Although cultural barriers to color-conscious policies are high, politicians and policy makers in France—as elsewhere—tend to respond to the demands of their constituents. If French civil society were to lobby for affirmative action, it may muster enough pressure to break through the philosophical opposition to such policies. There has, in fact, been a relatively strong and sustained antiracism movement in France, which at times has captured national headlines and has been courted vigorously by leading politicians. Yet although there has been grass-roots mobilization emphasizing ethnic criteria and even pressure for ethnic or gender equality of representation, concrete policy changes have been negligible. Potential vanguard groups such as liberal human rights organizations, minorities themselves, and women's groups have not been able to present a united and consistent political front and have not been able to overcome the cultural and political barriers against affirmative action.

The origins of the antiracism groups seem to militate against sympathy to ethnicity-conscious policies. Organizations such as the Human Rights League, the LICRA, and the MRAP[26] were founded prior to large-scale Third World immigration, principally to address problems of anti-Semitism in France and abroad. By the end of the 1970s, they had demonstrated strong support for French laws and policies that vigorously punished acts of racism but that favored integration and in no way countenanced ethnic categorization. In contrast to the American approach during the civil rights era (Skrentny 1996, 15), there was no implicit belief that the French antiracism law would bring about "proportional racial equality." Moreover, the very word *race* was nearly left out of the law because of some Parliamentarians' reluctance to include a term that might give succor to those who believe in the existence of races.[27]

If the human rights groups leading the antiracism movement until the 1970s tended to support the color-blind integrationist line, more recent pro-immigrant liberals and minorities themselves have exhibited a greater variety of positions on such policies. Immigrant and immigrant-rights groups began mobilizing in France following the mass protests and general strike of May 1968 (Blatt 1996). Momentum picked up during the 1970s, with these groups focused primarily on obtaining better living and working conditions and a more secure administrative status for immigrants living on French territory. By the early 1980s, however, some groups were building a more formidable challenge to the ethnically neutral French model. A series of political and policy changes had catapulted immigration and antiracism to the forefront of domestic politics during these years. The arrival of the Socialists in power in 1981 resulted in a series of pro-immigrant policies such as granting of ten-year residency permits and a legal revision that enabled foreigners to form officially recognized associations. On the opposite side of the political ledger, the far-right National Front (FN) made its first electoral breakthrough in 1983, consolidating its support in the following years. The shifting tectonic plates of French politics left immigrants and minorities searching for new issues. If, as in the United States, pro-immigrant and human rights groups[28] pursued divergent goals in earlier years (see chapter 2, this volume), by the early 1980s their interests and identities began to converge around the banner of antiracism.

The early 1980s saw the modest spread of "pluriculturalism" throughout France, exemplified by the government's support of re-gional cultures and by increasingly "intercultural" rhetoric in schools (Henry-Lorcerie 1983; Safran 1989). Within this context, antiracist groups began to call for the same "right to difference" that was being advocated for regions. Most significantly, second-generation immi-grants of North African heritage—known in French as *beurs*—began to organize around their ethnic identity and to seek common goals (see Blatt 1996; Bouamama 1994). A series of attention-grabbing marches in 1983, 1984, and 1985 boosted antiracism to a high-profile issue and served to highlight the role and activism of the beurs.[29] This new cluster of French citizens, self-defined by ethnicity and placing demands on government, prompted several observers to wonder if France was veer-ing down an American path toward ethnic identification and lobbying (Leveau and Wihtol de Wenden 1988; Pinto 1988).

Although there were some attempts to employ group mobilization for larger shares of both political and economic goods, there were only a few explicit calls for a direct analog to American affirmative action.[30] The main national organization of beurs sought instead to increase their ethnic group vote and thus to pressure political parties into putting more beurs forward for elected office. Local beur organizations, by con-trast, concentrated on tapping into social funding for job training, neighborhood-based economic renewal, and other welfare state provis-ions (Poinsot 1993). Working within the context of these pressures, the Socialist government of the 1981–86 period increased the FAS budget and reorganized its decision-making machinery to include representa-tives of different ethnic immigrant communities (Hargreaves 1995, 204–5). Yet the divergent goals of the beur movement proved irrecon-cilable, and the pressure for anything resembling affirmative action was not sustained (Blatt 1996, chap. six; Poinsot 1993).

Concurrent with internal divisions among beurs, another develop-ment limited the political impact of ethnic politics. Emerging in 1984, a rival antiracist organization—SOS Racisme—became an instant me-dia and political success in the joust for public attention. Selling a more traditional color-blind product and enlisting the support of both minor-ities and the majority, they emphasized opposition to acts of racism per-petrated against individuals, decried racist groups, and abhorred public expressions of racism, such as those manufactured in increasing quantity by the far-right FN. In keeping with the era, they also preached protection for the "right to be different" and stressed the benefits of ethnic diversity. The FN leadership, however, had proven adept at bending the discourse of difference to its own purposes, agreeing that difference was a value to be upheld, as long as "non-French" groups practiced their differences outside of French borders. From a discourse of inclusion, FN leader Jean-Marie Le Pen crafted a politics of exclusion, appealing to white French voters who felt marginalized in an economically troubled France.

Reacting to this turn of events, leading intellectuals such as Pierre-André Taguieff argued that the discourse of difference was damaging to the antiracist cause. Taguieff (1987, 328–29) asserted that "the recognition of the Other can only be hierarchical" and that any "right to difference" could lead to a "difference of rights," an intolerable situation given deeply cherished Revolutionary and Republican principles. Even leaders of SOS-Racisme began to publicly condemn the "community logic" of multiculturalism, further marking the declining fortunes of the "right to be different" (Désir 1991). Although the antiracism movement remains in France today, its character has changed. Not only has it fragmented, but the power of the early 1980s call for tolerance of difference and diversity has been greatly eroded. The strength of the FN and the rhetoric of intellectuals have brought the movement in line with the prevailing doctrines of the color-blind integration model. They have shifted the focus of antiracist activities away from substantive racial equality and recognition of difference and back to earlier themes of immigrants' rights and opposition to public racist statements.

If human rights and immigrant groups have not been successful in pressing for affirmative action, France's women's rights movements have until recently also been a less effective spearhead in lobbying for proportional representation and equal shares of societal goods than their counterparts in other developed countries (Gaspard 1997; Jenson and Sineau 1995). The notable exception to this rule has been the recent push for "parity" in Parliament that elicited a measure of popular support and sympathetic reactions from political leaders anxious to appeal to a large segment of the electorate.[31] Aside from the modest initiatives taken in the early 1980s (Jenson 1988, 160–64), however, French women's groups have not succeeded in instituting any official form of affirmative action in the spheres of education and employment. Moreover, leading activists for the movement deny that ethnic minorities are in any way analogous to women,[32] suggesting that whatever benefits accrue to women are unlikely to be automatically extended to minorities. In sum, neither the minorities' nor the women's push for elements of identity-based proportional equality have generated enough political support to overcome substantial ideological and political opposition to race-based affirmative action.

Problems of Discrimination

Accounting for approximately 5 percent of the total French population, minorities never had raw political numbers on their side. Yet, as important as such demographic pressure may be for policy making, straightforward lobbying was not the path to affirmative action even in the United States (Skrentny 1996). Rather, affirmative action—like any policy—can come about and be sustained as a solution to administrative, political, or societal problems.[33] As Skrentny (introduction, this volume) observes, proponents value affirmative action for a variety of reasons, whether moral, political, or economic. Nevertheless, strong support for affirmative action can also be based on purely practical grounds.

The pragmatic logic that typically undergirds arguments for affirmative action sees it as a solution to one or more high-profile societal problems. According to a common line of analysis, racial discrimination is a significant cause of disproportional allocation of jobs, housing, education, and other goods. Because minorities are victims of discrimination, they obtain such goods in lower quantities than one would expect in a discrimination-free world. Moreover, this line of reasoning is often extended by arguing that discrimination and disproportional allocation of goods contribute to social tensions and social disorder when unhappy victims turn violent. Working backwards in a reverse (and possibly—but not necessarily—spurious) logic, some observers view the existence of social disorder such as crime and rioting or the fact of nonproportional distribution of jobs, education, and housing, as prima facie evidence of discrimination. If riots erupt in the inner cities or minorities are unemployed in higher numbers than the majority, racism is argued to be at the root of the problems. In this context, affirmative action is seen to be an efficient means for overcoming the perverse effects of discrimination, for effecting a more proportional distribution of goods, and for maintaining social peace.

In order to examine why this logic does not function in France as it does in other contexts, it is necessary to examine how France deals with the interrelated concerns of discrimination, disproportional allocation of societal goods by race, and social disorder. Belief in the existence of serious and pervasive discrimination has long sustained affirmative action policies in the United States. Yet there has been a tendency among many observers to argue that discrimination is simply not a pressing social issue in France. Throughout the 1960s, the government avoided acting on antidiscrimination proposals by arguing that racism was not a problem in France and that what little racism existed was caught by the fragmentary laws in place at the time (Cohen 1980, 114). Moreover, the experiences of non-French commentators—such as James Baldwin—tended to lend credence to the view that there was simply no comparison between racism in the United States and in France (see Baldwin 1998). Even the domestic French proponents of antiracism legislation argued that the French were not as racist as other countries' nationals (Paraf 1964, 164-74). If discrimination is not a problem, then why bother with affirmative action as a solution?

If pressed, however, most agree that France is not an ethnic or racial utopia. In eight polls conducted between 1990 and 1996, never fewer than 89 percent of respondents stated that racism was either very widespread or relatively widespread in France (see table 1). Moreover, a 1996 survey showed that 32 percent of French respondents believed that racism was more widespread in France than in other European countries, as opposed to only 16 percent who felt it was less widespread (Commission Nationale Consultative des Droits de l'Homme 1997, 369).[34] Europe-wide data confirm this intuition, demonstrating that France ranks third of twelve (behind Greece and Belgium) in an "index of xenophobia" (Mayer 1996, 124). There have been periods in France with high-profile and persistent racial attacks, including a time during the early 1970s when a spate of aggressive acts against Algerian immigrants contributed to Algeria's decision to cut off migration flows to France (Benoît 1980, 363–64; Weil 1995a, 112–15). In addition, even in the current era, the consistent support of millions of French voters for the openly anti-immigrant National Front raises eyebrows and questions about the pervasiveness of racism in France.[35]

This evidence and acknowledgment of the many facets of domestic French racism, however, do not necessarily translate into an argument for affirmative action. Policy makers and intellectual elites largely concur that racism manifests itself differently in France than in the United States or in other countries. Whereas other nations frequently define their primary out-group based on skin color, they argue, the French tend to use other criteria. In keeping with the immigration paradigm, France exhibits more signs of xenophobia and cultural racism than of aversion based on color. The questions asked in Europe-wide surveys

TABLE 1
Opinions on the Level of Racism in France

	Feb. 1990	Oct. 1990	Nov. 1991	Nov. 1992	Nov. 1993	Nov. 1994	Nov. 1995	Nov. 1996
Very widespread	36%	38%	38%	36%	35%	34%	39%	41%
Relatively widespread	54	56	52	53	55	55	54	53
Relatively rare	7	5	7	9	7	8	6	4
Very rare	1	—	2	1	1	1	—	1
No answer	2	1	1	1	2	2	1	1

Source: Commission Nationale Consultative des Droits de l'Homme, 1997, 368.

may show France ranking high on aversion, but the questions are focused on attitudes toward people of "another nationality," not another race (see Mayer 1996). And survey data within France demonstrate substantially higher levels of antipathy directed toward "Arabs" and "Muslims" than toward "Blacks" and even show warm feelings for black French citizens (see tables 2 and 3).[36] The different bases for discrimination seem to reinforce the French perception that their problems are (and therefore their policies should be) different from those found in the United States and elsewhere.

Moreover, surprisingly few experts or observers make the connection between the types of racism that are known to exist in France and quotidian discrimination with regard to housing, employment, and educational and political opportunities. Much more than in the United States or in Britain, the prototypical racist act in France is understood to be either a racist statement by a far right (or a mainstream) politician, or else promulgation of a state policy that adversely affects immigrants.

TABLE 2
Opinions on the Number of Persons of Different Groups Residing in France

	Too many	Not too many	No answer
Arabs	61	31	8
Muslims	58	33	9
Blacks	38	51	11
Asians	30	60	10
Jews	20	67	13
Central Europeans (Poles, Romanians)	19	69	12
Mediterranian Europeans (Portuguese, Spaniards, Italians, Greeks)	17	73	10

Source: Commission Nationale Consultative des Droits de l'Homme, 1997, 375.

TABLE 3
Personal Attitudes Toward Members of Different Groups

	Subtotal, sympathy	Subtotal, antipathy	No answer
Mediterranean Europeans (Portuguese, Spaniards, Italians, Greeks)	89	5	6
French West Indians (Guadeloupe, Martinique)	85	8	7
Central Europeans (Poles, Romanians)	76	12	12
Black Africans	75	17	8
Asians	74	15	11
Jews	68	17	15
Young French of Maghrebi origin (Beurs)	54	35	11
Gypsies, travelers	50	39	11
Maghrebis	50	40	10

Source: Commission Nationale Consultative des Droits de l'Homme, 1997, 373.

The dominant response tends to be public marches and protests. By contrast, job discrimination garners much less attention than it would in the United States.

French institutions may themselves help perpetuate this situation by muting important problem indicators.[37] Punishing discrimination through the criminal law with its elevated standards of proof dissuades victims from filing complaints and limits the number of recorded convictions for such crimes to an average of fewer than nine per year between 1990 and 1994 (Commission Nationale Consultative des Droits de l'Homme 1997, 362–63; Costa-Lascoux 1994; Vourc'h, de Rudder, and Tripier 1996).[38] The low level of convictions, in turn, may divert attention from the pervasiveness of the problem. Although there is periodic attention focused on equal access to nightclubs, housing, or employment, there has been little sustained public interest in the specific types of discrimination problems to which affirmative action offers a tangible solution.[39]

If proof of discrimination is difficult to come by, disproportional distribution of goods by race or ethnicity is virtually impossible to observe. Because France collects no systematic data on race or ethnicity, it is very difficult to measure allocations of housing stock, placement in higher education, unemployment rates, or quality of job by race or ethnicity.[40] Moreover, there is little or no effort to do so. Whether because most minorities—as immigrants—are assumed to be of a lower socioeconomic status, or because minority citizens are presumed to be equal, France is not conscious of ethnic group differentials in the manner of the United States. Nobody in France, for example, measures the number of ethnic minorities in Parliament. French observers simply do not take for granted that race- or ethnic group–based representation and differentials are a meaningful tool for judging whether French society functions equitably. That minorities are almost certainly significantly underrepresented in the French establishment and at the more pedestrian levels of quality housing and jobs is simply not perceived as problematic, to the extent that it is perceived at all given the lack of data.

Finally, although there have been incidents of urban disturbances both in the early 1980s and in the early 1990s, such "riots" were interpreted through the color-blind integration filter. Rather than being cast as "race" disturbances pitting minorities against natives or the police, the troubles in the outskirts of Lyon in 1981 and 1990 in immigrant-dominated housing projects were seen as urban problems, not ethnic problems.[41] In the early 1980s, the state responded by creating a National Commission on the Social Development of Neighborhoods, which focused its attention on problems of housing (Schain 1993, 64). In 1990, the government created a new Ministry of Urban Affairs and provided additional funding to areas with high levels of social problems such as unemployment, poor-quality housing and neighborhood infrastructure, and tensions between police and local residents (Hargreaves 1995, 202). Although the effect of such policies disproportionately shifted resources to minority-populated communities, the policy targets were general social problems, and anybody—including nonminorities—residing in such areas benefited from state action. The state's responses thus demonstrated that it made the connection between disproportional allocation of societal goods and social disorder. Missing from the nexus outlined above, however, was a connection between these factors and racial discrimination. Because factors of race and discrimination are not seen to be relevant to major social problems, affirmative action is not perceived to be a valid policy solution.

Conclusion

Affirmative action has found no purchase in France. It has been delegitimized on ideological grounds, it was undercut on political grounds, and it is not viewed as justifiable based on problems of discrimination or social disorder. Though neither difference-blind nor devoid of racism, France has developed and maintained color-blind policies of integration of minorities-cum-immigrants that set it apart from its European neighbors and from the United States. For most political participants and observers in France, the color-blind approach has many desirable features. Perhaps most important, it encourages social solidarity by muting competition between groups defined by race or ethnicity. In addition, it addresses directly what many see to be the "true" problems of socioeconomic disadvantage.[42] The French approach may therefore provide a positive exemplar for advocates of color-blind policies in the United States.

Yet, it is not clear that the French model can easily be applied in America in the twenty-first century. America holds equality as one of its supreme values, as does France, but much of United States history has been marked by slavery and racial oppression. This history has provided a public justification for compensatory policies such as affirmative action that does not exist in France. In the United States, race-conscious policies are designed to benefit descendants of victims of slavery and of the institutionalized oppression of Jim Crow. In France, by contrast, the color-blind model is directed at mostly recent immigrants who never suffered openly racist government policy. American critics of affirmative action draw on normative rhetoric stressing equality of opportunity, meritocracy, and formal, legal equality to delegitimize preferential policies (see Patterson 1997, chaps. 1 and 3; Skrentny 1996, 1–63), but the extent and duration of the oppression of blacks makes this rhetoric less compelling in the United States. Of course, American affirmative action also applies to recent immigrants, but this participation remains obscure in the public debates despite its rapidly growing significance.

Second, the lack of affirmative action in France depends in part on the weakness of minority groups and on the reticence of a political Left that worries about playing into the hands of the far Right. The effects of interest group politics in America on the promotion of color-blind policy are very different. In the United States, advocates for color-blind policy are trying to end a policy already in existence, rather than prevent one from coming about. Ending policy is usually much harder than preventing policy. American conservatives play to the self-interests of groups whose members are demonstrably or purportedly injured by affirmative action (see Williams 1998). However, because many affirmative action regulations are closely tied to civil rights laws, American advocates of color-blind policy are regularly attacked as being against civil rights and worse, they are said to be racist. With public opinion at the turn of the century showing overwhelming support for civil rights in principle, it is exceedingly difficult for a politician to become successful in national politics if linked to racism (Skrentny forthcoming).

A third problem for an American advocate of color-blind policy not faced by his or her French counterpart relates to the perceived effectiveness of affirmative action and the legacy of years of racial data collecting in the United States. Unlike in France, racial statistics showing inequality are ubiquitous in the United States, buttressing defense of affirmative action as an effective and efficient remedy. With statistics regularly showing, for example, a black unemployment rate that is double that of Euro-American whites, color-blind policy can appear irresponsible.

Finally, unlike the French, many Americans value something approximating proportional racial equality, and many believe that the distribution of socioeconomic resources and life chances is linked to racial discrimination and perhaps even to social stability (see, for example, Bergmann 1996, 155–56, 164–65; Fiscus 1992; Hacker 1995; Sullivan 1986, 96–98). The 1964 Civil Rights Act itself aimed to overcome the perverse effects of racial discrimination on proportional equality (race differences in unemployment rates were then and now regularly discussed), and later policy developments were in part due to fears of 1960s-style riots (Button 1978; Skrentny 1996, 67–110). Affirmative action appears to many to be an efficient means for bringing about equality and integration, or at a minimum for offsetting the disadvantages associated with being a minority (see chapter 8 in this volume; Patterson 1997, 147; Skrentny 1996, 111–44). This observation raises the hypothesis that support for ending affirmative action is likely to be highest when such concerns are directly addressed. Opponents of affirmative action may need to search for alternative policies that produce the desired societal goals of compensating for existing or past discrimination, producing a measure of proportional racial equality, and preserving social order. Until then, proponents of a color-blind model leave open strong and persuasive arguments for continuing affirmative action.

Notes

1. In this chapter I follow Skrentny (1996, 7–8) who defines *affirmative action* as "race-conscious" rather than "color-blind." Specifically, affirmative action policies view race as "real," count anonymous minorities, reevaluate previously accepted standards of merit, and deemphasize discriminatory intent, while emphasizing representation, utilization, or employment of minorities.

2. See chapter 10 in this volume for the distinction between hard and soft affirmative action as applied to Britain.

3. France is divided into one hundred administrative units: ninety-six (Corsica included) constitute "metropolitan" France; four—Guadeloupe, Martinique, Réunion, and Guiana—are known as overseas departments (DOM).

4. On policy windows of opportunity, see Kingdon 1995.

5. A fourth possible rationale for affirmative action is that it is economically beneficial to industry (see chapter 4 in this volume). Because this does not enter into the French debate, I will not examine it in this chapter.

6. Foreigners therefore constituted 6.5 percent of the French population in 1975; Africans and Asians accounted for 2.5 percent of the 52.6 million total.

7. Maghrebis (Algerians, Moroccans, and Tunisians) make up by far the largest proportion of this group (619,923, 584,708, and 207,496, respectively) with Turks and other Africans (201,480 and 178,133, respectively) also contributing relatively large numbers. Of course, as in most European countries, immigrants tend to be concentrated in urban, industrial areas, raising their percentages in some regions well above the average (see Hargreaves 1995, 68; Weil 1995a, annex VI). The foreign population of France in 1990 was just over 3.6 million, or roughly 6.4 percent of the total French population (Weil 1995a, annex VI).

8. As of the 1990 census, the population of Antillian origin in metropolitan France was estimated at 330,168, or 0.6 percent of the total French population (Domenach and Picouet 1992, 185). These statistics were derived primarily from data on place of birth and place of current residence of French nationals.

9. The French model is commonly referred to as the "*creuset français*," or the "French melting pot." It should be noted, however, that French immigration policy has not always been purely color-blind. Elements of ethnic selection have at times entered into immigration calculations, most prominently during the 1930s and 1940s (see Weil 1995a, 41–91; Weil 1995b) and again in the late 1960s when quotas were imposed restricting Algerian migrants to France (see Blatt 1996, 75–78; Silverman 1992, 48–49).

10. Favell (1998, 46–62) notes, however, that prior to explicit reflection on integration, insertion was viewed less as a coherent model and more as a pragmatic approach to dealing with concrete immigrant problems at the local level.

11. Henceforth HCI.

12. Of course issues of compensation and proportionality are much disputed in the United States, as is the function of affirmative action more generally. The crucial point is that French law has limited itself to an extremely narrow interpretation of racism that involves an identifiable perpetrator rather than taking group attributes into account (see Fiscus 1992; Freeman 1978; Sullivan 1986).

13. Schain (1993, 62) notes that there have also been quotas limiting minorities in areas such as schools, summer camps, and winter ski schools.

14. Such goals have also been pursued in the United States; the Starrett City housing development in Brooklyn offers one example (Glazer 1987, xxiv).

15. Weil (1995a, 398–405) argues, however, that since poor housing stock was typi-

cally allocated first to immigrants, there were indeed "micro-ghettos" at the building level.

16. There are limits to such autonomy and recognition, however; these were clearly demarcated by the Constitutional Council (the French equivalent to the U.S. Supreme Court), which judged that the term "Corsican people" was contrary to Republican principles outlined in the Constitution (Granjon 1994, 24).

17. This, in spite of the insistence of the 1905 law regarding separation of church and state that the "Republic does not recognize or provide financial subsidies or salaries to any creed." For the text of the law and a brief introduction into church-state relations in France, see Haut Conseil à l'Intégration 1992. As this document shows, the state also recognizes congregations and provides financial support for religions under some circumstances, notably in schools.

18. In 1990, the Minister of the Interior set up the Council of Reflection on Islam in France in order to connect itself to the domestic Muslim community (Roy 1994). This organization was not wholly successful, however, and efforts to find Muslim interlocutors have subsequently continued through other channels (Favell 1998, 182–83; Hargreaves 1995, 206–8).

19. Confidential interview, Paris, 17 March 1997.

20. The course of French history is, however, littered with weighty exceptions to these principles. Women in the Third Republic were not allowed to vote, to give just one example.

21. France permitted slaves only in its overseas colonies, freeing them first during the Revolution and then once and for all during the Second Republic (Dubois 1998). Slavery has never been officially permitted in metropolitan France (Peabody 1996).

22. Interview with Charles Palant, former general secretary of the Movement against Racism and for Amity between Peoples (MRAP), 10 March 1997. Note that many minorities and pro-minority groups in both the United States and Britain were also opposed to collecting ethnic statistics at one time. The practice is now generally accepted as beneficial in both countries.

23. She measured both "ethnic belonging" (based on language use) and "ethnic origins" (based on parent origin). Because of the "French taboo against social scientific use of origins," she states that the completion of her project was uncertain for a long time (Tribalat 1995, 14–17). Recently, the taboo manifested itself in a book dedicated to denouncing collection of ethnic data as playing into the hands of the far Right (Le Bras 1998).

24. Confidential interview, Paris, 30 June 1997. Like France, Germany keeps no statistics on visible minorities, favoring instead data based on foreigners' country of origin (Forbes and Mead 1992).

25. As established in the first section, however, French state officials are less reluctant to bargain with representatives of established groups than they are formally to categorize group members.

26. The International League Against Racism and Anti-Semitism, and the Movement against Racism and for Amity between Peoples.

27. Interview with Alain Terrenoire, rapporteur for the law, 5 April 1997. See also

the French law 72-546 and National Assembly reports numbered 2357 and 2394 from the fourth legislature for the original bill and the Government amendments.

28. The closest (but still very distant) analog to liberal U.S. civil rights groups.

29. Although as Blatt (1996, 322–24) notes, by 1985, the *beur* march was a shadow of its former self and the movement had lost much momentum.

30. In a little-known 1985 article, George Pau-Langevin (1985, 54–55), then a vice president of MRAP (but not necessarily speaking for the organization), suggested that ethnic statistics could be used to aid disadvantaged minorities in the realm of housing and employment and even suggested that some public housing should institute priorities for "ethnic minorities, in the manner of programs called 'Affirmative Action' in the United States." The rarity of such a position in France cannot, however, be overstated.

31. On parity, see Gaspard et al. 1992; Jenson and Sineau 1995; *L'Express*, 6–12 June 1996; *Le Monde*, 8–13 March 1997; and Kramer 2000. Note that although the percentage of women in the National Assembly almost doubled following the 1997 elections, the total remained at only ten percent, leaving France with the second-lowest percentage of women Parliamentarians in Europe (Gaspard 1997, 5–7).

32. Communications with Françoise Gaspard, September 1997; February 1998.

33. In the case of the United States, affirmative action was useful in the search for bureaucratic legitimacy, as an effort to confound an opposition party, and as part of a design to quell riots and to maintain social order (Skrentny 1996).

34. Forty-two percent thought it was neither more nor less widespread and ten percent did not respond (Commission Nationale Consultative des Droits de l'Homme 1997, 369).

35. But see Mayer and Perrineau 1996 and Kitschelt 1995 for arguments about the full range of factors contributing to the rise of the National Front.

36. Substantial aversion to second-generation immigrants from North Africa, however, seems highly problematic for the color-blind model. Since the beurs are either citizens or citizens-in-waiting, and since they have been educated in France, widespread aversion to them is difficult to attribute to cultural factors. The only explanation compatible with French visions of the nation as a color-blind society is the possible (and probably fallacious) assumption by survey respondents that the beurs are practicing Muslims and therefore uphold what are seen to be "non-French" values.

37. On problem indicators, see Kingdon 1995, 90–94.

38. Moreover, as Costa-Lascoux (1994) reports, owing to the process of record keeping, these figures underestimate the total number of convictions, further muting this potential problem indicator.

39. There is some evidence that these issues are working their way up the public and administrative agenda in France (Haut Conseil à l'Intégration 1998).

40. Of course, it is possible to do so by immigrant status and nationality. In addition, Tribalat's (1995; 1996) recent work does compare certain measures of ethnicity to a broad range of socioeconomic variables.

41. In the United States, by contrast, problems of poverty and rioting were often viewed as co-extensive with issues of race. Moreover, although many U.S. policies were

color-blind on the surface, it was apparent that they were aimed at minorities, often in the hopes of quelling social disorder (Button 1978; Skrentny 1996, 98–99).

42. For an argument for class-based policies in the United States, see Kahlenberg 1996. The French model also focuses on issues relating to the cultural adaptation required of immigrants who do not speak fluent French or who are not familiar with French administrative institutions.

Acknowledgments

I am grateful to Keith Bybee, Laurent Dubois, Adrian Favell, Jane Jenson, Jennifer Pitts, Patrick Weil, and especially to John Skrentny for helpful comments on earlier versions of this chapter. For financial support I would like to thank the Mellon Foundation, the Social Sciences and Humanities Research Council of Canada, the Krupp Foundation, and the Center for European Studies at Harvard University.

References

Baldwin, James. 1998. *Collected essays.* New York: Library of America.

Bennett, Colin J. 1991. How states utilize foreign evidence. *Journal of Public Policy* 11:31–54.

Benoît, Jean. 1980. *Dossier E . . . comme esclaves.* Paris: Editions Alain Moreau.

Bergmann, Barbara R. 1996. *In defense of affirmative action.* New York: Basic Books.

Blatt, David Stuart. 1996. Immigration politics and immigrant collective action in France, 1968–1993. Ph.D. diss., Government Department, Cornell University.

Bouamama, Saïd. 1994. *Dix ans de marche des Beurs: Chronique d'un mouvement avorté.* Paris: Desclée de Brouwer.

Brubaker, Rogers. 1992. *Citizenship and nationhood in France and Germany.* Cambridge: Harvard University Press.

Button, James W. 1978. *Black violence: Political impact of the 1960s riots.* Princeton: Princeton University Press.

Cohen, William B. 1980. Legacy of empire: The Algerian connection. *Journal of Contemporary History* 15:97–123.

Commission de la Nationalité. 1988. Etre français aujourd'hui et demain. Paris: La Documentation Française.

Commission Nationale Consultative des Droits de l'Homme. 1997. 1996. La lutte contre le racisme et la xénophobie: Exclusion et droits de l'homme. Paris: La Documentation Française.

Costa-Lascoux, Jacqueline. 1994. French legislation against racism and discrimination. *New Community* 20:371–79.

Dekeuwer-Defossez, Françoise. 1985. *Dictionnaire juridique: Droits des femmes.* Paris: Dalloz.

Désir, Harlem. 1991. Pour l'intégration: Conditions et instruments. In *Face au racisme: Les Moyens d'agir,* edited by P.-A. Taguieff. Paris: Éditions La Découverte.

Domenach, Hervé, and Michel Picouet. 1992. *La Dimension migratoire des Antilles.* Paris: Economica.

Dubois, Laurent. 1998. *Les Esclaves de la république: L'histoire oubliée de la première emancipation 1789–1794.* Translated by Jean-François Chaix. Paris: Calmann-Lévy.

Fassin, Eric. 1999. "Good to think": The American preference in French discourses of immigration and ethnicity. In *Multicultural questions,* edited by C. Joppke and S. Lukes. Oxford: Oxford University Press.

Favell, Adrian. 1998. *Philosophies of integration: Immigration and the idea of citizenship in France and Britain.* London: MacMillan.

Fiscus, Ronald J. 1992. *The constitutional logic of affirmative action.* Durham: Duke University Press.

Fonds d'Action Sociale. 1996. *Etre acteur.* Nancy: Fonds d'Action Sociale.

Forbes, Ian, and Geoffrey Mead. 1992. *Measure for measure: A comparative analysis of measures to combat racial discrimination in the member countries of the European Community.* Sheffield: Employment Department.

Freeman, Alan David. 1978. Legitimizing racial discrimination through antidiscrimination law: A critical review of Supreme Court doctrine. *Minnesota Law Review* 62:1049–1119.

Gaspard, Françoise. 1997. Les Françaises en politique au lendemain des elections législatives de 1997. *French Politics and Society* 15:1–12.

Gaspard, Françoise, Claude Servan-Schreiber, and Anne Le Gall. 1992. *Au Pouvoir citoyennes! Liberté, égalité, parité.* Paris: Seuil.

Glazer, Nathan. 1987. *Affirmative discrimination: Ethnic inequality and public policy.* 2d ed. Cambridge: Harvard University Press.

Granjon, Marie-Christine. 1994. Le Regard en biais. Attitudes françaises et multiculturalisme américain (1990–1993). *Vingtième Siècle* 43:18–29.

Hacker, Andrew. 1995. *Two nations: Black and white, separate, hostile, unequal.* 2d ed. New York: Ballantine Books.

Hargreaves, Alec G. 1995. *Immigration, "race," and ethnicity in contemporary France.* London: Routledge.

Haut Conseil à l'Intégration. 1991. *Pour un modèle français d'intégration.* Paris: La Documentation Française.

———. 1992. *Conditions juridiques et culturelles de l'intégration.* Paris: La Documentation Française.

———. 1998. Rapport du Haut Conseil à l'Intégration Relatif aux Discriminations. Paris: Haut Conseil à l'Intégration.

Henry-Lorcerie, Françoise. 1983. Enfants d'immigrés et école française: A propos du mot d'ordre de pédagogie interculturelle. In *Maghrébins en France: Emigrés ou immigrés?,* edited by L. Talha. Paris: Editions du Centre National de la Recherche Scientifique.

Horowitz, Donald L., and Gérard Noiriel, eds. 1992. *Immigrants in two democracies: French and American experience.* New York: New York University Press.

Jenson, Jane. 1988. The limits of "and the" discourse: French women as marginal workers. In *Feminization of the labour force: Paradoxes and promises,* edited by J. Jenson, E. Hagen, and C. Reddy. Cambridge: Polity Press.

Jenson, Jane, and Mariette Sineau. 1995. *Mitterrand et les françaises: Un Rendez-vous manqué.* Paris: Presses de la Fondation Nationale des Sciences Politiques.

Kahlenberg, Richard D. 1996. *The remedy: Class, race, and affirmative action.* New York: Basic Books.

Kingdon, John W. 1995. *Agendas, alternatives, and public policies.* 2d ed. New York: HarperCollins.

Kitschelt, Herbert. 1995. *The radical right in western Europe: A comparative analysis.* Ann Arbor: University of Michigan Press.

Kramer, Jane. 2000. Liberty, equality, sorority. *The New Yorker,* 29 May, 112–23.

Lapeyronnie, Didier. 1993. *L'Individu et les minorités: La France et la Grande-Bretagne face à leurs immigrés.* Paris: Presses Universitaires de France.

Le Bras, Hervé. 1998. *Le Démon des origines: Démographie et extrême droite.* Paris: Editions de l'Aube.

Leveau, Rémy, and Catherine Wihtol de Wenden. 1988. La Deuxième génération. *Pouvoirs* 47:61–73.

Massey, Douglas S., and Nancy A. Denton. 1993. *American apartheid: Segregation and the making of the underclass.* Cambridge: Harvard University Press.

Mayer, Nonna. 1996. Is France racist? *Contemporary European History* 5:119–27.

Mayer, Nonna, and Pascal Perrineau, eds. 1996. *Le Front national à découvert.* 2d ed. Paris: Presses de la Fondation Nationale des Sciences Politiques.

Nieli, Russell, ed. 1991. *Racial preference and racial justice: The new affirmative action controversy.* Washington, D.C.: Ethics and Public Policy Center.

Noiriel, Gérard. 1988. *Le Creuset français: Histoire de l'immigration XIXe–XXe siècle.* Paris: Seuil.

———. 1994. "Civil rights" policy in the United States and the policy of "integration" in Europe: Divergent approaches to a similar issue. *Journal of Policy History* 6:120–39.

Omi, Michael, and Howard Winant. 1994. *Racial formation in the United States: From the 1960s to the 1990s.* 2d ed. New York: Routledge.

Paraf, Pierre. 1964. *Le Racism dans le monde.* Paris: Payot.

Patterson, Orlando. 1997. *The ordeal of integration: Progress and resentment in America's "racial" crisis.* Washington, D.C.: Civitas/Counterpoint.

Pau-Langevin, George. 1985. La Loi française contre le racisme. *Actes* 51:51–55.

Peabody, Sue. 1996. *"There are no slaves in France": The political culture of race and slavery in the ancien régime.* Oxford: Oxford University Press.

Pinto, Diana. 1988. Immigration: L'Ambiguïté de la référence américaine. *Pouvoirs* 47:93–101.

Poinsot, Marie. 1993. Competition for political legitimacy at local and national levels among young North Africans in France. *New Community* 20:79–92.

Rath, Jan, and Shamit Saggar. 1992. Ethnicity as a political tool in Britain and the Netherlands. In *Ethnic and racial minorities in advanced industrial democracies,* edited by A. M. Messina, L. R. Fraga, L. A. Rhodebeck, and F. D. Wright. New York: Greenwood Press.

Roy, Olivier. 1994. Islam in France: Religion, ethnic community, or social ghetto? In *Muslims in Europe,* edited by B. Lewis and D. Schnapper. London: Pinter Publishers.

Safran, William. 1989. The French state and ethnic minority cultures: Policy dimensions and problems. In *Ethnoterritorial politics: Policy and the Western world*, edited by J. R. Rudolph and R. J. Thompson. Boulder: Lynne Rienner.

Schain, Martin. 1993. Policy-making and defining ethnic minorities: The case of immigration in France. *New Community* 20:59–77.

Schnapper, Dominique. 1992. *L'Europe des immigrés*. Paris: François Bourin.

Silverman, Maxim. 1992. *Deconstructing the nation: Immigration, racism, and citizenship in modern France*. London: Routledge.

Skrentny, John David. 1996. *The ironies of affirmative action: Politics, culture, and justice in America*. Chicago: University of Chicago Press.

———. Forthcoming. Republican efforts to end affirmative action: Walking a fine line. In *Durability and change: Politics and policymaking in the 1990s*, edited by Marc Landy, Martin Levin, and Martin Shapiro. Washington, D.C.: Georgetown University Press.

Soysal, Yasemin Nuhoglu. 1994. *Limits of citizenship: Migrants and postnational membership in Europe*. Chicago: University of Chicago Press.

Sullivan, Kathleen M. 1986. Sins of discrimination: Last term's affirmative action cases. *Harvard Law Review* 100:78–98.

Taguieff, Pierre-André. 1987. *La Force du préjugé: Essai sur le racisme et ses doubles*. Paris: Éditions La Découverte.

Thernstrom, Stephan, and Abigail Thernstrom. 1997. *America in black and white: One nation, indivisible*. New York: Simon and Schuster.

Todd, Emmanuel. 1994. *Le Destin des immigrés: Assimilation et ségrégation dans les démocraties occidentales*. Paris: Seuil.

Tribalat, Michèle. 1995. *Faire France: Une grande enquête sur les immigrés et leurs enfants*. Paris: La Découverte.

———. 1996. *De l'Immigration à l'assimilation: Enquête sur les populations d'origine étrangère en France*. Paris: La Découverte.

Vourc'h, François, Véronique de Rudder, and Maryse Tripier. 1996. Racisme et discrimination dans le travail: Une réalité occultée. *L'Homme et la Société* 121–22:145–60.

Wacquant, Loïc J. D. 1993. De l'Amérique comme utopie à l'envers. In *La Misère du monde*, edited by P. Bourdieu. Paris: Seuil.

Weil, Patrick. 1995a. *La France et ses étrangers: L'Aventure d'une politique de l'immigration de 1938 à nos jours*. 2d ed. Paris: Gallimard.

———. 1995b. Racisme et discrimination dans la politique française de l'immigration: 1938–45/1974–95. *Vingtième Siècle* 47:77–102.

Weir, Margaret. 1995. The politics of racial isolation in Europe and America. In *Classifying by race*, edited by P. E. Peterson. Princeton: Princeton University Press.

Williams, Linda Faye. 1998. Race and the politics of social policy. In *The social divide: Political parties and the future of activist government*, edited by M. Weir. Washington, D.C.: Brookings Institution Press.

12

Affirmative Action, Caste, and Party Politics
in Contemporary India

. . .

S UNITA P ARIKH

On the spectrum of affirmative action policies discussed in this volume, policies in India can be placed near the extreme positive end in terms of time since initiation, groups covered, and level of implementation. Begun in the 1930s, Indian affirmative action policies, called "reservations," are used primarily in higher education and public employment. They are targeted at the lower castes, or "backward" classes. They take the form of hard quotas ranging as high as 50 percent, depending on the state implementing them (Parikh 1997, 9, 180).

For proponents, the Indian policies can be considered successful on many dimensions. This does not mean, however, that they are uncontroversial or universally accepted. They have been connected to episodes of violent social conflict, reservation debates have helped to destabilize and bring down governments, and opponents consistently assert that reservations reduce government efficiency and benefit the least deserving of targeted groups. Nonetheless, reservations continue to be institutionalized and supported by the courts, the major parties, and the public. By the end of the twentieth century, reservations became taken for granted, even by opponents. How and why did such controversial policies become an accepted part of the policy landscape in India?

I contend that affirmative action has endured in India in part because the size of the targeted group is much larger than in other countries, but not only for this reason. In addition to the large number of potential beneficiaries, the policy is significant as a political litmus test, and it is critical in creating both cohesive pro- and antireservation coalitions and the responses of political parties to these coalitions. Although the variation within the groups that are eligible for reservation benefits is great, differences are frequently subsumed to create a politically salient coalition termed "backwards" that sees itself in unified opposition to nontargeted groups, who call themselves "forwards." This dichotomy has a long history in southern Indian political mobilization but has only recently become important in northern India, and reservation policies have played a key role in the process.

Affirmative action policies in India provide a fascinating insight into the politics of ascriptive policies more generally and the way such policies develop over time. In the seventy years since their introduction there have been major changes in the composition of the eligible groups, in their popular support, in the political parties that support or oppose them, and in their range and scope. Their prospects for survival have ranged from highly uncertain to assured. To explain how reservations have remained a consistently important set of policies, I first trace their historical development, then discuss their expansion during one-party dominance and party competition, and finally evaluate their current importance in Indian politics. I conclude by suggesting how the Indian experience might help illuminate other cases.

The Origins and Early Development of Reservations

Reservation policies have a complicated history in India. Their origins lie in policies for indigenous representation developed by the British government during colonialism. They were codified and given legitimacy by a highly public set of negotiations between key Indian leaders during the independence movement, and they were written into the Indian constitution by the Indian National Congress. After independence, both the dominant Congress Party and the multiple parties that emerged after the end of Congress's political supremacy expanded reservations to new groups and new policy areas despite sustained and occasionally violent opposition by high-caste groups.

As I have discussed in greater detail elsewhere (Parikh 1997), reservation policies for untouchables (India's lowest castes) emerged as a byproduct of debates over the proper form of electoral representation for the major ethnic and religious groups, especially Hindus and Muslims. In the late nineteenth and early twentieth centuries, the British government introduced incremental changes in the political governance of India that were to have profound ramifications for the eventual development of reservation policies. These changes were predicated on the assumption that Indians, unlike their modern British counterparts, were defined by their ethnic or religious identity and therefore should not be treated as individuals in politics (Copeland 1945). Representation was therefore based on "communities of interests" rather than individual citizenship. When election rather than appointment of representatives was first considered in 1906, British officials extended the group-based selection process used for appointments to the new electoral system by establishing separate electorates for Muslims (Hardy 1971). This meant that only Muslims would vote for Muslim representatives. Ten years later, when reforms to the 1909 legislation were being considered, similar electorates were contemplated for other groups, including Sikhs, Christians, and untouchables. Untouchables were not seen as sufficiently organized at the time to take advantage of separate electorates, but the door was left open for them in the future (Government of Britain 1918).

Although the British sincerely viewed Indian society as irrevocably divided into ascriptive categories, they also had political strategic reasons for developing policies that reflected these views. Even though the vast majority of Indians posed little threat to British dominance, demands by elite Indian groups for greater representation in government service and the economy increased during the late nineteenth century (Seal 1971). If these groups were able to form a united front, they posed a greater threat to the British than if they remained divided. Therefore, policies that recognized and emphasized their differences aided the British. Separate electorates served this purpose, and the more groups that could be separated electorally, the better.

Not surprisingly, the Indian National Congress viewed these developments with severe misgivings. Opposed in principle to separate electorates for any group, they were particularly concerned about their award to untouchables. High-caste Hindus had to shoulder at least part of the blame for the potential success of the British strategy, since as late as 1911 there was still debate within the Hindu elite as to whether untouchables should be counted as Hindus at all (Galanter 1984). By the end of the 1920s, however, when untouchables had mobilized and developed a core of leaders, the Congress argued vehemently that separate electorates could not be granted to them. As Gandhi stated eloquently, "the claims advanced on behalf of the Untouchables, that to me is the 'unkindest cut of all.' . . . It will create a division within Hinduism" (quoted in Parikh 1997, p. 150).

The Congress's position was both principled and strategic. It was principled because the Congress's goal of an undivided electorate modeled on liberal democratic principles was severely compromised by the division of untouchables from higher-caste Hindus. It was strategic because the Congress's interests were diametrically opposed to those of the British colonial government. If the Congress were to maintain its position as the preeminent indigenous opposition to the British, it could not afford to lose any more groups from its support base. It might be able to overcome Muslim defections, but it would be severely compromised in British eyes by the untouchables' defection, and there was the possibility that a domino effect would not occur with Sikhs and other groups.

As a consequence, when the British government announced a new electoral policy in the Communal Award of 1932, the Congress could not afford to accept the provisions granting separate electorates to untouchables. Before the announcement Gandhi had made clear his position that if such a provision was included, he would be bound to resist it, and after the award was made public he communicated to the British government his decision to fast unto death. Though some British officials in London were skeptical of his resolve, both the government of India and the Congress leadership were deeply worried about the consequences of a fast for an already weakened, frail, and imprisoned leader. All the major Congress leaders, along with the preeminent untouchable leader, B. R. Ambedkar, convened in Poona, where Gandhi was in jail, to seek a compromise.

Both the Congress and Ambedkar had reason to compromise, the Congress because it needed to keep untouchables in the fold while fighting separate electorates, and Ambedkar because he could not afford the consequences, even within his own community, if Gandhi were to die for lack of a negotiated settlement. Reservations, which represented a compromise between completely open electorates and separated electorates, achieved each side's purposes. Electoral seats would be reserved within a general electorate, but they had to be filled by untouchables, that is, voting would be general but candidacy would be reserved (Tendulkar 1952).

The Poona Pact, as it came to be called, was a momentous event for the independence movement on a number of dimensions. Of all Gandhi's fasts, this was the one that came to be called "the epic fast." After negotiating the Poona Pact, Gandhi began his famous campaign to abolish untouchability and allow "scheduled castes" (a common euphemism for untouchables) to share caste Hindu temples, wells, and other community resources from which they had been historically excluded. And from a political point of view, the principle of reservations was given legitimacy by India's most revered leader.

The Poona Pact was succeed by a larger movement to improve conditions for untouchables in a variety of areas. Gandhi's "Harijan Uplift Campaign" stressed the abolition of discrimination against untouchables, most notably their exclusion from Hindu temples (Brown 1977). Though the campaign was not wholly successful, it brought greater public awareness to the issue, and it undoubtedly smoothed the way for the extension of reservations to other arenas, especially higher education and employment. By the end of the colonial period, a number of state and local governments had implemented reservations across several policy areas.

Gandhi's acceptance did not mean, however, that reservations were universally endorsed by the Congress's leadership, and Nehru in particular was deeply suspicious of them (*Constituent Assembly Debates [CAD]*, vol. 8). Given this ambivalence, why were they retained as policies in independent India, and even written into the constitution? After all, by the time the Constituent Assembly was convened to draft the new constitution, Gandhi had ceased to be a day-to-day player in party politics, and only months after independence he was assassinated. The "oligarchy," or the topmost leadership of the Congress Party, was divided on the merits of reservations, and even Ambedkar expressed concerns about giving reservations permanent status in the constitution (*CAD*, vol. 8).

Despite these scruples, there were practical and symbolic reasons for retaining reservations. Unlike separate electorates, which had been introduced by the British, reserved seats were an indigenous policy creation ratified by Congress leaders less than two decades previously. Their abolition might make the party more vulnerable to Ambedkar's accusation that the Congress, especially after Gandhi's death, did not represent the true interests of scheduled castes. There was no real reason to take such a risk from a party unity standpoint, because caste Hindus were not particularly opposed to reservations. The numbers of reserved seats were small and the power of scheduled castes minimal. The one concession to Nehru's antipathy, however, was to include economic and social criteria as a precondition for reservation privileges. This language would prove decisive in the expansion of reservation policy that occurred in subsequent decades.[1]

Reservations originated as a compromise between the separate electorates offered by the colonial government and the general electorates favored by the Indian National Congress. They were viewed as such from the time of their creation by the Poona Pact through the Constituent Assembly Debates, and although they covered a reasonably large target population (about 21 percent), the actual usage was often far lower. As a result, there was little opposition to reservations on the part of caste Hindus, and there was strong support for them among scheduled castes. The reiteration of their value in highly public settings throughout the independence struggle also invested reservations with a symbolic importance that political leaders recognized and confirmed. This symbolic salience was to prove to be much more difficult to manage once reservations spread beyond scheduled castes, especially in northern and western India. Moreover, during the colonial period and the early years of independence, the use of reservations was essentially a top-down policy. They were widely supported, but they were less widely utilized, and they represented a policy choice that upper and middle castes could bestow on relatively quiescent scheduled castes without much sacrifice. As segments of these groups became both economically better off and politically savvier, however, the policies became more controversial.

Reservations under Party Competition

During the 1950s and 1960s, reservations were by and large unproblematic for politicians, especially in northern India. In the 1950s there was an abortive attempt to extend reservations to low-caste groups (known after constitutional terminology as "Other Backward Classes," or OBCs) at the national level, along the lines of OBC reservations in southern states such as Tamil Nadu and Karnataka (then Madras and Mysore, respectively). A distinguished commission was appointed to investigate the prospects, but the difficulty of creating a nationwide OBC list soon became apparent, and the commission's report was tabled and never reintroduced in Parliament. These difficulties were to some extent practical but to a greater extent political. First, simply enumerating a consensually acceptable list of targeted groups was difficult; the problems that existed at the state level were simply compounded in the attempt to create a master national list because it involved comparisons of caste status. Second, the problem also was compounded by the local nature of caste. A caste that was in a low-caste ranking in one state might not have the same status in another state, but it was politically infeasible to target one state's population and not a population with the same caste name in the other state. The central government solved this conundrum by tabling the national discussion and allowing state-level initiatives. Therefore, to the extent that conflict over reservations occurred, it involved disputes between southern Indian states. These states had caste distributions that made it politically expedient to grant reservations to more than two-thirds of their population, which eventually led the Indian Supreme Court to set a ceiling of 50 percent on the number of reserved seats in *Balaji v. Mysore* (All India Reporter 1963 SC 649). But these conflicts, though important in defining the contours of constitutionally acceptable reservation policy, did not really touch northern and western India. The south, with its skewed distribution of a tiny Brahmin population, a huge OBC population, and no real middle castes, was clearly different.

After 1971, however, this fragile equilibrium broke down. The division of the Congress Party into the organizational (O) and the Indira Gandhi (I) wings had shattered the accommodations that had prevailed through the mid-1960s. Now no party could take for granted its vote base. While the Congress (O) continued, with little success, to mobilize voters along traditional lines, Congress (I) appealed directly to voters at the bottom of the caste and socioeconomic hierarchy—Muslims, scheduled castes, and OBCs—and one of the important planks in the platform was reservation policy. Indira Gandhi's resounding victory in 1971 and the victory of those who followed similar electoral strategies at the state level meant that they would have to deliver on their election promises in regions where reservations had hitherto been limited to scheduled castes (Manor 1977).

Attempts to implement state-level OBC commission recommendations in northern and western Indian states were met by widespread protests by middle and upper castes. In Gujarat, the introduction of 10 percent reservations for OBCs in employment and higher education touched off violent conflict between middle-caste groups and beneficiaries, including scheduled castes, whose reservations were never in doubt (Yagnik and Bhatt 1984). In Bihar, the introduction of reservations brought down the state government and led to widespread rioting, looting, and deaths. State governments responded in different ways: in Bihar the OBC reservations were withdrawn, while in Gujarat another commission was appointed (Government of Gujarat 1983). When that commission's recommendations were accepted by a government that depended heavily on OBC support, the subsequent rioting brought parts of the state to a standstill for up to six months (Mehta and Patel 1985).

It is worth noting that in every state the percentage of seats reserved was far below the targeted groups' proportion of the population, which regularly exceeded 50 percent. The discrepancy between the policy and population percentages was particularly great in Gujarat, where antireservation violence became endemic in the 1970s and 1980s. Yet state governments rarely abandoned reservation policies fully, leading to a cycle in which uneasy truces prevailed while commissions were convened and conflicts erupted once the new recommendations were taken up for consideration by the government in power.

At the national level, the experience of the 1950s was largely repeated in the 1970s, when a new commission was appointed. The Mandal Commission's report on OBC reservations at the center was commissioned by the 1977–79 Janata coalition government, received by the 1980 Congress (I) government, and subsequently tabled without opposition.[2] Yet no party ever fully abandoned its publicly declared support for reservation policies. What accounts for this paradox?

I argue that the answer lies in the nature of the uneasy coalition politics that developed in the 1970s and 1980s. In 1971 Indira Gandhi had been able to come to power by directly appealing to poorer groups in Indian society, unlike the old, dominant, undivided Congress's strategy of mobilizing through traditional ties and organizational links to local notables. She was successful at least in part because these underprivileged and poorly educated voters had nonetheless learned that their votes were important and sought after by politicians. Despite the persistence of traditional local power structures, the act of voting created a new political awareness in underprivileged sections of the society.[3]

These were not the only groups who had come to realize the importance of their votes, however. In northern and western India, the democratic electoral process had led to mobilizations of middle castes as well. In particular, the middle class "bullock capitalists" mobilized by Charan Singh and the growing political power of ritually backward but locally powerful groups had created new tensions within political coalitions (Rudolph and Rudolph 1987). During the period of undivided Congress rule, these potentially divergent interests had been present, but the use of local power networks and traditional ties by a party with no effective national rivals had muted both the potential for conflict and the ability of lower-status voters to act independently. Once they became mobilized outside this structure, their sense of their own interests crystallized and their demands grew accordingly.

This process of political differentiation was less easy to perceive in the 1970s because, except during the immediate post-Emergency period, Indira Gandhi was able to keep together coalitions that were developing internal contradictions. Challenges to her supremacy were often effective at the state level, but they rarely succeeded in posing a threat at the center. After her death in 1984, Rajiv Gandhi was increasingly less successful at using this strategy, and by the late 1980s the problems inherent in building a cross-caste coalition while supporting the Mandal Commission's recommendations were straining the strategic abilities of every party that attempted it. At the same time, however, support for reservation policies was becoming a litmus test for low- and scheduled-caste voters.

The Mandalization of Indian Politics

The odd history of the Mandal Commission report provides an illuminating glimpse into the way reservation policy politics changed during the 1980s and 1990s. As stated previously, the commission was formed under the Janata government, it reported to a Congress (I) government, and all major parties agreed to allow its recommendations to languish in out-of-print obscurity. At the same time, all major parties also subscribed to its recommendations (and to the need for OBC reservations at the national level) in their party platform. These dual strategies were necessitated by the controversial nature of OBC reservations outside southern India. If a party did not publicly support Mandal reservations, it risked losing necessary lower-caste support. But if it pushed for their implementation, it invited protests and more violent conflict by middle castes. Therefore, it was in almost no party's best interests to either repudiate or reintroduce the Mandal report.

Ironically, the Mandal commission had been convened to defuse the pressures of the 1970s. The Janata coalition's core parties and leaders were more conservative than the Congress (I) they replaced, and they needed to demonstrate their commitment to low-caste issues. By the time the commission issued its report, it delivered it to the resurgent Congress (I), which had defeated the Janata government in the 1980 elections. But despite the relatively greater reliance of Congress (I) on low-caste votes, it could not afford to alienate its high-caste backers by implementing the report. And since Congress (I) continued in power until 1989, they had no incentive to wade into the controversy that the Mandal report was bound to create.

This state of affairs came to an end in 1990, when the minority National Front government, led by V. P. Singh, announced that it would take up the Mandal report with a view to its implementation as soon as possible. The National Front government had succeeded in defeating the Congress (I) of Rajiv Gandhi in the 1989 elections, but it had failed to gain a majority of Parliamentary seats and therefore depended on the external support of the conservative, high-caste-Hindu Bharatiya Janata Party (BJP). Singh's reasons for reviving Mandal were fairly straightforward. As a party (or more precisely, an agglomeration of parties), the National Front relied heavily on lower-caste and minority votes. In June 1990, the removal of Devi Lal, an important OBC leader and deliverer of a critical OBC "vote bank," from the coalition made the National Front's commitment to OBC concerns more suspect, especially given the high-caste status of the prime minister. There is also reliable newspaper evidence to support the hypothesis that the National Front was concerned about the BJP's growing effectiveness at using the "Ayodhya" strategy to improve its fortunes and extend beyond its high-caste Hindu base (*Indian Express* 1990).

What came to be known as the Ayodhya strategy provided a counterpoint to the National Front's Mandal strategy. A focus on Ayodhya was designed to unite Hindus by reminding them of their similarities through the invocation of cherished Hindu icons, in this case the Hindu god Ram and his birthplace at Ayodhya. Obviously, it left out Muslims and other non-Hindu minorities, and it was problematic for scheduled castes because of its caste Hindu emphasis. The Mandal strategy, by contrast, accepted the high-caste versus low-caste cleavage, using reservation and other pro-poor policies to form a coalition of low-caste and scheduled-caste Hindus, Muslims, and other minority groups. It essentially gave up on all but the most left-oriented high and middle castes.

Although V. P. Singh's strategy may have seemed workable when contemplated, its effects were profound and destabilizing for the government. Almost immediately protests broke out in that time-honored hotbed of antireservation agitation, the state of Bihar. They might have been manageable if contained there, but conflict quickly spread to all parts of India, including the capital, New Delhi, where antireservation violence had never before occurred and where students quickly, and at first quite spontaneously, took to the streets. Within days Gujarat and other sites of previous conflict over reservations were also experiencing violent backlash against the government's proclamation.

One notable feature of the 1990 riots was that unlike state-level antireservation agitations in the past, this violence was directed almost exclusively at the government. Rather than looting the shops of low-caste people and torching their residential communities, protesters concentrated their attentions on government buildings and property, especially buses and trains. It was weeks before proreservation protesters joined the battle, and when they did they were far fewer in number. The violent events of 1990 were primarily directed at the government by voters unhappy with the policy choice.[4] It is noteworthy that by this time, reservations were seen by protesters as a government choice, not an occasion to pit one caste against the other in conflict.

Within the official political arena, parties were scrambling to adjust to the new policy and electoral calculus. The BJP, for whom caste-conscious policies were the most dangerous politically, was infuriated that V. P. Singh had made such an important policy choice without consulting it (as external supporters of the minority government). The opposition Congress party similarly deplored the hasty moves of the National Front. No one wanted to draw attention to their unanimous support in party platforms for Mandal's implementation, so they concentrated on issues of timing and consultation. They also offered behind-the-scenes support to protesters to continue the destabilization of the sitting government.

When the conflict failed to abate within a couple of weeks, V. P. Singh announced that he would suspend implementation until the issue could be debated. When this failed to appease protesters, he offered to withdraw the policy pending Supreme Court review. The Supreme Court handed down its opinion in late 1992. With some important modifications, it upheld the essence of the Mandal recommendations and pronounced them constitutionally legitimate (*Indira Sawney v. Union of India*, All Indian Reporter 1992 Supp. (3) SCC 217). Singh and the National Front government were long gone by this time, and it was up to a Congress government led by P. V. Narasimha Rao to make the policy decision. Contrary to the party position in 1990, Congress embraced the ruling, declared Mandal to be the law of the land, and promised quick and effective implementation. Remarkably, this pronouncement was greeted with little outcry by the previously vocal and violent antireservation lobby, and the few attempts to rouse opposition faded quickly.

What happened? It is difficult to pin down a single cause, but a few factors can be inferred. First, the passage of two years between the Mandal riots and the court's decision had created a space in which public acceptance could be developed. Second, the Supreme Court's decision was accepted as legitimate and reasonably argued. The court had supported reservations, but in doing so had mandated that economic considerations be taken into account, which defused a major issue of contention.[5] And third, the electoral arithmetic had begun to permeate Indian political consciousness. Despite the outcry by political groups and by influential media outlets such as *India Today* and the English-language dailies, it was clear that over half the Indian population supported reservations.[6] And for political parties, the salience of reservations as a signal of intentions toward OBCs was undeniable. Even the BJP, which was attempting with some success to replace Mandal with Mandir in order to create a cross-caste Hindu coalition, was afraid to speak out publicly against reservations.

By the end of 1992, the issue of Mandal, and of reservations more generally, was seen as settled. Although this may have been due to the events of December 1992 and the outbreak of the worst Hindu-Muslim violence since partition, Mandal has failed to reemerge as a significant arena of conflict. It has, however, redrawn the boundaries of the Indian electoral formula.

The Mandalization of Politics: Bihar

In the 1996 and 1998 Parliamentary elections, politicians and observers increasingly began to speak of the "Mandalization" of politics. At first it was unclear precisely what this phrase represented. Was it the importance of the OBC vote? The omnipresence of reservation policy in political discourse? Neither possibility seemed accurate or enlightening. But observing the 1998 elections in Bihar began to shed some light on the puzzle.

When Indians use the term *Mandalization* they are referring to the new political arithmetic created by the entrenchment of reservation policy in current politics. Until the implementation of the Mandal recommendations, reservation policy varied across states and remained, in the sense of implementation and discussions of policy choices, a state-level issue. After the Mandal implementation it became possible to speak of national coalitions based on the policy. The primary result has been to bifurcate the electorate into two groups: the targeted and the nontargeted. This distinction is at times more important than the multiple caste configurations of the recent past, and it has both practical and symbolic importance. Practically, it means that groups see themselves as sharing the interests of others that fall on their side of the division. Symbolically, it joins groups with potentially divergent interests against those whose interests are even further away on this single dimension.

It would be overstating the case to say that Mandal has realigned political coalition-building. Caste groups still see themselves as having differing or opposing interests, and voters will not support a politician whom they see as unresponsive to them simply because she is on the proper side of the Mandal divide. Nevertheless, two intriguing phenomena were apparent in Bihar during the recent election.

First, voters are unlikely to vote for a politician belonging to a party that is seen as on the opposite side of the Mandal divide. In Bihar, this meant that targeted group voters were not likely to vote for BJP candidates even when they were fed up with the chief minister, as many Biharis were. The BJP's surprising success depended on extending its traditional base at the same time that it formed a strong pre-poll alliance with the Samata Party, which has its base among the OBCs. Thus, the BJP brought in the high-caste Bhumihars, Rajputs, and Brahmins, while the Samata Party attracted the OBCs and some Yadavs. Voters were aware that in voting for the Samata Party they were implicitly supporting the BJP at the center, but this is still a step removed from casting one's own vote for the BJP.

Second, the most intense conflict is at the Mandal dividing line. The lowest high castes are pitted against the highest OBCs. In Bihar, this means that the main conflict is between the Yadavs and the poorer among the Rajputs and Bhumihars. The lower OBCs and the richer high castes are interested, but they are less engaged. Despite the great disfavor with which the government that dominated in the 1990s was regarded, Yadavs were only willing to desert when a sufficiently powerful Yadav or OBC candidate ran against the incumbent RJD Party. Other OBCs feel the Yadavs have disproportionately benefited under the government, whose chief minister is of the Yadav caste, but they are still willing to back Yadavs against nontargeted group candidates.

It is important to bear in mind that the groups closest to the Mandal dividing line probably have more in common with each other than with the more extreme members of their own side. They are, in some ways, analogous to the median voter of American politics, and they are the critical voters for Indian parties to win: The BJP, with its high-caste base, needs to find OBC coalition partners or woo the top layer of the OBC, while the OBC-based parties need to pull in some of the least privileged middle castes. Yet perhaps because these groups are so critical, their relations with each other are especially strained. And, unlike the median voter in the U.S. case, the salience of the Mandal division keeps the two symbolically separate.

The BJP has continued to gain ground even in caste-conscious Bihar, but it has done so because of the increasing weakness of the incumbent party and its own willingness to moderate its more extreme positions. The BJP's ability to form a government at the national level after the 1998 and 1999 elections was due in large part to its retreat from the most controversial Hindu-nationalist aspects of its platform. Similarly, in Bihar, it has increased its representation by playing down its high-caste roots.

Conclusion

Reservation policies today bear almost no resemblance to those created by Congress leaders during British colonial rule. They have evolved from protected political representation for scheduled castes to sweeping national- and state-level programs that cover more than one-half the Indian population in representation, higher education, and government employment. In one sense, reservations embody the story that highlights the unintended consequences of policy formulation and implementation.

At the same time, however, none of these divergences from the origins are difficult to understand or explain. Reservations began as a political (and undoubtedly sincere) response to an electoral incentive. Their growth has similarly been spurred by the changing electoral incentives faced by parties operating in the modern Indian political context. This was not an inevitable development; had political competition evolved differently, had individual politicians made other choices when building political coalitions, reservations might have played little or no role in structuring political strategies.

In an ethnically heterogeneous society, ascriptive policies are attractive because they appeal to voters who have already sorted themselves into groups. It is not necessary to build a sense of consciousness around caste or the have/have-not divide that results from the caste hierarchy. Therefore, it is not surprising that politicians competing for votes turn quickly to ascriptive appeals to gain support. It is important, however, to keep in mind what the potential consequences of such strategies are. The ironic result of the Mandalization of Indian politics has been to give the greatest leverage to those who are probably the least well sorted into the two categories. In Bihar, many OBCs will confide that Yadavs are not really like OBCs at all anymore, but they are still closer than Brahmins, Bhumihars, and Rajputs.

The Indian case offers important insights for scholars of affirmative action. The long view, nearly a century old now, provides a map of the paths that such politics can take over time. The ways in which the policies have changed since inception owe much to the changing configuration of politics and political groups. For parties, the willingness to accept reservations as a litmus test of commitment to low-caste political interests reinforced and increased their importance as policies irrespective of their success or failure. For political groups, this focus created new types of coalitions founded as much on symbolic as on material convergence among groups. When reservations were established in the Indian constitution, the great leader of the scheduled castes, B. R. Ambedkar, agreed that they should be subject to review after ten years so that they would be reevaluated and could be abolished when they were no longer necessary. At the beginning of the twenty-first century, it is almost impossible to imagine a political scenario under which the abolition of reservation policy might occur.

Notes

1. This discussion has centered exclusively on the development of reservations at the national level. There were reservations for non-Brahmins in political representation, public education, and government service across southern India from the 1920s. These, however, have not proved to be politically contentious for many of the reasons given in support of my argument. See Parikh 1997 for a fuller exposition.

2. From 1981 to 1989 the commission's report was out of print and almost impossible to obtain.

3. India has a first-past-the-post electoral system. Therefore, parties have an incentive to appeal to groups that are found throughout India rather than concentrated by region. Until very recently, it has been difficult for regional parties to gain national prominence, and even now it has come through the construction of successful coalitions.

4. Accounts at the time focused heavily on a wave of self-immolations that took place among youths across northern India. There is, however, only limited and unreliable evidence that the bulk of these acts, although horrible, were directly linked to attitudes about reservation policy.

5. Although reservations were supposed to take economic status into account, in a country where taxes are routinely evaded and assets are distributed among family members to keep them hidden, the practical problems of determining individuals' economic standing are enormous. The court attempted to address this problem by mandating that the best-off of each caste group, the so-called creamy layer, could not be targeted for reservations.

6. This support refers to reservations for caste groups. Although there is support for gender-based reservations, Parliament has been unable to agree on terms, even for the political arena. The problem stems in large part from the fact that women's reservations would not be divided according to caste status, which makes them unacceptable to low-caste groups. As a result, reservations for women are currently in place only at the local government level.

References

Brown, Judith. 1977. *Gandhi and civil disobedience.* Cambridge: Cambridge University Press.

Copeland, Reginald. 1945. *The constitutional problem in India.* Vol. 1. London: Oxford University Press.

Galanter, Marc. 1984. *Competing equalities: Law and the backward classes in India.* Berkeley: University of California Press.

Government of Britain. 1918. Report on Indian constitutional reforms. 06.18.90. Cd.9109, Parliamentary Papers VII.

Government of Gujarat. 1983. Report of the socially and educationally backward classes commission (A. R. Baxi, Chairman). 2 vols. Gandhinagar, Gujarat: Government Press.

Government of India. 1948–49. *Constituent Assembly debates.* Vol. 8. Delhi: Government Press.

Hardy, Peter. 1971. *The Muslims of British India.* Cambridge: Cambridge University Press.

Manor, James. 1977. *Political change in an Indian state: Mysore, 1917–1955.* New Delhi: Manohar Publishing.

Mehta, Haroobhai, and Hasmukh Patel, eds. *Dynamics of reservation policy.* New Delhi: Patriot Publishers.

Parikh, Sunita. 1997. *The politics of preference: Democratic institutions and affirmative action in the United States and India.* Ann Arbor: University of Michigan Press.

Rudolph, Lloyd I., and Susanne H. Rudolph. 1987. *In pursuit of Lakshmi: The political economy of the Indian state.* Chicago: University of Chicago Press.

Seal, Anil. 1971. *The emergence of Indian nationalism.* London: Cambridge University Press.

Tendulkar, D. G. 1952. *Mahatma: Life of Mohandas Karamchand Gandhi.* 3 vols. Bombay: Vithalbhai K. Jkaveri and D. G. Tandulkar.

Yagnik, Achyut, and Anil Bhatt. 1984. The anti-Dalit agitation in Gujarat. *South Asia Bulletin* 4:45–60.

13

Affirmative Action and Ethnic Niches:

A Legal Afterword

. . .

DEBORAH C. MALAMUD

This volume paints a valuable empirical portrait of affirmative action that is revealing on a number of levels—how it emerged (chapter 1), how it is viewed and practiced in private-sector employment (chapter 4) and higher education (chapter 5), what we as a nation believe about it (chapters 8 and 9), and how it is practiced elsewhere in the world (chapters 10–12). Most important from an American legal standpoint are the insights the volume offers on how the environment in which American antidiscrimination law operates has become increasingly complex due to interethnic conflict and immigration (chapters 2, 3, 6, and 7).

We lawyers and legal academics tend to view the world through the lens of litigation. Because not every social practice that *can* be challenged *is* challenged, however, litigation is hardly a reliable perspective. Just as there was a long hiatus in social science research on affirmative action[1] there was a long period without strong legal—or, for that matter, political—challenges to affirmative action as practiced. Similarly, ethnic niches in employment have long been a standard feature of American life, but only recently have they begun to attract legal attention.

Some of the social practices described in this volume may seem reasonable to Americans, but are patently illegal under current law. Some are of questionable legality. Some are plainly legal now, but may not be for long. My aim here is to describe the legal framework that would presently be brought to bear in judging them, and in so doing to reveal the gap that exists between the law and America's ethno-racial reality. In describing this gap, I do not mean to suggest that the right answer is for legal actors to change the law to accommodate newly pervasive social practices. I am, however, suggesting that actors within the legal system must learn to *see* the new realities of interethnic conflict and competition, and must develop a coherent response to them.

Affirmative Action

Several distinct but interrelated bodies of law govern affirmative action in the United States. The United States Constitution, federal statutes, federal executive orders, state constitutional provisions, state statutes, state executive orders, self-imposed restrictions by state bodies, and local ordinances all have things to say on the subject of affirmative action. Judicial decisions interpreting one source of law are not binding as to others but can be influential beyond their own borders. I cannot hope to survey the state of the law in general, but I will note some aspects of the law that have particular bearing on the empirical situations surveyed in this volume.

The Constitution

Levels of scrutiny. As interpreted by the Supreme Court, the Equal Protection Clause of Fourteenth Amendment to the United States Constitution subjects government programs to different levels of "scrutiny" depending upon the nature of the classifications they make.[2] "Strict scrutiny" applies to racial and ethnic classifications,[3] and it requires programs to be narrowly tailored to meet a compelling governmental interest. Gender-based discrimination is subject to "intermediate scrutiny,"[4] which requires a substantial relationship to an important governmental purpose.[5] The Court has rejected, in recent years, the claim that classifications aimed at helping traditionally oppressed groups ("benign" classifications) ought to be treated differently than classifications aimed at hurting these groups. Thus, affirmative action programs that expressly identify blacks and other ethnic minorities as their beneficiary class are subject to strict scrutiny— in other words, to the same level of constitutional scrutiny as programs that discriminate against blacks and ethnic minorities. Similarly, gender-based affirmative action is subject to intermediate scrutiny, because that is the level of scrutiny applicable to programs that discriminate against women. Despite the centrality of African Americans and their needs to our social embrace of affirmative action (chapter 1), affirmative action for women is markedly easier to defend than is affirmative action for African Americans and other racial and ethnic minorities.[6] Affirmative action based on economic factors ("class-based affirmative action") or on age or handicap, like discrimination on those grounds, is subject to "rationality review," which requires only a rational relationship to a legitimate government purpose.

The essays in this volume raise important questions about the kinds of racial and ethnic classifications that are routinely used in affirmative action programs. The common categories "Latino" or "Hispanic," "Asian American," and even "African American" mask socially important differences based on national origin (chapter 3), immigration cohort (chatper 2), and intermarriage. But at least as to the setting of levels of scrutiny for purposes of constitutional analysis, the law has not tracked the social reality. Race and ethnicity (and, swept in with it, national ancestry) are all subject to strict scrutiny. Furthermore, even if the levels of scrutiny *did* track the social reality, they would do so backwards, as if reflecting reality in a mirror. Absent a working concept of "benign discrimination," any hierarchy of suffering drawn to distinguish among American minority groups would simply backfire once affirmative action was on the table. If the legal system developed a sliding scale of levels of scrutiny to be applied to different racial or ethnic groups based on their relative level of suffering, and if the decision were made that Asian Americans were better off than African Americans, the odd result would be that public institutions would face a lower level of legal scrutiny for their pro–Asian American affirmative action programs than for their pro–African American affirmative action programs. That result would defy the remedial logic of affirmative action, but it would be dictated by the legal system's decision that there is no such thing as benign discrimination.

Treating unlikes alike may make no social sense, but it has beneficial effects on coalition building. If all ethnic and racial classifications are subject to strict scrutiny, there is reason for all minorities to stick together. But the pro–affirmative action coalition includes both minorities and women—and there, the doctrinal structure cuts against unity. The reason is the assignment of gender to the "intermediate scrutiny" category. The different status of women and minorities under the Equal Protection Clause gives a new dimension to the often-stated (though rarely empirically backed) proposition that women, and not minorities, are the primary beneficiaries of affirmative action in this country.[7] This claim is often made by civil rights activists and scholars who believe that affirmative action, like welfare, is negatively viewed by American whites as a program benefiting African Americans and is rejected for that reason. Much minority-instigated coalition building aims at increasing white women's self-interested support for affirmative action and at convincing white men to picture their own wives and daughters—

rather than blacks and Latinos—as affirmative action beneficiaries. If programs jointly proposed and designed to meet the interests of both women and minorities survive legal scrutiny as to women but not as to minorities, the coalition will break apart.

Think, in this light, of the typical program in government contracting that provides affirmative action benefits to businesses owned or managed by economically disadvantaged women and minorities. The program insofar as it applies to women would be subject to intermediate scrutiny, under which it would have a respectable but not easy chance for survival.[8] The program's application to racial and ethnic minorities would be subject to strict scrutiny and would face an exceedingly difficult road.[9] Yet in all probability the program was advocated for by informal pro–affirmative action coalitions and adopted by the legislature as an organic whole, and when it is challenged in court, it is likely to be challenged as an organic whole. When litigation is filed, however, tensions in the coalition come to the fore. The women's groups in the pro–affirmative action coalition are forced to decide whether to break ranks and remind the court that the program need only survive intermediate scrutiny for it to be legally sustainable for women. Sometimes litigants forego that argument, maintaining coalition in lieu of pursuing differential interests.[10]

"Compelling state interest": Different law for different domains. Another complex and coalition-stressing element of the Supreme Court's affirmative action jurisprudence concerns the specific uses to which affirmative action is put. There are distinctive bodies of case law under the Equal Protection Clause concerning affirmative action in higher education admissions, in federal contracting and licensing, and in employment.[11] Broad judicial statements about which governmental interests are sufficiently "compelling" to sustain affirmative action programs must be read in light of their programmatic context.

Take the case of higher education admissions, which was the subject of the *Hopwood*[12] decision against the University of Texas Law School and is the subject of pending litigation against the University of Washington and the University of Michigan—in all cases, under the sponsorship of the Center for Individual Rights (CIR). The *Hopwood* court agreed with CIR's position that *Bakke*[13] was no longer good law. One of its reasons was the Supreme Court's insistence in *Adarand*,[14] a federal contracting case, that only the remedying of past discrimination perpetrated by or "passively particip[ated]" in by government satisfies the "compelling interest" prong of the strict scrutiny test. As a result, the

Hopwood court held, *Bakke*'s reliance on "diversity" as a compelling governmental interest for purposes of higher education admissions could no longer stand. But the *Hopwood* court failed to recognize the context-specificity of much of the Supreme Court's affirmative action jurisprudence. There are plenty of reasons why the government might have a compelling interest in a diverse student body (chiefly centering on the educational mission of universities) but not have a similarly compelling interest in a diverse body of construction contractors. Decisions regarding state interests that originate in the domain of government contracting (like *Adarand*) cannot so simply be imported into the domain of higher education admissions (where *Bakke* still reigns).

There are, however, some cautionary implications from this insight. As we have seen (chapter 4), private businesses have wholeheartedly embraced the rhetoric of *Bakke* and proclaimed diversity to be necessary for the fulfillment of their business mission. We shall talk about the Title VII implications of that move shortly. But in constitutional terms, what if public employers (who are subject to constitutional challenge) were to follow suit? The problem they would face is that governmental interests that are seen as compelling in one setting may not be deemed compelling in others. *Bakke* does not mean that diversity is necessarily a compelling governmental interest. It remains to be seen whether the Supreme Court will accept diversity as a rationale for hiring (as opposed to student admissions),[15] and, if so, which types of government enterprises will be permitted to rely on it. Judge Richard Posner of the United States Court of Appeals for the Seventh Circuit, a judge whose influence far exceeds that of most of his fellow federal appellate judges, has taken a constitutionally lenient approach to race-based preferential hiring in an experimental corrections program.[16] Other judges have extended his reasoning to the fields of corrections and law enforcement more generally, using what is coming to be called the "operational need" rationale (Browne 1997). It remains to be seen whether this approach will be extended beyond the (perceived) extraordinary needs of the criminal justice system to enhance its (perceived) legitimacy by hiring minorities to police and incarcerate other minorities. Pending further developments, *diversity* is not a magic word.

Compelling state interest and proportionality. Many programs of affirmative action (in whatever legal domain) set "goals" or "targets" for minorities' or women's participation that are based on the proportion of these groups in a comparison group deemed to be relevant to the program. This is no accident. Take public employment as an example. Public employers know that they run the risk of being sued (under the Constitution, Title VII, or both) if their minority or female workforces fall significantly short of the proportion of minorities and women in the relevant labor market. To the significant extent that voluntary affirmative action is a response to the perceived threat of litigation, it makes sense that proportionality would be the ultimate aim of affirmative action programs.

In the constitutional analysis of affirmative action, the question often arises as to the adequacy of the government's proof of past and present discrimination against the beneficiary class. It is here that challenges to the proportionality principle fit in. There was a time when courts were simply willing to recite the nostrum (drawn from early Title VII pattern and practice cases) that absent discrimination, the proportion of minorities or women in the employer's workforce could be expected to match their proportions in the relevant labor market. That time has come and gone. Take, for example, the following analysis (by Judge Frank Easterbrook, also an influential jurist) of an affirmative action plan for the hiring of women as clinical psychology faculty at a midwestern university:[17]

> Where, for example, does the Dean's 61.8% target come from? . . . [I]t is the proportion of all doctorates in clinical psychology, awarded since 1980, that are held by women. . . . [I]f the Department had hired a large number of professors, say, 250 or 500, any significant departure from 62% female would be surprising and require justification to dispel the possibility that the departure was caused by sex discrimination (or a failure of outreach). But the Psychology Department is not large. In spring 1995, when it proposed to hire two additional tenure-track faculty, the department had ten members with tenure or on the tenure track. Four of the ten were women. If it had hired two more tenure-track faculty, to reach twelve, then a ratio of seven women to five men would have produced the closest approximation of 62% female. This appears to be the source of [the Dean's] statement that the Department needed an additional three women to meet its target. Suppose the University hired blindly from a pool that is 62% women. How likely is it that exactly seven of the twelve would be female? What the University appears to have in mind is a world in which the absence of discrimination means that every department would exactly mirror the population from which its members are hired. But that is statistical nonsense.

Statistical analyses in discrimination and affirmative action cases become increasingly sophisticated with every passing year. One can, for example, expect this volume's critique of the assumptions underlying disparity studies (chapter 3) to be mirrored in the testimony of expert witnesses in litigation for years to come.

Proportionality claims are particularly dangerous when "diversity" is put forward as the justification for affirmative action. We have seen (chapter 5) that the stated goal of the California legislature in 1974 was for the University of California "to reach parity between its total undergraduate enrollment and that of California's high school graduates." Such a parity goal would be highly suspect under *Bakke.* Justice Powell's plurality opinion in *Bakke* did not equate diversity with parity. Depending on the circumstances, an institution's diversity goals might require a higher or lower rate of representation of minorities than parity would require. Fixing goals based on parity is a sure-fire way to convince courts (and perhaps also political actors) that diversity talk is simply masking a desire (impermissible under current law) to remedy societal discrimination.

Narrow tailoring and inter- (and intra-)group distinctions. The constitutional approach to discrimination (and by extension to affirmative action) requires a two-part analysis: after one identifies the nature and strength of the government's interest, one must analyze how closely the government's program fits its stated justification. The "narrow tailoring" requirement might, as anti–affirmative action litigation becomes more sophisticated, become a locus for significant challenges to broad definitions of the beneficiary class.

For affirmative action programs that must be justified by demonstrating past or present discrimination, distinctions between groups already matter for purposes of "narrow tailoring."[18] This has been clear ever since the Supreme Court in *Croson* mocked the city of Richmond, Virginia, for extending affirmative action benefits to Aleuts (none of whom lived in Richmond). The problem exists not only in the case of groups without representation in the city's general population. Certainly a city cannot defend its affirmative action program solely by showing a pattern of discrimination against African Americans but then include Hispanics and Asian Americans in the program.[19] How, after all, does increasing the proportion of Hispanics and Asian Americans right the wrong of past discrimination against blacks? For minority groups that make up a sufficiently small proportion of, say, the population of available contractors, a requirement of group-specific discrimination data will be fatal.[20] To divide, for such cases, is in fact to conquer.

What about the fine-tuning of group definitions themselves—of the categories "Asian American" or "Hispanic"—the internal diversity of which we can now clearly see (chapter 3)? Courts are certainly aware of the social implications of their definitional task. As one court observed: "The most troubling facet of defining a group who have been the victim of prior discrimination is the derivation of the definition itself. . . . Because of the irrationality of the definitional process underlying social stereotypes, it is equally vexatious to develop a definition, or to criticize one that has been developed, without resort to the same stereotypes which application of the definition seeks to eradicate."[21] That being said, courts must decide the cases before them—and the issue raised in the quoted opinion was the constitutional validity of a definition of "Hispanic" that the city had borrowed from the Equal Employment Opportunity Commission. The EEOC's definition includes "all persons of Mexican, Puerto Rican, Cuban, Central or South American, or other Spanish culture of origin, regardless of race" and provides as well that included individuals must manifest "cultural and linguistic identification" with their heritage. It was attacked as both underinclusive (why include Argentinians and not Brazilians—why *Spanish* language rather than South American origin?) and overinclusive (why should Argentinians or Chileans benefit from the fact that Miami's large Cuban population has suffered discrimination?). The court's answer—after expressing its above-quoted frustration at having to answer the question—was that "prejudice against a group identified as Hispanics has existed which transcends the bounds of race and national origin." But there is no guarantee that such a decision will continue to hold force as social perception of intra-category differences—aided, perhaps, by social science—becomes more sharply defined.

The example of affirmative action in India (chapter 12) suggests just how much is at stake in these issues of group definition. What the Indian example shows is that much of the conflict over affirmative action is generated by the demands of those among the affirmative action ineligibles whose situation most resembles that of the affirmative action eligibles.[22] Suppose the eligibility line is drawn, say, between Cubans and Argentinians in Miami. If there is any truth to the court's notion that Hispanics in general face *some* discrimination in America, then Argentinians in Miami are likely to be worse off than non-Argentinian whites—even if they are less worse off than Cubans—and therefore likely to lose out to Cubans given a boost through affirmative action.

This may seem uncomfortably hypothetical, but there is one well-known case whose less-well-known facts present many of the perplexities of inter-minority competition and minority-group definition. That case is *Podberesky v. Kirwan*,[23] in which the United States Court of Appeals invalidated the University of Maryland's Banneker scholarship program for African Americans. *Podberesky* is known for its holding, not for its ethnically enticing facts and arguments. But it is indicative of the complexity of litigation to come.

The plaintiff, Daniel Podberesky, is identified in the opinion as "Hispanic." His grades and test scores would have qualified him for a Banneker but were short of the mark for a general merit scholarship (called the Key scholarship). He successfully challenged the use of race in reserving Bannekers for African Americans. That claim could have been made by any white person, of whatever national origin. What Podberesky *also* claimed in the district court—unsuccessfully—was that the university should have given special consideration to Hispanics under the Key program. The court observed, and rightly so, that this demand for special treatment for Hispanics was rather inconsistent with Podberesky's insistence that the Bannekers be race-neutral—and left it at that.[24] But it seems that Podberesky's real complaint was that special treatment was being given to blacks *but not to Hispanics.*

The pre-*Podberesky* history of the Banneker program illustrates what is at stake for African Americans in the drawing of eligibility lines. As originally adopted in 1978, the Banneker program was open to all racial minorities. At some point, nonblacks (most likely Asian Americans, if national patterns can be trusted) came to predominate, and the U.S. Department of Education insisted that the program be changed to more directly benefit African Americans. It is important to move beyond the "black-white binary paradigm" (Perea 1997) that has traditionally framed American race discrimination law. But it is equally important to recognize that when all members of minority groups are equally eligible for affirmative action, the best-off among them will prevail—and that the likely consequence is that African Americans will lose out.

Black-Hispanic (or Black–Asian American) conflict is not the only inter- and intra-ethnic dimension of the *Podberesky* case. Podberesky complained, in particular, that a Banneker had once been given to a Jamaican—not an American black, for whom we might feel some remedial sympathy.[25] Then again, Podberesky himself presented a complex picture as a "Hispanic." The court did not note (and may not have known) that Podberesky's father is an American-born, non-Hispanic Jewish lawyer and that his mother is an immigrant from Costa Rica or

Ecuador (sources conflict here)[26]—neither, I imagine, countries with a large presence or history of discrimination in the state of Maryland. His level of performance—high enough to comfortably outscore the other Banneker applicants, but not high enough to compete on equal terms with non-Hispanic whites for the Key scholarship—might well relate to his being part-Hispanic, and it might not. But his plea for something resembling a sliding scale of affirmative action is likely to be widely heard as the law becomes more sensitive to the definitional problems the social scientists already see. The best-off members of tradition-ally excluded groups (whether their status is due to their relatively-privileged national origin or to their mixed parentage) are not likely to be happy if the law leaves them to fend for themselves in open competi-tion against whites.

Narrow tailoring and race-neutral alternatives. Public universities that are no longer permitted to use race-based affirmative action (whether be-cause of court rulings, state constitutional amendments, or internal restric-tions) are experimenting with race-neutral alternative programs. Examples include the class-based affirmative action program designed by UCLA Law School and the state of Texas's decision to admit the top 10 percent of Texas high school graduates into the Texas system's flagship undergradu-ate institutions.[27] The results of these programs (which vary, both year to year and from program to program) have significant implications for constitutional litigation in jurisdictions which have not yet abandoned race-based affirmative action altogether.

With increasing zeal, courts are following the cues laid down by the Supreme Court in *Croson*[28] by using the "narrow tailoring" stage of constitutional strict scrutiny analysis to condition the use of affirmative action in hiring and contracting on the prior exploration of race-neutral alternatives. As one court put it, "Supreme Court decisions teach that a race-conscious remedy is not merely one of many equally acceptable medications the government may use to treat a race-based problem. Instead, it is the strongest of medicines, with many potentially harmful side-effects, and must be reserved for those severe cases that are highly resistant to conventional treatment."[29]

It is not yet clear whether courts will take the same approach in higher education cases, where Justice Powell's opinion in *Bakke* stands as an example of a court taking at face value a university's insistence that no race-neutral alternatives would produce the desired level of diversity. There is every reason to expect that the active consideration of race-neutral alternatives will travel across legal domains, however, because the question of whether affirmative action is in fact necessary is at the very heart of the concept of narrow tailoring.

If *Bakke*'s stress on the discretion of universities to pursue their educational missions is to be taken seriously, it should matter a great deal in higher education cases whether the proposed race-neutral alternatives will do as well as race-based affirmative action to preserve the academic quality of the institution. After all, elite universities could always have used their affirmative action programs to select the most economically disadvantaged minimally qualified minority candidates, or to select the top candidates from every de facto segregated school in the state regardless of the academic quality of the school and the resultant academic training of the candidate. The fact that they have generally opted instead to chose the best-qualified minority candidates, most of whom hail from the minority middle classes (and may well therefore have attended integrated schools where they did not land in the top 10 percent of the class), suggests that universities use affirmative action to attain diversity at the least possible expense to the strength of their academic programs (Malamud 1997a, 1997b). The question of how race-neutral alternatives will be assessed in the educational setting, like so much else in the law of affirmative action, remains an open question for now.

Soft versus hard affirmative action: What is a racial classification? Still another area of complexity concerns the fundamental question of what counts as a governmental "classification" subject to the Equal Protection Clause—or, stated more plainly, what counts as "affirmative action" for legal purposes. Several of the essays in this volume distinguish between "soft" and "hard" affirmative action (chapters 2, 8, and 10), and public support in the United States is stronger for the former (such as targeted outreach and training, broad recruitment) than for the latter (such as preferential hiring) (chapter 8).[30] If the government conducts (or insists that private actors conduct) outreach and recruitment efforts for women or specified minority groups, but does not insist on preferential selection of female or minority candidates, is there a governmental "classification" at all? If there is one, does it trigger the same level of scrutiny as would a full-blown preferential-selection plan?

Whereas Teles shows that the British would disagree, the American constitutional case law as it now stands suggests strongly that the line between "soft" and "hard" is not always easy to see. Take as an example the government contracting program at issue in *Adarand*. That program did not in fact require federal contractors to select minority contractors.

It merely tied financial incentives to their selection, up to a stated proportional goal. Is such an incentives program soft or hard—or somewhere in between? As a subsequent court noted, "although it was urged that such 'goals' should be treated differently than obligatory set-asides, the majority did not even pause to consider this argument."[31] If financial incentives are hard, are there other kinds of incentives that might be soft? What if failure to show progress or to meet minority selection targets leads only to administrative burdens (as opposed to financial sanctions)? What if there are financial sanctions, but they can be avoided by a showing of good-faith efforts? Courts are beginning to explore these issues, in both the hiring and government contracting and licensing contexts. The results do not bode well for those who would seek to design soft but effective programs in the American setting.

A recently emerging line of cases challenging outreach and recruitment measures is converging on the view that there is a "racial classification" subject to strict scrutiny whenever the government "induces an employer to hire with an eye toward meeting the numerical target."[32] This has been the approach taken, for example, to a complex Federal Communications Commission program under which the minority hiring of radio stations is closely monitored and failure to meet targets (set generally at 50 percent of minority labor market availability and at 25 percent for higher-level job classifications) triggers an FCC employment audit.[33] A similar approach was taken to hiring guidelines issued by the New Jersey Casino Commission for casinos it Atlantic City, where the court held that "We are convinced . . . that in setting employment goals for women and minorities, in monitoring compliance with these goals, and in providing for sanctions if casino licensees cannot demonstrate good faith efforts to comply with those goals, the regulations were intended to influence employment decisions generally and may, as here, affect concrete decisions; for example, which of two equally qualified job candidates will be hired."[34] To be sure, the programs at issue in these cases do more than simply call for aggressive outreach and recruitment. They monitor results. But they do so based on governmental experience that truly soft programs—programs that neither monitor nor tie consequences to results—do not generate sufficiently rapid changes in workforce composition—sufficiently rapid, that is, from the government's standpoint.[35]

There are only certain limited circumstances in which aggressive outreach can be expected to lead to rapid change. Outreach will produce rapid results when there are in fact women and minorities who could meet standard job or contracting qualifications, if only they knew the opportunities were available.[36] If the only problem facing women and minorities were "old boy" networks that limited access to information, outreach would be a fine solution. To the extent, however, that the problem runs deeper to include the concrete effects of past discrimination in economic opportunities and education, outreach alone cannot be expected to produce large numbers of acceptable candidates. Think of the now-standard image of two runners, one black, one white; the black runner has lived with his ankles shackled all his life; and the moment before the race begins, the shackles are removed and he is proclaimed to now have an equal chance to win the race. Limiting affirmative action to outreach and recruitment would be to change that image in only one respect: we would now commit ourselves to search far and wide—not merely through our usual recruitment channels—to find those especially talented blacks who could win the race. Why would we expect to find many that could? If we went further, and offered specialized training exclusively to the black runner before the race started, would that still be considered a soft program? Or would a concrete benefit now be allocated on the basis of race, fully subject to strict scrutiny? Again, that question remains to be examined by the courts.[37]

Title VII of the Civil Rights Act of 1964

Our consideration thus far has been of the status of affirmative action under the Constitution. It is important to recognize, however, that private employment has been a leading locus for voluntary affirmative action,[38] and that Title VII of the Civil Rights Act of 1964 governs private-sector affirmative action in employment.[39] As we have seen, employers in the private sector have broadly embraced the concept of diversity. Yet the Supreme Court has yet to hold that diversity is a permissible justification for affirmative action under Title VII.

The lead Supreme Court Title VII cases on affirmative action, *Steelworkers v. Weber*[40] (a race/ethnicity case) and *Johnson v. Santa Clara County*[41] (a gender case) set forth the governing legal standard. Unlike under the Constitution, the standard is the same for race or ethnicity and for gender. Under these decisions, employers are permitted to use affirmative action to correct a "manifest imbalance" in a traditionally segregated job category. The "manifest imbalance" need not be at a level sufficient to prove a prima facie case of discrimination, and the "segregation" of the job category need not be caused by the employer's own discrimination. In addition, the program must have as its goal to "attain" rather than "maintain" improved racial or gender balance, it must be temporary (meaning, in practice, that its goals must be sufficiently modest to be attainable within a reasonable period of time), and it must be designed so as not to unduly "trammel" the rights of non-beneficiaries.

But what of diversity? One might think that any time an employer needed to rely on affirmative action to attain diversity, it would be able to show a manifest imbalance in a traditionally segregated job category. But that is not true. In *Taxman*,[42] a New Jersey school district unsuccessfully defended its use of affirmative action in a decision to lay off a white teacher and retain an equally qualified and equally senior black teacher on diversity grounds. Even leaving aside the layoff issue—the Supreme Court had never embraced the use of affirmative action for layoffs under Title VII and had soundly rejected it under the Constitution[43]—the case was a factual nightmare. Black teachers were not underrepresented either in the school district or at the particular high school at issue, and there was thus no claim that affirmative action was necessary to correct a "manifest imbalance" in the *Weber* and *Johnson* sense. The problem was that laying off the black teacher would leave the school's small Business department without a black teacher. The *Taxman* court was unconvinced that diversity was a valid ground for affirmative action under Title VII.

Taxman governs in only three states (New Jersey, Delaware, and Pennsylvania), but it is certainly suggestive that employers relying on diversity as a rationale for preferential selection need to be very careful. This is particularly the case where race is at issue. Although the *Weber/Johnson* standard does not distinguish between race and gender, Title VII does distinguish discrimination on the basis of race and color from all other covered forms of discrimination in one important respect. Race cannot be a "bona fide occupational qualification" (BFOQ) for employment. *Weber* upheld race-based affirmative action notwithstanding the BFOQ provision. But using race-based affirmative action to correct manifest imbalances does not come as close to a BFOQ rationale as does using race-based affirmative action because an employer's own operational needs make it useful to have racial diversity in its workforce.[44] The BFOQ provision is not controlling, but it is suggestive that diversity may have a rough road ahead in Title VII cases.

Ethnic Niches

What Is an "Ethnic Niche"?

The term *ethnic niche* is generally used to mean a workforce in which immigrants from one country predominate, usually as a result of the use of informal word-of-mouth networks to fill job vacancies. In the purest ethnic niche cases, the business is owned by an immigrant and the employees are immigrants from the employer's group. By fairly natural extension, the term is extended to workplaces whose employers draw on several immigrant ethnic networks, resulting in the hiring of significant numbers of workers from several ethnic communities.

Ethnic job niches have existed for decades. For example, the Jewish-owned garment factories on the Lower East Side of Manhattan at the turn of the century, in which thousands of Eastern European immigrants gained their initial economic foothold in this country, would certainly fit the description of an ethnic niche—as, eventually, would the New York City teacher's union. But the potential application of modern antidiscrimination laws to ethnic niche hiring practices has gained public attention only in the last several years because of highly-criticized lawsuits the EEOC has filed on behalf of African Americans in cases like *EEOC v. Consolidated Service Systems*[45] (involving exclusive hiring of Koreans by a Korean-owned janitorial services company, as reflected in the absence of African Americans in the workforce).

Challenges to ethnic niches are controversial because they pit the interests of enterprising immigrants against those of African Americans. It seems absurd and unfair to many white descendants of immigrants to change the rules of the game for the new immigrants arriving in this country. Then again, it seems absurd and unfair to many African Americans and their allies to place the interests of new immigrants ahead of those of a people that has struggled in this country for a century to overcome the legacy of slavery. (See chapter 2 for the implications of broadening affirmative action eligibility at a time of broadened immigration.)

Another type of workplace ought also be treated as creating one or more "ethnic niches," but is rarely recognized as such. Employers create ethnic niches when they effectively reserve a particular type of job for members of a particular minority group. Sometimes the niche jobs consist of the lowest-tier jobs in the company, with the better jobs going to white workers. For example, in *Wards Cove Packing Co. v. Atonio*,[46] the job of "cannery worker" (meaning nonsupervisory jobs on the cannery line) was reserved for Asian American workers under the long-standing traditions of the industry, and filled by this particular employer by using the hiring hall of a Filipino American union local. These sorts of ethnic niches have existed for as long as segregation and social hierarchy have existed in this country. While challenges to them can take the form of outsiders from lower-status groups trying to break into the niche, jobs of this sort are undesirable enough that legal action is far more likely to be brought by niche employees trying to move out of the niche into the better jobs the employer reserves for whites (as was the case in *Wards Cove*, where the challenge was unsuccessful).

Reserved-job ethnic niches are not always workplaces in which only the very worst jobs are reserved for minority-group members. When ethnic niches are created by employers who desire to improve their political, market, and service relationships with members of minority communities, the resulting jobs can be of reasonably high quality. Examples include hiring blacks to police black communities, to counsel black university students, to sell goods and services to black customers, and to staff equal-employment-opportunity and public-relations offices in the corporate sector. Given the desirability of some of these higher-level ethnic niche jobs, whites can be expected to compete for them and sue when they are disappointed. Lawsuits are also occasionally brought by members of minority groups who have been stymied in their efforts to secure promotions to better jobs outside of the ethnic niche or who have been fired because the employer's needs for niche personnel have diminished.

In using the term *ethnic niche* to describe all of these situations, I am claiming that they have some things fundamentally in common. The commonalities are twofold. First, in all of these cases, employers restrict hiring to members of a particular group because they find it useful to do so. *Useful* means different things in different cases—for example, "cheap" or "comfortable" or "keeps my customers happy" or "keeps my employees safe." *Restrict* also has a range of meanings—such as "do nothing and only the right ethnics will come" or "if blacks show up, find some way not to hire them" or "assert a BFOQ and hope we can convince a court if we're challenged." But those differences are overshadowed by the common feature, which is that niche employers understand themselves as benefiting from placing race or ethnicity at the center of their hiring. Second, in all of these cases, employers perpetuate segregation—regardless of whether they do so at the level of the enterprise as a whole or by limiting minorities to those jobs within the enterprise that are labeled as niche jobs.

By asserting the commonalities among all ethnic niche situations, I also mean to suggest that the pervasiveness and public acceptance of one type of ethnic niche has the potential to influence public and legal attitudes towards the others. This is not a matter of ideology, so much as it is a matter of epistemology. Bobo (chapter 8) is persuasive in arguing that interest group considerations ("I care about the interests of blacks, so I disapprove of the Korean janitorial niche but approve of the hiring of blacks for diversity purposes") are more important than ideological considerations ("I believe in color-blindness, regardless of whose ox is gored by it") in shaping opinion in this field. But my proposition is not grounded on the expectation that people strive for ideological consistency. Instead, its basis is the uncontroversial observation (if there can be such a thing) that our experiences shape our expectations. If we routinely see race and ethnicity mattering to large corporations following a diversity management approach (as described in chapter 4), we come to accept that race and ethnicity matter and therefore see little reason to complain that race and ethnicity also matter to small business owners. If it becomes natural to think that jobs created by immigrant businesses "belong to" members of the owner's ethnic group, it becomes harder to question the notion that other jobs (like policing or counseling blacks) are also ethnic property. If we stress employer utility and downplay the rights of individual job seekers in one ethnic niche situation, it becomes difficult to subordinate employer utility to individual rights in the others.

What Is the Legal Status of Ethnic Niches?

Title VII of the Civil Rights Act of 1964 makes it unlawful to "fail or refuse to hire or to discharge an individual, or otherwise to discriminate against any individual with respect to his compensation, terms, conditions, or privileges of employment"[47] or to "limit, segregate, or classify . . . employees or applicants for employment in any way which would deprive or tend to deprive any individual or employment opportunities or otherwise adversely affect his status as an employee,"[48] because of the individual's race, color, religion, sex, or national origin. As Title VII practice has evolved, cases are evaluated under a number of judge-created proof structures that have not merely grown out of the language of the statute, but have supplanted it to a significant extent. Employment practices are sorted into those that are "intentionally" discriminatory (with "intent" subject to proof through a number of judge-made proof structures) and those that are facially neutral but have discriminatory effects on a protected group and are not justified by business necessity (called "disparate impact" cases).[49] There is no proof structure for dealing with segregation per se.

Intentional discrimination. For present purposes, there are two relevant types of intentional discrimination cases—for which I will use the nontechnical terms *covert* and *overt*. Covert intentional discrimination takes place when the employer considers race or ethnicity in its employment decisions but denies doing so. Overt intentional discrimination cases are those in which the employer admits that its decisionmaking was facially discriminatory but claims that its discrimination was legally justified. There can be no doubt that much of the observed segregation in and between American workplaces is of the covert sort, but the most attention-getting intentional discrimination in the ethnic-niche context is overt, and I shall restrict my comments on intentional discrimination here to overt discrimination.

The first-line standard defense for overt discrimination is to claim that membership in the preferred group is a bona fide occupational qualification (BFOQ). Most of the overtly discriminatory practices that this volume show to be commonplace in ethnic niche employment are not defensible as BFOQs.

First and foremost, the BFOQ provision in Title VII plainly provides that race and color cannot be a BFOQ. Most of my students find this fact about current American law totally absurd. It is, after all, the BFOQ defense that justifies hiring only female actors to play the role of women; the absence of a BFOQ for race or color would thus seem to require race-blind casting for all theatrical productions. Even students who can see the merits of race-blind casting of Shakespeare plays (a common practice in theater nowadays) tend not to extend their acceptance of the practice to more modern texts or media. Acceptance breaks down entirely when the discussion turns to casting a film about the civil rights movement, in which the Rev. Martin Luther King Jr. must certainly be African American and George Wallace must certainly be white for the story to work. And there are other cases in which real life resembles theater—the classic hypothetical being the undercover cop sent in to infiltrate an all-black gang, who must surely be (or look) black in order to survive.

As a practical matter, niche-outsiders simply do not file lawsuits to break into the kinds of jobs in which race or color seem most obviously to be BFOQs. The issue is far more likely to be discussed when blacks seek promotion or transfer to jobs outside of the niche and the employer claims a legal entitlement to keep them inside it. Most of these discussions have taken the form of "dicta"—discussions that turn out not to be necessary for resolution of the case. And the courts, in dicta, have struggled to wriggle their way out of the lack of a race BFOQ by ignoring the BFOQ provision and acting as though "business necessity" is available as a defense.[50] That strategy was eliminated in 1991, first by the Supreme Court[51] and then by Congress,[52] and no other strategy has taken its place.[53]

Even where the BFOQ defense is available—as is the case for national origin—it is quite narrow.[54] The fact that customers prefer being served by members of their own group is not sufficient to make group membership a BFOQ. For group membership to be a BFOQ, it must be "reasonably necessary to the normal operation of the particular business,"[55] and employers are not free to claim that their "particular business" is provision of a generally available service or product in a way calculated to appeal to a particular sector of the broader market. Southwest Airlines made such a claim years ago when it decided to market itself as the "Love Airline"—flying from Love Airport in Houston, dressing its (all-female) flight attendants in hot pants, calling drinks and peanuts "love potions" and "love bites." It learned the hard way that its "particular business" was and remained the provision of transportation services, and not, as it claimed, the provision of a sexually titillating flight environment to male business passengers.[56] Although not quite so colorful as Southwest's efforts, most of the ethnic-niche techniques of matching the workforce to the customer base look far more like forbidden catering to customer preference than like legitimate grounds for declaring national origin a BFOQ.

Just as customer preference is not the basis for a BFOQ defense, nor is co-worker preference. To see why this must be the case, one need only think of how many employers in the South could have made the argument in the 1960s that employees would be unhappy (and less productive as a result) if workplaces became integrated. Lichter and Waldinger (chapter 6) make a valuable contribution by detailing the many ways in which tensions between African Americans and members of other minority groups can interfere with workplace productivity. But Congress expected employers to work their way through the problem when the tensions were between blacks and whites, and changing the cast of characters would not seem to make any difference in that legal judgment.

Nor can these practices be defended as part of an affirmative action plan—at least not under existing Supreme Court decisions. Affirmative action under Title VII, as approved of by the Supreme Court in the past, has involved the development of formal plans. Neither the ad hoc exercise of hiring preferences in favor of members of minority groups nor the use of the racial and ethnic composition of a targeted customer base to determine the appropriate level of minority representation constitutes an affirmative action plan under Title VII standards.

We see, then, that the overt intentional discrimination that underlies the creation of ethnic niches is largely illegal under federal law. The question, then, is why it is so pervasive. The fact that ethnic-niche businesses tend to be small and that the smallest businesses in this country are not covered by Title VII is not a sufficient explanation. In New York, California, and Pennsylvania—the states studied by Lee and by Lichter and Waldinger—state and municipal fair employment practice statutes cover employers with very few employees, and their provisions are similar to those of Title VII in relevant respects. Explanation must be sought elsewhere. I shall offer a number of possibilities here, with the understanding that most of them are speculative and are offered as suggestions for future empirical research.

First of all, the facially discriminatory practices at issue here involve *hiring*. Although hiring decisions are covered by antidiscrimination laws to the same extent as are termination decisions, evidence shows that employers are far less likely to be sued over their hiring decisions (Donohue and Siegelman 1991). Litigation is expensive and time-consuming. People apply for (or are frustrated in attempts to apply for) numerous jobs, and have less of a stake in whether they are hired by any one employer than they do in whether their (only) current employer discriminates against them. People also tend to have less knowledge about the hiring patterns of employers they do not work for than they have about the employment practices of their own employer—making lawsuits harder to get off the ground for hiring cases as opposed to other types of employment discrimination cases. Ethnic niche hiring cases are thus a subset of a broader category of cases that are underlitigated.

Although no study has been done of the rate of case filings in ethnic niche hiring disputes, there is good reason to expect that the number is particularly low. Ethnic-niche businesses that hire through informal networks benefit from the fact that outsiders to the niche are largely unaware of the job opportunities inside the niche. Many ethnic-niche jobs are structured or compensated in a way that makes them undesirable to those outside the niche—an issue I will discuss below. And the leading civil rights litigating organizations that have been so instrumental in the development of federal employment discrimination law (groups such as the NAACP Legal Defense Fund and, increasingly, the

ACLU) may themselves be ambivalent about ethnic niches—either because they believe niches are important for the progress of immigrants or because they believe, as I have suggested, that they cannot attack the "bad" ethnic niches without undermining the "good" ones (however they define *good* and *bad* for these purposes). Conservative public interest groups (like the Center for Individual Rights) are interested in affirmative action, but they have not yet started to target the spurious use of BFOQ defenses in ethnic-niche settings.

Another possible explanation for the paucity of legal challenges to facially discriminatory ethnic niche practices is that much of the illegal conduct of the type these essays describe is shielded from the public eye. Certainly the problem of detection accounts for a good measure of underenforcement of legal norms of all sorts, and can be particularly problematic in antidiscrimination law. But one need only read the newspapers for examples of widely publicized employment policies that are arguably illegal under Title VII, but that go forward without legal challenge. Take for example the recent decision by New York City to replace fifty white members of the elite Street Crimes Unit that was responsible for the killing of Amadou Diallo, an unarmed black man, with fifty black and Hispanic officers.[57] In doing so, New York police commissioner Howard Safir was not declaring race a BFOQ for membership in the unit: even after the change, the unit would be 87 percent white. Nor would the replacement of fifty white incumbents with fifty black and Hispanic officers be legally acceptable as an affirmative action plan under existing constitutional or Title VII precedent. (Indeed, the city would have been on shaky legal ground even if it had created fifty new jobs in the unit and reserved them exclusively for minorities—an outcome that has far less visceral impact on whites than does the plan the city adopted.) Yet Mayor Rudolph Giuliani actively sought publicity for his new plan—not something he could have done if he feared an antidiscrimination lawsuit by disgruntled white incumbents. And he was probably right to conclude that his litigation risk is minimal. Why? In the specific case of the Street Crimes unit, there is likely to be great public acceptance of the notion that a unit with greater minority representation would not commit such blatant atrocities against blacks and Latinos. Any individual contemplating a challenge to the policy would likely encounter significant difficulty in finding a committed civil rights lawyer willing to go against so strong a surge of public support for the policy.

Despite the fact that "affirmative action" as such is under attack at present, there seems to be a broad public consensus that it is appropriate to hire members of minority groups to cater to the needs of minorities across a broad spectrum of public and private services. (It is only when minorities are given preferences that are not conditioned on their staying within their niche that diversity management techniques and affirmative action are generally seen as socially problematic.) It has, in fact, become a standard part of the liberal defense of affirmative action in education that minority medical and law school graduates are far more likely than are whites to provide services to minority clients. Segregation is taken as a given in this defense: the fact that programs could be structured to encourage or require whites to provide such services is forgotten. The same is true, even more dramatically, when New York decides that the best way to cure the barbarity of white police officers is to hire minority police officers instead. Thus when judges embrace the "operational needs" defense of race-based hiring, the message is that the cultural differences that separate the white and black communities are so great that they cannot be bridged by proper training. If that it what we believe, it is no accident that ethnic niches are not challenged more frequently and that the challenges are not more successful when brought.

If the consensus that ethnic niches are an inevitable characteristic of our society and labor market can be generalized to the job-applicant population, that fact itself goes a long way towards explaining why niche practices exist despite their illegality. Perhaps out-group applicants for these jobs don't sue because they aren't interested in the job (with "interest" being socially conditioned by reactions such as those I have described), or because they don't feel aggrieved by not getting the job (that is, they are interested in the job but realize they are abberant in their interest and that it's probably best for society in the end that the job go to minorities), or because they don't think anything unlawful has taken place (even if they think it is socially improper). These alternatives have different shades of meaning for the relationship between social conduct and the law, but they all amount to reasons lawsuits do not get filed and the law does not get enforced.

Disparate impact. What of the facially neutral practices that contribute to the ethnic niche phenomenon? We see from several of the essays in this volume how numerous facially neutral employer practices affect the ultimate ethnic composition of the workplace. The difficulty of legally challenging these practices is an important part of the reason ethnic niches persist.

The practice that is most often associated with ethnic-niche hiring is the use of informal ethnic networks rather than on-site hiring or newspaper advertisements to fill vacancies. As these essays note, the courts are actively debating the circumstances under which that practice is subject to legal challenge. Under a disparate impact approach, it is not necessary (in Lichter and Waldinger's terms) that the employers "know[ ] what they are doing": they need not *intend* the racial and ethnic results they obtain through informal hiring networks. But so far, the cases suggest that the more it can be said that the employer is not "doing" *anything*, the better insulated it is from legal challenge. Employers who actively encourage in-group referrals (through bonuses for new employees introduced to the company, for example) face a greater litigation risk.

This volume is particularly valuable to lawyers for bringing to light other practices that are discussed far less often but that also have the effect of producing an ethnically coded workforce. The employers interviewed by Lee and by Lichter and Waldinger suggest that African Americans will not work at wages and in working conditions that are acceptable to recent immigrants. If employers are right,[58] the implication is that employers essentially choose the ethnic composition of their workforce when they determine rates of pay and employment conditions. As Lichter and Waldinger also explain, employers also minimize the likelihood that they will hire and retain African Americans workers by permitting languages other than English to be spoken on the job.[59] Although not discussed in this volume, numerous other nuts-and-bolts decisions help to determine the ethnic composition of the workforce—the most important being the choice of where to locate the business. It is certainly possible that employers make these business decisions precisely because of their known ethnic consequences in mind—subjecting them to possible *intentional* discrimination suits if they are so foolish as to get caught.[60] But under Title VII, employers are supposed to be liable for practices that are *not* intentionally discriminatory but that have a disparate impact on members of protected groups and are not justified by business necessity. We should therefore expect to see disparate impact challenges to these kinds of decisions. But we do not—just as we do not see challenges to many of the facially discriminatory practices that sustain ethnic niches.

Would challenges to these sorts of practices likely succeed under the disparate impact proof structure? Probably not. As James Atleson (1983) has explained in his important critique of American labor law, American courts are tremendously protective of the prerogative of management to determine the shape of its business. Certainly management power is subject to legal constraint. American labor law requires employers to negotiate with duly elected unions over wages and working conditions, and Title VII bars employers from discriminating against members of protected groups in wages and working conditions. But the willingness of the courts to read the antidiscrimination provisions of Title VII broadly is shaped by their retained conservative sense that Title VII is a limited restriction of what is a retained management right to run the business. Stated a different way, courts are not likely to apply disparate impact analysis to fundamental business decisions unless they are deeply enough disturbed by their effects to be willing to substantially unsettle their own background expectations about the reach of Title VII. In general, courts are not sufficiently disturbed by ethnic niches to take that step.

Courts are reluctant to use disparate impact analysis to upset ethnic niches for another reason as well. There is an increasing tendency in the courts to view the disparate impact cause of action as a tool that ought to be reserved for circumstances in which there is reason to believe that impermissible intentional discrimination is taking place.[61] It may well be that courts view the immigrant-business ethnic niche as so natural and normal that it is unlikely to be the product of intentional discrimination, or that they do not view "own-preferences" as being as dangerous as "other-aversions" (see chapter 6). Or it may simply be the case that courts are so committed to these ethnic niches as part of the ongoing success story of American immigration that they are unwilling to use the powerful tool of disparate impact litigation to dismantle them.

The fact that the law has done so little to root out the facially neutral practices that create and maintain ethnic niches has implications for the enforcement of the laws against intentional discrimination that are plainly applicable to ethnic niches. If facially neutral business decisions that are not (or not yet) subject to Title VII challenge are perpetuating a labor market in which racial and ethnic segregation is an everyday occurrence, then labor market segregation continues to be accepted as natural and normal. The segregation caused by intentional discrimination does not stand out as clearly as it otherwise would; it just becomes another thread in the segregated fabric of American life. And segregation, which we still claim to reject in principle, becomes ever more accepted as fact.

"Absurdities" Revisited

Is it absurd or anachronistic, in light of these observations, for Title VII to apply with full force to new immigrant businesses? I think not.

It is certainly true that new immigrant businesses are burdened by layers of legal regulation of their labor relations that were lacking when earlier generations of immigrants came to this country. But why are the anti-discrimination laws of the 1960s less important (or less presumptively relevant) to these business than are the other labor laws from which immigrant businesses can claim no legal immunity? Surely immigrant businesses would be more successful if they did not have to pay workers' compensation and unemployment compensation and overtime and the minimum wage. But that has not convinced us to ask about whether *these* laws are anachronistic because of the multiethnic nature of American society.

Perhaps the difference is that the immigrant workers themselves are the beneficiaries of enforcement of these other labor laws, whereas members of excluded minority groups (chiefly African Americans) are the beneficiaries of Title VII enforcement. But that overstates the contrast. If enforcement of wage and hour laws (and other nondiscrimination-related labor statutes) raises labor costs, fewer immigrants can start businesses and fewer immigrant workers will be hired. This means that the benefit to "immigrants" from better working conditions is unevenly distributed: some new immigrants get better jobs, while others get no jobs. If enforcement of antidiscrimination laws diversifies the workforce in immigrant businesses, fewer immigrants will work inside the former ethnic niche. Some of those immigrants will search harder for (better) jobs outside the niche and will obtain them. Some will remain unemployed. But those who remain inside the former niche will benefit from the presence of the outsiders. The outsiders may bring with them greater knowledge of the rights of American workers and greater willingness to challenge the owner's employment policies due to the absence of the bond of ethnic solidarity. And the contact across cultural lines may well speed the immigrants along to the development of skills and contacts that will lead to better jobs in the broader economy. The costs and benefits story is thus a complex one, and does not account for the difference.

Is it absurd or anachronistic for Title VII to maintain its strong stance against BFOQ defenses for race and color discrimination? Again, I think not. Congress was certainly aware that there are circumstances—such as theatrical authenticity—in which race genuinely is a BFOQ. But Congress fundamentally did not trust American society of the 1960s to keep a race BFOQ a narrow one. Can we be trusted to do so now? I do not think so. We are less likely now than we were in 1964 to say that *whiteness* is a BFOQ for serving the white community.

But we are, in fact, more likely now than we were in 1964 to say that only blacks can deliver core services (be they teaching and counseling or policing and incarceration) to the black community. Increasingly, similar claims are made about Latinos and Asians. That is a dangerous path if integration remains the desired goal. Sometimes it is better to keep an absolutist rule in place, and to trust common sense to be the guarantor against the filing of insane lawsuits (like the hypothetical suit, never filed to the best of my knowledge, by the white cop who wants to try to infiltrate the hypothetical all-black gang—or by the white actor who insists on being cast as Dr. King). At least that way the employers who keep black employees in their niche-defined places because that is where they are the most "useful" will have less reason to believe that the law endorses their view that the law's central concern is their utility—rather than minority employees' rights.

This is not to say that we should revert to color- and ethnicity-blindness as the only acceptable stance under Title VII. We should, however, recognize that legalization of the forms of color-consciousness we endorse also tends to make it more difficult to abolish the forms of color-consciousness we abhor. The correct stance in light of the double-edgedness of color-consciousness is to exercise genuine, legally reviewable care in the use of color-conscious employment strategies. Make the employers who genuinely believe that their jobs can only be done by members of a particular racial or ethnic group think very carefully about that judgment, as they only do when there is considerable risk that a court will decide they were wrong. If that is our stance, we should continue to distinguish between genuine affirmative action plans and ad hoc racial preferences, and between BFOQ and customer preference. Anything less promotes segregation by dressing it in the garb of diversity.

Conclusion

I began this chapter with the observation that the gap between American law and American multiethnic reality does not necessarily mean that the law must do all the changing. In the field of affirmative action, it is too soon to tell whether the reawakening of litigation and political activity will result in pervasive legal change. A few things are, however, certain. Affirmative action will continue to be drawn out from the cloak of darkness under which it has operated for so long and will be subject to highly fact-specific inquiry in the courts. Social science will play a crucial role in the current wave of affirmative action litigation and politics—whether its contribution is to provide expert testimony on the need for diversity in higher education or to provide advice to pollsters and activists on how the framing of questions about affirmative action shapes the results of polls and popular initiatives. And the multiethnic and immigrant nature of American society will play an increasingly important role in the affirmative action debate.

The social forces described in this volume all point toward the need for American judges to move beyond the "black-white binary paradigm" out of which our civil rights laws grew. I wish to suggest that urging the legal system to move beyond that stale and outdated paradigm is dangerous if it means that judges will no longer focus on the needs of the beleaguered African American community. Lichter and Waldinger are right when they say that history points immigrants "to the advantages of adopting the Euro-American prejudice against African-Americans." Judges need to remember that new immigrants' exclusion of blacks and whites' oppression of blacks are related phenomena, that permitting the former perpetuates the latter, and that both may have the same end result.

Notes

1. See Hochschild 1999, 345: "Americans' elaborate and sophisticated legal and normative debate about the legitimacy, desirability, and impact of affirmative action has taken place in something close to a factual vacuum."

2. The Fourteenth Amendment applies by its terms only to the states, but the Fifth Amendment, which applies to the federal government, has been held implicitly to include in its Due Process Clause protections coextensive with those of the Equal Protection Clause. Constitutional standards generally apply only to governmental actors, but they are also applied to some private entities deemed to be "state actors." Most significantly for our purposes, constitutional standards govern the actions of private universities receiving federal funds.

3. *City of Richmond v. J. A. Croson Co.*, 488 U.S. 469 (1989); *Adarand Constructors, Inc. v. Pena*, 515 U.S. 200 (1995). Race and ethnicity are recognized in the social and biological sciences as imprecise and contestable terms but are nonetheless routine terms in legal discourse.

4. This is subject to some dispute in the case law, but the better-reasoned cases come out on the side of intermediate scrutiny.

5. The intermediate scrutiny standard was restated to an extent in the VMI case, *United States v. Virginia*, 518 U.S. 515 (1996), where the Court held that the explanation must be "exceedingly persuasive." But as the court explained in *Engineering Contractors Ass'n of South Florida v. Metropolitan Dade County*, 122 F.3d 895 (11th Cir. 1997), the VMI majority continued to use the traditional formulation as well. For the argument that the

"exceedingly persuasive" standard lies somewhere between traditional intermediate scrutiny and strict scrutiny, see Skaggs 1998.

6. Courts are aware of the irony: see, e.g., *Ensley Branch, NAACP v. City of Birmingham*, 31 F.3d 1548 (11th Cir. 1994): "While it may seem odd that it is now easier to uphold affirmative action programs for women than for racial minorities, Supreme Court precedent compels that result."

7. There is no doubt that white women have benefited from affirmative action, but to take the next step and say, as many do, that women (or, even stronger, *white* women) have been the *major* beneficiaries of affirmative action (see, e.g., Delgado 1998; Strossen 1997), would seem to require more empirical support than is offered for the proposition. Lawrence and Matsuda (1997), for example, make the claim (167) based on a single study of public-sector affirmative action in the state of Washington that hardly unambiguously supports their claim (Washington State Commission on African American Affairs 1995–96). The part of the Washington study that deals with employment seems to suggest, for example, that women of color most often received additional consideration under the program, followed by Vietnam veterans, and only then followed by white women. The part of the study that focuses on higher education contains no gender breakdown at all. In any event, it concerns not "affirmative action" in the conventional race- and gender-conscious sense, but all "alternative admissions" of students below a specified combination of grades and test scores. Schools designate a broad range of purposes for alternative admissions candidates, including parental socioeconomic status and the needs of the institution (one supposes that athletes and bassoonists come in here). In the study of government contracting, "participation by white women lagged that for minorities in 1992 and 1994. In 1994, however, white-women-owned firms garnered only 4.37 percent . . . of the participation base while minority-owned firms garnered only 4.18 percent." The study is thus hardly a basis for claiming that women are the primary beneficiaries of "affirmative action" in Washington.

Even at the intuitive level, the strong claim is not obviously correct. Certainly there are more women than minorities in the United States. But affirmative action has played different roles for women than for minorities. In the early years of affirmative action, blacks were the EEOC's major concern, and early uses of affirmative action were significant in opening up large numbers of unskilled manufacturing jobs to blacks. Similarly, in the field of undergraduate admissions, affirmative action was a major tool for the integration of college campuses. It is doubtful that women will enter traditionally male skilled crafts, for example, in anywhere near the numbers that blacks entered unskilled manufacturing jobs in affirmative action's early years. And women have not been major beneficiaries of affirmative action in college admissions. Even where women have benefited from affirmative action, one would want to know, when making the strong claim, whether women received as significant a competitive boost from affirmative action as did blacks. Thus, the fact that women outnumber minorities takes one only part of the way.

8. See, e.g., *Ensley Branch*, note 6 above, where the court held that "one of the distinguishing features of intermediate scrutiny is that, unlike strict scrutiny, the government interest prong can be satisfied by a showing of societal discrimination in the relevant economic sector."

9. Only if the program applied to *all* businesses owned or managed by the economically disadvantaged, regardless of race, ethnicity, or gender, would it be subject to rationality review and be almost be assured a legal green light.

10. See, e.g., *Milwaukee County Pavers Ass'n v. Fiedler*, 922 F.2d 419 (7th Cir. 1991), where the state failed to make the argument for intermediate scrutiny. One cannot tell whether this was an oversight or a strategy, however.

11. There are of course also affirmative action cases that do not fit into any of these domains. Examples include the use of affirmative action for *secondary* school admissions, *Wessmann v. Gittens*, 160 F.3d 790 (1st Cir. 1998), and for the setting of salaries on university faculties, see, e.g., *Maitland v. University of Minnesota*, 155 F.3d 1013 (8th Cir. 1998).

12. *Hopwood v. Texas*, 78 F.3d 932 (5th Cir. 1996).

13. *Regents of the University of California v. Bakke*, 438 U.S. 265 (1978).

14. *Adarand Constructors v. Pena*, 515 U.S. 200 (1995).

15. This issue was left open in the Court's opinion in *Wygant v. Jackson Board of Education*, 476 U.S. 267 (1986). As Justice O'Connor there notes, the diversity justification was not raised in *Wygant* and the word *diversity* doesn't appear in the majority opinion.

16. *Wittmer v. Peters*, 87 F.3d 916 (7th Cir. 1996). See also *Patrolmen's Benevolent Ass'n of New York City v. City of New York*, 74 F. Supp. 2d 321 (S.D.N.Y. 1999) (using operational needs approach in case involving involuntary transfer of black police officers to district in which Abner Louima had been sexually assaulted by white police officers).

17. *Hill v. Ross*, 183 F.3d 586, 591–92 (1999). The analysis goes on to drive the statistical point home in great detail.

18. The issues discussed here are also at times dealt with as going to the question of whether the government has a "compelling interest" in remedying discrimination against the group in question.

19. *Alexander v. Estepp*, 95 F.3d 312 (4th Cir. 1996).

20. *Contractors Ass'n of Eastern Pennsylvania v. City of Philadelphia*, 6 F.3d 990 (3d Cir. 1993) (finding that Asian American and Hispanic contractors constitute only .27 percent of the city's pool of contractors, and holding that the fact that such a small percentage of firms received no contracts "does not rise to the 'significant statistical disparity' *Croson* requires").

21. *Peightal v. Metropolitan Dade County*, 26 F.3d 1545 (11th Cir. 1994).

22. Parikh argues that "the most intense conflict is at the Mandal dividing line. The lowest high castes are pitted against the highest OBCs. In Bihar, this means that the main conflict is between the Yadavs and the poorer among the Rajputs and Bhumihars. The lower OBCs and the richer high castes are interested, but they are less engaged. . . . It is important to bear in mind that the groups closest to the Mandal dividing line probably share more in common with each other than with the more extreme members of their own side."

23. *Podberesky v. Kirwan*, 38 F.3d 147 (4th Cir. 1994).

24. "Baffling" and "all but paradoxical" were the words used by the district court. 764 F. Supp. 364, 377 (D. Md. 1991).

25. As the court noted with some sarcasm, "The University gives African-American a hemispheric meaning."

26. For the claim that Podberesky's mother was from Ecuador, see Chang and Culp 1997. For the claim that his mother was from Costa Rica and that he grew up in a comfortable all-white community, see Rodriguez 1994. Both sources (and numerous others) identify his father as Jewish. The legal scholar Michael Olivas is quoted in Rodriguez 1994 as saying that "Podberesky is only nominally a Latino."

27. For an exchange on the UCLA program, see Malamud 1997b; Sander 1997a; Malamud 1997c; Sander 1997b. For an account of the Texas program, see Orentlicher 1998.

28. See *Croson*, 488 U.S. at 507, 509; see also *United States v. Paradise*, 480 U.S. 149, 171 (1987).

29. *Engineering Contractors Association*, note 5 above. See also *Patrolmen's Benevolent Association*, note 16 above (requiring a factual showing that no "viable less burdensome alternatives" existed).

30. For a recent empirical study tracking the use of affirmative action in recruitment versus in hiring, see Holzer and Neumark 2000.

31. *Lutheran Church-Missouri Synod v. Federal Communications Commission*, 141 F.3d 344, 391, *reh'g denied*, 154 F.3d 487, *reh'g en banc denied*, 154 F.3d 494 (D.C. Cir. 1998) (Edwards, C.J., and Tatel, J., dissenting).

32. 141 F.3d at 291. Not all U.S. courts agree. For a discussion, see Millenson 1999. Teles (chapter 10) suggests that in the United Kingdom, monitoring proportionality, even for purposes of outreach and training, would be problematic.

33. *Lutheran Church-Missouri Synod*, 141 F.3d at 291.

34. *Schurr v. Resorts International Hotel*, 196 F.3d 486, 493 (3d Cir. 1999). For a similar approach in the contracting setting, see *Bras v. California Public Utilities Commission*, 59 F.3d 869 (9th Cir. 1995). Although these cases involve the question of the plaintiff's constitutional standing rather the ultimate question of the programs' constitutionality, the question of whether the programs involve racial classifications would apply to both stages of the analysis.

35. See, e.g., *Bras*, 59 F.3d at 875.

36. See, e.g., Fischbach and Hunt 1999, 1242 (attributing rising women's medical school enrollments to rising ambition rather than to affirmative action).

37. Although this chapter is not considering legal developments under California's Proposition 209 (now embodied in the California state constitution), one lower appellate court in California has held this provision bars a contracting program that requires contractors to use special outreach techniques that "give personal attention to and consideration of minority and women businesses that need not be given to non MBE/WBEs" and that provides that a contractor may not "unjustifiably reject as unsatisfactory bids prepared by minority or women business enterprises." This protection from arbitrariness, uniquely given to women and minorities, was held to "alone gran[t] a distinct [unlawful] preference." *Hi-Voltage Wire Works v. City of San Jose*, 84 Cal. Rptr. 2d 885 (Ct. App. 1999) (review granted).

38. The concept of voluntariness requires some degree of stretching in the leading

Title VII case dealing with private employment: in *Steelworkers v. Weber*, 443 U.S. 193 (1979), the affirmative action program at issue was adopted with the wolf (that is, the Office of Federal Contract Compliance) at the door.

39. Title VII also covers public employers. In many cases, Title VII claims and constitutional claims are brought together. Some public-sector plaintiffs, for whatever reason, bring only Title VII claims. Two leading cases—both of which will be discussed in text—arose in that posture. See *Johnson v. Transportation Agency of Santa Clara County*, 480 U.S. 616 (1987); *Taxman v. Board of Education of the Township of Piscataway*, 91 F.3d 1547 (3d Cir. 1996).

40. See note 38 above.

41. See note 39 above.

42. See note 39 above.

43. *Wygant v. Jackson Board of Education*, 476 U.S. 267 (1986).

44. See Browne 1997.

45. 989 F.2d 233 (7th Cir. 1993).

46. 490 U.S. 642 (1989).

47. 42 U.S.C. sec. 703(a)(1).

48. 42 U.S.C. sec. 703(a)(2).

49. The distinction between intentional and disparate-impact discrimination has procedural and remedial implications under the Civil Rights Act of 1991: juries and monetary damages are available in intentional discrimination cases but not in disparate impact cases. Racial and ethnic harassment (properly regarded as a type of intentional discrimination) can be used as a tool for maintaining ethnic niches—by making it extremely difficult for minorities to survive placement in jobs outside of the ethnic niche. In a fuller treatment of niche issues, I would discuss the question of whether the proof structure for racial and ethnic harassment is or should be the same as that for sexual harassment, which has a far better developed case law.

50. An example is *Miller v. Texas State Board of Barber Examiners*, 615 F.2d 650 (5th Cir. 1980), where an African American barber shop examiner challenged his assignment to inspect only black barber shops. The court used the Dr. King/George Wallace theatrical example to explain both why it was absurd for there not to be a BFOQ for race and of why it was important to find a doctrinal way out of the bind.

51. The Supreme Court held in *International Union, UAW v. Johnson Controls*, 499 U.S. 187 (1991), a gender discrimination case, that the business necessity defense is available only in disparate impact cases, and that facial discrimination (outside the context of affirmative action) must be justified, if at all, as a BFOQ.

52. Under the Civil Rights Act of 1991, "a demonstration that an employment practice is required by business necessity may not be used as a defense against a claim of intentional discrimination." 42 U.S.C. sec. 703(k)(2).

53. See *Patrolmen's Benevolent Association*, note 16 above (reviewing the case law and rejecting a BFOQ exception for race-based transfers based on law-enforcement operational needs).

54. Note that the law groups race and ethnicity together for some purposes and differentiates between them for other purposes. Racial and ethnic classifications are both sub-

ject to strict scrutiny under the Equal Protection clause, but Title VII's BFOQ provision distinguishes between race (no BFOQ defense) and ethnicity—insofar as it is expressed in "national origin" rather than in "racial" terms.

55. *Western Air Lines v. Criswell*, 472 U.S. 400 (1985).

56. *Wilson v. Southwest Airlines Co.*, 517 F. Supp. 299 (N.D. Tex. 1981).

57. *New York Times*, 27 March 1999.

58. The "lack of interest defense," as it is sometimes called, is much maligned in the legal academic literature, particularly where race is concerned. See Schultz and Petterson 1992. More empirical work directed at its core assumptions in different employment settings would be of great value to the legal community.

59. Of course, employers may someday seriously risk liability for *not* permitting other languages to be spoken on the job, but under current case law those risks are minimal.

60. *Hazen Paper v. Biggins*, 507 U.S. 604 (1993).

61. Id. (suggesting for this reason that disparate impact analysis might not be appropriate in age discrimination cases).

References

Atleson, James. 1983. *Values and assumptions in American labor law*. Amherst: University of Massachusetts Press.

Browne, Kingsley. 1997. Nonremedial justifications for affirmative action in employment: A critique of the Justice Department position. *Labor Lawyer* 12:451–73.

Chang, Robert S., and Jerome McCristal Culp. 1997. Nothing and everything: Race, *Romer*, and (gay/lesbian/bisexual) rights. *William & Mary Bill of Rights Law Journal* 6:229–59.

Delgado, Richard. 1998. Rodrigo's roadmap: Is the marketplace theory for eradicating discrimination a blind alley? *Northwestern University Law Review* 93:215–45.

Donohue, John, III, and Peter Siegelman. 1991. The changing nature of employment discrimination litigation. *Stanford Law Review* 43:983–1033.

Fischbach, Ruth L., and Marion Hunt. 1999. Behind every problem lies an opportunity: Meeting the challenge of diversity in medical schools. *Journal of Women's Health and Gender-Based Medicine* 8:1241–47.

Hochschild, Jennifer L. 1999. Affirmative action as culture war. In *The cultural territories of race*, edited by Michele Lamont. Chicago: University of Chicago Press.

Holzer, Harry J., and David Neumark, 2000. What does affirmative action do? *Industrial and Labor Relations Review* 53:240–71.

Lawrence, Charles, III, and Mari Matsuda. 1997. *We won't go back: Making the case for affirmative action*. Boston: Houghton Mifflin.

Malamud, Deborah C. 1997a. Affirmative action, diversity, and the black middle class. *University of Colorado Law Review* 68:939–1000.

———. 1997b. Assessing class-based affirmative action. *Journal of Legal Education* 47:452–71.

———. 1997c. A response to Professor Sander. *Journal of Legal Education* 47:504–11.

Millenson, Debra A. 1999. W(h)ither affirmative action: The future of Executive Order 11246. *University of Memphis Law Review* 26:679–737.

Orentlicher, David. 1998. Affirmative action and Texas' ten percent solution: Improving diversity and quality. *Notre Dame Law Review* 74:181–210.

Perea, Juan. 1997. The black/white binary paradigm of race: The "normal science" of American racial thought. *California Law Review* 85:1213, published concurrently at *La Raza Law Journal* 10 (1998): 127.

Rodriguez, Roberto. 1994. Latino groups say leave Banneker, other programs alone. *Black Issues in Higher Education* 11 (19), available on Westlaw at 1994 WL 14361131.

Sander, Richard H. 1997a. Experimenting with class-based affirmative action. *Journal of Legal Education* 47:472–503.

———. 1997b. Comment in reply. *Journal of Legal Education* 47:512–13.

Schultz, Vicki, and Stephen Petterson. 1992. Race, gender, work and choice: An empirical study of the lack of interest defense in Title VII challenging job segregation. *University of Chicago Law Review* 59:1073–1181.

Skaggs, Jason M. 1998. Justifying gender-based affirmative action under *United States v. Virginia*'s "exceedingly persuasive justification" standard. *California Law Review* 86: 1169–1210.

Strossen, Nadine. 1997. Women's rights under seige. *North Dakota Law Review* 73:207–30.

Washington State Commission on African American Affairs. 1995–1996. *Affirmative action: Who's really benefiting?* Olympia: Washington State Commission on African American Affairs.

Index

Page numbers in italics refer to tables and figures.

ACLU (American Civil Liberties
Union), 20, 66, 333
Adarand Constructors, Inc. v. Pena: classification in, 85, 339n. 3; Clinton and,
54, 101; compelling state interest
and, 316–17; hard vs. soft affirmative
action and, 323–24; strict scrutiny
in, 68n. 3
administrative pragmatism concept, 6
admissions process. *See* student admissions affirmative action
Adolph Coors Company, 219
affect (emotion), measurement of, 197
affirmative action (British): electoral system and, 260–61; government centralization and, 255–57; immigration
and, 251–54; minorities' status and,
248–51, 258–59; outlook for, 262–
65; response to riots and, 246–48;
status of, 242–46; type of, 18–19,
241, 246, 270; welfare state structure
and, 259–60
affirmative action (Indian), 2, 18; constitutional status of, 298, 301; early, in
southern states, 302–3, 311n. 1; eligibility for, 297–98; hard quotas in,
20; implications of, 310–11, 320;
Mandalization of politics and, 304,
305–10; origins and development of,
298–302; party competition and,
303–5
affirmative action (U.S.): approach to, 2,
48–49, 338–39; beliefs about costs/
benefits of, 191–204; beyond U.S.
borders, 17–20; British compared to,
241, 244, 245, 246, 254, 264–65;

civil rights linked to, 90–91; components of, 192, 218; debate on, 8–10,
234–35; decline of, 67–68, 99–101;
definitions of, 4–6, 39, 91, 265n. 3,
289n. 1; discrimination distinct
from, 11; diversity compared to, 105,
106; French compared to, 271, 279;
goals vs. methods of, 223–25; groups
included in, 8–12, 16, 25n. 13, 258,
340n. 7; for group vs. individual,
228–29; immigration policy and,
53–57; justification for, 6–7, 60, 97–
99, 229, 283, 288, 292n. 33; legal
status of, 21–22, 96, 313–26; opportunity-enhancing vs. outcome-
directed, 48, 193, 215, 218; plans
for, 92, 96, 317–19, 331–32; quotas
linked to, 218–23; recast as diversity
initiatives, 89, 100–107, 111–13; resistance to, 32, 40–41, 43, 277–79;
soft vs. hard, 59–61, 68n. 2, 215,
218, 323–25. *See also* antidiscrimination policies; classification; color
lines; public opinion; student admissions affirmative action
Africans, as immigrants to France, 272–
73
Afro-American-owned businesses: hiring
practices of, 177–78, 181; on immigrant workers, 182–83; income of,
24n. 6; in-group/out-group concept
and, 170, 172
Afro-Americans: attitudes toward affirmative action, 15–16, 33, 43, 192,
197–209, 224, 225; on/as beneficiaries of affirmative action, 215,

Afro-Americans (*continued*)
225–26, 228, 321, 340n. 7; in construction trades, 42, 47; on discrimination, 229–31, 232; ethnic niches
for, 328; expectations of, 179–84,
335; Hispanic and Asian tensions
with, 64–66; immigrants and, 12–
14, 148, 254; occupational choices
and, 34–35, 84; own-preferences/
other-aversions of, 148; in parity
model, 137–38, *139;* preferences for
hiring, 14, 168, 170, 172–85; on
quotas, 220–21; unrest of, 37–38,
47; use of term, 23n. 1; workplace
conflict of, 155–60
Afro-Caribbeans, 249–51, 261, 266n.
14
age, in construction trades, 41
airlines, BFOQ defense of, 331
Aleuts, 83
Algerians, 284
Ambedkar, B. R., 300, 301, 311
American Civil Liberties Union
(ACLU), 20, 66, 333
The American Dilemma (Myrdal), 35
American Institute for Managing Diversity, 102, 107
American Society for Training and Development, 108
ancestry. *See* national origin and
ancestry
antidiscrimination enforcement: ambiguity in, 90–91; detection as precursor
to, 333; expansion of, 91–94, 110;
institutionalization of, 88–90; in new
immigrant businesses, 336–38; rise
and decline of, 87–88, 95–96, 101,
111–12
antidiscrimination policies: characteristics of, 7, 89–90; demand for, 37–
38; ethnic niches and, 327–28; failure of post–New Deal, 31–32; federal efforts in 1950s–1960s, 38–40;
in France, 270; in immigration policy, 58–59; shift from soft to hard,
59, 60–61; shortcomings of, 36–37,
47–48; as threat, 43–48; white resistance to, 32, 40–41. *See also* em-

ployer response to affirmative action;
equal employment opportunity
antiracism: law on, 274; politics of,
279–83
ANT (National Agency for the Insertion and Promotion of Overseas
Workers, French), 276
apprenticeship programs, 39, 46–47
armed forces, affirmative action in,
68n. 2
Asian Americans: attitudes toward affirmative action, 15–16, 197–209,
223, 225, 233–34; on beneficiaries
of affirmative action, 226, 228; black
and Hispanic tensions with, 64–
66; classification of, 11, 62, 76, 82;
differences among, 82–83, 231;
on discrimination, 229–31; educational achievements of, 24n. 7;
ethnic niches for, 328; income of,
62–63; in parity model, 128–29,
137–38, *139;* proof of discrimination against, 72; on quotas, 218–
19. *See also specific groups*
Asian Indians: businesses owned by,
24n. 6; inclusion of, 73; status in
Britain, 249, 251, 253, 266nn. 10, 11
Asians: as immigrants to France, 272–
73; on immigration to Britain, 266n.
14; political support from, 261. *See
also* Asian Americans; *specific groups*
assimilation, use of term, 273
*Associated General Contractors of Ohio v.
Columbus,* 85
Associated General Contractors v. Drabik,
76, 77
*Association for Fairness in Business v. State
of New Jersey,* 76
Atleson, James, 335
AT&T, 108
Avon (company), 108
Ayodhya strategy, 306–7

Balaji v. Mysore, 303
Baldwin, James, 284
Belgium, racism in, 284
Bell, Derrick, 225–26
Bell, Myrtle P., 215, 219, 230